T0344998

Institutional Foundations
of Impersonal Exchange

Institutional Foundations of Impersonal Exchange

Theory and Policy of Contractual Registries

BENITO ARRUÑADA

The University of Chicago Press
Chicago and London

Benito Arruñada is professor of business organization in the Department of Economics and Business at Pompeu Fabra University in Barcelona.

The University of Chicago Press, Chicago 60637
The University of Chicago Press, Ltd., London
© 2012 by The University of Chicago
All rights reserved. Published 2012.
Printed in the United States of America

21 20 19 18 17 16 15 14 13 12   1 2 3 4 5

ISBN-13: 978-0-226-02832-3 (cloth)
ISBN-13: 978-0-226-02835-4 (e-book)

ISBN-10: 0-226-02832-1 (cloth)
ISBN-10: 0-226-02835-6 (e-book)

Library of Congress Cataloging-in-Publication Data

Arruñada, Benito.
  Institutional foundations of impersonal exchange : theory and policy
of contractual registries / Benito Arruñada.
      pages ; cm
  Includes bibliographical references and index.
  ISBN-13: 978-0-226-02832-3 (cloth : alkaline paper)
  ISBN-10: 0-226-02832-1 (cloth : alkaline paper)
  ISBN-13: 978-0-226-02835-4 (e-book)
  ISBN-10: 0-226-02835-6 (e-book) 1. Land titles—Registration and
transfer. 2. Right of property. 3. Conveyancing. 4. Contracts. I. Title.
  K754.A77 2012
  346.04'38—dc23
                                                                    2011051048

♾ This paper meets the requirements of ANSI/NISO Z39.48–1992
(Permanence of Paper).

To Marisa

CONTENTS

ILLUSTRATIONS

ACKNOWLEDGMENTS

Several fortunate circumstances prompted me to write this book. The first was the creation of the International Society for New Institutional Economics (ISNIE), an interdisciplinary forum that pointed to the demand for this kind of interdisciplinary effort. In fact, the first outline of the book was presented at my presidential lecture at ISNIE. This was an early attempt to organize my thoughts on the application of theoretical insights to policy discussions in the area of contractual registries. Such thoughts had repeatedly benefitted from interaction in the field with what I consider to have been flawed policies in institutional reform, promoted by international organizations that include the European Commission, the World Bank, and the Inter-American Development Bank. The project then started to crystallize when I received a generous offer from the Mercatus Center at George Mason University and, in particular, Claire Morgan and Brian Hooks, to organize a Mercatus conference around the first draft of the manuscript. The commitment this entailed spurred on my writing efforts. David Pervin and the anonymous reviewers at the University of Chicago Press not only saw promise in the project at such an early stage but later on guided several rounds of extensive and fruitful revisions.

During the whole process, I have benefitted greatly from the advice, comments, and criticism of many scholars and policy experts. It would be impossible to list here all those who made valuable contributions. Those who read and discussed draft versions of different chapters include Yoram Barzel, John Bruce, Robert Ellickson, Victoria Elliot, Nuno Garoupa, Ricard Gil, Fernando Gómez Pomar, Henry Hansmann, P. J. Hill, Philip Keefer, Amalia Kessler, Dean Lueck, Carlos Manzanares, Richard Messick, Nicolás Nogueroles Peiró, Pamela O'Connor, Joyce Palomar, Henry Smith, Giorgio Zanarone, and, most especially, Fernando P. Méndez González.

Moreover, many correspondents in different countries were willing to graciously share with me their information and opinions on specific issues and cases. Let me thank especially Robert Abbey, Jesús Alfaro Águila-Real, Veneta Andonova, Petar Balachev, Sander Baljé, Diether Beuermann, Karol Boudreaux, Max Bradford, Eric Brousseau, Tony Burns, Mike Calder, Wade Channell, Elizabeth Cooke, Stephen Copp, Thomas Cutler, Klaus Deininger, Antony Dnes, Jane Dokko, John Drobak, Luis Fernández del Pozo, Klaus Gaensbacher, Sebastian Galiani, Eduardo García Martínez, Francisco Garcimartín, Jean-Michel Glachant, Jack Goldstone, Yadira González de Lara, John Greenwood, David Grinlinton, David Haddock, Marc Hameleers, Stephen Hanssen, Christian Harm, Ron Harris, Gijs Hesselink, Paul Holden, Miguel Jaramillo, Steve Kelway, Fredrick Kerr, Stuart Kerr, Rolf Knieper, Gerry Korngold, Amnon Lehavi, Gary Libecap, Jonathan Lindsay, Nelson Lipshutz, Rouhshi Low, Francisco Marcos, José Massaguer Fuentes, Bruce McKenna, Liliana Miranda, Stephen Moulton, Robert Muir, Antonio Nicita, Janet November, John Nye, Claus Ott, Joyce Palomar, Cándido Paz-Ares, Christofer Peterson, Carlos Petit, José Manuel Pinho Martins, Craig Pirrong, Carla Revilla, Joaquín Rodríguez Hernández, Maribel Sáez Lacave, Jolyne Sanjak, Jason Sorens, Rod Thomas, Xosé Henrique Vázquez, Ainhoa Veiga, Leon Verstappen, John Wallis, Richard Webb, Manfred Wenckstern, James Young, and Joan Youngman.

Some parts of the book were presented not only at the Mercatus Center monographic conference but also at various seminars and conferences, including the Center for the Study of Public Choice at George Mason University; the David Berg Institute for Law and History at Tel Aviv University; the German Development Institute; the French *Conseil d'État*; Goethe-Universität; the Italian Society of Law and Economics; the Justice Reform and Land Administration Groups at the World Bank; the Lincoln Institute of Land Policy; the Millennium Challenge Corporation; the Radzyner School of Law at the Interdisciplinary Center (IDC), Herzliya; the Reflexive Governance Workshops at Paris and Rome; the Society of European Contract Law; the Department of Economics at the University of Bologna; the University of Paris West–Nanterre La Défense; and the World Bank Annual Conference on Land Policy and Administration. Discussants and participants at these meetings contributed highly valuable insights, criticisms, and encouragement.

Making the manuscript intelligible would have been well-nigh impossible without the masterful assistance of Jenny McDonald and the editorial staff at the University of Chicago Press.

The book stems from previous research supported by several grants from the European Commission and the Spanish Government, and work on the book itself has received generous support from the Spanish Ministry of Science and Innovation through grants ECO2011-29445 and ECO2008-01116, which I heartily appreciate.

Finally, I acknowledge permission from the publishers of my previous research to elaborate and include materials from it in this book. Chapter 2 draws on "Property Enforcement as Organized Consent" [*Journal of Law, Economics, and Organization* 2003, 19(2): 401–44], by permission of Oxford University Press. Chapter 3 draws on "Institutional Support of the Firm: A Theory of Business Registries" [*Journal of Legal Analysis* 2010, 2(2): 525–76)], by permission of Harvard University Press. A section of chapter 5 draws on "The Choice of Titling System in Land," coauthored with Nuno Garoupa [*Journal of Law and Economics* 2005, 48(2): 709–27], by permission of University of Chicago Press; and "Property Titling and Conveyancing" (in K. Ayotte and H. E. Smith, eds., *Research Handbook on the Economics of Property Law*, Cheltenham: Edward Elgar, 237–56). Chapter 6 draws on "Market and Institutional Determinants in the Regulation of Conveyancers" [*European Journal of Law and Economics* 2007, 23(2): 93–116], with kind permission of Springer Science and Business Media; except for the section on title insurance, which in part draws on "A Transaction Cost View of Title Insurance and Its Role in Different Legal Systems" [*Geneva Papers on Risk and Insurance* 2002, 27(4): 582–601], with permission of Palgrave Macmillan. Parts of one section in chapter 7 draw on "Pitfalls to Avoid when Measuring the Institutional Environment: Is 'Doing Business' Damaging Business?" [*Journal of Comparative Economics* 2007, 35(4): 729–47], by permission of Elsevier B. V.; and "How Doing Business Jeopardizes Institutional Reform" [*European Business Organization Law Review* 2009, 10(4): 555–74], by permission of T. M. C. Asser Press. Lastly, a section on technological change draws on "Leaky Title Syndrome?" (*New Zealand Law Journal* April 2010: 115–20), by permission of LexisNexis.

I warmly thank all these colleagues, professionals, and institutions for helping to make this a better book. I alone hold responsibility for any remaining errors of fact or judgment.

Misguided Property Titling and Business Formalization Policies

Discussions on economic development have lately focused on the role of institutions in protecting property rights and reducing transaction costs. In particular, the idea has taken root that development would benefit from facilitating access to legality. It is thought that, if those in possession of even small buildings and plots of land have good titles, they will enjoy better incentives to invest and can use these real assets as collateral for credit. Similarly, if business entrepreneurs are able to "formalize" (for our purposes, publicly register) their firms easily, they will benefit from operating them as legal entities. For instance, they will have access to the courts for enforcing contracts and settling disputes, and will also be able to obtain credit and invest more. Consequently, firms will grow faster and be more productive.

These simple ideas, inspired by the works of Ronald Coase, Douglass North, and Oliver Williamson, and reminiscent of widespread arguments in the most advanced economies of the nineteenth century, have motivated thousands of reform and aid programs in developing countries, where the state of legal institutions is often considered to be inadequate. Some authors have even held that providing better institutions would lead to greater development. Similar ideas have also influenced reform policy in developed countries, where some of the institutions for registering property and businesses have become outdated or captured by private interests. Simplifying administrative procedures was expected to have considerable impact on economic activity.

However, outcomes from these efforts in institutional building and reform have often been disappointing, failing to fulfill their promise of economic growth and even that of improving the institutional environment. Common mistakes have often been committed, such as seeing registries' controls as mere entry barriers to legality, forgetting that they must be reliable to be socially useful. This has often led to reforms that emphasize quantity and speed, thereby sacrificing quality and making registries speedy but useless. Of course, registries, like any other institution, can be used to capture rents and deter competition. This possibility must be considered and avoided, but it only imposes one more policy and organizational constraint—it does not define registries' function and should not therefore be treated as their only design factor.

In other cases, the error comes from mixing up cause and consequence when assuming that informality is causing poverty instead of the other way around. This has led, for instance, to the building of universal land titling systems that spend huge amounts to little effect, as they usually miss key objectives, such as the use of land as collateral for credit. In fact, given that formalization incurs fixed costs, informality may be appropriate for low-value assets and small, incipient firms. Registries are not silver bullets for development. Decision on the creation and coverage of registries must be guided by considerations of costs and benefits, which depend on the particular circumstances of each country.

How Public Registries Reduce the
Transaction Costs of Impersonal Trade

I submit that these failures are rooted in a poor understanding of the role of registries and, consequently, of the demand for them and of their organizational requirements. I have written this book in the hope of correcting this shortcoming. First, I develop a theory of contractual registries that explains their rationale as an essential part of the institutions that make truly impersonal trade feasible, the trade in which contractual performance depends on assets instead of persons. Second, I use this theory as a basis for analyzing the main policy questions posed by the creation and organization of registries.

Opportunities for economic development are greater when trade is impersonal instead of limited to known people. To be fully impersonal, contractual performance must be independent of parties' characteristics, including not only their reputation and wealth but also their legal authority to contract. Such fully impersonal trade therefore requires contractual enforcement to be based on assets, which poses a conflict between those holding and those acquiring property rights, between owners and buyers. (More precisely, between owners seen retrospectively as buyers and owners seen prospectively as potential victims of future expropriation by, e.g., a fraudulent seller.) In short, making contractual performance hinge on assets reduces transaction costs but may endanger the security of property. Overcoming this conflict is the role of contractual registries, a crucial role, because both secure property and low transaction costs are necessary conditions for economic development and would collide in the absence of registries.

This conflict can be better identified by considering legal remedies. Property rights are the foundation of economic incentives and prosperity. It therefore makes sense to enforce them strictly, so that in case of conflict goods are always returned to their legal owners unless they had granted their consent—treating them as rights *in rem* (from the Latin word *res*, thing). But such *in rem* enforcement would increase transaction costs by worsening the information asymmetry suffered by acquirers of all sorts of rights, who would always have to gather the consent of the legal owners. Enforcing rights *in rem* might therefore endanger trade. It would also endanger specialization, because specialization is often based on having agents acting as owners' representatives, and acquirers would have reasons to doubt the legal authority of sellers. Economic development therefore requires this conflict between property enforcement and transaction costs to be overcome, so that both owners and acquirers are protected. Owners' property rights need to be protected to encourage investment, and the transaction costs faced by acquirers need to be lowered to encourage them to trade and thus improve the allocation and specialization of resources.

Achieving both goals is straightforward when the consequences of private contracts are easy to verify: all it requires are clear adjudication rules between owners and acquirers. This is what usually happens in commercial trade of movable goods, for which Western law has been able to effectively overcome the conflict between property enforcement and transaction costs since the Middle Ages. Generally speaking, when one firm gives possession of movable goods to another, the legal system understands that it authorizes the receiving firm to sell the goods. Third parties acquiring from a firm are therefore secure and do not need to worry about the authority of the seller. Owners are protected because it is they who choose the seller. And they cannot renege from their decision because the transaction produces a verifiable consequence: the transfer of possession.

Protecting third parties without damaging owners is harder when contracts remain private. This is what happens in transactions such as mortgages or those involving companies, which lack verifiable consequences. History suggests that achieving both goals in these cases requires effective, independent, public registration of property rights or private contracts. Only such reliable registers can ensure that owners of resources have publicized their property rights (so that acquirers can find out about them before contracting) or have consented voluntarily to a weakening of their property rights with respect to innocent acquirers (so that owners cannot opportunistically renege from such consent). When purchasers of land and mortgage lenders rely for their contracts on the information filed with the registry, developed legal systems protect their acquisitions even against unregistered legal owners. A similar function is performed by company registries with respect to personal and corporate creditors, so that, for instance, if a company has remained unregistered this should not damage third parties. In both cases, these protections in fact eliminate the information disadvantage suffered by third parties and thus reduce transaction costs, making trade easier. Furthermore, well-functioning registries achieve these feats without damaging the property rights of landowners or shareholders.

The role of contractual registries can be more easily clarified by considering that most economic transactions are interrelated sequentially. In the most simple sequence, with only two transactions, one or several "principals"—such as owners, employers, shareholders, creditors, and the like—voluntarily contract first with one or several economic "agents"—possessors, employees, company directors, and managers—in an "originative" transaction. Second, the agent then contracts "subsequent" transactions with third parties.

These sequential exchanges offer the benefits of specialization in the tasks of principals and agents—between landowners and farmers, employers and employees, shareholders and managers, and so on. But they also give rise to substantial transaction costs, because, when third parties contract with the agent, they suffer information asymmetry regarding not only the material quality of the goods or services being transacted but also the legal effects of the previous originative contract. In particular, third parties are often unaware if they are dealing with a principal or an agent, or if the agent has sufficient title or legal power to commit the principal. This constitutes a grave impediment, especially for the impersonal transactions that are necessary to fully exploit the advantages of specialization.

Moreover, principals also face a serious commitment problem when trying to avoid this asymmetry because their incentives change after the third party has entered the subsequent contract. Before contracting, principals have an interest in third parties being convinced that agents have proper authority, but, if the business turns out badly, principals will be inclined to deny such authority. This is why the typical dispute triggered by sequential transactions is one in which the principal tries to elude obligations assumed by the agent in the principal's name, whether the agent had legal authority or not.

Judges can adjudicate in such disputes in favor of the principal or the third party. I will refer to favoring the third party as enforcing "contract rules," as opposed to the seemingly more natural "property rules" that favor the principal.

The effects of these rules are clear. Take the simple case in which an agent exceeds his legal powers when selling a good to an innocent third party (i.e., a good-faith party who is uninformed about the matter in question). If judges apply the "property rule" that no one can transfer what he does not have, they rule to have the sold good returned to the "original owner," and the innocent third party wins a mere claim against the agent. Owners will feel secure with respect to this contingency, because this outcome maximizes property enforcement, but it worsens the information asymmetry suffered by all potential third parties with respect to legal title.

Conversely, judges can apply an indemnity or "contract rule" so that the sold good stays with the third party and the principal only wins a claim against the agent. This will minimize information asymmetry for potential third parties but will also weaken property enforcement, making owners feel insecure. Enforcing contract rules thus obviates the information asymmetry usually suffered by third parties and encourages them to trade. In so doing, contract rules transform the object of complex transactions into legal commodities that can be traded easily, thus extending the type of impersonal transaction that characterizes modern markets. However, contract rules weaken the principals' property rights, endangering investment and specialization in the tasks of principals and agents.

The choice of rule therefore involves a tricky conflict between property enforcement and transaction costs.[1] This conflict puzzles some economists because the economic literature on property rights has been interested in problems such as violence, externalities, and the tragedy of the commons, which can be successfully analyzed using a simplified view of property enforcement. In particular, these problems are independent of the legal remedies that are made available to the rightholder in case of a dispute or, in particular, the type of protection—real or personal—the law gives to different entitlements.

These remedies are of two types: either the rightholder gets a real right, a right *in rem*, or a personal right, a right *in personam*—in legal terms these are called, respectively, property and contract rights. The enforceability and thus the value of these two types of right are often markedly different, because, while rights *in personam* are only valid against specific persons, *inter partes*, rights *in rem* are valid against all individuals, *erga omnes*. The latter, therefore, provide the strongest possible enforcement: without the consent of the rightholder, the rights *in rem* remain unaffected. However, as already mentioned, this makes transactions more risky for acquirers, endangering impersonal exchange. Without the supporting institutions, which are the object of this book, enforcing rights *in rem* is incompatible with the multiplication of rights and frequent transactions needed for specializing and allocating resources. The function of registries is precisely to make rights *in rem* viable without increasing transaction costs.

To achieve this feat of overcoming the conflict between *in rem* property enforcement and transaction costs, expanding the set of viable contractual opportunities without damaging property rights, the law applies property or contract rules depending on conditions that provide proper safeguards. In essence, for judges to apply property rules, which favor owners, owners must have publicized their claims or rights, which should protect acquirers. That is, principals can opt for a property rule to make their rights safer, but, thanks to publicity, third parties suffer little information asymmetry. Conversely, for judges to apply contract rules, which favor acquirers, owners must have granted their consent, which should protect them. That is, when principals choose a contract rule, third parties' rights are safe, whereas principals' rights are weaker. But this weakening of property is limited, since principals choose the agent whom they entrust with possession or appoint as their representative, this being the moment when they implicitly "choose" a contract rule.

Smooth operation of this conditional application of rules poses varying degrees of difficulty for different transactions. The difficulty is minor when the originative transaction inevitably produces verifiable facts, such as the physical possession of movable goods or the ordinary activity of an employee. For these cases, judges can base their decisions on this public information, which is produced informally. What judges or legislatures have to do is to clearly define efficient contract rules to be applied. The difficulty is greater when the originative transaction produces less verifiable facts, making informal solutions harder to apply. Such informal solutions may even be impossible if the contract remains hidden and its consequences are not verifiable. Consider, for example, the difficulties for clearly establishing by purely private contract the existence of a corporation, distinguishing the corporation's assets from the personal assets of its shareholders.

In such contexts of harder verifiability (verifiability referred here not to the parties' performance on the contract, as it is usual in the economic analysis of contracts, but to the content of the contract itself), defining contract rules is not enough because applying them requires information on originative contracts, which, in principle, are not always verifiable. To make them verifiable, it is necessary to enter and preserve at least some information on them in a public registry, which is costly to start up and operate, and must enjoy independence and public access.

First, the costly nature of registries means that their existence is not always efficient. Therefore, as often happens with institutions, they are supportive of markets and may even be a necessary condition, at least of the most impersonal type of transaction. But they are not a sufficient condition.[2] Reformers have to be attentive to signals indicating whether demand really exists for new institutional development. Public intervention without such demand is wasteful and may even have negative consequences: if these attempted institutions fail, reforming them in the future will often be more difficult than starting from zero.

Second, to prevent interested manipulation, the registration process must be independent of all the parties involved, including parties to the originative contract. This requirement of independence makes registration wholly different from the documentary formalization performed by lawyers and conveyancers, which is mainly designed to safeguard the relation between parties to the same contract but lacks the public element required to have full *in rem* effects in the context of a sequence of contracts.

Third, the key features of the originative contract need to be made available to the public or at least to potential third parties, so that they know beforehand which rules are applicable to any subsequent contracts. In essence, registration thus becomes the means to make the voluntary choice of market-enabling contract rules verifiable by courts and therefore to commit principals to their choices.

These three attributes of efficiency, independence, and effective access summarize the organizational requirements of public registries. They are not automatic or easy to achieve—they must be consciously pursued. Furthermore, registries suffer from two structural weaknesses. First, because of their public nature, they are subject to all the limitations of public organizations. Second, because, by drastically reducing transaction costs, they also reduce the demand for providers of palliative services such as lawyers, notaries, and conveyancers, these professionals have an interest in impeding the development of effective, independent public registries.

Organization of the Book

The book follows a logical theory-policy order, developing a theory of registries in the first three chapters and applying it to policy oriented issues in the last four substantive chapters. Thus, the first chapter describes the analytical framework presenting a general theory of public contract formalization, which is then developed in the second and third chapters to explain, respectively, how the different types of property and company registries perform their functions.

The remaining chapters mostly apply this framework to the key strategic, policy, regulatory, and organizational questions posed by property titling and business formalization institutions. Thus, chapter 4 ponders essential strategic issues, such as the conflict between legal orders and the logical sequence to be followed in formalization reform. Chapter 5 considers the main design choices for registries, including how to consider the demand for formalization institutions, how to introduce them, and how to choose between different types of property and business registry. Chapter 6 analyzes the nature of conveyancing services and their interactions with registries and outlines a proposal for regulating conveyancing and other complementary services. Lastly, chapter 7 deals with five organizational issues with a more managerial content: the use of information and the design of information systems for sensible decision making in this area; the synergies and risks of integrating contractual and administrative formalization; the challenges posed by technical changes in information technology; the need to apply strong incentives in the organization of public registries, seeing them as an organizational hybrid between private enterprise and public administration; and the importance of considering the self-interests of all participants and managing these by means of counterbalancing incentives. A brief closing section recapitulates the main arguments and conclusions.

Methodology and Exposition:
Approach, Assumptions, and Caveats

The book develops the theory with the aim of understanding problems and enlightening policy. Its interdisciplinary approach relies on concepts and analytical tools from law, economics, and organization. This blend of theoretical perspectives should be productive, but is bound to create some misunderstandings and to occasionally make some readers feel unhappy with different sections. To avoid these misunderstandings, especially regarding what this book is and is not about, readers will appreciate an explanation beforehand of the boundaries, assumptions, and methodology of the analysis, though most of these aspects will be revisited as and when necessary.

Focus on General Rules and Institutional Support

Given the pragmatic purpose of the book, I have strived to portray an accurate map of the institutional forest, often sacrificing attention to particular trees and hoping this does not distort the overall analysis and its conclusions. I thus plead the sympathy and understanding of specialists, who may often feel that particular species of trees have not been adequately treated. This is particularly so in regard to the book's focus on the cases and solutions that are prevalent in the population of routine transactions instead of those most represented in the litigated sample. Intentionally, most exceptions will be treated lightly to focus on the general rules that support modern impersonal markets.

This focus on the prevalent cases and general rules departs from both legal scholarship and law and economics to the extent that these two disciplines often pay more attention to disputed judicial decisions than to the real contractual process.[3] The same emphasis on judicial disputes sometimes leads analysts to base theories on pathologies instead of the prevalent solutions, framing general rules in terms of the exceptions or even taking the exceptional regimes as general rules. This selection bias might be behind the focus of the literature on, for instance, the theft of movable property and the presence of informed or bad faith third parties, or the marginal treatment given to standard commercial transactions when introducing the transfer of movables.[4]

Similarly, the literature focuses on judicial decisions within oversimplified institutions that do not modify the informational structure, while my focus lies on the institutional support: the main issue is how to provide judges with verifiable information on rightholders' consent. Consequently, the book departs from previous work by focusing on the role of institutions in modifying the problem's information structure instead of on how parties' incentives and costs drive the local optimality of alternative rules.

Assumptions on the Existence of Property, the State, and the Judiciary

The book also differs from much of the literature on the institutions of property rights in that for the most part it covers private property. It does not focus on the origins and foundations of property but on the institutions needed to make property compatible with modern impersonal markets. Most of the book thus assumes the existence of private individual property, which implies at least a nonpredatory state plus an allocation of property rights to

individuals. Consequently, most of the analysis will be less useful for economies with dysfunctional or nonexistent states, for which the priority is to
protect property from public expropriation and private violence. In this respect, the book's theme has more to do with private as opposed to public
expropriation—it mainly deals with the risk that acquirers may lose their
rights and therefore be reluctant to trade. Analysis of public expropriation
plays a secondary role and focuses on how formalization institutions may
be used by governments to damage private property. Most of the book also
assumes that property is already allocated to individuals.

Focus on the Legal Concept of Property, Real or In Rem, Rights

My theory of contractual registries relies on basic concepts from property law
and the economics of property rights. Both disciplines are complementary
and indispensable to understand how property institutions work. But they
hold different perspectives and emphasize different aspects. Furthermore, they
use the same names to designate disparate concepts, mainly that of "property right" itself, which has a more precise meaning in law than in economics. This combined use of law and economics is therefore fruitful but poses
conceptual and language difficulties, which I should clarify from the start.

The analysis in the book relies extensively on a key legal distinction: that
between what the law understands as property (real, *in rem*) and contract
(personal, *in personam*) rights and, consequently, what I call property and
contract rules. This may discourage readers tempted to skip legal distinc-
tions, especially economists accustomed to mixing up property and contract
rights and calling both of them "property rights," which is fine for some
analyses but would cause considerable ambiguity here. Patience is advised,
as the analysis of formalization institutions in general and registries, in particular, needs to rely on this distinction to be useful. For a start, observe
that the value of property and trade hinges on enforcement and that this
distinction—being given a right *in rem* or *in personam*, a right on things or a
right against some person—usually makes a total difference in enforcement
and, therefore, value. When the thing is a parcel of land, the difference often
ranges from full value for the party being adjudicated the land to zero value
for the party being given a claim to be indemnified by an insolvent person;
similar differences arise in business and corporate contexts, where a parallel distinction is often made, framed in more general terms, not in terms
of rights but in terms of legal priority. This enforcement advantage is valuable so legal systems rely heavily on it. However, enforcing rights as rights
in rem—in general, granting priority to current rightholders—endangers

trade because their potential adverse enforcement places aspiring acquirers of rights at an informational disadvantage and subjects them to the risk of purchasing less than they paid for. Registries are costly but they allow the law to overcome this conflict. They exist to make *in rem* property rights possible without endangering trade, providing the basis for truly impersonal trade. The distinction between rights *in rem* and rights *in personam* therefore lies at the very core of the role of registries, which is essential to my inquiry.

Conventions of Terminology and Exposition

The subject of the book also makes it necessary to use a few polysemous words: mainly, the words "title," "registration," "formalization," and "conveyancing." I try to use these words univocally except for cases where the meaning can easily be inferred from the context. For instance, "title" may refer to a legal right or to the evidence of it, often a deed (a written and signed document). Similarly, "registration" is often used to refer to any lodgment of documents and to their subsequent filing in a public registry or to the filing in a specific type of register that first checks the legality of the intended transaction. Ambiguity may arise because of the different types of registry and their different legal effects. For instance, within property titling, the registry may simply establish the date of lodgment and store the documents (in what is then better called "recording" or "recordation" of documents or deeds). Alternatively, it may also check the transaction and file only those that do not collide with any other right in what will here be called a "register of rights." Occasionally, when the context resolves the ambiguity, just "recordation" and "registration" are used to refer to each of them.

Likewise, the term "formalization" often describes three types of distinctive process: (1) giving private contracts a certain form, which may include a written document and the presence of witnesses and lawyers; (2) filing them in a contractual registry with public access but with the function of facilitating private contracting; and, mainly in the business area, (3) performing certain administrative procedures, such as enrolling a firm in a tax registry, with a more public function (see figure I.1). The book focuses on the second process, that of contractual registration (or, simply, "registration"), for which use of a "public" qualifier would be ambiguous: even if registration relies on publicity as a means, its goals are essentially private. To avoid confusion, I will identify these three processes by adding objective qualifiers, referring respectively to "documentary formalization," "contractual registration," and "administrative formalization."

I also rely on a broad concept of "agency," closer to the economic than

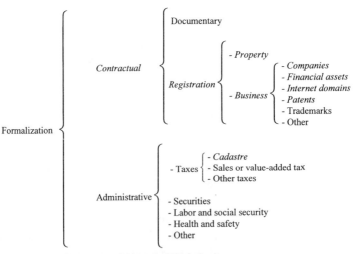

NOTE: Italicized terms indicate areas explicitly analyzed in the book.

Figure I.1. Types of formalization

the legal concept, to draw up a general theory of contractual registries that can encompass both property and company registries. This use of agency language for describing property cases may puzzle readers familiar with the legal concept of agency. However, it seems a low price to pay in order to reveal the commonality of the business and property transacting problems.

Naming concepts is further complicated because of the wide scope and interdisciplinary nature of the book. The book's coverage of business and property transactions poses semantic difficulties because each of these two areas tends to use its own words to refer to functionally similar concepts, starting with the use of "business formalization" and "property titling" to name the institutional solutions applied in each of these areas. Moreover, the different disciplines used in the analysis refer to similar concepts with different words. For instance, the term "business formalization" is commonly used in development circles to refer to what in law is often named "business" or "company registration," but often also includes administrative formalization.

Lastly, the word "conveyancing," which often refers to the whole process of transferring land, will be narrowly used in the book as the private services provided usually by legal professionals to help parties in the transfer and mortgage of real property. Most often, "conveyancers" will be used to refer to such professionals, including not only lawyers, solicitors, and notaries, but also licensed conveyancers and land brokers.

Some other conventions adopted in the book stem from its intention to reach a diverse audience. For instance, to avoid causing confusion and at the risk of redundancy, key specialized terms will be repeatedly clarified. In addition to explaining them in the text, footnotes explain any remaining ambiguities. Moreover, in cases where doubts might persist, two consecutive labels are often used, sacrificing grace to clarity (e.g., as in "property *in rem* rights"). Some other conventions are made for the sake of simplicity. Thus, whenever possible, more concrete terms such as "registration" or "registries" will be preferred to terms such as "formalization." A distinction is also made between "registry"—to refer to the registration office and institution—and "register"—the latter referring to the registered information. Also for simplicity, the text often talks about owners and ownership even though the analysis is more generally applicable and refers to all types of rightholders and property rights. Lastly, given the broad coverage of the book, its chapters aim to be relatively self-contained. This may occasionally annoy comprehensive readers, who are kindly requested to skip and forgive these repetitions.

Degree of Technical Detail

The book aims to clarify real problems, so some minor aspects, including elegance and uniformity of rigor and style, have occasionally been sacrificed. In particular, to be effective the analysis needs to go into technical details and rely on other disciplines in addition to economics. For example, chapters 2 and 3 analyze how the different institutional machineries work. They solve an economic problem, analyzed in chapter 1, but in both cases the analysis also relies on law and organization theory. In a sense, their perspective is closer to a sort of "institutional engineering," whereas chapter 4 and especially chapter 5 look more economic because they analyze the costs and benefits of the main design choices. Chapter 6 will again look too technical to economists. However, without a technical understanding of the functions played by registries and conveyancers, the discussion of alternative possibilities of design and regulation (e.g., how to deal with electronic technologies) would not advance.

Choice of Historical and Current Casuistic Evidence

In general, I focus on historical evidence about European instead of American institutions because the problems faced today by those creating institutions in many developing countries are similar to those faced when the liberal state was designed in Europe. For example, in the area of real property, the disentailment processes that occupied European elites for several centuries posed similar difficulties to those posed today by customary land rights in developing countries. American settlers, on the other hand, were lucky to find weak preexisting institutions or none at all. For this reason, lessons learned in the creation of institutions in the United States are hardly applicable to countries with old but strong institutions, comparable to those found in Europe at the end of the ancien régime.

ONE

The Role of Verifiable Contract Publicity in Impersonal Trade

People prosper when investors feel secure and are therefore willing to invest in productive activities. But they prosper even more if they can trade beyond their personal circles of known people, as producers invest and specialize more when they can sell their production in a larger market.[1] Good institutions facilitate these two key factors for development, as they not only make investors feel secure in their investments but also enable everybody to trade impersonally,[2] thus creating wealth. Most of this book focuses on a subset of these institutions: those for contract registration, which makes it possible to ground contract enforcement directly on assets, in such a way that transacting parties need no personal information about each other and can therefore trade impersonally.

Impersonal Exchange Requires Rights on Assets, Not Merely on Persons

Reaching specialization advantages requires transferring all sorts of rights to the most productive user. It therefore requires exhausting the opportunities for exchange. Unfortunately, profitable exchange opportunities may be lost because potential parties do not trust each other.

To avoid distrust, parties display plenty of ingenuity to bond their own future behavior with a variety of safeguards and to learn more about their prospective contractual partners. When parties know each other well, they suffer less information asymmetry about the value of each other's promises; thus, conflicts are less likely. They also know about the safeguarding mechanisms that will be activated if a conflict eventually arises, and which may be based on public or private "ordering"—that is, mainly with or without help from an independent judiciary. This knowledge facilitates economic exchange, but only of a personal nature, as parties need to know each other's characteristics, including their solvency and reputation. In brief, they need local knowledge.

This personal nature of exchange is a more or less continuous attribute, derived from the more or less personal nature of the safeguards used to enforce contractual performance. In turn, the nature of these safeguards affects the amount of personal information that parties need to gather before committing themselves to the exchange. Going from the most to the least personal (and omitting individual moral traits[3]), the starting points are expectations of future trade and market-observable reputation, then systems for indirect liability (including the use of assurance intermediaries and community responsibility), and, lastly, impartial judicial enforcement of contractual agreements.

First, most trade between parties who know each other is fully personal as it relies on their mutual knowledge and expectations of their future trade. This generally affects private ordering solutions (Williamson 1985, 163–205). Likewise, much of the trade with strangers also requires gathering information to know what performance assurances—for instance, their track record and reputation—they offer. So it, too, is mainly personal.

Second, trade also remains personal when performance assurances are not produced by the parties themselves but by assurance intermediaries, such as financial institutions, credit bureaus, credit and title insurers, rating agencies, auditors, and so on. In such cases, trade remains personal to the extent that it is based on the reputation of the intermediaries and their knowledge of their clients. Similarly, trade is also personal under community responsibility systems, when all members of a group (e.g., all merchants of a particular city in late medieval times) are liable for the behavior and contractual obligations of each of the group's members.[4] Such a system allows strangers to trade with group members, but they do so based on limited personal information, just enough for them to unambiguously know which individuals are members of which groups and which groups are dependable. Moreover, such a system also requires monitoring individuals' characteristics within each group. Both assurance intermediaries and community responsibility therefore make transactions more impersonal but still retain important personal attributes.

Lastly, trade is often considered to be impersonal when it relies on independent judges.[5] But this reliance only reduces the amount of personal information required for transacting, as parties still need to ascertain at least how solvent their obliged counterparties are. Even with perfect judges, creditors must worry about how likely it is for their debtors to become judgment proof—that is, even after a court order states their debts, their creditors still cannot collect any money. Insolvency carries little stigma today but even in old times, when insolvent debtors ended up in prison, jailing them must have provided little joy to their creditors. As before, therefore, judicial enforcement still depends on personal attributes, and judicially supported trade still remains substantially personal in nature.

To the extent that personal attributes are present in all these cases, parties must spend resources on developing personal safeguards and producing knowledge about them. Also, to the extent that such safeguards remain weak, contractual enforcement is unreliable, prone to conflict and thus costly. Lastly, where there is a risk of contractual default, parties withdraw and waste trade opportunities. Therefore, relying on personal exchange precludes profitable exchanges between unknown parties and limits specialization opportun-ities and efficient reallocation of resources, reducing economic growth.

To expand the scope of transactions and fully exploit the benefits of comparative advantage, parties must be able to trade without any knowledge of personal characteristics. This requires making contractual performance independent of such characteristics, a feat that can only be achieved by granting acquirers rights directly against the acquired assets instead of against the sellers, that is, rights *in rem* (from the Latin *res*, thing) instead of *in personam*. However, providing this *in rem* protection to acquirers would endanger the rights of owners, who might be left holding mere claims against persons, rights *in personam* (e.g., against a fraudulent seller). Take the example of a simple asset sale when the seller is not the owner. The acquirer is better off if she is granted a right *in rem* against the asset itself, so that, for instance, possible defects as to the relationship between owner and seller do not affect her purchase. In contrast, were she given a right *in personam*, such defects might require her to return the asset to its owner, leaving her with a mere claim against the seller. Obviously, the opposite is true for owners.

In sum, legal systems face a hard choice, as rights on assets are needed for both the security of owners and impersonal exchange. But these two goals conflict because they entail protecting, respectively, current owners and acquirers, leaving the other party unprotected. And the choice is not made easier by the fact that today's owners are yesterday's acquirers: even though they share a common interest in abstract terms, their interests clash in any specific conflict. Protecting the interests of both owners and acquirers requires institutions and, in particular, contractual registries. For instance, if judges grant assets to those registered as owners in a public register, acquirers can avoid their information asymmetry by simply checking the register.

Before explaining in more detail the rationale behind contractual registries, I will examine in the next two sections what it means to define rights directly on assets instead of on persons, the comparative advantages of both enforcement strategies, and how they are handled by the two disciplines called on to support the analysis: the economics of property rights and property law.

The reason why I focus on the asset-versus-personal dichotomy is because it is key for contractual registries. But, of course, given that assets are not physically homogenous, eliminating personal elements does not exhaust the possibilities of commoditization that make trade easier. Establishing standard physical measures of assets greatly facilitates exchange—as, for example, when developing production standards useful in subcontracting manufacturing tasks (Arruñada and Vázquez 2006) or when demarcating land using a uniform grid (Libecap and Lueck 2011a and 2011b). In contrast, removing personal elements and defining rights on assets comes close to commoditizing the key legal, instead of physical, attributes.[6]

What Do Rights on Assets Mean? The Difference between Rights on Assets and Rights on Persons

A right *in rem* is more valuable than a corresponding right *in personam* even when both allocate to the holder the same set of asset uses—that is, the same decision rights about what to do with the asset—because rights *in rem* are easier to enforce.[7] It will be useful to examine several examples illustrating this enforcement advantage.

Imagine, first, a lease of real estate, which in many jurisdictions may be structured either *in personam* or *in rem*, as either a contract or a property right.[8] Imagine also that both of these define and allocate the same uses for the asset, including its possession.[9] However, if the lease is a property right, which is generally the default rule in the United States, the lessee keeps the right of occupation unless she consents to leave. It is then the land buyer who will have a claim for compensation against the seller if the sale was made free of leases. From the viewpoint of the lessee, the buyer simply replaces the seller without any change to the lease, which is said to "run with the land" from the seller to the buyer, surviving intact after the sale. Conversely, if the lease is a contract right, as in Roman law, the lessee loses the right of occupation when the leased land is sold during the life of the lease, following the principle of *emptio tollit locatum* or "sale breaks hire." Instead, the lessee gains a right to be compensated by the lessor.

The same happens when using property to guarantee the owners' debts. For example, a landowner may use her land as collateral for a loan by granting a mortgage to the lender. Alternatively, she may contract an unsecured personal loan. In both cases, the creditor has a right to be paid from the land, conditional on the borrower's default. However, the mortgage lender keeps the same claim on the land even after the debtor sells it or contracts a second mortgage on it. By contrast, when a landowner borrows personally, the land is also safeguarding the transaction but much more weakly, as the lender is granted only conditional *in personam* rights on the borrower's assets. Therefore, when the debtor defaults on such a personal loan, the lender is allowed to trigger the seizure and sale of debtors' property in order to be paid, but only if such property has not been legally transferred to an innocent third party before the debtor's default. The personal creditors' claims do not run with the land.

Finally, perhaps the most important example is ownership itself, which, even if held by the same person, is distinct from the right to use and enjoy the asset (usufruct in civil law) and from control of the asset (broadly equivalent to legal possession). Therefore, were someone purporting to be the owner to sell the land in a fraudulent sale, the true legal owner would recover it, and the buyer would thus get only a personal claim against the fraudulent seller. In fact, ownership is so much the ultimate *in rem* right that talk of the *in personam* owner seems awkward. However, it is *in personam* ownership that a claimant holds when a judge finds (or would find if asked to decide) that an alternative claimant is really the legal owner; thus, this alternative claimant is (or would be) given ownership of the land, the *in rem* right on it.

As shown in these examples, property *in rem* rights enjoy decisive enforcement advantages, as they define more direct relations with regard to things. They are thus claimable against the thing itself and therefore oblige all persons, *erga omnes*. This universal obligation means that, in the examples, the new owner who has purchased the land—whoever she is—must respect the *in rem* lease and the mortgage: in particular, the lessee's possession and the mortgagee's right to foreclose if the debtor defaults. And when she buys from a nonowner, she gets only a claim against the seller, without touching the owner's right on the land. This is why property rights run with the land—they survive unaltered through all kinds of transactions and transformations dealing with other rights on the same land or on a neighboring parcel. Enforcement of a property right *in rem* is independent of who holds this and all other rights on the same land, including ownership, because "rights and duties *in rem* do not refer to persons . . . in the sense that nothing to do with *any particular individual's personality* is involved in the normative guidance they offer" (Penner 1997, 26, emphases in the original).

A consequence of particular importance for specialization and thus for the functioning of the economy is that *in rem* owners do not suffer the possible moral hazard of their agents. For instance, when the owner cedes possession, she does not risk losing the asset if the agent poses as owner and sells it to a third party. *In rem* rights may certainly weaken enforcement in one dimension: all current owners have been acquirers and they can lose the asset against potential claimants with a better legal title. But this risk is delimited, being a risk from the past, and also diminishes with the lapse of time, due to the operation of rules that automatically purge titles, such as adverse possession and the statute of limitations.

In contrast, mere contract rights define obligations between the contracting parties and thus are enforceable only against these specific persons, *inter partes*. Moreover, persons last less and move more than durable assets, and their reliability suffers from all kinds of additional risks. In terms of the examples, if the lease were contractual, the lessee would have to attain an indemnity from the lessor, who might well have disappeared or be insolvent. The same might easily happen with insolvent debtors and fraudulent sellers.

Consequently, contract, *in personam*, rights provide little security and their value depends on who the obliged persons are and how they will behave. Information on these specific persons is thus necessary to alleviate the information asymmetries potentially causing adverse selection and moral hazard. Furthermore, the performance of contract rights remains conditioned on all these personal elements even if it ends up being materialized in uses of the asset—for example, an *in personam* land lease materializes in the same use of the land as an *in rem* lease, but with lower enforceability. This personal mediation in accessing assets compares badly in terms of enforceability with *in rem* rights, whose asset uses are enforced independently of any personal condition. So rights *in rem* are intrinsically different and more valuable than the mere addition of a corresponding set of rights *in personam* defining the same uses (Merrill and Smith 2001b, 786–87).

Rights *in rem* enjoy this enforcement advantage because they can be damaged only with the consent of their rightholder. This ensures enforcement but is costly when multiple, potentially conflicting rights are held in the same asset. In particular, potential acquirers of rights suffer additional uncertainty because, if they are sold more than the seller holds, adverse *in rem* rights will survive their acquisition. Such potential adverse rights are all those that conflict with the intended transaction. In our previous examples, they are the rights held by the lessee and the mortgagee when the land is sold purportedly free of *in rem* leases and mortgages. In the case of a fraudulent sale, the adverse right is the ownership held by the legal owner. In all these cases, if rightholders have not consented to the transaction, their rights survive intact, and the acquirer gets a claim against the grantor for the unfulfilled difference (which is all she gets in a fraudulent sale).

From this perspective, parties and institutions have to manage a tricky interaction between enforcement and transaction costs, between *in rem* property rights and the transaction costs they cause. Rights *in personam* offer less enforcement but are easier to contract over, given that they only affect the transactors. In contrast, rights *in rem* offer stronger enforcement but are harder to contract over, given that they affect and therefore require the consent of everybody.[10] Moreover, the difference is important because the value of a given use right enforced *in rem* is greater than the same use right enforced *in personam*. Individuals may even be judgment proof, which would make *in personam* rights unenforceable. Different legal systems provide parties with ways to contract *in rem* rights more or less easily, so that parties can benefit from their enhanced enforceability. Otherwise, they have to rely on mere personal rights. There are, therefore, two distinct tradeoffs at the social and individual levels. First, society must decide how much to spend on institutions that ease *in rem* contracting, such as, for instance, contractual registries to make mortgages public. Second, given these institutions, parties must then decide how much to spend on transaction costs (e.g., examining the register) so that they transfer *in rem* rights or, in continuous terms, rights with a greater *in rem* content and thus enhanced enforcement.

This interaction between *in rem* enforcement and transaction costs, which lies at the core of property law, fits poorly in the economic analysis of property rights, which, when considering property enforcement, tends to disregard what may well be its essential element: the legal remedies available to owners. For economists, enforcement is often a matter of precisely defining the scope and allocation of rights, two aspects that should generally reduce the costs of transacting—that is, greater precision should reduce transaction costs. My next step is to clarify this divide between economics and property law which, far from being merely semantic, reveals their widely different but complementary perspectives.

Differences between the Economic and Legal Views on Enforcement— Or Why Economics Chose to Ignore Legal Property

Everybody agrees that security of property is essential for development. All owners want their rights to be universally respected. If they do not feel secure, if their rights are weak, they will be unwilling to invest, and this will hinder economic growth. However, property security has many dimensions, of two major types, public and private, attached to what can be seen, respectively, as political and market failures.[11]

Economics has mainly focused on the public aspects. First, as emphasized by North and coauthors, a well-organized polity will preclude violence and confiscation, and subject owners' expropriation to strict conditions, including proper compensation.[12] Second, as analyzed by many works influenced by Coase (1960), the law and, to a large extent, government and politics set the initial allocation of rights, which enables parties to freely transact in the market and thus reach a more efficient allocation of resources. Many of these economic analyses focus on how political failures lead to bad institutions. Their central concern is that property may be endangered by political failure because most governments not only prove unable to allocate property rights clearly and to preclude violence and defend private rights against private encroachment but are also prone to confiscating their citizens' property.[13]

Property law, instead, focuses on private aspects.[14] In particular, it is mainly concerned with the fact that property can also be endangered by market failure, when individuals misuse transactions to grab the property of others. This may happen because owners acquire their property from someone else and will, at some point and especially in a modern economy, transfer it to others. But transfers pose risks to both owners and acquirers, so that owners will fear being dispossessed of their rights and acquirers will fear being cheated on their purchase. To prevent their mutual fears and encourage them to invest and trade, even impersonally, a market economy requires institutions providing more than an initial allocation of rights—they must also provide effective *in rem* enforcement and, as a consequence, what in the Coasean setup can be labeled as "recurrent allocations of rights."

However, little attention has been paid by the economic analysis of property rights to *in rem* enforcement and the need for clarity in these reallocations in the context of frequent market transactions. The primary reason is that this economic literature, much of which "remains ignorant of property law" (Lueck and Miceli 2007, 187), by omitting the distinction between rights *in rem* and rights *in personam*, that is, between what the law calls, respectively, property rights and contract rights,[15] is in fact dealing only with rights *in personam*.

This omission makes sense in these economic analyses because they focus on the emergence of property and the analysis of externalities. Their main issues have been the transition from regimes of open access and common property to private property and the requirements for bargaining around externalities, disregarding the more mundane but no less important problem of routine transactions on ordinary private property.[16] For these objectives, it makes sense, adopting a simplistic view of Coase (1960), to see property as a mere bundle of use rights and to consider that these are strong if well defined, if their content is precisely delineated, and if they are clearly allocated to individuals. This amounts to treating rights on assets as valid only against specific persons, *in personam*. In other words, no distinction is made between the strength of the right and the size of the set of parties it can be enforced against, disregarding that a crucial element of a right's strength is that it can be enforced against all persons. Instead, enforcement tends to be equated to effective judicial decisions and police actions, ignoring that many individuals are judgment proof. Therefore, remedies remain undefined in a key dimension. Although the question of the proper level of indemnity in different situations is carefully analyzed, little attention is paid to the more basic problem of having the obliged person pay it.

In contrast, property law focuses on standard transactions on private property and emphasizes *remedies* as the key dimension of enforcement. Consequently, it tackles this basic problem head on, by obviating persons and establishing rights directly on assets, *in rem*. These are strong rights because the consent of the rightholder is required to affect them, establishing the strongest link possible between holders and assets.

This enforcement by consent provides a conceptual link with the Coasean contractarian framework because all relevant consents must be granted to acquire rights *in rem*, and this involves several consequences for the contractual process and its support institutions. First, as acquirers are interested in acquiring *in rem*, they try to gather all pertinent consents, and institutions are structured to make such gathering possible. Contracting then becomes a two-step process: a first, personal step, in which the parties to the contract agree on the intended transaction; and a second, real step, in which holders of *in rem* claims conflicting with the intended transaction grant their consent. For instance, the buyer of a house does not only contract with the seller; if both parties want to transfer the house free of an existing *in rem* lease, they must first obtain the consent of the lessee.

Second, the acquirer might still be unsecure about the universality of the gathered consents. Reducing this remaining uncertainty requires institutional solutions that, in essence, publicly reallocate rights *in rem*. The acquirer will be especially worried about the possible existence of any adverse abstract rights, such as mortgages, that might remain hidden. Furthermore, ownership itself is also abstract and may cause the greatest loss. Therefore, the acquirer will be especially queasy about the identity and authority of the seller because, in the worst case, she would be getting nothing *in rem* but only a mere claim on the seller, and the value of such an *in personam* claim will often be zero. Understandably, this remaining uncertainty has driven the provision of institutional solutions. A common strategy, often used for mortgages, consists of requiring that, to be enforced *in rem*, rights be made public in a registry. This obviously facilitates more thorough gathering of consents. Alternatively, either registers with a quasi-judicial function or judges themselves are called on to explicitly establish this allocation of *in rem* rights. In any case, when *in rem* rights are involved, initial allocation of rights is not enough and there will be implicit or explicit recurrent public allocations. In short, given that *in rem* rights oblige everybody, acquisition of *in rem* rights cannot be achieved by purely private contracting between parties but must include a public intervention to reallocate rights. (Alternatively, it could be said that rights *in rem* can be acquired privately but commit *in rem* only the parties to the transaction. However, this makes little sense considering that the essence of *in rem* enforcement lies in the universal duties it creates.)

Lastly, it is worth mentioning that the focus of property law on assets, on *in rem* remedies, makes this branch of law the main institutional foundation for impersonal exchange, given that only such remedies make truly impersonal exchange possible. This link between impersonal exchange and rights *in rem* comes naturally to property law (e.g., in Penner 1997). In contrast, conventional economic analysis of (*in personam*) "property rights" inspires a distorted view of the division of labor between property and contract law, in which property law is seen as serving merely to allocate resources and contract law to handle transactions. For example, a survey of the economic analysis of contract law asserted that

> while the law of property determines the configuration of entitlements that form the basis of production and exchange, and the law of torts protects those entitlements from involuntary encroachment and expropriation, it is contract law that sets the rules for exchanging individual claims to entitlements and, thus, determines the extent to which society is able to enjoy the gains from trade. (Hermalin, Katz, and Craswell 2007, 7)

This view is valid only with respect to part of the economic analysis of property rights, that which focuses on the initial allocation of rights, paying little attention to transaction and enforcement difficulties. It holds no water with respect to the functions of both branches of law.

Specialization and Transactions Require Multiple Rights on Each Asset, Hindering Impersonal Trade

As the previous examples show, difficulties arise from the presence of multiple rights (in the examples, leasehold, mortgage, and ownership) on the same asset. If only one right were held on each asset, *in rem* enforcement would be easy to provide without increasing transaction costs. Governments and judges would only have to guarantee the peaceful possession of assets, preventing individuals from being deprived of them against their will by violence or fraud. But in that case actual possession—direct, physical, and intentional control—would be the only possible right on assets, precluding multiple and abstract rights, as well as impeding even the most simple types of specialization.[17]

Understandably, multiple rights are instead pervasive, as the drive for specialization leads parties to voluntarily define multiple rights on the same assets. This process includes all arrangements separating ownership and control, which pursue specialization advantages by defining rights on particular uses or for limited periods of time. They span from the simplest landlord-tenant contract in real estate, in which owners usually cede all the uses of the land, to sophisticated structures of corporate governance, in which millions of shareholders jointly and indirectly own assets controlled by a team of professional managers.[18] Moreover, multiple rights are also created as an often involuntary consequence of defective transactions: for instance, when a seller sells more than she owns, conflicting *in rem* claims will exist on the same asset. Before the conflict is resolved and to the extent that such claims may win in court, the asset is subject to multiple and colliding rights *in rem* (even of the same nature as, for instance, in cases of disputed ownership).

Whatever the voluntary or involuntary origin of multiple rights, the information asymmetry suffered by acquirers is made worse by the very multiplicity of rights when they might be enforced *in rem*. For a start, the individuals using the asset are in possession of it and can therefore easily pose as owners. This means, for instance, that purchasers are never fully sure that they are dealing with an owner, as they cannot infer ownership from possession; therefore, even true legal owners face difficulties when trying to sell directly, and transaction costs are present in all transactions, both with and without selling agents: all transactions are de facto multilateral. Similarly, sellers can hide from prospective acquirers the existence of *in rem* rights that conflict with the rights they are purporting to sell. Also, in this case, as acquirers are uncertain, the shadow of possible burdens will hang even over unburdened assets. And, in general, the more *in rem* rights there are, the greater the possibility of cheating and conflict.[19]

The risk is especially acute and hard to overcome for parties alone because both the voluntary and involuntary multiplication of rights generate rights that are abstract in nature and may therefore remain hidden. Thus, voluntarily giving possession to nonowners makes ownership an abstraction, and financial specialization leads to abstract rights in the form of mortgages and security interests, as well as to corporate relationships. Similarly, disputed claims may remain hidden for a long time before coming to light.

In sum, multiple rights are indispensable for specialization and are pervasive in today's economies. Because multiple rights increase the transaction costs caused by *in rem* rights, transactors need institutional solutions, such as registries, that allow them to achieve the advantages of both multiple rights and *in rem* enforcement. For example, if judges establish ownership based on a public register, mere possessors will have a harder time posing as owners to deceive innocent acquirers.

Generalizing the Analysis

To find out the nature of these solutions and make the analysis more general, I now consider the sequential structure of transactions, using a framework of economic agency. This allows me to clarify how rights are recurrently allocated and show that the interaction between enforcement benefits and transaction costs is widespread in all sorts of economic transactions.

Information Structure of Single and Sequential Exchanges

Judges solve two main types of contractual conflict, which correspond to two different exchange structures: *single* and *sequential* exchanges. Single-exchange conflicts involve only one transaction—for instance, a client and a seller who provides a good or a service to the client. Sequential-exchange conflicts involve at least two interrelated single exchanges. Consequently, in addition to the relation between the client and the seller, the judge will need to consider the relation between the seller and the owner of the good or between the seller and her employer.

Sequential exchange therefore involves at least three parties in two single transactions that I will call *originative* and *subsequent*. Labeling the parties according to their economic role, the originative transaction takes place between a *principal* (the owner or employer in the example) and an *agent* (the seller), while the corresponding subsequent transaction takes place between the agent and a third party (the client) external to the originative

Figure 1.1. Timeline of generic sequential exchanges with two transactions and three parties

transaction. Consequently, the agent plays a contractual function and not only a productive function. As depicted in figure 1.1, both single and sequential exchange give rise to conflict; but in each type of exchange the information asymmetry causing the conflicts is different, so dealing with it requires different types of institutional support.

Information asymmetry in single exchange is well represented by Akerlof's (1970) influential analysis of the market for "lemons," in which the owner of a used car is trying to sell it. Understandably, prospective buyers are reluctant to buy because, given that owners know the quality of their own car best, used cars on sale tend to be those of poorer quality. In such situations of adverse selection, which are much more common than the car example suggests, information asymmetry with respect to material quality poses a serious threat to trade. Therefore, parties must devote plenty of resources to producing solutions, disclosing and obtaining information and providing all sorts of quality assurances.

Many of these solutions may be implemented by parties themselves by, for example, writing contracts (here termed "documentary formalization"), verifying quality and investing in reputation. They can also rely on a judge to complete and enforce the contract. In particular, parties will define the promised performance of the car. Also, the seller can guarantee a minimum level of quality, promise to pay for future repairs, or return part of the price in case of a major breakdown. Specifying and verifying these relevant dimensions of performance is costly. For instance, parties have to agree on the terms, write them down, and safely keep a copy of the contract for future use. But, if contract obligations are not fulfilled, the aggrieved party can call on the judge to enforce the contract, using it as a source of primary evidence for the judge's decision.

A variant of this example of single-exchange "lemons" illustrates the information asymmetry problem posed by sequential exchange. How does the buyer know that the seller is really the owner or, in general, has legal power to sell the car? If she does not have such power, the buyer faces the loss of the full purchase price. Therefore, this information asymmetry about what I will be referring to as legal "title" (i.e., the prior originative transaction between the previous owner and the current seller) may be even more serious than that about material quality, which most often only causes a partial loss.

A key point for my inquiry is that this type of information asymmetry is also harder for parties to solve by themselves because, however much title examiners strive to clarify and assure title, title evidence may remain hidden in the absence of public registries. And developing registries faces the standard collective-action problems. Creating them generally exceeds the power of individual parties and thus requires a public initiative. Moreover, once in operation, individuals would benefit from having a reliable register, but each individual would benefit even more if the register were selectively reliable, being, for instance, lenient with the individual but strict with her counterparties.

The task of the judge is also harder and more critical. Harder because the judge must decide based on the originative contract between the principal-owner and the agent-seller, which they can easily manipulate, especially if it has not been available to the acquiring third party. More critical because, instead of simply solving a conflict between the parties to the contract by comparing actual and promised performance, the judge now has to adjudicate the asset as belonging to one of the two allegedly innocent claimants, either to the previous owner, applying a property rule, or to the buyer, applying a contract rule. The judge will grant the losing party a mere claim for indemnity against the seller, who will often be judgment proof. And, in fact, most cases of title conflict start because such a claim is much less valuable than its alternative.

Effects of Sequential Exchange on Trade and Specialization

This gap in value explains that this type of judicial decision has substantial effects throughout the whole sequence of transactions. Expectations about similar cases define the incentives of all parties potentially involved with this type of asset when they invest, trade, and specialize. Potential buyers will be more reluctant to purchase at time 1 if they think judges will rule at time 2 for the owner; but at time 0 owners will be less willing to invest and specialize if they think judges will rule for the buyer (see figures 1.1–1.3). Both will also take more precautions if they fear that judges might rule against them: buyers will investigate title more and will prefer to contract with people they know. Consequently, there will be less impersonal exchange.

In particular, owners' attempts to avoid putting themselves in a position where they may risk being dispossessed will hinder specialization. They will contract more directly instead of using intermediaries, given that it is separation of ownership and control (i.e., possession by nonowners) that creates such a risk. And they will be more careful about choosing contractual agents, preferring those they know personally or who, more generally, offer good personal guarantees. Moreover, this reduced separation of ownership and control is only the most basic example of a much larger phenomenon: it will be privately profitable to define fewer rights on each asset, with a consequent loss of the specialization opportunities. Furthermore, many of these effects impose costs in terms of lost trade opportunities and will therefore remain invisible, so that developing proper solutions will be harder.

All these effects mean that judicial decisions on sequential exchange cases exert a major impact on key economic decisions. Moreover, sequential exchange is prevalent, affecting most economic activity, as I will conclude after exploring in the next section a representative survey of business and real property transactions. It is therefore crucial that judicial decisions on them be based on reliable contractual evidence.

This survey of typical transactions will also reveal how the degree of difficulty for solving this evidentiary problem varies across transactions, requiring different solutions. Verifiable evidence on originative contracts is easily available for some types of transaction but not for others.[20] In this context, the essential function of contractual registries is to provide evidence for judicial decisions when it is not readily available as a byproduct of the contracting and productive processes. Using this evidence, judges can safely decide litigated cases by applying rules that favor innocent, uninformed parties, which should encourage them to trade impersonally and, in turn, encourage all participants to specialize. Furthermore, reliable evidence allows judges to apply such rules efficiently, without damaging property rights, even when multiple and abstract *in rem* rights are defined and enforced on the same asset.

Prevalence and Varying Contractual Difficulty of Sequential Exchange

The scope of single exchange is severely limited because most specialization necessarily involves a sequence of interrelated transactions, both originative and subsequent, and a given transaction may have many originative transactions. For a start, transactions on durable assets are inevitably sequential, as, due to their durability, claims on them are potentially valuable. Therefore, claimants prefer to enforce their rights *in rem* rather than *in personam*. Even simple transfers of such assets implicitly involve originative transactions in the form of previous total or partial transfers, as well as "principals" in the form of alternative claimants—for example, potential "true" legal owners and, usually, any potential claimants of other rights on the asset. More generally, most exchanges also involve several parties in a sequence of transactions because of the desire of economic participants to reach specialization advantages. This is all the more evident when one of the parties to the contract explicitly acts as an economic agent for someone else.

In all these cases, exchanges thus involve at least three parties in a sequence of at least two transactions (figure 1.1).[21] This sequential exchange is necessary to specialize the tasks performed by principal P and agent A, including all types of delegation and separation of ownership and control— for example, between shareholders and managers, owners and possessors, and mortgagors and mortgagees. But specialization creates new transaction costs, driven mainly by the risks that the agent may lack or exceed the powers to commit the principal or that either the owners or the acquiring third party, T, may be dispossessed or deceived. These acquiring third parties now suffer much greater information asymmetry than if there was only uncertainty about the material quality of the good or service being delivered by the agent. And this information asymmetry about the agent's legal title or power to contract needs to be overcome for impersonal markets to function properly.

Sequential Exchange in Business Transactions

Perhaps the simplest sequential exchange is one in which a producer relies on a distributor to sell its products to the distributor's customers (figure 1.2, row a). First, an originative transaction takes place between the producer, P, and the distributor, D, and then there is a subsequent transaction between the distributor and the customer, C. This arrangement achieves specialization advantages because using distributors allows producers to focus on production and to reach a larger market. In turn, distributors can focus on distribution, sell a wider set of products, and be closer to their customers.

But it also causes transaction costs. In principle, customers are unaware of the quality of the seller's legal title. Ideally, in case of a dispute (arising, for instance, from default of payment by the distributor to the producer), they would like the judge to decide that the goods remain with the customer, with the producer getting only a claim for indemnity against the distributor. This is probably a sensible solution if the producer has chosen the distributor voluntarily, especially if both the producer and the distributor are professionals repeatedly making similar choices. Producers then will have good incentives to choose reliable distributors, and distributors will have good incentives to develop proper safeguards.

0	1	2

Originative transactions: $P \rightarrow A$	Subsequent transactions: $A \rightarrow T$	Judicial decisions: P vs. T
a) Distribution transaction $P_r \rightarrow D$	Sale by distributor $D \rightarrow C$	P_r vs. C
b) Employment $E_r \rightarrow E$	Contract by employee $E \rightarrow T$	E_r vs. T
c) Organization as LLP $LP \rightarrow GP$	Credit transaction $GP \rightarrow CC$	LP vs. CC
d) Incorporation $P_1, \ldots P_n \rightarrow M$	Sale of shares $M \rightarrow P_{n+j}$	$P_1, \ldots P_n$ vs. P_{n+j}

NOTE: Arrows represent agency relationships, not transfers. Numbers 0, 1, and 2 indicate time 0, time 1, and time 2, respectively. A, agent; C, customer; CC, company creditors; D, distributor; E, employee; E_r, employer; GP, general partner; LP, limited partner; M, manager; P_r, producer; P_{n+j}, new shareholders; and T, third party.

Figure 1.2. Timeline of a sample of typical business sequential exchanges in business

The second business case is equally simple: employment relations consist of an originative transaction by which employer E_r hires employee E, leading to subsequent transactions in which the employee interacts with a third party, T (figure 1.2, row b). (Note that there is no need for the subsequent transaction to be contractual. For example, E may commit E_r because his actions damage T, generating tort liability to E_r due to the fact that E is an employee of E_r.) In any case, the third party should worry about the power of the employee to commit the employer, as well as how the judge will decide when the employee exceeds such power. As in the producer-distributor case, it will be sensible for the judge to protect the third party. The rationale, as before, is that employers are the ones freely choosing and controlling employees.

In these two cases, the judge has little difficulty verifying that both the producer and the employer had consented to be committed by, respectively, the distributor and the employee. Such consents are made verifiable by the visible fact that the goods had been entrusted to the distributor and the employee had been publicly acting as such.

In contrast, company contracts often lack such public, verifiable consequences. Imagine, for instance, a third case in which two partners create a limited liability partnership, LLP, with a general partner, GP, under unlimited liability and a limited partner, LP, under limited liability (figure 1.2, row c). Consider the possibility that, in a subsequent transaction, the general partner borrows from company creditors, CC, falsely claiming that the limited partner is subject to *unlimited* liability. In a case like this, the judge will face serious difficulties if the originative contract remains private and, as a consequence, does not produce unequivocal consequences. In the two previous cases, possessing a good and acting as an employee were publicly observable facts. But in this third case, a partner's liability regime is an abstract feature of the originative organization contract, which might remain private and therefore be manipulated in an opportunistic manner. Such a regime would, at least, need to be explicitly included in all subsequent contracts for them to be implemented with a modicum of guarantees, and such an inclusion would be costly.

Many other corporate transactions pose similar difficulties, as it is often unclear who has legal power to commit a company. Typically, partners or shareholders delegate to a corporate board or manager M, who then enter into all sorts of contracts with third parties: they may, for instance, sell unauthorized shares to new shareholders P_{n+j} or exceed the limits of the company's legal purpose or "objects clause" (figure 1.2, row d). For some companies and transactions, the authority of the company agents may be easy to verify; for many others, however, it will remain hidden and nonverifiable. And additional attributes of companies may also be hard to verify. In particular, both companies' and partners' creditors will be most interested in knowing which assets are owned by the company and which by its partners. Furthermore, participants are often motivated to behave opportunistically. Besides incentives to exaggerate the assets at the time of contracting credit, shareholders also have incentives to move assets in or out of the company depending on company and personal circumstances.

In principle, as with partners' and shareholders' limited liability, clauses on all these aspects could be explicitly included in subsequent company and personal contracts. But this inclusion would be costly and unreliable. As analyzed below, filing originative corporate contracts and legal acts in a public registry usually provides a more efficient solution. Even if costly, registering these contracts implicitly includes them in all subsequent contracts in an easy-to-verify (i.e., hard-to-manipulate) manner.

Sequential Exchange in Real Property Transactions

Time now to come back to real property in order to reformulate the initial analysis of property rights in terms of the general framework.

The deep structure of real property exchanges is identical to that of the previous business cases: (1) a principal and what in the economic sense of the word is still an "agent" enter into an originative contract selling, mortgaging, leasing, or somehow transferring or dividing rights on a piece of real estate; (2) the agent contracts with a third party in a subsequent contract—for instance, the owner sells or mortgages the land again; and (3) a judge may be called to decide who gets the land. In real property cases, the agent often cheats by hiding or distorting the previous relevant transaction

0	1	2
Originative transactions:	Subsequent transactions:	Judicial decisions:
$P \to A$	$A \to T$	P vs. T
a) First sale	Second sale	
$B_1 \to O$	$O \to B_2$	B_1 vs. B_2
b) First mortgage	Second mortgage	
$M_1 \to O$	$O \to M_2$	M_1 vs. M_2
c) Sale of land on credit	Buyer sells before paying	
$O \to B_1$	$B_1 \to B_2$	O vs. B_2
d) Leasing	Owner sells	
$L \to O$	$O \to B$	L vs. B
e) Leasing	Lessee sells	
$O \to L$	$L \to B$	O vs. B

NOTE: Arrows represent agency relationships, not transfers. Numbers 0, 1, and 2 indicate time 0, time 1, and time 2, respectively. A, agent; B, buyer; L, lessee; M, manager; O, owner; P, principal; and T, third party.

Figure 1.3. Timeline of a sample of typical sequential exchanges in real property

and pretending to transfer a given right that is apparently unaffected by the hidden transaction; pretending, for example, to convey full title or to grant a first mortgage, or to sell the land free of encumbrances. As in the previous business exchanges, the judicial decision will, in essence, allocate a right on the property, between the principal and the third party, awarding the losing party a mere claim against the agent.

However, in real estate exchanges, as compared to those in business, the roles of principal and agent are more implicit and alternating. For example, in a double sale of land, the owner who sells the same land twice can fruitfully be seen as cheating on his duties as an agent of the first buyer, to whom he has a duty to not sell again (figure 1.3, row a). The judge will give the land either to the principal (the first buyer) or to the third party (the second buyer), while leaving the losing party with the right to claim an indemnity from the former owner (the agent). Something similar happens with second mortgages: the first mortgagee acts as principal, the owner as agent, and the second mortgagee as the third party (figure 1.3, row b).

Understandably, when applied to property, this "agency" language, based on the broad economic concepts of principals and agents,[22] may puzzle readers more familiar with the legal concept of agency. Both concepts are closer and the agency structure is clearer in business than in property transactions because, for many business transactions, there is a more explicit agency or employment relationship. In contrast, for property, which party plays the role of agent or of principal even depends on the type of deception considered in each transaction. But the agency structure is also present in all property transactions. Observe, for instance, that in a second sale the seller is acting as an economic agent for the first buyer, even if this use of the agency concept is unconventional in legal terms, since the first buyer does not intend the seller to act in this capacity and the seller does not portray herself as an agent of the buyer.

Moreover, in addition to being implicit and atypical, for many originative transactions in real property, both buyers and sellers alternate in the roles of principal and agent in different circumstances, with respect to different subsequent transactions. In fact, each of the previous cases presents a typical conflict in each transaction and not the transaction itself. For example, in a double sale, the owner, O, is an agent with respect to his obligation not to sell the land to another buyer, B_2, after selling it to the first buyer, B_1, who acts as a principal (figure 1.3, row a). However, a buyer of land may also act as an agent with respect to the obligation to pay a deferred purchase price to the owner. Imagine, for instance, that the buyer, B_1, resells the land to an innocent third party, B_2, before paying the agreed price to the owner-seller, O (figure 1.3, row c). Similarly, a lease may pose risks in both directions, to both the lessor and the lessee. The owning lessor, O, may sell the land to a third party, B, who might then try to evict the lessee, L, or get only a claim against the seller if the judge so decides (figure 1.3, row d). In the opposite direction, a lessee might abuse possession, posing as an owner and selling the land to someone else (figure 1.3, row e). Furthermore, these alternating roles are common because the survival of property makes long chains of transactions possible so that, in most property cases, a current subsequent transaction will be the originative transaction of future subsequent transactions on the same asset. Similarly, what is now an originative transaction was in the past the subsequent transaction of a previous originative one.

Information Problem of Sequential Exchange and Solving It by Selective Application of Property and Contract Rules

The Problem: Information Asymmetry in Subsequent Transactions

All these business and property transactions therefore share a common structure: specialization and trading decisions by owners and their agents lead to originative transactions that multiply and reallocate rights, creating information asymmetries that may hinder subsequent impersonal transactions, as third parties may doubt the legal title of the agent to commit the principal. Fraudulent subsequent transactions are made possible because, as a consequence of the originative transaction, agents become in possession of assets or are placed in a position in which they seem to have power to contract on behalf of the principal. For example, an employee will tend to be seen as authorized to commit the firm. Similarly, a lease gives the lessee the possession of the land and puts her in a good position to pretend to be the owner when selling to an innocent third party. These situations create tension between protecting owners with property rules, thus enhancing investment and specialization, and protecting acquirers with contract rules, thereby enhancing impersonal exchange.

This can be expressed in terms of Coasean bargaining by observing that, in a sequential exchange, the judge will at some point adjudicate *in rem* and *in personam* rights of widely different value. To the extent that this adjudication is based on originative contracts, it is these contracts that determine the information structure and the difficulties of subsequent transactions. Perspectives that emphasize the initial allocation of rights risk obscuring this process, as most contracting relates to rights that were at least privately reallocated in a previous originative transaction. And the fact that *in rem* rights are more valuable than *in personam* rights leads market participants to demand recurrent public allocations—that is, a judicial adjudication or, at the least, verifiable information on how such reallocation will be decided. Providing this verifiable information is the minimum and essential function of contractual registries, especially about originative transactions producing abstract rights, which may easily remain hidden.

Note that my focus has been different in business and real property cases, but the problems they pose are not really different. For business transactions, I have assumed that the agent did have a legal right to contract, whereas, for land, I have focused on cases in which the agent did not have such a right. But I could equally have compared the case of a merchant who contracts for another merchant to take custody of some merchandise with an explicit agreement not to sell it, a case which would resemble more closely that of a buyer of land who allows the seller to remain in possession of it. Even if in most legal systems possession produces different legal effects for movables and immovables, this does not affect the structure of the problem. Nor is there a difference in the potential for collusion between parties to the originative contract: it is just as possible in a company as in a second sale or a second mortgage. In these latter cases, the parties simply hide the previous contract until the money changes hands in the subsequent contract, cheating the innocent acquirer. They can even choose opportunistically according to the evolution of the market price, especially if the indemnity is not defined by the market price but by the selling price.

Moreover, characterization in terms of *in rem* rights is apparently inexact for some business transactions, as no assets are directly involved. Many business transactions do directly involve rights on assets, for instance, on all sorts of goods, negotiable instruments, or company shares; but others do not, when the transactions only redefine the priority of personal obligations (e.g., tort liability), making the principal liable. However, even for the latter, the informational structure of the problem and the institutional solutions are the same. Strictly speaking, the law does not achieve fully impersonal exchange, but it does achieve much safer personal exchange, given that the exchange remains impersonal with respect to the agent: acquirers know who is liable for the agents' actions, so parties can have reliable individuals and firms (especially firms, because they often are more durable and reliable than individuals) acting as principals. It also makes it easier to safeguard trade by means of reputation and with help from assurance specialists.

Observe also an implicit assumption in the analysis: subsequent transactions are assumed to be more impersonal than originative transactions. This is consistent with reality in that, for example, the set of originative transactions that makes up the firm (including incorporation, employment, and links with suppliers) can be assumed to be relatively of a more personal nature—being mostly based on repeated interactions—than subsequent transactions with third parties. In other cases, such as land, all transactions are equally impersonal when taken individually. However, even in this case, principals and agents have better information than third parties about previous transactions, which causes information asymmetry, putting third parties at a disadvantage and making the subsequent transaction different. In other words, impersonal transactions de facto become personal when they are originative of future subsequent transactions.

Lastly, for real property, instead of an originative "transaction" there will sometimes be a simpler allocation of rights, which can either be explicit, stemming from some political power (as in, e.g., Crown grants), or implicit (e.g., from first possession). In fact, going back through the historic chain of title, there will always be at least one initial allocation of this type; and often many more, not only when there are breaks in the contractual chain of title, but also when parties call on the state to clarify title—that is, to clearly allocate rights *in rem* (remember the demand for public recurrent allocations analyzed above).

Despite these nuances, all conflicts triggered by these sequences of business and property transactions are of the same nature, as the judge has to adjudicate either *in rem* rights to an asset (the property), leaving the losing party with the much less valuable possibility of claiming an indemnity from the agent; or, in those business cases in which *in rem* rights are not involved, adjudicate to the third party an *in personam* right against the principal or merely against the agent. If judges always rule in favor of the uninformed acquirer, applying a contract rule, they will make the information asymmetry irrelevant for third parties, but owners will be in danger of dispossession. This would even be bad for acquirers: they would be secure against possible claims by past owners but insecure with respect to misbehavior by possible future agents. Similarly, if judges always rule in favor of the principal-owner, applying a property rule, the information asymmetry suffered by third parties will hinder impersonal trade. Even true legal owners would have difficulties in selling or using their assets as collateral for credit. In a way, reducing transaction costs require the weakening of property rights, and strengthening property rights increases transaction costs.

Therefore, I will use these concepts of "property rule" and "contract rule" to identify the two solutions in which the judge grants the legal owner a claim, respectively, superior or inferior to the conflicting claim of a good faith acquirer for value. It seems sensible to consider as a property rule the solution in which priority is granted according to legal property, and as a contract rule the alternative in which it is granted according to the transfer contract. This may cause confusion but some confusion is in any case inescapable, given that both property and contract rights are allocated in all cases. For instance, by enforcing a contract rule, judges grant owners a contract right and acquirers a property right. Therefore, any way of labeling the rules suits a certain perspective better and risks being perceived as confusing when seen from the alternative perspective of the other specific party in the transaction. In particular, the labeling I will be using in this book is more intuitively coherent with the perspective of former owners, because property rules confirm their property *in rem* rights. It might seem less coherent for acquirers, as it is the contract rule that leads them to acquire property instead of contract rights. But I apply the labels to the allocation rules and not to the allocated rights, which are always *in rem* for the winner and *in personam* for the loser. And my usage, by implying that the true legal owner is given a contract right, emphasizes the *voluntary dilution of property rights* that I consider an essential feature of impersonal markets.

In addition, these rules are similar but distinct from the "property" and "liability" rules defined in a classic work by Calabresi and Melamed (1972) because, instead of a taking that affects only two parties, here the rules are defined in the context of a three-party sequence of two transactions. Moreover, my analysis focuses on the role played by the parties in each transaction, disregarding that current third parties will often act as principals in a future sequence of transactions. Consequently, when good-faith third parties win a dispute over their acquisitive transaction (i.e., when they are given a property *in rem* right), they do not win as a consequence of applying a property rule, which—by definition—would have given the good to the original owner. In such a case, the third party does not pay any monetary damages to the original owner, as in Calabresi and Melamed's liability rule. A final difference is that Calabresi and Melamed's property rule is weaker, referring only to the ability to force a would-be taker to bargain for a consensual transfer similar to specific performance, which thus arguably has little to do with a right *in rem*.

The Solution: Third-Party Protection and Verifiable Consent

Returning to the main discussion, remember that the essential choice seemed to be between protecting owners and protecting acquirers—that is, between granting *in rem* enforcement of property rights and lowering the cost of transacting. Applying property rules would favor earlier owners to the detriment of later owners and, vice versa, applying contract rules would favor later owners to the detriment of earlier owners. However, economic growth benefits from and may often require both secure property rights to encourage investment, and low transaction costs to improve the allocation and specialization of resources. Therefore, it is often efficient to develop institutions that, at a cost, are capable of *overcoming* the tradeoff, maximizing value for acquirers without damaging owners.

Such institutions achieve this by applying contract or property rules in a given context but with the appropriate conditions, which greatly reduce damaging side effects for, respectively, security of property or transaction costs. Broadly speaking, contract rules, which favor acquirers, are conditioned to verifiable owners' consent to protect owners; and property rules, which favor owners, are conditioned to contract publicity and verifiability to protect acquirers.

When the law applies a contract rule, it does so after the owner has consented, and granting or denying their consent allows owners to protect their property. This, for instance, was the solution invented in the Middle Ages under the law merchant: when merchants entrusted possession of their merchandise to other merchants, the judge would grant the goods to innocent third parties acquiring in subsequent transactions. Similarly, when shareholders incorporate a company and appoint its representatives, they are consenting to their property rights being weakened in favor of any third parties who contract with the company. Since this potential weakening of property rights is decided by their owners, it should not cause much damage.

Conversely, when the law applies a property rule, it does so only after the owner has complied with publicity requirements that ensure judges' ability to verify originative contracts and reduce transaction costs for all potential third parties in the market. For example, in a double sale of land, the judge will give the land not to the first buyer but to the first buyer to make the purchase public. In other words, by not making the purchase public, the first buyer is implicitly consenting to his property right being weakened, so that a contract rule will be applied to adjudicate a possible second sale that is made public first. Similar solutions are applicable to all previous examples.

The key issue is that the judge does not apply these rules automatically: they are subject to conditions, which are needed to overcome the tradeoff between property enforcement and transaction costs. In particular, given the sequential nature of the exchange, all systems must make sure that principals remain committed to their choices. To illustrate this, imagine a merchant who, after placing his merchandise in the hands of a distributor who does not pay him, claims that the distributor was not authorized to sell it; or take a shareholder who grants full powers to a manager but, when the manager makes a huge mistake, reneges from her and claims that she lacked legal powers. If their points were upheld by the judge, the third party would get only a claim for indemnity against the distributor or the manager. Commitment is the key in these examples, as it is also in land transactions. For example, in a double sale of land, the owner and the first buyer could easily collude and emerge with the first sale only when land value moves above the expected indemnity cost. Moreover, when a property rule is to be applied, commitment must also reach all potential third parties.

The common condition is that the judge has to be able to verify some element of the consent given or the publicity produced in the originative transaction. This can be done informally, when the originative transaction itself or the activities it triggers inevitably publicize the relevant information as a byproduct. An informative transaction in this regard is, for example, one that leads to a commercial seller gaining possession of merchandise. Similarly, the scope of employees' powers can often be easily ascertained by observing them perform the usual tasks involved in their jobs. Otherwise, explicit and costlier organizations and procedures need to be implemented to, in essence, make public the consensual elements affecting third parties. Such elements include, at least, the date and the information necessary to apply the corresponding rule. For example, the incorporation of a company requires the date, name, founders, capital, decision rules, and so on; and purchases and mortgages of land require, at least, the identification of the parcel and the transactors.

Therefore, the solution is to rely on public knowledge of originative contracts and, when such knowledge is not available, to publicly register such contracts to make their content verifiable (figure 1.4). Broadly speaking, when the law applies a contract rule, which directly eliminates risk for

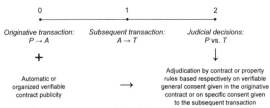

NOTE: Arrows between parties represent agency relationships, not transfers. Numbers 0, 1, and 2 indicate time 0, time 1, and time 2, respectively. *A*, agent; *P*, principal; and *T*, third party.

Figure 1.4. Role of verifiable contract publicity in sequential exchange

acquirers in subsequent transactions, it protects owners by having them choose the agent and triggering the contract rule only as a consequence of the agent's appointment. Conversely, when the law enforces a property rule, which guarantees *in rem* enforcement of owners' rights, it does so with the condition that the originative transaction has been made public, which reduces risks for acquirers and transaction costs for subsequent transactions. Of course, many situations are not all-or-nothing and, instead, there is a continuum. For instance, some degree of automatic publicity may be sufficient for low-value transactions and, in other cases, a mixture of publicity mechanisms is applied for different dimensions. For example, possession of real property may play a publicity-and-verifiability role for some *in rem* rights that produce notice (e.g., most leases), but not for others that are abstract in nature (e.g., ownership, mortgage). In any case, having some elements of the originative contract public and verifiable ensures either that parties to that originative contract are committed to the contract rule (i.e., rightholders cannot deny they have given consent to weakening of their rights) or that enforcing the property rule will not harm innocent third parties. In essence, it makes sure that judges and third parties base their decisions on the same information.

A key characteristic of these judicial decisions is that they are based on information about the consent given by rightholders, not about the possible values of the disputed resources in their competing uses.[23] The law, and registries in particular, therefore allow the market to function without any judicial valuation of alternative uses, avoiding the danger that judges and governments may in fact be determining the allocation of resources according to their own preferences and subject to their limited ability to ascertain value. Allocation is driven, instead, by rightholders' consents, given either in the originative transaction, when they appoint an agent and therefore trigger the eventual enforcement of contract rules in subsequent transactions;

or, in cases in which the law enforces property rules, at the time of the subsequent transaction, when they agree to transfer their rights to acquirers. The essential element of private contracting—voluntary consent—is therefore not only preserved but enhanced. This ensures that owners will be better off than under an alternative legal system that, by always ruling in favor of true legal owners, would hinder specialization and trade.

Conclusion and Next Steps

In conclusion, the law follows two strategies to handle the tradeoff between the enforcement benefits and transaction costs inherent in rights *in rem*: (1) to enforce property rules—that is, to rule disputes in favor of owners—conditioned on publicity and verifiability of such rights or (2) to enforce contract rules—that is, to rule disputes in favor of third parties—conditioned on owners' verifiable consent. In broad terms, these are the main strategies applied, respectively, in land and in business, which I analyze separately in the next two chapters. This separation suggests that the reason for the strategies has to do with the business versus civil nature of transactors and, in particular, principals, an aspect that I analyze in chapter 3.

These different strategies involve a series of consequences for the treatment of most land and business transactions. First, owners grant their consent in widely different manners. For business and, in particular, corporate transactions, consent is granted in the originative transactions so it applies to many possible subsequent transactions. For land transactions, owners, by making evidence of their rights public, preserve their power to exercise their consent in the future, granting or denying *in rem* effects in any aspect of subsequent transactions which collides with their own rights. Consent will be granted or denied at the time of subsequent transactions and specifically for each transaction.

Second, the reallocation of rights is thus more automatic in business than in land transactions. The enforcement of contract rules means that *in rem* rights conflicting with the intended subsequent transaction are automatically transformed into *in personam* rights. Therefore, a reallocation takes place with every subsequent transaction. For land transactions, a similar reallocation takes place only under land registration, whereas in systems of privacy and recordation conflicting claims may subsist unless parties call for the judge to intervene.

Third, the main assurance activity of acquirers (i.e., parties contracting with all sorts of agents) also differs between business and land transactions. For business transactions, given that the law enforces contract rules and consents are granted in advance, acquirers do not need to gather such consents but just check that they have been granted in such a manner that, if necessary, they would be verifiable by a judge. In contrast, given that for land the law enforces property rules, acquirers of *in rem* rights need to gather rightholders' consents for the intended transaction; this they are either able do to (when the law requires independent publicity, in systems of land "recordation") or must necessarily do (when the law allocates rights after each transaction, in systems of land "registration").

This third consequence for the type of assurance necessary to contract safely explains many of the differences observed between the land and company registries that are the focus of the next two chapters.

TWO

Institutions for Facilitating Property Transactions

Mortgages ensure that lenders will get their money back, so they eliminate default risk and should therefore reduce interest rates. Consequently, in some countries interest rates on mortgage loans are very close to those paid on government bonds, which are supposedly free of default risk. Yet, in many other countries, adding a mortgage guarantee to a loan only slightly reduces its interest rate. A main reason for this is that different owners and prior mortgages may appear once the loan is granted. As a result, the collateral value of land remains unfulfilled; there is less credit and more of it remains in the sphere of personal exchange.[1] Why, then, are so many countries in the world unable to provide institutional support for mortgages?

The answer is, simply, that providing such institutional support is not easy. Even in the United States, many transactions on foreclosed houses had to be halted as a consequence of the foreclosure crisis that erupted in the fall of 2010, because it was unclear who were the actual owners of the foreclosed properties. This meant that insurance companies were reluctant to issue title policies, lenders were unwilling to lend, and buyers were unwilling to buy. The crisis posed the risk that the whole property financing system would collapse, taking with it most of the major US banks. Yet, the United States probably has the most sophisticated mortgage market in the world, so how was this possible? It turned out that the giant US mortgage market had weak institutional foundations. As I explain when revisiting the case at the end of this chapter, the root of the crisis lies in the fact that the United States has poor institutions for publicly recording land transactions. They are plagued by the obsolete design of public recording offices, the poor incentives of the bureaucrats in charge of them, and the vested interests of conveyancers and title insurers.

This chapter examines how functional land registries enable impersonal markets. Mortgages facilitate impersonal lending because they are directly defined on assets. As argued in the previous chapter, truly impersonal exchange must be grounded on this type of *in rem* right (*rem* from the Latin word *res*, meaning thing, asset), so that innocent third parties can trade safely, without spending resources on determining how reliable their counterparties are. But when multiple rights are defined on the same asset, this advantage can be attained only if institutions are capable of avoiding information asymmetries and collisions among rights *in rem*, such as the alternative ownership claims and prior mortgages mentioned in the examples given above.

Moreover, gains from *in rem* enforcement are greater for assets such as land, which is relatively more durable, harder to remove, and easier to identify than many other assets. But these characteristics of land, which make *in rem* enforcement more valuable, also increase the benefits of having different people simultaneously holding rights on the same land. Multiple and abstract rights on land are therefore prevalent: to reach specialization advantages, it is common to allocate physical possession, different use rights, and legal ownership of land to different sets of persons; to divide land ownership in several ways (e.g., the land, its buildings, and the mineral resources beneath it may belong to different persons); and to define other abstract rights to exploit the collateral value of the land (e.g., mortgages, including their securitization). Also, owners often hold certain *in rem* rights on neighboring land, either individually (e.g., rights of way) or through political bodies (e.g., zoning restrictions).[2] This multiplication of rights makes contracting harder by increasing information asymmetry and transaction costs, especially because many of these rights are abstract in nature (e.g., ownership claims and mortgages).

Understandably, given the gains attainable, ingenious solutions have been devised. This chapter analyzes how these different solutions are organized.[3] According to the dominant strategy observed in legal systems, their function is seen as reducing the cost of finding out about adverse property claims, gathering and contracting the relevant consents, and systematically, or at least occasionally, producing a public reallocation of rights. Starting with the regime of purely private transactions, this chapter focuses on the main public titling solutions in use today: the recordation of deeds with or without title insurance, found in the United States and France, respectively, and the registration of rights available, for instance, in Australia, England, Germany, and Spain. Although the objective of this and the next chapter is to examine how the different systems of property titling and business formalization work and the nature of the tradeoffs involved in their design, chapters 4 and 5 ponder issues of organizational choice between the different alternatives.

Private Titling: Privacy of Claims as the Starting Point

Under the Roman Law tradition of private conveyance that was dominant in Europe until the nineteenth century, private contracts on land had *in rem* effects on third parties, even if they were kept secret. The baseline legal principle was that no one could deliver what they did not have (*nemo dat quod non habet*), which was closely related to the principle "first in time, first in right." So, in a double sale such as the one represented in row *a* of figure 1.3 (see chapter 1), in which an owner O sells first to buyer B_1 and later to B_2, the land belongs to B_1 because, when O sold to B_2, O was not the owner. In cases of conflict, the judge will allocate property and contract rights between both claimants (B_1 and B_2)—that is, will "establish title"—on the basis of evidence on possession and past transactions, whether or not these transactions had remained hidden.[4]

This potential enforcement of adverse hidden rights made gathering all relevant consents close to impossible, hindering trade and specialization. Most transactions in land therefore gave rise, totally or partially, to contract rights, and the enforcement advantage of property rights remained unfulfilled, especially with respect to abstract rights, such as mortgages. These difficulties are clear in the functioning of the two sources of evidence traditionally used to establish title under privacy: possession and the "chain of title deeds."

Reliance on Possession

First, the use of possession—that is, the fact of controlling the asset—as the basis for establishing property rights is a poor solution for durable assets, because for such assets it is often valuable to define multiple rights, at least separating ownership and possession. However, relying on possession to establish ownership makes it possible for possessors to fraudulently use their position to acquire ownership for themselves or to convey owners' rights to third parties. In such cases, owners will often end up holding a mere contract right, an *in personam* right, against the possessor committing the fraud. Understandably, under such conditions, owners will be reluctant to cede possession impersonally, for fear of losing their property.

Similarly, credit will involve contractual, personal guarantees provided either by the debtor or by the lender. This is because the only way of providing some type of *in rem* guarantee to the lender is by transferring ownership or possession to him, thus leaving the debtor subject to the lender's moral hazard and safeguarded only by the lender's contractual guarantee, which is weaker and costly to produce. Moreover, this technique does not allow the same land to be used to secure debts with several lenders unless third-party administration is used, with the added conflict that this solution will often cause.

Documentary Formalization through the Chain of Deeds

Second, some of the problems posed by possession are solved by embodying abstract rights, such as ownership and liens, and even complementary consents in the conveying contracts, which then form a series or "chain" of title documents or deeds ("chain of deeds," for brevity) that is based on what I have been calling "documentary formalization." This evidencing of rights with the chain of deeds facilitates some degree of separation of ownership and control because it is the content and possession of deeds that provide evidence of ownership. Therefore, title experts can examine the history of transactions going back to a "root of title," which is proof of ownership in itself—either because it is an original grant from the state or, more often, because of the time that has lapsed beyond the period of prescription or the statute of limitations.

This solution has also been used for a long time. For example, in the Demotic titles used in Ptolemaic Egypt between 650 and 30 BCE, the consent of affected rightholders (usually the wife and coheirs of the vendor) was stated in a specific clause (Manning 1995, 254–55). But relying on the chain of deeds also creates problems. Above all, new possibilities for error and fraudulent conveyance appear, giving rise to multiple chains of title, which leave acquirers with contract rights against the fraudulent grantor and the professionals involved in the transaction. Moreover, titles are less effective than possession in reducing the asymmetry of acquirers, as possession is observable but adverse chains of title remain private to the acquirer.[5] Furthermore, acquirers remain fully unprotected against any hidden charges that are not voluntarily contracted, such as judgment and property tax liens.

Similarly, the chain of deeds also serves to enforce a security, by pledging the deeds with the lender, a practice already found in Mesopotamia during the second millennium BCE (Silver 1995, 123–24). But this solution is also defective, as it burdens the debtor with the lender's moral hazards (the lender could impede a sale or even sell) and causes switching costs that make mortgage subrogation difficult. Nor does it lend support to the possibility of contracting second mortgages with different lenders.

In general, multiple rights are hard to implement through the chain of deeds. The absence of multiple rights is precisely what makes documentary formalization viable for powers of attorney and negotiable instruments, such as bills of exchange. I examine this below.

Traditional Conveyancing in England: Solicitors and the Chain of Deeds

Despite these difficulties, transactions on unregistered land in England heavily relied on the chain of deeds up until the last decades of the twentieth century. Typically, ownership was proved by possession and the whole series of deeds, which was often kept by the owner's solicitor. And mortgages were formalized by pledging the deeds with the lender.[6] This privacy system was able to survive, despite its shortcomings, because agricultural land ownership was relatively concentrated in a few hands, which made personal transactions easier (Pottage 1998).[7] In addition, the flaws of privacy were palliated in England by parliamentary interventions that reorganized obsolete and overly fragmented property rights (Bogart and Richardson 2009), an example of large-scale public reallocation of rights.

The English case also illustrates a constant feature of privacy regimes: to contain fraud, private conveyancing services provided by solicitors and notaries tend to develop into professional monopoly. First, it seems natural to impose stricter requirements on the documentary formalization process producing the title deeds. Reserving this to a certain legal profession—lawyers and notaries—and requiring the signature of witnesses have been the most common outcomes. Second, the need to guarantee professionals' quality provides a ready argument for restraining entry into the profession and regulating its practices. Lastly, the profession is also interested in developing formal and informal arrangements to share information in order to reduce the possibility of having several contradictory chains of title. This has been a common solution among notaries, as illustrated by the contemporary attempts by Andorran notaries and the old story of French notaries that I examine next.

Traditional Conveyancing in France:
The Role of Notaries in the Ancien Régime

Under privacy, notaries public in civil law countries play a similar role to that of English solicitors, with the advantage that each notary office keeps an archive with the original of all the titles it notarizes. This gives notaries privileged access to information on the transactions that each office has authorized. After describing how French notaries in the eighteenth century used this knowledge to support credit transactions and the use of land as collateral, Hoffman, Postel-Vinay, and Rosenthal (2000) conclude that

notaries could provide a substitute for mortgage registries because they accumulated information about individual debtors and creditors in the course
of drawing up contracts. They simply had all the relevant information about
assets and liabilities, and they could provide it more cheaply than any mortgage registry. (21)

However, this conclusion is doubtful, mainly because notaries' information about individual debtors was incomplete. Not only did property transfers not require notarization (Weill 1979, 603–5), but the enforceability of
general mortgages (those on all the assets of an individual) substantially
reduced the informational effectiveness of the chain of deeds: in essence, it
allowed the creation of a contradictory chain of title for all the assets of any
individual. Therefore, even notaries as a group did not have all the relevant
information. Moreover, no individual notary had access to all notarized
transactions but, instead, had to rely on the willingness of other notaries
to share their information. And this sharing was bound to create all sorts
of uncertainties, especially considering that notary fraud and bankruptcy
were prevalent in France even much later. The links between these incidents
and notaries' financial activities (Suleiman 1987, 63–75) suggest that, with
regard to financial intermediation, the incentives of notaries are not particularly sound.

Notaries did, however, have better information than other intermediaries because of their monopoly of mortgage deed notarization. And they
apparently used this position to diversify into financial reporting and intermediation. But their comparative advantage was based on exploiting the
information obtained by the profession as the monopoly producer of documentary judicial evidence. Once this information was widely shared, their
privileged position disappeared, as revealed by notaries' failure to compete
with banks after the 1798 mortgage credit law and the Napoleonic 1804 Civil
Code created a functional public registry of mortgages. After then, mortgages
still required a notarial deed but they became ineffective against third parties unless they were registered (Coing 1996, 519–20). Consequently, once
the register became publicly accessible, notaries' information advantage
disappeared.

Lastly, the superiority of public titling was clear to observers in the France
of the ancien régime, as they could see it in operation in some northern and
eastern regions of France that had Germanic institutions based on judicial
filings (*les pays de nantissement*) and in Brittany (Patault 1989, 206–8; Serna
Vallejo 1996, 979–96). Failure of the Crown to implement public titling, despite repeated attempts, mainly in 1581 and 1673, has been attributed, as in

England, to the opposition of the nobles, who did not want their debts to be known, and that of the notaries, who did not want to lose their monopoly.[8]

Limitations and Palliatives of Privacy

Limits of Privacy with Respect to *In Rem* Rights

Whatever the system of documentary formalization for private conveyance contracts, conveying parties will always try to contract relying on the evidence that will eventually be used by the judge to establish title. Under privacy, however, given that courts may enforce *in rem* rights that have remained hidden, examination of title quality is based on potentially incomplete evidence, as represented in part (a) of figure 2.1, which I will use to compare the structure of titling systems. Therefore, removal of title defects and contradictions, as well as any adjustments to the terms of the private contract, are informed only by the limited and hard-to-verify publicity provided by possession and by documentary formalization (the chain of deeds), and are motivated by the risk the grantor faces when giving title warranties on a defective title.

Acquirers have limited possibilities of knowing what they are buying. They, in fact, acquire residual property *in rem* rights plus a contract *in personam* right against the grantor for the difference between the *in rem* property rights effectively granted and what the grantor had promised to deliver. This is applicable to all kinds of rights and transforms the affected right into a contract right, a transformation that will be total or partial, depending on the nature of the hidden competing claim. For example, a buyer may lose all the *in rem* property rights if a hidden legal owner emerges, or only some of them if the hidden adverse right was an easement or a mortgage. Having been acquired subject to these uncertainties, all rights have a contract, *in personam*, element—their value thus depends on the wealth of the grantors and the enforcement of contract, *in personam*, rights against them, so they lose all or part of their *in rem* efficacy.

Understandably, legal systems try to counterbalance this chronic incompleteness of property rights in their *in rem* dimension under a privacy regime by adopting private and public means to strengthen contract *in personam* rights, such as granting formal guarantees, expanding the scope of criminal sanctions, and even relying on bonding and slavery. Moreover, legal systems also provide specialized judicial procedures capable of purging title—that is, establishing which rights *in rem* are alive and who holds them—thus producing a public reallocation of rights that should be useful at least for the most complex and valuable cases.

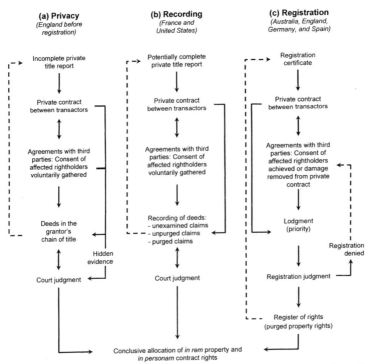

(a) Privacy
(England before registration)

(b) Recording
(France and United States)

(c) Registration
(Australia, England, Germany, and Spain)

NOTE: Dotted lines represent information flows; continuous lines, decisions with respect to demanding a report on title, purging contradictory rights, and keeping evidence out of the chain of title, as well as court and registration judgments.

Figure 2.1. Comparison of privacy, recordation of deeds, and registration of rights

In rem contracting therefore requires two contractual stages: first, the private contract between the transactors; and second, the agreements between one or all of these transactors—usually the grantor—and the third parties holding rights being affected by the private transaction, by which these third parties consent to the said private transaction.[9] As explained below, this second stage is driven by different voluntary and mandatory rationales in each system, and uses increasingly complete information about which rights are affected and therefore require consent. This information is also processed in a different manner and by a variety of private and public agents who produce different inputs for the contracting process.

Making Up for *In Rem* Rights by Strengthening Personal Rights

As information on adverse rights is inevitably incomplete under privacy, parties run a serious risk of ending up holding contract, *in personam*, rights. Understandably, acquirers strive to reinforce these, usually by means of title warranties. Because such warranties, which were already common in ancient Babylonia (Silver 1995 124; Ellickson and Thorland 1995, 383), create only contractual *in personam* obligations, they tend to be underwritten by a well-reputed third party to make them stronger. Historically, this was mostly done implicitly, by making extended families responsible for their members' debts. For example, it was common to make sellers' households liable for the deeds of their members to strengthen the enforcement of personal obligations.[10] But there are also some explicit arrangements of this kind, such as holding witnesses personally liable on a subsidiary basis, or contracting specific third-party eviction guarantees, a precedent of modern title insurance, a solution once common in England. Finally, in addition to reinforced warranties, which are common for land transactions, credit is also secured in many societies, even today, on the basis of personal indenture and contractual slavery. Children continue to be used as bonds, and slavery is still a common consequence of unpaid debts.[11]

Moreover, public enforcement of contract rights is also strengthened by different means, including debtors' prison and bonding. This was the case in ancient Rome, where the law granted special powers to creditors to control debtors' conduct and also mandated double damages for eviction (Jackson 1908, xxii–xxiii; Watson 1984, 16). Different forms of debtors' prison, which played a key role in England until the middle of the nineteenth century (Harris 2000, 131–32), are still common in many jurisdictions. For example, personal loans are often formalized as postdated checks to make default a criminal offense, one that often leads to imprisonment. This happens, for instance, in Bolivia (Fleisig, Aguilar, and de la Peña 1997, 74–78). Some criminal law enforcement also persists, where debtors can be forced to disclose their assets through an action to recover debt and may even be imprisoned if caught in perjury.

This reliance on such rough measures as indentures and criminal law contrasts with the tendency of more developed legal systems to relax the enforcement of contractual obligations as, for example, in personal bankruptcy. It is often claimed that this weaker enforcement avoids inefficient signaling and motivates risk-taking initiatives by providing a degree of limited liability at the personal level.[12] Conversely, the need to rely on such harsh mechanisms for enforcement provides a glimpse of the opportunity costs caused by a lack of proper institutions for conveyancing land and securing credit.

Public Reallocation of Rights through Judicial Purging of Titles

In a situation of systematically unclear title of the sort that may be fostered by a privacy regime, many individuals demand that the legal system afford them greater security for their rights, especially owners who plan to make additional investments or to sell land to third parties who may be unsatisfied by personal guarantees. To fulfill this demand for greater security, legal systems often provide summary judicial procedures that aim to call on all possible claimants and solve any possible contradiction in their claims, proceeding to what in terms of the concepts used in chapter 1 is a public reallocation of rights. For example, before the consolidation of recordation and registration systems, many countries in Europe resorted to special judicial procedures for clarifying title, such as the French *purge* (Cabrillac and Mouly 1997, 732) and the Spanish *purga* (Pardo Núñez 1993).

Unsatisfied demand for greater security is also behind the fake lawsuits that parties resort to with the objective of clarifying title when the law does not provide for specific summary procedures. A famous example was the English "fine," a simulated lawsuit that allowed the transaction to be entered in the books of the court and made it binding on everybody after a short period of limitation. It was used from the twelfth century until 1833 (Kolbert and Mackay 1977, 241). This type of fictitious and amicable lawsuit is found in different historical contexts, from the Bible (Ellickson and Thorland 1995, 385) to colonial Massachusetts (Konig 1974, 160–61). Unfortunately, however, both specific purges and fake lawsuits are insecure under a privacy regime, because judges must rely on proclamations to identify all claims, given that many rights remain hidden. Therefore, their effects in many jurisdictions are not general but are limited to any identified claims.

Publicity of Claims

Whatever the palliatives applied, the costs of contracting true property *in rem* rights under a regime of pure privacy are so high that modern systems of property law have abandoned privacy in an effort to lower them. At a minimum, the law induces or requires the independent publicity of contracts, which makes them verifiable, as a prerequisite for them to attain *in rem* effects—that is, to convey property rights and not mere contract rights. If they keep their claims private, rightholders lose or risk losing *in rem* effects. Private contracts may create obligations among the conveying parties but do not bind third parties: all other rightholders and, especially, potential future buyers and lenders. Independent publicity therefore facilitates finding out which property rights are alive and which will be affected, thus making it possible to gather consents, purge titles, and reduce information asymmetries between the conveying parties. At a maximum, in addition to requiring publicity of contracts, the law also requires a complete purge of conflicting claims for each transaction. Because this purge is supervised by a public registrar acting in a judicial capacity, the registry not only provides publicity of claims but also produces and publicizes rights.

Specific laws therefore vary substantially with respect to how and when any contradiction with other property rights must be purged by obtaining the consent of the holders of these affected rights. This second contractual step may be postponed indefinitely or may take place at the time of the private contract. In the latter case, it may be either voluntary or compulsory and total; and, if voluntary, it may also be total or partial. Moreover, jurisdictions also differ in what their registries produce, as they may either simply publicize the deeds evidencing potentially contradictory claims or certify fully purged property rights. Lastly, there is also a logical adaptation of the specific devices needed to produce these outcomes in each environment, the set of rights enforced as property rights, and the adjudication rules in cases of disputed title.

I now examine this variety, starting with the primitive versions of publicity of claims.

Old Forms of Publicity Suitable for Local Transactions

Physically marking the assets is perhaps the simplest way of providing publicity of claims. However, the symbolic nature of marking makes it especially suitable for abstract rights, such as ownership and security interests. This explains why it has been used extensively for enforcing ownership in the absence of possession, as in valuable movables such as livestock, automobiles, and books.[13] It has even been used for spouses, with wedding rings being only a pale remnant of the variety of devices traditionally used to "give notice" of marital status.[14] More revealing still is the use of marks to disclose security interests in land. In classical Athens, a slab, known as *horos*, was posted on the land itself, to be removed only by releasing the encumbrance (Finley 1952). These *horoi* contained the essential data of the encumbrance: always, the nature of the *horos* as security and often, but not always, the existence of a written agreement, the name of the creditor, and the amount of the debt. In some cases, it also contained the name of the person who kept the document of the transaction, supposedly to make it possible for third parties to collect more information. This system was one of the first to make an *hypotheca* possible—namely, the use of land as collateral without temporarily transferring ownership or possession to the lender.[15]

Another simple way of providing publicity is by using conspicuous contractual procedures. It is well known that, after 1066, English conveyances followed the continental practice of delivering possession through a ritual known as *livery of seisin*. In essence, the grantor gave the grantee a clod of earth from the land, a twig, or a key, and loudly said he was conveying the estate. Several features support the idea that this ceremony had a publicity function. First, it took place on the land or looking at the land. Second, numerous witnesses were required who, originally, had to be neighboring, and therefore potentially affected, rightholders. Lastly, until the Statute of Uses (1535), people preferred to contract uses as a way of avoiding the *livery of seisin* and thus escaping taxation, which shows that this ceremony gave notice to tax collectors.

Publicity was also likely the aim of practices as remote as those used for land transactions in Babylonia, which triggered controversy as to whether the "secondary sellers" present in them were really sellers or mere witnesses (Silver 1995, 122–27). An intermediate interpretation seems more consistent: even if they were not sellers, strictly speaking, they might have been holders of affected rights. Their presence in the transaction would assure that pertinent notice had been given to them and that they had granted their consent. This kind of practice could also be related to the custom of paying "witnesses" found in some primitive tribes (Diamond 1975, 259).

The publicity function was even clearer in the practices followed in other European regions, where laws mandated sophisticated procedures of publicity "before the church" and "at the gate of town walls" for rural and urban land, respectively, as well as some judicial registration.[16] Historical evidence on similar forms of publicity dates back to the ancient societies of the Middle East, around 2500 BC (Ellickson and Thorland 1995, 383–84). The requirements of repeated proclamations and the existence of a waiting period for the contract to reach *in rem* effects cannot be explained as mere providers of contractual proof to transactors.

These old practices for reaching consent and purging property rights were effective likely because transactions mainly took place between neighbors. For neighbors, it is easy to notice announcements and public deals, especially for the kinds of rights common in rural and traditional societies, many of which were linked to family matters. It is revealing that the effect of publicity "before the church" was immediate for the rightholders who were present but was delayed for one year and one day for those absent. Costlier knowledge was apparently balanced with longer time, suggesting that these systems could hardly support impersonal trade.

Recordation of Deeds

The next logical step in the provision of publicity is to deposit private transaction documents ("title deeds") in a public registry so that this evidence on property claims can then be used by the courts to verify them and allocate property, *in rem*, rights in case of litigation. Moreover, by making the register publicly accessible to potential acquirers, these can ascertain the quality of the sellers' title, thus reducing their information asymmetry.

After many failed attempts, such as the Statute of Enrollments issued by Henry VIII in 1535 but never enforced, and the Massachusetts 1640 Recording Act, recordation eventually started to succeed in the nineteenth century and has been used in most of the United States, part of Canada, France, and some other countries, mostly those with a French legal background. The key for its success was to switch the priority rule, because other incentives failed in convincing people to record. Historically, recordation systems thus became effective only when, in deciding on a conflict with third parties, courts determined the priority of claims from the date of recording in the public office and not from the date of the deed. This means that, instead of the conventional "first in time, first in right" rule, courts adjudicated according to the rule "first to record, first in right." For instance, in terms of a double sale such as the one depicted in row *a* of figure 1.3, the judge would give the land not to the first buyer, B_1, but to the first buyer to record the purchase.

This change in the priority rule not only protects acquirers but also avoids incomplete recording, which hampered many of the first recordation systems.[17] The reason is that the switch in the priority rule effectively motivates acquirers such as B_1 to record from fear of losing title through a second double sale or any other granting of rights (e.g., a mortgage) by the former owner to an innocent acquirer such as B_2 (e.g., a lender) who might record his claim first. Consequently, all relevant evidence on property rights is available in the public records. From the point of view of third parties, the record, in principle, is complete (part [b] of figure 2.1). Other claims may not be recorded and may well be binding for the parties who have conveyed them, but these hidden claims have no effect on third parties.[18]

The inclusiveness of the record of deeds makes it possible to assess the quality of title by having experts examine all relevant deeds, that is, only those that have been recorded, and producing "title reports." If there is sufficient demand, a whole title assurance industry will develop for examining, gathering consents, purging, and assuring title quality. This industry may take different forms. It is composed, for instance, of notaries public in

France and of title insurers in many of the United States, while abstractors, attorneys, title insurance agents, and title insurance underwriters perform separate functions in other US states. Despite their different names and differing degrees of vertical integration, the industry performs similar functions in all countries, as it mainly reduces information asymmetry between the conveying parties and encourages them to voluntarily purge the title. In particular, experts search for title defects, which can thus be removed before contracting by obtaining the relevant consent. Alternatively, if not removed, the grantee will not transact or will insist on modifying the content of the private contract, reducing the price or including additional warranties, in compensation for the survival of the defect. To motivate experts' diligence and technical innovation and to spread remaining risks, a standard close to strict liability is often applied to such examination and assurance activities. Consequently, experts are strongly motivated to find any defects on the title and a substantial part of the remaining title risk is reallocated from acquirers to title experts and their insurers. (A section in chapter 6 analyzes the role of title insurance in different contexts.)

Moreover, as under the privacy regime, both contractual and judicial procedures are used to remove title defects. Compared to privacy, deed recordation provides more possibilities for contracting the removal of defects, because defects are better known to buyers and insurers. The identification of rightholders also gives greater security to the summary judicial hearings that serve to identify possible adverse claims and publicly reallocate *in rem* rights. These summary hearings continue to exist today in, for example, the French judicial *purge* and the US "quiet title" suit. In addition to purging titles directly, the existence of such a court-ordered purging possibility also reduces bargaining costs indirectly by encouraging recalcitrant claimants to reach private agreements (Cabrillac and Mouly 1997, 732–40).

However, the recording office accepts all deeds respecting certain formal requirements (mainly, the date of the contract and the names of the conveying parties), whatever their legality and their collision with preexisting property rights. In fact, the recording office is often obliged by law to file all documents fulfilling a set of formal requirements, regardless of their legal status. For example, according to Article 27201 of the California Government Code, "the county recorder shall not refuse to record any instrument, paper, or notice that is authorized or required by statute or court order to be recorded on the basis of its lack of legal sufficiency."[19] The public record may therefore contain three kinds of deed. First, those resulting from private transactions made without previous examination. Second, those granted after an examination but without having all defects removed. Finally, those that define purged and noncontradictory property rights.

Transactors who record clouded titles therefore produce a negative externality for all future transactors.[20] Experts examining the title of a parcel do not know a priori which kinds of deed are recorded concerning it. For each transaction, they will thus have to examine all relevant deeds dealing with that parcel in the past, even those which may have been perfectly purged in previous transactions.

The cost of this repeated examining of deeds can be reduced with proper organization of the registry. In the short run, the easiest way to organize the information is by relying on indexes of grantors and grantees to locate the chain of transactions for a given parcel. However, this method is subject to errors, such as, for example, those caused by identical names and misspellings. This explains the steps taken, for instance, in 1955 to create the *fichier immobilier* in the French Registry and to forbid recording a deed if the grantor's title is not recorded.[21] Another way of reducing costs when public records are poorly organized is to build privately owned, indexed databases (known in the United States as "title plants"). These plants replicate public records in a more complete, reliable, and accessible manner by transferring and abstracting relevant documents lodged at the public registries and building tract indexes to easily locate the relevant information for each land parcel. In principle, computerization of public land records should reduce this dependency on title plants by making it possible to directly search the public registries for all documents referring to any given parcel (Bayer-Pacht 2010, 340–44 and 357–60), but the dispersion of public records, their incomplete computerization (e.g., limited time), and their varying quality mean that title plants are still necessary.

In any case, in deed recordation, disputes on title are solved using a property rule but conditioned on recordation. If the seller's right is shown to be defective, the buyer loses the property right to the benefit of the true legal owner. The buyer is then left with contract *in personam* rights against the seller, the title examiner, or the title insurer. This motivates buyers and, indirectly, all transactors to produce information and gather the consent of affected rightholders. Moreover, setting priority by recordation in fact means that the property rule is applied only if the private contract is recorded and thus made public. Otherwise, acquirers, whatever the quality of their grantors, may not become owners: for instance, they lose the land if the grantor sells for a second time to an innocent third party who records first. This obviously motivates acquirers to record as soon as possible.

Registration of Rights

Registration of rights (hereafter referred to as "registration," and often confusingly called "title registration"[22]) goes one crucial step further than recordation of deeds: instead of providing information about claims, it defines the rights.[23] To do this, it performs a mandatory purge of claims before registering the rights. As in deed recordation, claims stemming from private transactions gain priority when transaction documents are first lodged with the registry. They are then subject, however, to substantive review by the registrar in order to detect any potential conflict that might damage other property rights (part [c] of figure 2.1). New and reallocated rights are registered only when the registrar determines that the intended transaction does not affect any other property right or that the holders of these affected rights have consented. When these conditions are met, the change in rights caused by the transaction is registered, antedating the effects of registration to the lodging date. (In a sense, any registry of rights thus contains a recording of deeds: its "lodgment" or "presentment" book is a temporary record of claims.) Otherwise, when the consent of an affected rightholder is lacking, registration is denied, and the conveying parties have to obtain the consents relevant to the originally intended transaction, restructure it to avoid damaging other rights, or desist.

Registration aims to eliminate all uncertainties and information asymmetries, as information in the register is simplified in parallel with the purge of rights. Ideally, rights defined in each new contract are registered together with all surviving rights on the same parcel of land. Extinguished rights are removed or deleted, making it easy to know which are the valid rights. Production of information is a key element. As pointed out by Baird and Jackson, "[i]n a world where information is not perfect, we can protect a later owner's interest fully, or we can protect the earlier owner's interest fully. But we cannot do both" (1984, 300). The assertion is accurate but the assumption is crucial: registration intends to produce perfect information and thus protect *both* the earlier and the later owners.[24] The goal is to abide by three principles traditionally deemed desirable for a titling system, according to which (1) the register reflects the reality of property rights, so that potential transactors do not need to look out of the register ("mirror principle"); (2) the register reflects only valid rights, so that transactors do not need to perform a title search in the chain of title ("curtain principle"); and (3) losses caused by a registry's failure are indemnified ("assurance, insurance, or guarantee principle").

To the extent that these three principles are achieved and given that any contradictions are purged before registration, the registry is able to provide "conclusive," "indefeasible" title, meaning that a good faith third party "for value" (i.e., one who pays for the property rather than receiving it as a gift) acquires a property right if the acquisition is based on the information provided by the registry.[25] If the seller's right is later shown to be defective, the buyer keeps the property *in rem* right and the original owner gets contract *in personam* rights against the seller and the registry. The property right is allocated in these exceptional cases to the acquirer, by applying a contract rule, in contradiction with the property rule. However, this happens only when there has been a failure in the registry, and in most cases no contradiction should appear, so property enforcement is based on rightholders' consent.

Reallocation of Private Property Rights under Registration

For each transaction, registrars therefore oversee a full "reallocation of rights," using the Coasean perspective introduced in chapter 1. This reallocation is complete because, in contrast to a privacy regime, all necessary information is public, and, in contrast to a recording office, the registry does not register any right that would conflict with any other preexisting *in rem* right on the same land. When functioning correctly, the register is thus able to provide potential transactors with a complete and updated account of the *in rem* rights alive on each parcel of land. Given the enforcement advantage of *in rem* rights, this accounting amounts to commoditizing the legal attributes of rights on real property, which makes impersonal trade much easier.

Registration therefore interferes little with private property,[26] as registry intervention focuses on the timing and completeness of the reallocation of rights implicit in any purge. Registration is controlled by registrars, but ultimate decisions are made by rightholders by giving their consent. Privacy and recordation allow conveying parties more discretion on timing and heavier reliance on privately produced information. They therefore seem to rely more on private decisions, but this perception is deceptive because even recorded rights are in fact mere claims. They retain a higher contractual content, given the survival of conflicting claims *in rem*. Additional intervention by the court, also subject to the possibility of allocation failure, would be required to transform them into property rights at an *in rem* level equivalent to that provided by registration. In sum, as compared to recordation, it is useful to see registration as a quasi-judicial step, which in other titling systems is in any case necessary to reach full *in rem* enforcement.

This similar degree of public involvement helps explain why both registration and recordation have taken root in countries with different legal traditions and why there is little correlation between titling systems and legal traditions (Arruñada 2003a, 416–20). Trading cities in the late Middle Ages were the first to enact effective registration systems (the German Hanseatic cities of Hamburg and Bremen) and demand them from their sovereigns.[27] But, since the late eighteenth century, registries of rights have been created not only in countries with a German legal tradition (Prussia, 1783; Austria, 1794; and Germany, 1900) but in many others (e.g., Australia, 1858–1875; Spain, 1861; and England, 1862), including the "Torrens" variety usual in common law jurisdictions.[28] They have also been introduced in most former socialist and developing countries (Deininger and Feder 2009, 244). Similarly, recordation has taken root in countries with such different legal traditions as France and the United States.

Organizational Features

The functioning of registration depends on the way it is organized, the key aspects being tract indexes, the degree of registration completeness, and avoiding registration failure.

First, to be effective in finding which rights might be affected by an intended transaction that the conveying parties want to register, the register must be organized on the basis of a tract index to locate all rights in each parcel. Each parcel must therefore be unequivocally identified. This has always been relatively easy for buildings but used to pose a harder problem regarding rural land, especially in areas in which, in the absence of distinctive natural or man-made landmarks, the traditional metes-and-bounds method of identifying and delimiting the different tracts of land was less reliable. Modern technologies for surveying and mapping, such as aerial photography and GPS, have greatly facilitated these tasks. Property rights can be secured and land markets developed without precise surveying, as even the International Federation of Surveyors (FIG) admits (e.g., Onsrud 2002, 9). When "learning from the past," the Commission on Legal Empowerment of the Poor (CLEP) also considers that "assuming that titling always has to be cadastre-based and rest upon expensive survey and mapping" is one of "the lessons [to be learnt] from mistakes related to land and real property" (2008b, 82–84).

Second, registration systems will be more or less complete; therefore, their workload will vary depending on the number of *in rem* rights allowed, as well as on the depth and scope of the review they perform before changing the register. They differ, first, in the degree to which the law mandates the number and content of property rights and, correspondingly, reduces transactors' freedom and registrars' discretion. If property rights are more narrowly defined by law, limiting the type of such rights (with a closed number or *numerus clausus* of such rights),[29] collision between rights is less likely and the affected parties are more easily identified by the registrar in order to check that the conveying parties bring the consents of affected third parties. For example, the 1925 property and registration reform, which boosted the English Land Registry, drastically reduced the preexisting variety of property rights (Bostick 1987, 77) but not enough, as reflected in the additional reduction introduced by the 2002 Land Registration Act. Conversely, when more attributes of property rights can be defined by private contract, collision is more likely, and it becomes more cumbersome for the registrar to identify who the affected third parties are. Second, registries differ in the depth of the review they perform. Their task is made harder and their output more valuable when they are required to verify the transaction's cause. An extreme case is that of the German *Grundbuch*, which frees the registry from checking or even mentioning the cause of the registered transactions. Others (such as the Austrian, Swiss, and Spanish registries) are, however, required to verify the cause and make it explicit in the registered entry. Third, a registry's workload also depends on how exhaustive the register is with respect to *in rem* rights, both private and public. The work of the registry is made simpler, but its output less valuable, when the legal system enforces more rights *in rem* than those that are registered (e.g., the English overriding interests), or when (as in Austria, Germany, and Switzerland) the register only contains a limited set of information so that, for some rights, the register must refer users to the relevant deed or document, which is kept in the registry and also must be examined before future transactions (Nogueroles Peiró 2007, 126–33). A registry's workload also increases when it is required to enforce public rules, for example, when the law mandates that registration be refused if the lodger lacks a building permit or has not paid taxes. In principle, it seems sensible to define a stricter *numerus clausus* and a lighter workload for less capable registries—a crucial aspect when creating functional registries in less developed countries. These issues are also of some consequence for the implementation of electronic conveyancing and registration, which is easier in systems with a stricter *numerus clausus* and often requires some sort of additional standardization.[30]

Finally, given the application of a contract rule that favors innocent acquirers to the potential detriment of legal owners, registration failures would reduce enforcement of preexisting rights. For this reason, such failures must be rare. Otherwise, judges would be reluctant to enforce contract rules and go back to applying property rules when adjudicating rights.

Consequently, registries of rights would soon turn into mere recordation of deeds. Judges would be able to revert to the previous practice because, even in civil law legal systems and especially under common law, they can interpret more or less leniently the conditions for good faith or lack of notice that are commonly required of third parties in order to consider them innocent acquirers and grant them the protection of contract rules. Furthermore, if judges did not prevent a high rate of registration failure from leading to expropriation of owners, owners would avoid registering their rights and would lobby legislators for a change in the rules. One way or another, the end result would be the demise of registration.

Land Titling Systems Compared: Promise and Reality

A main theoretical argument in the old controversy about the relative performance of recordation of deeds and registration of rights is that recordation incurs lower costs but is less effective than registration.[31] In critically revisiting this argument, I identify factors that substantially modify these apparent comparative advantages in practice. My interest is not so much to reach an absolute verdict about relative performance as to find ways of evaluating performance, making the systems more efficient and managing the transition between different systems

The Dubious Cost Advantage of Recordation of Deeds

Even considering the cost incurred for lawyers, title agents, title insurers, notaries, and the like to privately examine, purge, and assure title quality ("title assurance services" or, for short, "assurance services"), recordation of deeds may be less costly than registration of rights because of stronger incentives in both the demand and the supply sides of the industry. Under recordation, titles are examined and purged voluntarily, and most supporting services are provided on the basis of private enterprise. Conversely, registration requires a full purge, which is privately arranged but controlled by the registry. A main benefit of an optional purge is that any defects not worth purging can be insured on a casualty basis, either by the conveying parties themselves or by an independent insurer. Under registration, the requirement to remove these minor defects may cause holdouts with substantial bargaining costs.[32] Recordation is also thought to enjoy the advantage of private incentives in the supply of title assurance services,[33] because titles are examined and purged, gathering the relevant consents, by business firms or professionals paid with a residual profit. Assuming competition, costs will tend to be minimized and efficiency achieved, including rapid innovation and adaptation to changes in technology and demand.

However, given the actual incentives of both users and suppliers, these cost advantages may be illusory. Voluntary title assurance may incur higher costs than those of public registration because of the nature of the demand for assurance, leading to "overtitling," duplicated efforts, and lost economies of scope. Private organization of assurance services may also be inefficient because many of these services are natural monopolies and are heavily regulated.

Excessive private expenditure on title assurance arises in all titling systems because individuals base their decisions on the losses that bad titling might cause them. And such individual losses are greater than social losses because part of the individual loss is only a transfer between individuals.[34] This private overtitling thus reduces the potential advantage that recordation might otherwise enjoy with respect to registration as a result of the greater scope it grants to voluntary purging. Furthermore, the scope for corrective (i.e., supramarginal cost) pricing may be lower under recordation, given the greater role played by private services in the whole of the assurance and titling process.

Recordation also suffers a substantial degree of duplication of several kinds. First, the private databases known as "title plants" have to file information on all transactions and relevant facts and not only on the rights being transacted or examined. Consequently, being able to choose the timing and completeness of the purge provides little advantage. Second, title plants only serve companies' internal administrative functions, as they have no legal effect. This means that the whole chain of title is often examined for each transaction, at least when the title insurer was not the previous insurer. (Marketable title statutes limiting the time required for title searches reduce this cost but may also threaten the security of property rights.) Lastly, in the United States, not only do private title plants duplicate the information of the public registries but also different title plants may do so in parallel, given that in many areas several titling companies operate one title plant each. Some of these duplications can be avoided with better-organized recording offices—mainly, by using tract indexes; and automation also makes it easier to gather data from public records and reduce the extent and cost of archive duplication. But indexes do not reduce duplication in the repeated examination of the chain of title, and automation aggravates privacy concerns and is unlikely to avoid the need for filtering this information.

Similarly, potential economies of scope in producing information and purging rights are also hard to reach under recordation. Information on the quality of titles is underused and has to be produced repeatedly. This is also caused by the voluntary nature of purging, as in some cases title defects are not removed after being identified by the title report. Moreover, even when defects are removed, the information on the records is not necessarily simplified. The public record accumulates information on all kinds of claims, defective and clean, dead and alive. And acquirers suffer asymmetry of information with respect to sellers on the quality of the relevant titles. Worse still, rightholders may have incentives to make the information hard for future acquirers to discover even if they examine the record (as argued for unrecorded cases by Ayotte and Bolton [2011, 3422–23]). This mix of claims increases the cost of future title searches. Potential savings will therefore be incomplete and will depend on hiring the same expert to search the title. Private title plants can simplify their information, but they still face similar problems.[35] Moreover, even if in principle statutory law usually limits the time required for title searches, making it unnecessary to examine the whole chain of title, searches often have to consider longer periods. For example, thirty states in the United States have marketable title acts setting periods of between thirty and seventy-five years (Boackle 1997). But, even if the statutory number of years is thirty, if the most recent title transfer was fifty years ago, the title search must go back to that "root of title" and then search everything subsequent to it. And the title must be searched all the way back to the first conveyance from the government for exceptions contained in the acts, such as easements, subdivision restrictive covenants, rights of parties in possession, mineral rights, and rights of or conveyed by the federal government (Palomar 2003, §563).

Furthermore, with respect to suppliers' incentives, the two main types of title assurance industries developed under recordation of deeds have been heavily regulated. In both France and the United States, these industries—notaries and titles insurers, respectively—are subject to pricing regulations, entry barriers, and comprehensive rules on products and processes, partly as a result of incidents of fraud and bankruptcy.[36] In particular, since title plants enjoy decreasing unit costs,[37] suppliers are good candidates for becoming natural monopolies. Understandably, their behavior has been repeatedly scrutinized and sanctioned by competition authorities.[38]

Lastly, the relative performance of recordation is affected by the fact that registries of rights are not necessarily slow and ineffective bureaucracies. Countries with registration of rights display a variety of incentive structures and results in terms of, at least, apparent productivity. Some of the most appalling results were produced by registries with standard, fixed-salary bureaucracies (Cook County, which includes the city of Chicago in Illinois;

England, before the reforms introduced in 1990; and Puerto Rico, where registration was created with variable salaries but moved to fixed salaries early on). More professional, judicial-style bureaucracies, as in Germany or Scandinavia, seem to produce better outcomes although—whatever the type of registry—they are especially productive when each registrar is compensated with the profits of his or her office, as in Belgium, some regions of Brazil, France, Luxembourg, and Spain.

Risk of Ineffectual Registration of Rights

It is also commonly believed that registration, though more costly, at least provides more security for property rights, enhancing investment and impersonal trade. These effects come about mainly because registration makes it possible to use a contract rule, instead of a property rule, fully protecting good faith acquirers. In contrast, the protection granted by recordation is in principle intrinsically inferior in that it is largely contractual (i.e., *in personam*) in nature and thus does not take advantage of all the enforcement benefits of property (i.e., *in rem*) rights. The promise in registration is therefore one of transforming property rights into legal commodities that are easier to trade impersonally. This should provide better incentives to invest, drastically reduce the cost of future land transactions, and increase the value of land by itself and as collateral for credit. Owners have better incentives to invest because they enjoy a high level of security. For the same reason, when rights are transferred, transactions no longer require a costly legal analysis of previous transactions because the registry certifies which rights exist and who holds them. Similarly, land is more valuable as collateral for credit because such value depends on whether the debtor is the true legal owner, whether there are any previous mortgages and whether, in case of default, the mortgage is easy to foreclose; and registration helps in all three dimensions. Lastly, as argued above, the protection given to registered rightholders by a surviving registration system cannot be detrimental to current rightholders. And, if it fails to protect owners on a significant number of occasions, its chances of survival are limited, and it will be transformed into a recordation system.

However, despite these promises, effectiveness of registration is far from guaranteed, especially when creating a new registry. Even established registries often fail to fulfill the promises of registration by being slow and incomplete. Oddly, they also fail by being too effective. I look at slowness and incompleteness first.

Some registries take a long time to examine transactions. Meanwhile, private deeds are given priority conditional to final registration so that, during the time lapse between completion of the transaction and its registration at the registry (the "registration gap"), the register functions as a record of deeds. The registries of Cook County, England, and Puerto Rico saw chronic episodes of registration delay, which resulted in different outcomes—closure, structural reform, and title insurance and recurrent reform, respectively. Later, some of the projects introducing electronic conveyancing even toyed with the idea of making transaction completion and registration simultaneous, running a substantial risk of transforming the registration of rights into a recordation of deeds (as analyzed in chapter 7). The lesson is that, for registries to function properly, governments must be prepared to provide registrars with sound and strong incentives.

Incompleteness of registration is driven by both legislative and judicial decisions that lead to enforcing as property—*in rem*—rights interests which are not registered.[39] This already causes some difficulty with respect to those "overriding interests" that are easily observable (such as possessory rights), but poses a more serious problem for abstract overriding interests (such as tacit liens produced by operation of the law, held by employees and governments, for instance).[40] Proposed solutions come up against the opposition of bureaucrats, conveyancers, and judges. Bureaucrats prefer not to be required to file legal claims. Conveyancers protect their market, and the weaker the effects of registration, the greater the demand for their private assurance services. And judges are often inclined, both for the sake of fairness and to preserve their discretion, to deny the conclusiveness of registration, especially when the registries are not part of the court system.[41]

Finally, registries of rights may also be at risk as a consequence of their effectiveness, because governments find it useful to use effective registries as gatekeepers for all kinds of public obligations.[42] For instance, enforcement of land use regulation substantially increased in Spain after a 1986 law ordered the land registry to check for building licenses as a requirement for registration. In general, it is tempting for governments to require even minor obligations to be fulfilled before a right can be registered. In addition, governments are making registered information freely available to the public rather than only to those with a legitimate interest or those so authorized by rightholders. This public availability may have similarly doubtful effects, now aggravated by the power of new technologies to bring together data from disparate sources.

Creators of public titling systems in the eighteenth and nineteenth centuries were well aware of the risk of relying on registries to enforce taxation. Their decision to place the registry within the realm of the Ministry of Justice (as in Germany or Spain) was germane to their primary goal of making the registry an instrument for private contracting instead of tax collection (as in Napoleonic France, where it was placed under the Ministry of Finance). Similarly, today, the increasing public-good burdens placed on registries might result in a serious risk. By making the registry more costly for users, its contractual function may be endangered and rightholders may even choose to avoid it. Moreover, when such public burdens are inefficient, there will be demand for more lenient enforcement, without necessarily distinguishing between private and public rights.

Organizational Requirements: Registries' Monopoly as a Safeguard of Their Independence

According to the analysis in chapter 1, contracting *in rem*, which is desirable because of its enforcement benefits, requires a recurrent reallocation of rights that must be public because it affects third parties. This explains why decisions on property *in rem* rights are made by bodies or agents that are independent from transactors, which usually implies that they are organized on the basis of territorial monopoly: parties are not free to choose a registry or a judge but are assigned to them on a geographical basis. The reason is simple. Property, *in rem*, rights, oblige everybody and, to protect everybody's interests, those creating them or determining their creation must be independent from all actual and potential parties to both originative and subsequent transactions. Verifiability requires independent publicity. By contrast, a similar constraint would not make sense for contract, *in personam*, rights because agreeing to exchange contract rights only obliges the parties to the agreement, who thus can be left to care for themselves. For the same reason, transactors are generally allowed to freely choose which individual professional, if any, they will retain to prepare their conveyancing contracts.

This requirement of independence must be satisfied by all titling systems, even if they create property *in rem* rights in different ways and at different moments. In essence, privacy and recordation delay producing them to an eventual judicial intervention, whereas registration produces them at the time of the private contract. However, in all three systems, independent agents decide which rights will be enforced as property rights and which rights will be merely contractual. Under privacy and recordation, this includes the judge, who eventually decides on title matters, as well as, under recordation, the recording officer, whose decisions establish title priorities. Under registration, it is the registrar who decides when choosing between registering and requiring additional consents as a condition for registration.

Consequently, incentives for all these decision makers, whether judges, recorders, or registrars, have the same objective: to make them independent with respect to all the parties.

Impartiality is needed not so much between the parties to the private conveying contract but mainly between them and third parties, that is, those holding property *in rem* rights affected by the conveyance—impartiality is required between parties to both originative and subsequent transactions. Because these potentially affected third parties are not present, are frequently not even aware of the situation, and are often dispersed, it is understandable that the parties to the private contract should not be allowed to choose the providers of recordation, registration, or judicial services. Take, for instance, the possibility of a lender determining who will decide the priority of his mortgage among other competing mortgage claims. Freedom to choose cannot protect rightholders who are not choosing. All kinds of land recorders and registries are thus organized as territorial public monopolies both when they produce evidence determining future judicial decisions, as recorders do, or when they decide directly on property rights, as registries of rights do.

Alternative solutions to costly monopoly seem to be insufficient to guarantee effective independence. Apparently, it is not enough to make the rules of priority mandatory to all those applying them, probably because such rules leave substantial scope for potentially partial interpretation and abuse. Neither is it viable to imitate the dual organization of liberalized utilities, including telecommunications, railroads, and electricity, in which several competitive providers use the same monopoly distribution network. This paradigm could theoretically be applied to registries because, in addition to providing legal services and decisions, registries also keep an archive of deeds or rights. This archiving activity enjoys decreasing unit costs, thus generating a situation of natural monopoly. By itself, this monopoly would not preclude free choice of judges, recorders, or registrars, who could share a common archive to reach economies of scale, in a fashion similar to utilities which channel the services of several providers. But this arrangement is not viable for registries because such free choice by conveying parties would endanger the interests of third parties, a problem which does not exist for utilities because there are no important externalities between consumers.

Exceptions to Monopoly Confirm the Argument

Multiple recorders or registries are used only in circumstances in which there are no third parties or these third parties remain unprotected. Therefore, when studied carefully, these apparent exceptions to monopoly only reinforce the argument.

First, still in the area of real property, the argument is consistent with the fact that US title plants lack effects on third parties. Private abstracts of title were used at least once, after the 1871 Chicago Fire, for reconstructing the public records that had been burned, but in that case the private abstracts had been produced before the fire, when those choosing their abstract provider could not have guessed the future public use of such abstracts. Therefore, even this remote exception confirms the rule.

Second, for registries of financial assets and to eliminate delays between settlement and registration, best practice advises having a single clearing agency and depository acting also as a registry (Bank for International Settlements-International Organization of Securities Commissions [BIS-IOSCO] 2001, 13). This is, for example, the solution adopted in the United States for the Depository Trust & Clearing Corporation (DTCC). Only a few countries, including Spain, rely on an alternative called "indirect holding" systems based on two-step registration, with a central depository and multiple custodians. However, when these custodians also act as first level registries, they are chosen by the issuer of the securities; therefore, transactors themselves have no choice. Furthermore, when the issuer switches registry, he has to gather the consent of third parties (such as lien holders), in a process supervised by the central registry. Additional precautions are also taken to avoid conflicts with the registry itself, mostly by the drastic measure of preventing the existence of third parties. For this purpose, rights with a potential to cause conflict are simply not enforced as *in rem* rights (e.g., second liens). In addition, the central registry is the sole registry with legal effects for all securities owned by entities with registration functions.

Third, the registration of Internet domains also ties in with the argument. On the one hand, registries of geographic top-level domains, such as ".de" or ".es," which do exert preregistration review are also monopolies. On the other hand, problems with the registration of other domains illustrate the consequences of a lack of independent registry review. For each top-level domain (all those ending in, e.g., ".com"), there is only one registry, but users choose freely among multiple so-called registrars who in fact act as recorders. The system allocates the domains on a first-come, first-serve basis, without controlling potential damage to third parties, mainly holders of intellectual rights in the name. The only review it performs aims to avoid name repetition, but this is in the interest of the party asking for registration, which thus has the potential to damage third parties' interests, as shown by the extent of "cybersquatting"—the registration of prominent names with a view to later selling them back to their trademark owners when said owners wish to start operating online. The system only started to provide additional protection for third parties who complain when it began to enforce the Uniform Domain-Name Dispute-Resolution Policy or UDRP (Internet Corporation for Assigned Names and Numbers [ICANN] 1999). This policy, which applicants to certain top-level domains have to accept, is designed in a way consistent with my argument, since disputes are not decided by "registrars" but by a panel selected from among the arbitrators approved by ICANN. Moreover, statistical evidence indicates that, at some point, free choice of arbitrator by challengers might have been biasing the results, causing substantial differences in the ratio of successful-to-unsuccessful challenges across arbitrators (Mueller 2001).

Lastly, the need for those deciding on property *in rem* rights to be independent from all the parties is also shown by the expansion of constraints on private property in connection with zoning and environmental protection (e.g., Epstein 1995, 275–305). This expansion is partly caused by failing to separate parties and decision makers. In essence, zoning and environmental regulators act as both custodians and holders of property rights that allow them to prevent certain uses (e.g., building, filling a wetland, or logging a forest). As with any rightholder, their consent is required to use the land affected by the regulation. However, as custodians, they also decide whether their rights are affected by the proposed use or transaction, carrying out a function that is similar to that of a registry of rights. Unsurprisingly, these rights have been expanded beyond initial expectations because the rightholders are also acting as registrars. Leaving aside the controversy on the optimal allocation—or expropriation—of such use rights, a more rational system would place the custodian role with independent bodies, be they the legislature, the registry, or the courts. Separation should help prevent unlimited expansion of rights and facilitate the exchange of regulatory consent for compensation. And it should be consequential, as can be inferred from the fact that the expansion of environmental rights has been smaller in areas in which agencies' powers are constrained by law—for instance, where the law limits the level of risks or the types of control techniques that regulators can impose (DeLong 1997, 151–52).

Scope for Free Choice between Land Titling Systems

Thus far the analysis has dealt with the different legal systems for enforcing property *in rem* rights as mutually exclusive alternatives. The previous section has also examined the impossibility of free choice of registry within a given system. The present section explores the possibilities and difficulties of granting individual rightholders freedom of choice between titling systems, an issue with important practical consequences.

As always, the rationale supporting free choice is mainly one of improving allocation of resources. Given that legal systems incur different costs for gathering the necessary consents and provide different levels of enforcement, freedom might produce a better match of demand and supply, as well as competition between different systems. The rationale against freedom of choice is also based on standard considerations of costs, external effects in the form of damages to rights held by third parties, and adverse selection. First, freedom of choice requires sustaining several titling systems, and even two filing systems. Some degree of duplication will be inevitable for the law, the judiciary, and the conveyancing industry if they are to support several titling systems, and some economies of scale will be lost. But costs in terms of potential damage to third parties and self-selection processes are even more important.

Both of these effects and their costs vary with the type of freedom granted to owners. First, they may be free to choose between privacy and public titling and, within public titling, between its different forms. Second, at least theoretically, the law could allow both choices to be made only once for each parcel or right, or once for each transaction. Third, voluntary procedures may be used as a palliative to complement public titling systems. In them, two modest but useful applications of choice are the procedures for fully purging a title within recordation and, conversely, the presence of some optional elements of recordation in a registration system. On the one hand, when a low-cost judicial purge is viable in recordation, it provides conclusive title when this is most needed. On the other, when possessors are allowed to register their possessory rights, these rights, if unchallenged, become conclusive after a period. Registration of possessory rights therefore produces legal effects intermediate to those of recordation and registration, including priority and most often an expectation of ownership after a certain period of time. Registries of rights can thus be designed to function with three levels of freedom: registered rights, registered possessory rights, and unregistered possessory rights.[43]

Fortunately, a comprehensive examination of all these possibilities is unnecessary, as it would involve repetition and some of them are empirically irrelevant. Therefore, I only discuss two sets of choices: (1) freedom to switch between privacy and publicity and (2) freedom to switch between recordation and registration, focusing on externalities and adverse selection.

Third-party Effects Caused by Freedom to Switch
between Privacy and Public Titling

Unrestrained freedom to switch between privacy and publicity would cause serious damage to other rightholders, under both registration and recordation. The powerful effects of registration make the act of registering or deregistering a parcel of land potentially damaging for rights held on that parcel and neighboring ones. For example, rights kept private may be destroyed in their *in rem* nature by registration or by renewing a "broken tract" on the same parcel, or may be substantially damaged by registering the boundaries of a neighboring parcel incorrectly. Supporting evidence on these effects is provided by the additional precautions that registration systems take with respect to initial registration, as well as the cautions they introduce regarding deregistration, which often is simply forbidden. When allowed, deregistration of a land parcel requires a purging procedure, in which all rightholders *in rem* can object. For example, Massachusetts made it possible to voluntarily deregister more types of land from its Torrens registry as from February 11, 2001. Consistent with the argument, before such deregistration can be approved, an examiner of title is appointed to ascertain whether mortgagees or lessees are affected and to give them notice, thus providing an opportunity for them to object (MCA 2001). US registries have generally resisted deregistration (Shick and Plotkin 1978, 95 and 139). In England, the 1925 reform definitely eliminated the possibility for transfers out of the registry that had momentarily been opened by the judicial decision in *Capital & Counties Bank Ltd. v. Rhodes* (Sparkes 1999, 79). In most other jurisdictions, deregistration has always been impossible. In a recordation system, opportunistic filing and de-filing of deeds, if allowed, would pose similarly serious hazards through the operation of the priority-in-recording rule. Given that, under recordation, there is no active registrar, the risk is partly offset only by putting stricter requirements on buyers for them to be considered in good faith or to be more diligent in producing information on adverse possession.

However, both registration and recordation do indirectly allow a sort of optional privacy, to the extent that the law relies on possession as evidence in conflicts on property rights. For instance, when, to be considered in good faith, acquirers are required to diligently inspect the land regarding adverse possession, rightholders can keep possessory rights unrecorded or unregistered. In such cases, all other rights remain on file and thus are unaffected by the choice of keeping the new right private. Removal of these rights from the public record or register is in fact allowed, but in a direction that cannot damage property rights already held by third parties. (This objective to protect third parties is also shown by the right that registration systems often grant purchasers and foreclosing mortgagees to compel registration.) Moreover, it hardly matters for this aspect of free choice if registration is compulsory, as, for example, in England, or not, as in Spain, because this distinction is much less important than the legal treatment of possessory rights. When the law is willing to enforce "overriding interests" and similar possessory rights *in rem*, as in England and to a lesser extent Spain, property rights that oblige all people can in fact be created without a public filing.

Self-Selection Caused by Freedom to Switch between Recordation of Deeds and Registration of Rights

Given the different levels of security provided by recordation and registration, granting owners freedom to choose between them could be beneficial. Theoretical models have shown that, under sensible assumptions, the more defective the title and the more valuable the land, the more landowners would opt for registration.[44] This result finds empirical support in the choices effectively made in jurisdictions with both systems in the United States (Shick and Plotkin, 1978). The best known experience of this type of selection is that of Cook County, where a record of deeds and a Torrens register of rights were functioning simultaneously until 1997. Empirical results show that rightholders self-selected into one of the two systems and that registered land had a higher price than would have been expected had it been recorded, all other things being equal (Miceli et al. 2002, 2011). Similarly, land newly registered under possessory rights in Spain over the period 1900–44 was of lower average value than that newly registered under ownership (Arruñada 2003b).

A complementary rationale for granting freedom between recordation and registration is that this freedom could provide some degree of competition between the two systems. However, this competition would be unlikely to function properly. First, given the conclusive nature of registered title, the more freedom registering parties have, the more serious the adverse selection problem suffered by the registry. This would increase operating costs and cause losses for its insurance fund. Shick and Plotkin confirm this risk by pointing out the proclivity of owners with doubtful titles to apply for registration in the three main Torrens registries they analyze, those of the Twin Cities, Massachusetts, and Cook County (1978, 93–95, 118, and 141). Pricing risks correctly would become crucial to avoid adverse selection, but a public bureaucracy will find this type of fine-tuning of prices hard to achieve. For instance, prices were not adjusted to the substantial difference in the costs of running each system in Cook County (136), which might explain the deficit experienced by its Torrens operation (138). Particularly striking was the registrar's fee for initial registration of only $30 (135). A second reason why competition would not function properly is that it would take place between the state registration agency and the private conveyance and assurance industries, with the latter being both a user and a competitor of the filing office. This duality would likely cause conflict, as registration reduces the potential market for private assurance. Especially if the registry is organized as a standard state agency in which registrars are paid fixed salaries, their relatively weak incentives might easily lead to the registry being captured or degraded by the industry.

An Example of Voluntary Privacy: The Electronic Registration of Mortgages in the United States

Choice between privacy and public titling is behind the mortgage foreclosure crisis that arose in the United States in the fall of 2010. A major role in the crisis was played by Mortgage Electronic Registration Systems (MERS), a private structure created by the mortgage industry to support the private trading of mortgage loans in the secondary market. Owned by two dozen of the largest US lenders and used by around three thousand financial services firms, it was managing about sixty-five million mortgages in 2010, well over half the US mortgages, when it became the focal point of that crisis.

In the previous decade, MERS had become a major component of the securitization process followed by most US mortgages. In essence, securitization interposes several specialists between ultimate lenders and borrowers. Mortgage loans are pooled with other similar loans, the pool is sliced by risk characteristics, and the different slices sold to investors with different risk appetites. A trustee bank then oversees the operations of the pool and channels borrowers' payments to investors. Lenders also appoint a firm as loan servicer, to interact with the borrower and collect monthly payments on behalf of the lender.

Lenders had created MERS between 1993 and 1997 to facilitate securitization, reducing the costs and times involved in public filings. It was designed to circumvent the public registries by performing two main functions: (1) acting as an agent of lenders at the public recordation office and (2) providing lenders, if they so wish, with a private computer record for their loan trades. Before MERS, every time a mortgage loan was reassigned, transfers had to be recorded in the particular county record office. As loans are typically assigned several times, these local recordings were costly in terms of fees and time.[45] Furthermore, when assignments hastened in the 1990s, some city recording offices almost collapsed. Moreover, the decentralization of record offices made efforts to reform them well-nigh hopeless.[46]

MERS avoids the need of repeated filing, as well as the associated costs, fees, and taxes by being appointed with the acquiescence of the borrower as "nominee" or agent for the lender and any future buyer of the loan. MERS mortgages are first given identification numbers and filed at the county's recording office with MERS named as the first assignee or as the original mortgagee.[47] Lenders may then assign to other parties the beneficial owner-ship without recording these assignments in the public records.

Therefore, MERS mediation provides a legal interface, allowing its members to perform low-cost *in personam* loan assignments without putting their *in rem* property claims at risk or having to file the assignments in the public record to avoid such a risk. MERS mediation thus can be interpreted as a way of organizing private transactions on recorded rights: mortgagees keep their rights private but do not risk losing *in rem* rank.

THREE

Institutions for Facilitating Business Transactions

When you buy a new computer in a store, you do not check whether the salesperson has the legal power to sell it; and, when you pay for it, you do not worry that the salesperson might keep the money instead of giving it to the store or that the store might not pay the manufacturer. Even if the employee or the store fail to comply with their duties, you know that you will keep the computer. The store would have to recover the money from the salesperson and the manufacturer from the store. But you would keep the computer; thus for you the relationships among the salesperson, the store, and the manufacturer are almost irrelevant. In fact, many other possible relationships are also irrelevant. For instance, most stores are now part of corporations, legal entities that simplify a complex web of legal relationships. When you contract with their representatives, such as managers and salespersons, all these relationships are also irrelevant. These simplifications greatly facilitate exchange and, in particular, impersonal exchange: as a customer, you can focus on the computer, because proper legal institutions make sure that you are able to buy an *in rem* property right on it. Similarly, when you invest in a company that has recently issued new shares, you do not worry that some shareholders might contest the issuance decision; even if the decision failed to follow corporate rules, your purchase will be protected.

In most business contexts, the law therefore enforces "contract" rules, granting *in rem* rights or priority to third parties and greatly facilitating impersonal exchange. This protection of third parties dilutes owners' property rights, but this dilution is controlled by owners' decisions: it is owners who select and monitor the agents whose conduct might trigger the economic consequences of dilution. In the example, it is the store owner who selects its agents and salespersons, and it is the manufacturer who selects its distributors.

The functioning of this mechanism for protecting both owners and third parties requires that judges are able to reliably verify owners' decisions. This is easier when originative transactions, such as the one between the store and the salesperson, are publicly known. It is harder for other transactions that might remain hidden, such as many of those related to corporations. In this chapter, I explain these mechanisms, focusing on how independent registration of originative contracts and legal acts allows courts to apply market-friendly contract rules when settling disputes on subsequent corporate contracts with third parties. I start by examining why contract rules are needed in business transactions, emphasizing the common structure of the information problem and the prevalent solutions adopted in the three areas of movable property, agency, and corporations. Then I explore how the verifiable evidence needed to efficiently apply contract rules can be produced by different means in these three areas and establish a common requirement: independent publicity. When originative contracts and legal acts are known as a byproduct of market activity, they are made public informally. If they were to remain hidden, some formal publicity—independent registration— is required to prevent parties from opportunistically manipulating the relevant evidence affecting the choice of rules. Thus, the key question in all areas is the organizational requirement for independence from parties to both originative and subsequent contracts. And, as shown by history, the main difficulty in company registries is collective action among entrepreneurs.[1]

Prevalence of "Contract Rules" in Business Exchange

Contract rules protecting innocent third parties are applied in the three main types of business exchange, that is, those aiming to (1) transfer the ownership of movable property, (2) exercise employment relationships, and (3) conduct corporate transactions. In the terms developed in chapter 1, all three are sequential exchanges in which, first, originative transactions take place between principals acting as owners, employers, and shareholders, and agents acting, respectively, as sellers, employees, and managers; and, second, subsequent transactions occur between these agents and third parties who are strangers to the originative transaction. For each of these three types of exchange, contract rules are generally efficient because the enforcement advantage that would be provided by alternative property rules is less valuable than the cost of the information asymmetry they cause. Such asymmetry would lead to high costs in gathering or confirming the owner's consent. Imagine, when buying the computer from the store, that you have to first check with the store's shareholders and the computer manufacturer. This would be costly, if not impossible, and avoiding these costs easily makes up for the loss in enforcement suffered by their property rights.

Movable Property

Assume first that a third party, T, purchases a movable good from an agent, A, who is not the owner and is not entitled to sell it. Applying the traditional legal rule that grantors cannot transfer more rights than they legally hold (*nemo dat quod non habet*), if the real owner, P, claims the good, T will have to hand it over and can only ask for compensation from A.[2] However, in order to facilitate market transactions and at the risk of weakening property rights, the law predominantly chooses to ensure that innocent purchasers keep the good even if the seller was neither the owner nor entitled to sell it. This is so in most commercial contexts, in which the judge will confirm ownership for an innocent third party who bought the good from a "merchant" (in practice, now a business firm) who had been entrusted with possession.[3] For example, the Uniform Commercial Code (UCC) in the United States, adopted by almost all states, establishes that "any entrusting of possession of goods to a merchant who deals in goods of that kind gives him power to transfer all rights of the entruster to a buyer in ordinary course of business" (UCC §2–403[2]). Something similar happens in civil law jurisdictions.[4] This means that the former legal owner will only hold a personal indemnity claim on the selling merchant and will not recover the good bought for value and in good faith by the third party.

A particular set of exceptions to this application of the contract rule in commercial contexts clarifies its rationale. In many countries, a property rule is applied to some transactions with merchants, including sometimes the obligation for the owner to compensate the purchaser for the price paid by the latter to the seller.[5] Such exceptions are frequent for transactions in which the selling merchant's supplier—usually the owner of the good—is an individual and not another merchant, as in used goods stores, art galleries, and auction or pawnshops. As a result, even innocent purchasers lose ownership of the goods they have acquired in such establishments when a legal owner appears whose right had been violated. For example, when defining whether a purchaser acts "in ordinary course of business," UCC §1–201(9) requires the seller, in addition to good faith and lack of knowledge, to be "in the business of selling goods of that kind." And its mention of pawnbrokers was interpreted as creating an exception (Baird and Jackson 1984, 307, n. 22), an interpretation that was later confirmed by the revision of the UCC. Moreover, purchases in art galleries are generally treated in the United States in the same way as those in auction houses and pawnbrokers, so that a good-faith purchaser of a stolen work of art will probably have to relinquish it if the legal owner appears.[6] In many countries, the owner is entitled to restitution but only after refunding the price paid for the good by the good-faith purchaser. This applies for lost or stolen movables that have been purchased in a public sale, as well as those bought from authorized pawnbrokers.[7]

In sum, legal systems tend to attribute the property right to the good-faith purchaser when *the owner* is a merchant. This solution is well adapted to a commercial context. Basically, application of one rule or the other alters purchasers' incentives to determine the true legal ownership, as well as owners' incentives to protect their property, whether this protection is a matter of physical possession or legal title. Moreover, both the cost and the effectiveness of these three activities of information and ownership protection change depending on whether the owner is a merchant.[8] First, if the owner is a merchant, it is usually more difficult for the purchaser to investigate the ownership of the good, because in most cases there will have been a whole chain of transactions, such as those between manufacturers and wholesale and retail distributors: "[t]he rapid circulation of movables makes it difficult, if not impossible, to trace their legal origin. If every purchaser were compelled to investigate his predecessor's title, the circulation of movable property would be seriously hampered" (Sauveplanne 1965, 652). Second, both economies of scale and specialization in commercial activities reduce the cost of protecting physical possession. Third, merchants are better able to protect their legal ownership because most of the risks for ownership arise when giving possession of the goods to a third party, and merchants have comparative advantages in such transfers of possession—they gain knowledge with experience, carry out repeat transactions, and may put safeguards in place. So, the key in commercial transactions is that, with regard to enforcement, owners who are merchants are in a good position to choose reliable sellers.[9] Therefore, retaining a property right over the goods would be less valuable to them than to owners who are not merchants. Moreover, with regard to the costs of gathering the owner's consent, when the owner is a merchant, it is most likely that there will be a chain of transactions; therefore, such costs will be greater than when the owner is not a merchant. Both factors thus advise against applying a property rule in the commercial ambit.

Agency

The law also applies contract rules for legal representation through agents, generally employees. The traditional principle that no person can commit another—equivalent to the principle of property law according to which owners cannot transfer more rights than they have—is thus turned round so that the agent does commit the principal (*respondeat superior* or "Master-Servant Rule"). This switching of rules protects innocent third parties acquiring rights on the firm's assets, who thus will be more willing to contract since they do not need to ascertain whether the agent is or is not legally empowered to commit the firm. In addition, third parties who are affected noncontractually by the firm's activities enjoy greater protection of the rights they now hold.

The argument used in the preceding section to explain the use of a contract rule in commercial sales and purchases can also be applied when the firm acts through an agent. The value of the additional enforcement that rightholders would obtain if a property rule were applied would be limited, whereas the cost of gathering all the relevant consents would be high. It therefore makes sense to apply a contract rule. Although such a contract rule reduces enforcement, principals and employers have effective tools for containing such a reduction, because they can select and supervise their agents and employees. Conversely, if a property rule were applied, purchasers would have to check both the consent of any entrepreneurs acting through agents, which would be costly, and the identity of those acting independently.

In particular, the entrepreneur is generally liable for damages caused by the firm's employees to third parties. Moreover, this attribution of liability is not left to the will of the parties, unlike other damages that only affect them, because such contractual freedom would make transactions harder for all market participants. For example, if the courts were to enforce a contract whereby an employee bears all liability without the affected third party being able to take action against the employer, then the information asymmetry for all contracting parties would increase. Furthermore, such asymmetry would increase not only for that firm's parties but also for all market participants, who would have to start producing information on the liability regimes contracted by each and every employee and their employers.

Corporations

The sequential nature of corporate contracting is more complex than for movables and agency because corporations are artificial constructs—legal entities—that need to be identified, have specific mechanisms defined to make their decisions, and own a set of assets to operate. Originative transactions thus include not only incorporation but also later changes in both the corporate decision-making process and capital structure. Subsequent transactions include any dealings the company has with third parties, although the dealings that are of particular interest to this section are those that affect the relative legal position of shareholders and third parties.

In addition to the contractual problems of property transfer and agency existing when the firm is a sole proprietorship, new problems arise when the firm is a company. In this case, third parties may suffer new types of information asymmetry in regard to the very existence of the company, how the corporate will is produced, and how priorities are set for the firm's and the shareholders' assets: the "incorporation," "corporate will," and "asset partitioning" problems.[10] Information asymmetries in these three areas would dissuade possible contractual partners.[11] To reduce such asymmetries or eliminate the damage they might cause to third parties, rules governing these three areas are changed from the traditional property rules to contract rules.

First, company existence is generally determined with a view to protecting innocent third parties, so that, if a company has not been legally incorporated or has been used as an alter ego, this cannot be used to the detriment of innocent third parties. The contract rule is applied either by (1) asserting the legal existence of a corporation placed in doubt by its shareholders in order to elude an obligation entered into on their behalf or (2) piercing the corporate veil to attribute the duties of a corporation to its shareholders. Contract rules are applied in both sets of cases as the interests of innocent third parties are favored over those of shareholders. For example, according to section 2.04 of the US Model Business Corporation Act (MBCA), "all persons purporting to act as or on behalf of a corporation, knowing there was no incorporation under this Act, are jointly and severally liable for all liabilities created while so acting." Generally speaking, protecting innocent third parties makes sense in these cases because shareholders know more about the condition of the incorporation process and can also easily avoid most defects in it.

Second, third parties tend to remain unaffected by possible legal defects in the corporate decision-making process.[12] For example, when a company decides to increase its capital, if the terms of the company charter are not respected (regarding, e.g., the prospectus, the quorum, or the shareholders' assent), such a defect will not affect the rights of investors who buy the new shares [e.g., MBCA §6.21(c)]. Also, the law usually protects third parties when the decision-making body goes beyond the limits of its powers or the objects clause.[13]

The rationale behind this application of contract rules is similar to that of the previous cases. In company transactions, the value of the additional enforcement that would be provided to rightholders (usually shareholders) if the property rule were applied would be limited, whereas the cost of gathering all the necessary consents would be high. In regard to enforcement, switching the rule applied to decisions by company governance bodies reduces the rights of shareholders who then may only act against the company directors and officers but without damaging any third parties who have entered a contract with the company. However, this potential reduction is made up for by attributing voting rights to shareholders, which not only allows them to exert some control over company appointments and extraordinary decisions but also allows the functioning of the takeover market. Moreover, investors choose with whom they want to associate when deciding to buy shares in one company rather than in another, so they can choose reliable partners. Since investors are in a position to choose, this should also motivate issuers of shares to provide efficient safeguards. In regard to the costs of gathering consents, use of the contract rule avoids the heavy costs for third parties of checking with all shareholders.

Third, in order to facilitate the contracting of capital, shareholders' assets are separated from those of the firm, making it possible to switch from property to contract rules, and allowing each set of assets to back its own set of debts. This is achieved with two special versions of contract rules: limited liability and what Hansmann, Kraakman, and Squire (2006) call "entity shielding." These two corporate rules depart from the legal principle of unlimited liability, whereby persons are liable with all their assets for their debts. Limitation of liability protects shareholders' assets from their firms' debts, while entity shielding protects firms' assets from any debts personally taken on by shareholders. Not only do the firms' creditors have priority over the firms' assets but usually the shareholders' personal creditors are not entitled to liquidate the firm in order to claim their debts. At most, personal creditors may step into the shareholder's role as an owner of shares in the company.

These two rules are functionally similar to the contract rules described in previous sections. By virtue of entity shielding, company creditors know that their rights over the company's assets will not be damaged by the shareholder's individual obligations toward personal creditors who might otherwise—in the absence of the rule of entity shielding—have priority over such assets or might have the company liquidated. The relationship between the personal creditor and the shareholder is thus transformed in a similar way to that between an owning merchant and a selling merchant after a good has been sold to an innocent third party: the owner retains a personal right against the seller but has lost any property right on the good, which will be kept by the third party. Similarly, the shareholder's personal creditor has a personal right over him, but not over the firm's assets, which are only within reach of the firm's creditors.[14]

In a symmetrical way, limited liability safeguards personal assets, thus protecting personal creditors against the firm's creditors. Therefore, the two types of creditor simultaneously play different roles as principals and third parties regarding the two types of asset—personal and corporate. Corporate creditors act as principals and consent to lose priority regarding personal assets (because of limited liability) but gain priority regarding corporate assets (by virtue of entity shielding). It is the other way around with personal creditors who act as principals regarding the corporate assets over which they consent to lose priority.

As with movable property and agency, the rationale for applying these contract rules in asset partitioning depends on the balance of enforcement benefits and consent costs in comparison with the alternative application of property rules. On the one hand, regarding the enforcement benefits, entity shielding causes little damage to personal creditors of investors. When the investment is in cash, the contract rule hardly affects the creditor because an opportunistic individual has better ways to keep funds out of the reach of his creditors than investing in a company. It is true that, for nonmonetary investments, the rights of these creditors are reduced because of entity shielding and to the extent that shares in closed corporations are not liquid. However, most nonmonetary contributions take the form of real estate, identifiable movable goods, and financial assets, so personal creditors will have had the opportunity to protect themselves by asking for them to be posted as collateral. Similarly, limited liability does not change the guarantee of company creditors unless the money is transferred to shareholders, a circumstance that may often lead courts to pierce the corporate veil and make shareholders personally liable. Moreover, when limited liability would make it harder for corporate creditors to collect their debts, they can easily reintroduce unlimited liability by contract.

On the other hand, regarding the costs of gathering consents, both rules reduce information asymmetry and facilitate the firm's contracts with third parties, expanding opportunities for trade and specialization. Therefore, under limited liability, potential investors who are thinking about buying shares in the firm no longer need to worry about the wealth of other shareholders, and they also know their losses will be limited to the amount invested. Moreover, if the entity is shielded, a potential creditor who is thinking about lending it some money will no longer have to worry about the solvency of the individual shareholders, because the latter's personal debts do not affect the position of the firm's creditors regarding the firm's assets. In this case, too, some of the information asymmetry is avoided, that referring to the greater knowledge that individuals have of their own assets.

Summing Up: The Verifiability of Originative Contracts Simplifies Sequential Contracting

Independent publicity of business contracts makes them verifiable, allowing judges to apply rules that are suitable for agents when contracting with poorly informed third parties, thus facilitating impersonal transactions. This is so for the three sets of relations I have just examined—commercial sales, employment, and corporate. In addition, the rules applied in each of these three areas share the same structure. From an economic perspective, all these relations can be considered "agency" relations between different participants in the firm: owners and sellers, employers and employees, shareholders and company bodies, companies and their representatives, or creditors and shareholders. In all these relations, contract verifiability makes it possible to simplify the corresponding originative agency relationship so that third parties are protected against any possible defects that might exist in it—in a sense, they contract with the principal. Consequently, they will not care about their information asymmetry with respect to the agent's title and will be more willing to contract, enhancing trade and specialization between principals and agents. This functional simplification of agency relationships provides a sort of legal modularity that allows market participants to treat business firms as black boxes, using little information about what is going on inside them.[15]

Therefore, in all these relations, contract publicity makes it possible to apply rules that are suitable for the market and especially for impersonal market transactions. This is achieved by adding to the originative private contracting between the parties an element of independent publicity. For example, the sale contract between a supplying merchant and a buying merchant is followed by a transfer of possession. Similarly, the subscription of a company formation agreement by founding partners is followed by public registration. The contract is purely private and, as such, only generates legal effects between its parties, whereas independent publicity determines the rights of third parties who are strangers to the private contract. Publicity may be an automatic byproduct of the private originative contract, such as the appearance obtained when transferring possession of movable goods or the notoriety (i.e., informal common knowledge) produced when allowing the firm's employees to carry out their functions. Alternatively, it may be a formal process, as when the private contract or an extract of it is entered in a public register. In any case, it is independent and it affects all subsequent contracts. In essence, by making their private contracts public, rightholders consent and (given the public element) implicitly but firmly commit to having contract rules applied to future transactions with innocent third parties. This consent is often more constructive than real. When a merchant transfers possession to another or an employer places employees in contact with third parties, they are implicitly consenting to their rights being relegated to those of, respectively, future purchasers or any third parties dealing with such employees in the ordinary course of business. For the same reason, the rights of shareholders defer to those of any parties contracting with the company once it has been registered.

Requirements for Applying Contract Rules: The Rationale of Formal Publicity

Although contract rules have generally been adopted for all these commercial transactions, judges base their decisions on different types of information: for movable property, they rely mostly on informal notoriety; for agency contracts, on a combination of informal and formal criteria; and for corporate contracts, predominantly on public registers. I now examine the logic for this reliance on formal and informal solutions for different types of transaction.

Movable Property

As argued above, the rationale for applying a contract rule in transactions on movable property depends on the commercial nature of the owner of the good, although the legal formulation for its application is often approximated in terms of the commercial or noncommercial nature of the seller or of the transaction, thus using subjective or objective criteria (Tallon 1983). Moreover, the commercial nature of the owner is also used to establish the exceptions (e.g., auctions, art dealers, and pawnbrokers) to which some variant of the property rule is usually applied, especially in common law. All the same, in both the general rule and its exceptions, informal criteria are most often used to establish who is a merchant. In fact, today most legislations use criteria of professional dedication, habitualness, and notoriety to identify individual merchants, and public registration is only required for companies. For example, the UCC defines a merchant as "a person that deals in goods of the kind or otherwise holds itself out by occupation as having knowledge or skill peculiar to the practices or goods involved in the transaction or to which the knowledge or skill may be attributed by the person's employment of an agent or broker or other intermediary that holds itself out by occupation as having the knowledge or skill" (UCC §2-104[1]).[16]

Contract rules are therefore applied to transactions on movables by individual merchants without it being necessary for them to register as merchants and to commercial acts carried out by nonmerchants. This makes sense, first, because individual merchants are natural persons and are easier to identify than legal entities, as is the commercial nature of their activity. Second, in principle, goods belonging to a natural person also are relatively easy to identify. This is indicated by the legal requirement that individual merchants formalize and make public certain transactions that, were they to remain hidden, would affect their liability and obscure how much guarantee their assets provide for third parties. Such is the case, for example, of general powers of representation, marital authorizations, dowries, and legal incapacitation, as well as some marriage contracts. Lastly, movable property poses fewer difficulties for informal publicity because there are usually few rights on them, thus granting greater information value to possession (Baird and Jackson 1984), unlike what happens with immovable property (Arruñada 2003a, 406–7). These three factors thus indirectly reveal why registration is more necessary for legal entities and, in particular, for companies, which constitute a paradigm for both abstraction and multiplicity of rights.

Agency

The same rationale of specialization and delegation advantages that explains the efficiency of applying a contract rule for agency relations also explains why informal criteria are used to define when to apply such a rule: in essence, in transactions habitually performed by employees. More precisely, in such transactions, the contract rule is applied based on the law of actual and apparent authority without any need for registration.[17] In particular, employees are generally considered to enjoy apparent authority if they have been notoriously acting on behalf of the principal, even if they lack actual authority (Menéndez Menéndez 1959, 282). Notoriety thus plays a publicity role that is similar to that played by possession in sales and purchases of movables. This is possible because acting as legal representative is easy to observe, not only for third parties but also for the entrepreneur, who is able to prevent recurrent deception or misuse. For movable goods, owners regulate the effects of the contract rule when they decide to which merchant they entrust possession of their goods. For agency and employment relations, entrepreneurs do the same when selecting and supervising their agents and employees.

Exceptions also confirm the argument. The rule is not switched for transactions that go beyond the usual competence of the agents as in the case of a sales assistant selling the cash tills. Also, for habitual transactions, the entrepreneur may (but not always, as exemplified by the German *Prokura* and European company officers) prevent rule switching by means of appropriate publicity. This publicity adopts forms ranging from notices affixed in the actual establishment in such a way as to destroy the effects of the appearance (as achieved, e.g., by the Roman *condicio praepositionis* or by signs still stating "Fixed price" or "Pay here," which alert the customers that the sales assistants are not empowered to either apply discounts or collect payment for the goods sold) to formal solutions, such as the proclamation and entry in a public register of the powers of the agent, as practiced, for example, in Italian cities during the Middle Ages (Menéndez Menéndez 1959, 281–305; and Fernández del Pozo 2008).

Corporations

Both in the movable property and agency areas, informal publicity criteria predominate for triggering the application of contract rules. However, formal publicity—namely, registration—plays the predominant role in corporate transactions, most clearly in company incorporation and asset partitioning, with informal criteria playing an important role only with respect to the representation component of the corporate will, which can, in fact, be seen as an issue of agency.

First, with regard to incorporation, when corporate charters were granted by specific legislative acts, incorporation was publicly known as a byproduct of the legislative process and the ordinary publication of the chartering acts. The charters themselves established that contract rules would be applied to future transactions by the corporations by granting them not only a clear legal position (Coornaert 1967, 247) but also entity shielding and limited liability (Hansmann, Kraakman, and Squire 2006, 1378). However, this publicity function has often been neglected because most analysts focus on the role of charters in imposing entry barriers in economic activity (their licensing function). Consequently, after incorporation was liberalized in the nineteenth century, analysts were inclined to see registration as a substitute for licensing and not as what it mainly was—a substitute for the publication of the chartering legislative acts, which until then had been essential to allow judges to safely apply contract rules to subsequent corporate contracts.[18] Registration has been performing this function since then, given that "registration and notice of that registration are in all legal systems the borderline; when crossed, the entity is formed" (Buxbaum 1974, 19–20). For example, according to section 2.03(a) of the US MBCA, the existence of a corporation begins when the articles of incorporation are filed. A similar effect is produced with respect to third parties by Article 3.5 of the First European Directive 68/151/EEC (Article 3.6 in Directive 2009/101/EC), which establishes that companies cannot rely on unregistered documents to be used against uninformed third parties. Consequently, once it is registered, a corporation has all the necessary elements for acting as a legal entity, it is empowered to sign binding contracts, and counterparties are able to litigate against it. In essence, the new entity becomes easily identifiable and traceable because all registries make sure that the corporation has a distinctive name, a physical location, and, at least, a contact agent for legal notifications (e.g., MBCA §2.02[a]).

Second, incorporation creates a decision-making authority, enabling it to exercise its corporate will. In particular, it determines that such authority exists and constrains its structure, mainly by drastically limiting shareholders' rights and centralizing decision rights with the board of directors (Clark 1986, 21–23). Countries differ as to how much detail about representation mechanisms is disclosed in the public record. Typically, the corporate will is first structured by naming at incorporation the initial directors and officers [e.g., Article 2.1(d) of the First European Directive; currently Article 2(d) of Directive 2009/101/EC] or, at least, by naming the incorporators who then must hold an organizational meeting to elect directors and complete the organization (MBCA §2.05).

Third, incorporation is the key condition for asset partitioning. The articles of incorporation do not only describe the capital structure of the company (in particular, the types, numbers, and rights of authorized shares [e.g., MBCA §2.02(a)].) Once a company has been incorporated, it is also clear how the corporate will is to be exercised and what its consequences are. This makes it possible to separate changes in corporate assets and liabilities from changes occurring in shareholders' personal assets and liabilities. Consequently, incorporation is essential for both limited liability and entity shielding. In particular, filing of the articles is conclusive with respect to limited liability for those transacting on behalf of the corporation. If the articles have not been filed, the law generally imposes personal liability on those prematurely acting as or on behalf of a "corporation," at least while they know that the articles have not yet been filed (e.g., section 2.04 of the US MBCA and Article 7 [now 8] of the First European Directive). Similarly, entity shielding also requires registration: a majority of votes of incorporators, initial directors, or shareholders is necessary to trigger voluntary dissolution of a registered corporation (e.g., MBCA §§14.01 and 14.02). Conversely, the law may allow individual incorporators to trigger the dissolution of unregistered corporations (e.g., Article 16.1 of the Spanish Corporate Act).

Lastly, changes in all these elements must be registered. For instance, in the United States specific filings are needed in connection with structural changes, such as amendments of articles of incorporation (MBCA §10.06), mergers (§11.06), issuances of shares (§6.02[c]), and dissolution (§14.03).

Most company registries require additional information and perform additional functions. However, the analysis in this chapter is not affected by these differences, since it focuses on the core functions of company registries, which are common to all jurisdictions and represented in the above description by a minimalist registry such as the one proposed by section 1.25(d) of the MBCA, which since 1984 has treated the role of company registries as purely ministerial. The argument here is that even such a minimalist registry plays an indispensable legal function by safely switching the legal rules applicable to corporate transactions. And this essential function of the registry is not merely that of providing "notice," that is, allowing parties to check company documents. It is mainly a judicial-support function, allowing courts to verify such documents and to apply contract rules without inflicting on property rights any harm that has not been consented by the rightholder.

Differences across registries should not obscure the universal presence of this common core of minimum functions that are performed by all of them, and the essentially legal nature of such minimum functions. This universal presence suggests that the rationale for these core functions is rooted in reducing private transaction costs. The rationale for registering additional information or having registries perform additional compliance review, in addition to being more related to positive externalities,[19] is probably subject to a tradeoff of costs and benefits that may differ for different countries. The efficiency of having such additional functions performed by registries is addressed in chapter 5.

Difficulties Involved in Organizing Company Registries: Independence and Collective Action

The common core of registries' functions is essential for corporate contracting. Without it, it would be difficult to ensure the independent publicity that makes originative contracts verifiable, and corporate contracting would be either unfeasible or much more costly. This section analyzes this independence requirement, examines why documentary formalization is insufficient, and explores the main difficulty faced by business registries. This difficulty is that registries place entrepreneurs—when acting as principals—in a typical collective action dilemma: they all want effective registries to exist but at the cost of other entrepreneurs.

Independent Publicity Required

Enforcement of contract rules involves a reallocation of property rights with each subsequent transaction: third parties are protected, and principals are left with a less valuable right against agents. This dilution of principals' rights is triggered by their consent to originative transactions but requires independent publicity, whether formal or informal, to make originative contracts verifiable. Otherwise, parties might try to opportunistically deny or alter originative contracts (and, consequently, the rules to be applied) in accordance with the evolution of the business. In general, before contracting, principals and agents in originative contracts will choose the option that suits third parties in subsequent transactions, so that the latter will be willing to contract. However, subsequently, they will do everything possible to ensure that the rule applied is the most favorable to their own interests. For example, during much of the nineteenth century, individual merchants tried to resort to whichever legislation and jurisdiction—civil or commercial—were most favorable to them (see, e.g., for Spain, Menéndez Menéndez 1990, 30 and 54).

This possibility of gaming the rules to be applied poses a pervasive moral hazard in corporate contracting. For example, a company and its shareholders are interested in convincing third parties that a person has sufficient authority to commit the firm in a specific operation. But, if the operation turns sour, then the company and its shareholders may allege that that person was not its legal representative or lacked sufficient authority. The judicial history of unincorporated companies prior to the creation of the English Company Registry in 1844 provides many examples of this type, because "third parties were in the dark, in many circumstances, as to the status of the person they were dealing with. They could not be certain whether a person pretending to be a director, officer, or clerk could act for the company, its capital, or its shareholders" (Harris 2000, 144). In a similar way, companies may offer unlimited liability to make credit cheaper but, when the company becomes bankrupt, shareholders would prefer to allege limited liability. A version of this type of problem, which had considerable historical relevance (causing, e.g., much litigation in France and Spain for centuries), was the hidden limited partnership in which the limited liability of a wealthy partner was concealed until the firm became bankrupt.[20] Similarly, companies will often want to create the impression of having more capital than they in fact have because that would allow them to borrow under better terms.

Given this interest of parties to originative contracts in choosing rules opportunistically, mechanisms that are independent of such parties are required in order to make such contracts verifiable by judges and establish, without any risk of manipulation, the rules to be applied when deciding on conflicts in subsequent transactions. To guarantee independence, different types of publicity are required in different contractual situations. When the originative contracts themselves or their consequences are notorious, this very notoriety provides the required independence. Notorious facts are observed by all sorts of operators and result in ample proof that, if necessary, can accredit the legal reality of originative contracts, which are therefore relatively easy for judges to verify. For example, when employees act in representation of their employers, their work is often observed by everyone dealing with them. Such people could testify to the employee's actions and thus refute an employer who attempted to repudiate the obligations that the employee has reached with third parties. Something similar occurs with corporate officers, at least for ordinary affairs.

On the other hand, when originative contracts remain hidden and especially when they generate intangible consequences, the latter cannot be observed by independent third parties who will not be able to provide reliable information in a possible judicial process. For example, if the courts were to enforce company formation agreements against third parties so that the partitioning of company and personal assets could remain secret, it would then be easy for shareholders to cheat such third parties, opportunistically adjusting the distribution of assets between those of the company and those of the shareholders. Third parties would struggle to find out which assets really back which obligations and would be reluctant to contract unless they receive additional guarantees. To avoid this, ensuring verifiability, publicity needs to be produced using formal mechanisms that guarantee independence—usually company registries. The basic guarantee of their independence with regard to the parties is that parties are not free to choose between alternative registries. As analyzed in chapter 2, when parties are able to choose jurisdiction, once their choice is made, they are not able to choose a registry. In general, when parties are seen as choosing registries, this is in fact a choice of jurisdiction and, when there is a switch of registries, specific precautions are taken to protect third parties.

In summary, the key for making contract rules possible—i.e., both effective in protecting third parties and triggered by principals' consent—is independent publicity of the originative transactions and legal acts, so that principals remain committed to their choices. Such independence results automatically as a byproduct of some transactions, but, when this is not the case, registration is needed. Without it, not only would third parties to subsequent contracts be facing adverse selection before contracting, but they would also suffer moral hazard afterward. The reason is that the relevant originative contracts would remain secret; principals and agents thus could alter them in order to choose the rules that suit them best at any one time, to the detriment of third parties. Independent registration avoids this risk by making it possible to verify the consents given by principals—the property rightholders in such originative contracts and legal acts. This enables judges to apply contract rules and thus protect third parties without damaging the enforcement of property rights, which remain safe by requiring rightholders' consent.

Two Exceptions That Confirm the Argument: The Viability of Documentary Formalization by Means of Negotiable Instruments and Powers of Attorney

Apparent exceptions to independent publicity of originative contracts, such as negotiable instruments and powers of attorney, reinforce the argument, because independence is absent only when third parties retain contractual evidence preventing manipulation by either the principal or the agent.

Negotiable instruments, such as promissory notes and bills of exchange,[21] and those governed by similar rules (e.g., securities, letters of credit, bills of lading, and IOUs) also facilitate impersonal market transactions using the same formula as for transactions on movables, with agents and by companies: assigning rights in such a way that the third party's information asymmetry becomes irrelevant. In general, the third party who acquires a credit formalized in this type of instrument is safe against defenses that the debtor (who acts as the "principal" in my framework) could plead against the "agent." For example, in bills of exchange and promissory notes, the obligation to pay is separated from the underlying transaction, such as the sale in regard to which the bill was issued, unless the instrument returns to the agent. Therefore, a third party who has acquired the instrument in good faith has an unconditional right to be paid by the maker, even if the maker has a valid defense against the original payee (Méndez González 2007).

This is achieved without making the originative contract—that is, the instrument—public. Principals' commitment to the originative contract is ensured by a simpler procedure: transferring possession of the instrument, once it has been signed by the principal, first to the agent and then to the third party, when the agent cedes it. Consequently, the principal cannot cheat the third party by manipulating it. The solution is viable because the instrument involves only one obligatory right (that of being paid). So, there are none of the usual difficulties arising from the existence of multiple *in rem* rights on the same asset as, for instance, with mortgages, in which the principal retains not only ownership but also possession of the mortgaged land or, worse still, when previous hidden mortgages might be enforced, a market-killing risk in a regime of contractual privacy (as argued in chapter 2). Nor are there several third parties who might be interested in possessing the instrument to protect their rights, with potentially damaging consequences for all others. Consistent with the legal nature of the right involved, such instruments are used for personal transactions safeguarded by knowledge of the debtor's solvency.

Significantly, modern forms of secured finance that allow multiple rights on the same movable assets (including accounts receivable) and thus need to prioritize such rights rely on registries, such as the one established by Article 9 of UCC on secured transactions.[22] Alternative solutions to public filing establish priority by the dates of the competing agreements to assign, protecting the first assignee, or by the date on which an assignee notifies the debtor or receives acceptance from him, protecting the first assignee to notify (Kötz 1992, 93–99). Both solutions are poor because they do not inform potential assignees about possible previous assignments. Moreover, the cost of notification increases with the number of debtors, making it impossible for a large number of transactions. The missed opportunities will increase the cost of credit and hinder securitization.

Powers of attorney also fully commit the grantor (the principal) in legal acts signed by the proxy (the agent), with and without publicity in different cases. First, a variety of publicity mechanisms are used to ensure that the principal remains committed and cannot deny the existence of the proxy. As argued above, notoriety in the exercise of representation provides sufficient independent publicity for the usual functions of entrepreneurs' agents. In addition, registration is often required of powers of attorney for general representation (i.e., those in which proxies remain in force after being used) and organic representation of companies.

Second, mere documentary proxies are used, in which representation figures in a document but there is neither notoriety nor the need for registration. Legal systems often require such documentary proxies to meet certain requirements: for example, their form must be at least that of the act to be carried out by the proxy (*equal dignity rule*), the grantor may be required to consult with experts, and granting of the proxy may need to be authenticated by the presence and signature of lawyers and witnesses. These safeguards aim to ensure that the grantor understands the risks involved in granting power to the proxy and to provide convincing proof of the granting. They seem less effective, however, for protecting future third parties because it is the grantor who chooses the persons who authenticate the proxy, so they are dependent on him, especially when they compete with each other. Nor are they effective for avoiding false proxies, which would explain why cases of fraud involving documentary proxies are so common.

Nevertheless, in spite of the privacy maintained in documentary proxies and the dependent relationship of the authenticators, representation of individuals is largely based on this type of proxy. The principal's commitment is ensured by similar means to those used for bills of exchange. On the one hand, the third party checks the proxy and retains, if not the proxy, at least documentary and often (at least in civil law countries) authenticated evidence. On the other hand, a revoked proxy continues to commit the grantor toward good faith third parties, as it is understood to generate an appearance of representation that third parties can trust.

This efficacy of revoked proxies avoids the main risk for the third party, that of opportunistic behavior by the principal who may renege on the agent's act if such reneging suits him. In the terms used above, when granting a proxy, the principal accepts being committed by the agent not only during the validity of the proxy but also afterward, until such time as the power is taken back. Here again, the viability of this documentary solution depends on the existence of a single right (that of acting in representation of the principal). Revocation poses a problem that is to some degree equivalent to dispossession for a bill holder. But the solution is simpler than what is required for the latter, because of the personal nature of representation, in contrast to the real nature of the relation between the holder and the bill.

However, the efficacy of revoked proxies only transfers the risk to the grantor. In particular, the grantor is in a difficult position if, after revoking the proxy, the agent does not give it back. In such cases it will be hard for the grantor to destroy the appearance of representation power that the proxy may still give to innocent third parties, which may harm the grantor. Avoiding such consequences may be easier for special proxies that authorize representation in a single transaction. This helps to explain why general proxies tend to be publicly registered. In addition to saving costs in repeated uses of proxies, registration provides a reliable way of revoking them. Without registration, grantors would tend to rely less on proxies, hindering specialization.

Lastly, it is worth mentioning that both exceptions—negotiable instruments and powers of attorney—thus involve single rights where third parties can retain the contractual evidence, which prevents possible manipulation of originative contracts by principals. Therefore, they reinforce the argument that independent publicity is essential in the general case in which multiple rights are present.

Collective Action and Commitment in Business Registration

The main difficulty for achieving this independence when registration is necessary stems from the nature of the registry as a public good.[23] Entrepreneurs are truly interested in the registered information being credible, as this is the only way of making it trustworthy for courts and, consequently, for their contractual counterparts. However, they face a collective action problem because they prefer others to contribute to the registry, contributing as little as possible themselves. They are obviously reluctant to finance the functioning of the registry, to disclose information, to have it subject to what is often slow scrutiny, and to have registration denied, with the consequent need to revise their originative contracts.[24] Less obviously but often more importantly, given the legal function of the register with respect to the rules applicable to subsequent contracts, entrepreneurs are reluctant to commit themselves in the originative contracts that they file, preferring to remain free to choose ex post whatever option turns out to be the most favorable to them. Yet they do want other entrepreneurs to remain fully committed.

Consequently, they all want an independent registry but, ideally, they would prefer this independence to be exercised only with respect to others. They thus demand what I will call "selective laxity," by which they would be treated leniently or even allowed to alter ex post their legal attributes (e.g., the name of their legal representative or their company's assets) so that, in any subsequent contract, judges would apply whichever rule or option is most favorable to the entrepreneur. If such selective laxity of the registry did not significantly damage its average effectiveness so that judges and thus contracting parties still relied on it, the entrepreneur would benefit in two ways. First, when acting as a third party, he would be protected by strict operation of the registry. And, second, when acting as a principal, his originative contracts would not undergo tough scrutiny and would not be delayed or rejected by the registry. In the extreme case, he would not remain committed and would be able to opportunistically choose a posteriori, potentially damaging third parties who had relied on the register when they contracted with the entrepreneur's agents. Obviously, no entrepreneur would want to be in this situation when acting as a third party, so they all want the registry to commit other entrepreneurs but not themselves.

This demand for "selective commitment" regarding legal rules poses a more serious collective action problem than that caused by mere funding or information disclosure, as it involves a risk of creeping but radical subversion of the registry. If a significant proportion of entrepreneurs is successful in achieving special treatment—avoiding commitment—the registry will no longer be effective and will turn into a useless burden for firms. It is therefore necessary to include additional precautions to protect the independence of registration decisions. The solution is not only to define the information to be filed but also to establish independent control to ensure that at least the required contractual information is filed, that such filing is independently dated, and that the information is preserved. This is not an easy task, as shown by the slow development of registries.

Lessons from Four Historical Cases

Thus far, I have discussed the role and requirements of company registries. I now analyze four historical cases to illustrate the fundamental aspects of the discussion and to draw some lessons for the organization of registries. In particular, the cases, presented in their logical order, confirm that it would be too costly to organize corporations by purely contractual means. They also indicate how the effectiveness of company registries depends on making them independent from parties and on resolving the collective action problem suffered by entrepreneurs.

Feasibility and Costs of Private Incorporation: The English Unincorporated Companies

Before the act creating the Company Registry in 1844, English companies could only be incorporated by specific acts of Parliament or royal charters or Letter Patents, which were difficult to obtain. This meant that so-called unincorporated companies took on increasing importance, despite being exposed to all sorts of complications, including the uncertainty of judicial decisions, as analyzed by Harris (2000).[25] Their experience confirms the difficulties that arise when companies are created without registration, based only on private contracts and informal publicity, since these unincorporated companies had to use increasingly complex legal engineering, based on the structure of general partnerships to which they gradually added various elements of trusts and corporations. Promoters first created them by signing an initial agreement and then searching, often publicly, for additional passive partners. A deed of settlement was then drafted and signed by all promoters, specifying the joint-stock capital of the company, how it was to be raised and divided into shares, and under what conditions the shares were transferable, as well as everything relating to the administration and representation of the firm. The most fully developed versions also created a trust with all the firm's assets, designated trustees, and established rules for their appointment and decision making (Harris 2000, mainly 39–40).[26] Perhaps the most famous example organized in this way was Lloyd's insurance market, which only obtained sound legal status with the Lloyd's Act of 1871. Interestingly, the launching of new companies involved substantial, decentralized publicity campaigns addressing potential subscribers of shares. These campaigns used all sorts of means, including public meetings, prospectuses, circulars, letters, and newspaper ads, and relied on bank networks and previous subscribers to reach new subscribers (Harris 2000, 124–27).

This English experience with unincorporated companies reveals that creating companies based on private contracting and informal publicity comes up against three main types of difficulty: (1) high transaction costs for the partners to contract both among themselves and with third parties; (2) heavy judicial costs and uncertainty; and (3) substantial opportunity costs, since contracting has to be limited to certain industries and based to a large extent on personal guarantees.

First, the parties faced high transaction costs for contracting the desired conditions, such as entity shielding or limited liability, as well as for ensuring that the corporate will was well defined (in many cases, all the partners had to sign). They found it difficult to limit their liability. Even for insurance companies, in which the practice of including limited liability clauses in their policies came to be widespread, "the limitation of liability was only partial, and in other sectors, in which there was no practice of drafting standard written agreements, almost no limitation was in fact achieved" (Harris 2000, 143–44). Given that they were not considered legal entities, there was also little continuity and they had to be re-created when one of the partners died or went bankrupt, as every one of the partners could commit the firm. The use of trusts relieved this problem but did not solve it because trusts were more appropriate for real estate (Harris 2000, 141–59).

Unincorporated companies also involved heavy judicial costs. First, since they lacked legal entity, it was necessary to litigate against all the partners. According to Ker (1837), "the principal difficulty in the present law arises in legal proceedings taken by or against partners, or in suits *inter se*, where the partners are numerous" (3). Second, evidentiary difficulties were pervasive. For example, judges had to resort to contracts and notoriety as the main sources of evidence, especially to establish priorities among personal and corporate creditors in bankruptcies. Obviously, court decisions entailed great uncertainty, as made clear in a long series of contradictory court decisions (Harris 2000, especially 230–49). Unsurprisingly, disputes and litigation were intense (Copp 2002, 363; Ker 1837). Apparently, the courts were unable to find a way to make the creation of joint-stock companies effectively viable using purely contractual methods, without the need for either specific state charter or public registration.

Finally, these high contractual and judicial costs led to a substantial opportunity cost, because many transactions and firms turned out to be unfeasible. Unincorporated companies either relied on additional personal guarantees or carried out low-risk activities. Their contracts were based to a large extent on personal guarantees, both among partners and with personal and company creditors; as well as on the debtors' prison system, which played an essential role in England until the 1869 Debtors Act (Harris 2000, 131–32). Moreover, their presence was limited to not-for-profit activities and low-risk sectors, that is, those needing little borrowed capital and those in which fixed assets predominated so that default risk was low (Harris 2000, 165–67 and n. 71).

The Registration Solution: The 1844 English Company Act

To resolve these difficulties, in 1844 Parliament passed the Act for the Registration, Incorporation, and Regulation of Joint Stock Companies, enabling companies to be created freely, provided they met certain requirements for registration and information disclosure, both at the time of incorporation and in subsequent reports that had to be registered every six months. Also, the law authorized the registry to issue a certificate conferring full legal entity status on the company, but only after ensuring that the registered documents complied with the law and contained all required information. The latter referred, among other things, to the company's objects and capital structure, as well as the names and addresses of both shareholders and the company's officers and auditors. The act required that all companies with transferable shares or more than twenty-five members be registered.

The registry was a success from the start. During the fourteen months subsequent to entry into force of the 1844 Act, 1,639 companies were registered, that is, more than double the number that had existed in England two years before (Harris 2000, 288). It had two main consequences: (1) it eliminated preexisting barriers to entry and (2) it resolved the legal problems for incorporating companies, thus expanding contractual possibilities.

First, as analyzed by North, Wallis, and Weingast (2009), given the paucity of incorporation charters granted by Parliament and the drawbacks suffered by unincorporated companies, lack of access to the corporate form of enterprise constituted a serious barrier to entry before 1844. These authors claim that "[c]harters created rents even when charters did not confer monopolies, because the ability to access the corporate form in itself was a substantial advantage to any economic organization" (2009, 217). They are right when considering that English unincorporated companies suffered anticompetitive constraints because they could not obtain a corporate charter. However, the charter formula was difficult to apply widely and probably amounted to a poor solution for reducing transaction costs. And the contractual solution was no easier, as can be seen from the difficulties faced by unincorporated companies. This explains why the number of companies increased not when one of the main prohibitory laws (the Bubble Act) was derogated in 1825, but when effective institutions for company contracting were implemented (i.e., as from 1844, the year the Company Registry was set up). According to this argument, the main accomplishment of registration is not to liberalize incorporation but to make it feasible.

This episode holds an important lesson for today's debate on business formalization and bureaucratic simplification. As in the England of the nineteenth century, effective institutions need to not only liberalize company incorporation but also facilitate the enforcement of legal (contract) rules that enable impersonal market transactions. This requires implementing an effective company registry. In the same way, current reforms cannot be limited to just making formalization cheaper or faster without considering the quality of formalization institutions, thus condemning companies to use mere contractual methods similar to those used by unincorporated companies in England in the first decades of the nineteenth century. In view of the English historical experience, company formalization appears not only or even mainly as an entry barrier, as seen by De Soto et al. (1986, 1989), Djankov et al. (2002), and the "Doing Business" project (World

Bank, 2004–11), but also as a necessary condition for the effective functioning of legality.

Second, the registry expanded contractual possibilities by making it possible to limit liability contractually, something that unincorporated companies had been unable to do. On limited liability, the 1844 reform was timid, and until the enactment of a further law in 1855, registration did not entail limited liability. However, in contrast with the inability of unincorporated companies to limit the liability of their shareholders contractually (as explained above), registered companies were indeed able to limit their liability after 1844 (Hansmann and Kraakman 2000, 429–30).

Despite these achievements, the positive role of the registry in resolving the problems for incorporating and operating companies in England is often disregarded. For example, Hansmann, Kraakman, and Squire (2006) blame legal conservatism and the shortcomings of bankruptcy institutions for such problems and, more generally, for the English legal system's incapacity to meet the economy's demand for companies with full-fledged legal entity status. They argue that it was impossible or, at least, very costly, to shield the entity and, to a lesser extent, to limit liability without "organizational law"—mainly, corporate law. However, the lack of a law changing the rules to be applied should not in itself hold back the adoption by courts of such new rules, at least not in common law, especially according to the extensive literature on the adaptability of common law. What seems to have been most difficult was to set up the organizational mechanisms for formalization (i.e., registries) that judges require in order to apply these rules efficiently: preserving rightholders' consent and thus property enforcement, while also ensuring commitment so that, when judges adjudicate subsequent contracts, principals cannot opportunistically choose whatever rule they prefer.

In addition, Hansmann, Kraakman, and Squire (2006) seem to attribute the growth of companies in the United States to more specific, more recent factors, such as corporation tax, modern accounting techniques, and obligations for disseminating information (1394–99). These considerations have been criticized by Lamoreaux and Rosenthal (2006) for not taking into account developments in continental Europe, where it had been possible to shield entities earlier through limited liability partnerships, a figure whose roots went back to the medieval *commenda*. However, in their critique they also disregard the role of registration: in particular, the serious problems that judicial enforcement of hidden limited liability partnerships used to cause before registration was effectively required. The supposed superiority of continental law over Anglo-Saxon law is therefore debatable, at least in countries that did not have an effective company registry, in that the judicial enforcement of company contracts was often achieved at the cost of damaging the interests of third parties.

This English experience suggests that effective company law requires two inseparable elements—not only a set of market-enabling rules but also an organization, the public registry, without which it is difficult to apply such rules. For example, section XXX of the 1844 English Company Registration Act established that acts by a director whose appointment was defective are still binding on him and the company. Moreover, section XLIV affirms the validity against the company of contracts signed by its officers, even if they fail to meet certain requirements (in writing, signed by two officers, sealed and so on) that otherwise nullify them. These are simple rules but they are easier to apply safely if the incorporation and appointments have been registered and thus are easy to verify. Therefore, the essential element of the English Company Registration Act of 1844 was the organization of an effective registry. To apply these new rules without previous company registration, the courts would have had to resort to notoriety in the incorporation and the exercise of the office, which would provide a much weaker basis. It seems reasonable for judges to be reluctant to make such a radical departure from the usual rules on the basis of informal publicity when this is unreliable. So, redefining by law or precedent the rules to be applied by judges is insufficient for ensuring that they will be enforced. Efficiently applying market-enabling contract rules requires effective registration of originative private contracts and legal acts. This becomes indispensable when notoriety does not provide verifiable evidence on originative contracts and thus commitment to them by principals. Essentially, the registry ensures the quality of judicial evidence, allowing the application of market-enabling contract rules to subsequent transactions.

Importance of Organization: The French 1673 Registry

Unfortunately, effective registration is not easy to achieve because a functional, independent registry is hard to organize and because business registration and disclosure suffer from collective action problems. As discussed above, firms and entrepreneurs usually want others to make their contracts public but are reluctant to do it themselves, unless they are obliged to do so, and this obligation has to be enforced. Moreover, they may fall in a vicious circle: when the registry is ineffective, they are less interested in registering and, since many people do not register, the registry then becomes even less effective.

All these problems are illustrated by the difficulties suffered, and by the practical irrelevance of the company registry created in France in 1673. The main reason for setting it up was the need to establish a firmer basis for companies to contract with third parties, avoiding the main problems faced by trade at the time, which required clarifying who the company's partners were and what assets backed their contractual commitments (Kessler 2007, 163–64). These requirements were implemented in the *Ordonnance Commerciale* of 1673 issued under Jean-Baptiste Colbert but drawn up by merchants, especially Jacques Savary, a former businessman, civil servant, and author of a classic treatise on the subject.

According to the *Ordonnance*, companies in France were to be created in two steps. First, the partners were to sign a written agreement (*acte* or *traité de société*) and, second, register a summary of the agreement with the merchant court and post it publicly (Kessler 2007, 162–63). Testimony on oral agreements could not be used to contradict the written agreement. But these requirements were almost always violated, and the set penalty of nullity was not applied. As early as 1681, eight years after publication of the *Ordonnance*, the Paris Court issued a ruling recognizing the legal existence of a nonregistered company. Also, the court stated repeatedly that it was against the obligation to register.[27] Most companies failed to comply with the writing and publicity obligations.[28] Conversely, written letters and witness testimony sufficed to establish company existence (Kessler 2007, 162–66). Other evidence usually considered by judges in other jurisdictions to determine the existence of a tacit company contract were the partners keeping accounts in common, business taking place after expiry of the period set in the company contract, and withdrawals of money being made from the company's treasury (Petit 1979, 90).

The immediate cause for this failure to use the registry was that, by imposing nullity on noncompliance with the obligation to register, the penalty became impossible to apply in practice. It was unfair because it was mainly imposed on innocent third parties, and imposing the penalty would have gone against the very purpose for which the registry was created (Girón Tena 1955, 159–63). Moreover, the law allowed unrestricted access by the general public to the content of the register, which went against the then prevailing desire for privacy. However, the failure of the registry stemmed from the typical collective action drama analyzed above. This French registry had been created at the initiative of businessmen, and we can assume they wanted the registry to succeed, but with others registering. They themselves were unwilling to register, and sanctions were ineffective in forcing them to do so.

Resistance to register is also easier to understand when it takes place in a context of transition as with the French registry, in which most companies were personalistic, so informal publicity was still somewhat effective, and most transactions still had a highly personal element.[29] In fact, many participants did not understand the advantages of facilitating impersonal transactions.[30] This is illustrated by the above-mentioned response of the Paris Court. When criticizing the proposal made by the *députés de commerce* to strengthen the public company registry, the Paris judges asked:

> Why can this matter [company registration] not be left to general good faith, as it always has, and to the mutual trust that is the soul of trade? *A person who trades is assumed to know the trading partner.* If this is not the case, then there should be no trade, or the person wishing to trade should request the opposite partner to make himself known. If this precaution is not taken and the merchant relies on general, public good faith, then the only person to blame is himself for trusting someone he did not know sufficiently well.[31]

This response underscores the role played by public registries in making impersonal transactions viable. In 1748, it was not as clear as it is today that economic development is based precisely on the possibility of carrying out the sort of impersonal transactions that the French judges rejected outright.

Some decades later, the 1807 *Code de Commerce* restored the by then all-but-forgotten registration requirement with a nullity sanction. Contemporary doctrine tried to make nullity for failure to register unexceptionable against third parties, but this only became consolidated gradually and was not set in law until 1935 (Girón Tena 1955, 129–34). However, the registry had partly succeeded by the nineteenth century. For example, thanks to the public registration of partnerships, partners in nineteenth-century France could delegate management to one or some of them, limit their power to commit the firm, require that certain types of contract, such as debts, be signed by more than one partner, or even prohibit one person from signing altogether (Lamoreaux and Rosenthal 2005). Their freedom to do these things was based on the willingness of judges to enforce these restrictions against third parties, provided that the partnerships had been registered.

Private Interest in Mandatory Registration: The Bilbao Company Registry of 1737

Entrepreneurs are interested in having registries that will reduce transaction costs, especially those of companies for which informal solutions based on notoriety are ineffective, to the point that "all the possible effects of registration [in the commercial registry] have developed initially in response to the interests of private individuals and only subsequently to those of public interests" (Tallon 1983, 110). This private interest is exemplified by the appearance of the first modern company registries stemming from the evolution of the *lex mercatoria*, as illustrated by the French case analyzed above. It is not unique. For example, beginning in 1737 merchants in the Spanish city of Bilbao voluntarily, although with state support, adopted mandatory commercial regulations—known as the *Ordenanzas de Bilbao*—which, in order to achieve "preservation of good faith, and public security of Commerce in company," obliged them to file with their Consulate a testimony of the company contract that could be accessed by any legitimate interested parties. This requirement soon led to the filing of the contract itself.[32] Moreover, from 1791 on, the filings were reviewed by the Consulate Syndic, who could demand disclosure of additional information of special interest to third parties. This included, at a minimum, the following: the identity of the partners and officers; the company signature and that of its representatives; the duration of the company; and, in practice, the regime for capital and profit sharing, limited liability, and other matters relating to accountability, restrictions on trading by partners outside the company, the books, and the criteria for liquidating the company (Petit 1979, 83–107). The main reason for their insistence on registration was the problem previously caused by the existence of hidden limited liability partnerships, which resulted from the lack of a clear distinction between the different types of companies and the presence of limited partners in companies claiming to be general partnerships (Girón Tena 1955, 164–65).

Along these lines, the *Ordenanzas de Bilbao* illustrate two aspects that might well be forgotten today since registration now is a legal imperative. First is the private interest of entrepreneurs in introducing an independent registration system with mandatory registration of the fundamental elements of company contracts. These eighteenth-century entrepreneurs decided to commit themselves to resolve the collective action problem that existed and continues to exist today regarding registration. This was achieved by voluntarily setting up a system that obliged them to register information on the aspects of their company contracts that were relevant to third parties. Furthermore, they ensured the integrity and verifiability of registered documents by making the Consulate Syndic responsible for preserving the files, and empowering him to determine that the filings were sufficient, to require additional information when necessary and to impose penalties in the form of fines and closures.

Second is the high degree of compliance with the registration requirements laid down by the *Ordenanzas de Bilbao* (Petit 1979, 98–103), which is in contrast with the poor compliance, as described above, with the French *Ordonnance Commerciale* of 1673. The difference seems to be due to two factors. On the one hand, the French *Ordonnance* raised the private costs of registration because, unlike in Bilbao, the register was open to all rather than just to those with legitimate interests (Petit 1979, 98). On the other hand, although failure to register could result in a more serious penalty, that of absolute nullity of the company contract (which could be claimed not only by third parties but also by partners among themselves and against third parties), such penalties proved to be unenforceable because of their harshness and because they damaged the interests of the same innocent third parties whose interests the rule was designed to protect (Girón Tena 1955, 129). The penalties in Bilbao, though weaker, proved to be more effective and consisted, initially, of fining and then closing the establishments of unregistered companies. More importantly, perhaps, they punished the unregistered company instead of the innocent third party.

Conclusions on the Historical Evidence

In summary, these historical experiences teach us several lessons. First, the difficulties faced by English unincorporated companies indicate that it is necessary to formalize a company's originative contracts in order to facilitate judicial action on subsequent contracts and, more specifically, to allow the enforcement of market-friendly rules. Private interest in establishing a registry is also clear from the French and Bilbao initiatives, which arose in the sphere of the law merchant. However, both these episodes also reveal the need for legislative intervention to solve the collective action problem in the creation of registries. Similarly, the history of the French registry throws light on the need for independent enforcement. Lastly, the effectiveness of such enforcement is clear in both the English registry, where it was based on a legal mandate, and the Bilbao registry, where it was arranged by the entrepreneurs themselves.

Registration and the Theory of the Firm

By explaining how business registers help reduce transaction costs without endangering property rights, the analysis provides a rationale for the institutional foundation of the firm. This rationale complements the contractual emphasis that dominates most theories of the firm,[33] in which the role of the state is limited to providing a set of default rules for contracts; a judiciary that ensures contract enforcement; and a range of mechanisms to correct externalities, often seen as not being part of corporate law. This contractual emphasis is quite visible with respect to corporate law. For example, Posner (1976) states that "the primary utility of Corporation law lies in providing a set of standard, implied contract terms" (506). Similarly, in reply to the question as to why corporate law exists, Easterbrook and Fischel (1991) state that "the short but not entirely satisfactory answer is that corporate law is a set of terms available off-the-rack so that participants in corporate ventures can save the cost of contracting" (34). Consequently, the scope of corporate law is often limited to companies' internal affairs. As summarized by Ramseyer (1998),

> Corporate law governs the internal affairs of the corporation. More specifically, it governs the ties among a firm's shareholders and its senior managers—its officers and directors. Functionally, it governs the relations among the residual claimants to the firm's assets and the agents they directly or indirectly appoint to manage those assets. Necessarily in doing so it governs only a small part of a firm's business activities. Banking and commercial law, for example, govern its relations with its creditors. Labour law governs its relations with its lower-level employees. Contract law governs its relations with its trade creditors, and tort law with its involuntary creditors. (503)

There is little need in these views for business registration. Because they tend to disregard the two types of contract in sequential contracting, they do not feel any need to make originative contracts verifiable in order to reduce transaction costs in subsequent contracts. Consequently, both normative and positive discussions of the mandatory content of corporate law also tend to disregard the mandatory element in registration: for example, even when incorporators are free to structure the articles of incorporation, they still have to register them.[34] Essentially, these views tend to focus the analysis on the parties to the originative contract, disregarding the difficulties they face to contract with third parties. Something similar happens with broader analyses in the theory of the firm that place the distinctive nature of the firm on how the law treats employment as compared to commercial contracts (Masten 1988), or on what Williamson (1991) calls "forbearance," the refusal of courts to hear disputes between firms' divisions.

Conversely, the analysis presented in this chapter has emphasized the relation with third parties. From this point of view, the ability of agents and third parties to commit the principal provides an additional criterion for defining the nature and boundaries of the firm. The analysis thus provides an alternative explanation as to why the corporate form of enterprise needs the support of institutions and what type of support is needed: not only rules but also organization. It must be possible for judges to apply market-enabling contract rules to subsequent contracts, reducing transaction costs without damaging property rights. Organized registries accomplish this by providing a verifiable record of the decisions made by property rightholders to weaken future property enforcement. This preserves rightholders' consent and commits them to their choices.[35]

The analysis confirms that, although strong (meaning, *in rem*) property rights are essential for economic development, they may act as a deterrent for trade when innocent third parties are imperfectly informed on their nature and scope. Solving the problem requires more than clear legal definitions and strong judicial enforcement of property rights. In addition to these two key ingredients, good corporate law also requires effective organization—functional company registries—to make private originative contracts verifiable by judges and thus to provide a safe ground for subsequent contracts with third parties and judicial decisions on them.

FOUR

Strategic Issues for Creating Contractual Registries

In the previous chapters, I have developed a theory of formalization institutions and, in particular, contractual registries and identified some major features in their design and regulation. In the remainder of the book, I apply and extend these findings to build a practical framework for creating, developing, and regulating registries. In the present chapter, I address the most general questions, such as (1) how to interact with preexisting legal orders often best adapted to local markets, (2) the most logical sequence in developing institutions for impersonal trade, (3) priorities for reform, (4) lessons to be learnt from reforms in the areas of property titling, and (5) business formalization. In subsequent chapters I address more specific issues in the creation of registries, including choice of the type of registry, organization of registries, the challenges posed by new technologies, and the regulation of complementary services.

Understanding Conflict between Local and Wider Legal Orders

Titling reforms often cause conflict with customary property rights. This happened in Europe with the feudal system of property rights, the remains of which were for centuries a serious impediment to individual property. Meanwhile, European urban owners kept requesting the creation of land registries from their rulers. Between 1535 and 1925, England alone devised twenty-nine laws to create a real property registry (Sparkes 1999, 1–3). Similarly, as early as 1528, the cities represented in the Castilian *Cortes* asked King Carlos I to introduce mandatory registration of *censos* (a sort of indefinite leasehold). However, these demands were always left unsatisfied. Effective registration was not in place in England until the twentieth century, and effective registration was only enacted in Castile in 1861. A main reason for these failures was the opposition of nobles and lawyers. Similarly, in developing countries today, customary property rights often collide with attempts to assign a fuller set of property rights to individuals.

The cost of registers is an important factor in this type of delay, but the particular nature of demand and private interests often play more essential roles. Trade opportunities opened by institutional reform are not available to all and beneficiaries of the old system may have little to gain in the new one. Consequently, economic demand does not necessarily imply sufficient political demand for institutional change. Moreover, the demand for change likely correlates with the strength of alternative institutions, which are suited to different forms of production that rely little on markets or only on personal transactions and local markets. In these cases, institutional change is often resisted by those with vested interests in the traditional order, be they tribal chiefs in a primitive region, organizers of squatters in an urban slum, or nobles and conveyancers in the European ancien régime.

I argue in the next sections that contemplating these situations as conflicts between legal orders, which are more or less adapted to different markets or even economic systems, will help prevent the common mistake of overestimating the capacity of customary institutions to adapt. Such a perspective will also reveal the limits of private initiatives to overcome the maladjustment between the scope of the available institutions and the desired extent of the market, be they the different versions of collective responsibility systems or intermediation constructs, such as the ones devised by the US mortgage industry to overcome the deficiencies of county registries. Finally, this perspective will also demonstrate how prevalent the problem is, as even developed market economies generally suffer a similar but subtler problem: the predominance within mainstream law of a personal-exchange view. This view often takes legal solutions suitable to personal exchange as general (e.g., arcane concepts of ownership transfer), while it relegates those suitable for impersonal exchange (e.g., indefeasible title) as exceptional. This confusion results in legal complication, greater demand for lawyers, and the waste of impersonal exchange opportunities.

Integrating or Superseding Local Legal Orders?

Even primitive societies have developed sophisticated legal solutions for formalizing transactions,[1] including independent publicity and rudimentary registration. For example, local economic activity in Tanzania relies on a myriad of private contractual tools and public institutional arrangements. Private tools include contracts for purchases, debts, and partnerships, as well as safeguards, such as representation proxies, accounting records, and reference letters. Public arrangements include arbitration and judicial mechanisms, as well as public archives.[2] Solutions of this sort perform formalization functions that are useful within a local market, as they make originative transactions verifiable and are effective in supporting transactions at their local level. For example, some of these systems provide for publicly recording land contracts so that acquirers can obtain information on the title held by the seller.

Using such solutions as building blocks is tempting when creating a legal system for a wider national market. For example, the European Union Task Force on Land Tenure (EUTFLT) concludes that, "even if the aim of the state is to develop a formal system of individual titles, the focus should be on favoring progressive evolution which builds on existing rights and gives them legal recognition" (EUTFLT 2004, 13). De Soto (2000) even claims that failure to recognize and incorporate informal systems is the main reason why many titling efforts failed in the past. Coherently, he urges governments to "determine how these dispersed grassroots extralegal procedures can be pulled together, systematized, codified, and harmonized with the existing legal system" (De Soto 2006, 57).

But local legal orders are ineffective in supporting transactions outside the local market. The local nature of their enforcement mechanisms often precludes them from supporting transactions in wider markets, those with parties external to the local community. The source of their legitimacy and power is local, which endangers their impartiality when external parties are involved. The wise man acting as judge in a village would have obvious difficulties deciding on a case involving a villager and an outsider. For this reason, local institutions tend to collide with those created by the state to support such a wider market.

The problem is tough because it is not weak but strong local enforcement that precludes trade. An extreme example was reported by Lanjouw and Levy (2002) in urban Ecuador when observing that the presence of a male in a household makes their land harder to sell, possibly because their claims are better enforced and buyers fear that they might be able to claim the land back. Conversely, it is easier for them to rent the land. The opposite happens with female-only households. The legal "order" in their case is the most local one: pure self-enforcement by owners. From this perspective, titling programs should be targeted at communities with weak informal legal orders, reinforcing the argument that titles are also more valuable for young communities without strong "organizers."

The conflict therefore has little to do with informality or with the less formal nature of local institutions. It is a conflict between jurisdictions, the same type of conflict that has historically hindered the emergence of effective judicial enforcement (Greif 2006b). And it is also a modern concern. Even in the United States today, state courts tend to rule in favor of local parties. For instance, Tabarrok and Helland (1999) find that, when deciding in tort cases and in comparison with nonelected judges, elected judges are prone to redistribute wealth from out-of-state businesses to in-state plaintiffs.

What markets need are effective institutions for the scope of the intended type of transaction—local versus national or international. And suitable institutions are more easily provided by political entities matching the scope of the market. For example, Anderson and Hill (2004) relate how cattlemen's associations in the US West were effective in the last decades of the nineteenth century in enforcing property rights at the local level. But they had to rely on government intervention to make cattle branding effective, because cattle were traded across large territories. Cattlemen therefore moved governments to create brand registries, to enact laws forbidding the driving of unbranded cattle from its accustomed range, and to regulate and inspect cattle and brand sales (Anderson and Hill 2004, 28, 141, and 149–51). The lesson is clear: nonlocal, impersonal transactions require nonlocal institutions, and developing them is generally easier for a political entity with effective authority over the intended market. The solution adopted tends to be a hierarchical structure in which the higher political entity constrains local jurisdictions through common rules. For land, this often also means introducing a *numerus clausus* that nullifies or degrades some customary and communitarian property rights. In such hierarchical structures there might be little, if any, integration of the local legal systems, which often mostly disappear.

Limits of Private Palliatives for Overcoming
Local Legal Orders and Enhancing Impersonal Trade

When a political entity covering the scope of the intended market does not exist, lacks authority, or is otherwise unable to create the necessary institutions, but at the same time there are enough potential gains from impersonal trade, local political entities or private parties themselves may develop palliative solutions to make some forms of quasi-impersonal trade viable.

Two prominent examples are the centuries-old systems of collective responsibility and the contemporary arrangements developed in the United States to make a national market in mortgage loans possible, on the basis of essentially local property institutions. Both are highly informative regarding the possibilities and limitations of private palliatives for impersonal trade.

Collective Responsibility as a Means of Channeling Local Enforcement toward Impersonal Trade

In the absence of a capable political authority willing to implement a vertical solution, local market participants may structure palliative horizontal solutions that resemble the "community responsibility system" supporting late medieval European trade (Greif 2002, 2004, 2006a). At that time, all merchants of a city could be made liable for each other's obligations in trade abroad, overcoming the tendency of local courts to be partial. Today, fairly similar solutions are found in many microcredit initiatives (Besley and Coate 1995; Bhole and Ogden 2010). An interesting example is the system of community mortgage lending established in Indonesia under the name *Kredit Triguna* or "triple function" loan, which is granted not to individuals but to low-income communities to buy land, build houses, and finance productive activities (Suyono and Juliman 1999). First, the community shows its commitment and ability to pay by providing a counterpart fund (Dana Mitra) that can take the form of cash savings or other value, including land. Every month, in addition to repaying part of the loan, each individual contributes to a collective reserve fund (Dana Solidaritas) that shoulders possible individual defaults. If any member defaults, the creditor is paid from the reserve fund and the defaulting member is dealt with under the rules of the community. If there are no defaults, the reserve fund remains with the community. (Microcredit initiatives also apply some of these features to favor the enforcement of *in personam* contract rights.)

Community responsibility provides a connection between local and wider legal orders. Without community responsibility, many transactions with outsiders would be made impossible by the strength of the local community, which leads to imperfect enforcement of contracts between locals and outsiders. For example, mortgage lenders would anticipate that the local legal order would make it impossible to foreclose on local defaulting mortgagors and would therefore be unwilling to lend. It is the strength of the local community that makes such transactions with outsiders impossible. Systems such as *Kredit Triguna* positively channel this strength to make them possible. The low default rates observed in microcredit schemes also point to their effectiveness.

However, the nature of these community responsibility solutions also hints at their limitations. It helps if the local community enjoys some legal standing, which in many cases—for example, communities of squatters—will require some political formalization (not dissimilar from company incorporation, whose historical antecedent lies in the incorporation of local entities). Moreover, community responsibility does not provide a general safeguard to all potential transactors but only to those covered in the agreement between the local entities. This constrains the ability of individuals to leave their local communities and sometimes makes it difficult to verify community affiliation. In the Middle Ages, registration was used to distinguish between burghers and mere inhabitants, who had less rights and were required to provide additional safeguards (Kadens 2004, 46–47, n. 34). Other arrangements used for verifying affiliation in medieval trade included having merchants of each city—those subject to the jurisdiction of that city—traveling and lodging together, as well as acting as witnesses in each others' contracts (Greif 2006a, 227). Understandably, these arrangements became less effective with the growth of cities (229).

Moreover, community responsibility relies on the personal ties between members of the local communities, which tends to weaken with trade and development. As argued by Greif to explain the demise of the medieval system of collective responsibility, enforcement will be increasingly costly to participants as the economy, the number, and the heterogeneity of participants grow. The very success of community responsibility thus endangers its future. In particular, when the community is unable to impose strong social sanctions, collective responsibility may encourage strategic individual behavior in the form of voluntary default, as pointed out by Besley and Coate (1995). Reputational networks without central enforcement mechanisms face similar difficulties, as indicated, for instance, by the decline of the merchant coalition in Mexican California (Clay 1997, 223–25).

Private Intermediation as a Substitute for Institutions in the US Mortgage Market

The foreclosure crisis in the United States, already mentioned in chapter 2, constitutes another contemporary showcase of the tricky interactions between local and wider legal orders in the development of institutions.

The US system of land recordation was developed at the local level by counties and states. One may therefore expect it to be well adapted only to local markets, so it is unsurprising that, in the second half of the twentieth century, it became increasingly inadequate for the national secondary mortgage market. From the early growth of this secondary market after World War II, it was felt by market participants that the land recording system did not provide a sufficiently uniform level of legal security. Hence, the early practice of requiring mortgages to be sold in the secondary market with a title insurance policy for the lender. Such policies provided a standard-izing complement that made it possible to package and sell mortgage loans even if they originally afforded uneven security. Later, the secondary mort-gage market developed much more complex transactions and faster turn-over, which were hard to process through filings of mortgage loan assign-ments in the local recording systems, in terms of both time and monetary costs. The industry therefore created the Mortgage Electronic Registration Systems (MERS) between 1993 and 1997 as a way of decoupling the local and national sides of the market and providing another commoditizing interface, in addition to title insurance. At the local level, MERS was to be the lender's representative, holding the rights *in rem*, enforced through the recording offices. At the national market level, MERS could also act as a registry of transactions for its members, keeping a record of *in personam* rights held by lenders if they so wished. Crucially, MERS was owned and controlled by lenders, protecting them against the risk that MERS might use its stronger *in rem* position to defraud them, as an independent rightholder might otherwise be tempted to do.

The 2010 crisis was at least partly caused by bad incentives and poor performance by MERS and the mortgage industry's members,[3] as well as their apparent oblivion of the judicial and political risks ever remaining on the enforcement of home foreclosures against apparently "weak" parties. However, the abundance of cases in which judicial rulings against MERS were later overturned on appeal also suggests that local courts took a narrow legalistic position against MERS in order to protect local interests—those of borrowers. As suggested, for example, by Korngold (2009), "an unarticu-lated concern over residential owners losing their homes or hard-pressed borrowers in general may underlie anti-MERS rulings" (743). To this extent, the foreclosure crisis, at least with respect to MERS, can be understood as one more case of conflict between local and wider legal orders, respectively, supporting local and wider markets.[4]

More generally, the crisis shows that these private palliative mechanisms tend to suffer the permanent threat of local enforcement. A likely solution to the foreclosure crisis might be to grant MERS what would amount to essen-tially public effects through an *ad hoc* political decision by the US Congress.[5]

Mainstream Law as a Local Legal Order
Hindering Institutional Development

The difficulties for building a solid institutional support for trading mort-gage loans in the United States show that the conflict between local and wider legal orders is not exclusive to emerging market economies. In fact, the difficulties that customary law and local legal orders in undeveloped countries pose to the development of legal institutions suitable for impersonal exchange are similar to the resistance that mainstream law often poses in more developed countries. In both cases, there are two different contractual technologies suited to two types of market. And the predominance of the law of personal transactions in mainstream law often acts as a main impediment to the institutions suited to impersonal transactions.

A difference in the mainstream law case is that the economic groups resisting change are not general social or economic classes—tribal chiefs, the nobility, land tenants, and current debtors[6]—but the professionals specialized in providing palliative services to support impersonal exchange. This difference helps to explain the paradox that colonial powers such as France and the United Kingdom in Africa, as well as the United States in the Philippines, introduced land registration in their colonies while keeping more traditional systems of privacy and recordation in their homelands. Apparently, colonies had stronger bureaucracies and weaker professions.

But professionals' vested interests alone can hardly explain the endurance of the law of personal exchange in legal scholarship. The inertia embedded in the use of conceptual and theoretical models is also an important obstacle to market-enabling legal institutions, whose creation and renewal are hindered by path dependency in legal evolution, given the inevitable piecemeal nature of legal reform, and registries' need for effective and costly organization. Most conceptual and instrumental resources in mainstream law were indeed originally designed for facilitating personal exchange. When institutional development in the form of creating contractual registries did not keep pace with the growing demand for impersonal exchange, some of these resources were adapted as palliatives (of the type used, e.g., by property chains of title and the unincorporated English companies analyzed in chapter 3) to support such demand for impersonal exchange. When registries finally developed, they often were articulated in a pragmatic, empirical, and gradual manner by introducing minimal changes and slotting them into conventional law. Their key rules were treated as mere exceptions to the previous legal framework, which was still presented as general, neglecting the relative weight of both frameworks in real market transactions. Such neglect was initially reasonable where both systems were working in parallel, especially while the old system was predominant. However, the neglect continued when these conditions were no longer present. So law school curricula and textbooks keep focusing on traditional legal principles and procedures well after they have become obsolete. For example, as late as

1999, "no major land law text had yet been published [in England] which recognized that the majority of titles were registered" (Sparkes 1999, 1). Similarly, the first Australian textbook on property law to treat the Torrens land registration system as central was not published until 1971, more than a century after the system was introduced (Sackville and Neave 1971). And, everywhere, the law of impersonal exchange (mainly, property by publicity or registration and the application of contract rules) is presented as an exception to the supposedly general principle of unconditional property rules.

Most legal resources are therefore still adapted to personal exchange. This includes not only the human capital of scholars, judges, and law practitioners but also other intangible assets, such as conceptual frameworks and academic curricula. Above all, most foundational legal analyses still take as their references legal effects that are triggered by private contract alone. They thus disregard effects on third parties, which are essential for impersonal trade, and the fact that, for most transactions in today's impersonal economy, private contracts alone do not have effects on third parties. For example, typical analyses consider that transactional documents that provide evidence of the originative contract between property transactors or company founders actually transfer property rights or incorporate a company, when, in fact, in modern legal systems such documents either have no effects on third parties or have them only exceptionally.[7] In these analyses, the framing role of the traditional paradigm is preserved only by presenting the exception as the general rule and the rule as an exception.[8]

As argued in chapter 1, this neglect of impersonal exchange by the law has been partly replicated in economics, which has also focused on the type of transaction that hardly needs registration. Both disciplines have focused on solving the problems between parties to a single-exchange contract. Both tend to overlook sequential exchange and thus the key problem for impersonal transactions: the information asymmetry that third parties face when entering into a transaction affected by a previous, originative, transaction. This applies to economic analyses that (as analyzed by Merrill and Smith 2001a, 2011) do not distinguish between *in personam* contract rights—valid only against specific persons—and *in rem* property rights—granted directly on the asset and valid against everybody—dealing instead with contract rights that are enforceable only between the parties to the originative contract, or, most often, with the conditions for private rights on property, whether they are enforced *in personam* or *in rem*. These focuses on single exchange and contract rights are consistent with the widespread consideration as impersonal of any judicially supported exchange. By emphasizing the initial allocation of rights, such focuses also have unexpected consequences in terms of policy. For instance, by disregarding the recurrent reallocation of rights, they may be seen as lending support to policies that start title systems with extensive surveying and mapping efforts, and to favor universal instead of voluntary titling, two policies that are often unsustainable, as shown by owners' reluctance to register second transactions.

Consequently, registries have been paid uneven attention: substantial by development experts aware of the problems in the field and little by students of both law and economics. Both legal and economic analyses thus fail to provide a consistent understanding of the function and organizational requirements of registries. Analyses continue to be framed within the traditional paradigm, which means that the role played by registries is underestimated and, correlatively, that of palliative documentary formalization and informal solutions, such as possession and apparent authority, is overestimated. This makes it difficult to develop formalization systems to meet the demands of the modern economy and explains both the time it often takes for new laws to take root[9] and the survival of unfounded legal exceptions, which generate gray areas in which impersonal contracting becomes impossible.

Instead, emphasizing the contractual problem of parties to the originative contract and paying little attention to third parties lead formalization systems too often to support myriad private palliatives, both prior to and subsequent to the contract—mainly, lawyering to draw up personal safeguards and validate private contracts (documentary formalization) or to litigate in any additional conflicts arising. But these idiosyncratic solutions are costly and offer doubtful effectiveness and variable quality. They can be judged as "artisan," in contrast to the "industrial" solutions required for impersonal transactions, which require low unit costs and standard legal attributes for subsequent transactions. This institutional development is similar to the standardization achieved by mass production in the nineteenth century and the secured quality provided by "zero-defect" manufacturing in the late twentieth century. This is the type of solution that nineteenth-century legal experts started to build but which their successors do not always grant all the value that it deserves.

The struggle for market-enabling legal institutions is therefore still often a battle between two different technologies and the specialized resources using them: the artisan manufacturing of contracts and palliatives by lawyers and notaries, supported by established legal scholarship, and the industrial production of "legal commodities" by default contract rules and registries, often supported by market participants. In this context, something close to a Luddite attitude is observable when legal professionals oppose standardization of legal acts and services, or when they claim that personalized service offers higher quality. It is revealing that the law merchant, by which contract rules were created, developed without relying on and, in fact, in disdain of the established legal professions: "In all types of commercial courts. . . . not only were professional lawyers generally excluded but also technical legal argumentation was frowned upon" (Berman 1983, 347). Consistently, the desire to preserve rents and quasi-rents therefore constitutes a major barrier for most efforts to create or reform public registries. The added twist in this "Institutional Revolution" is that Luddites are not opposing business entrepreneurs, as they did in the Industrial Revolution, but mostly civil servants. In this conflict, the side of modern technology is especially weak, even after a registry is created, when registrars are paid a fixed salary and, consequently, have little interest in providing a valuable service. Understandably, in many countries registries end up being captured by and subordinated to lawyers and notaries.

Following a Logical Sequence of Reform

Because market-supporting institutions, such as different registries and courts, are interrelated, it is hard to decide which institution should be created or reformed first. Yet reformers must often choose not only because resources are scarce but also because the ordering of their efforts may substantially affect their outcome. I discuss here some factors that they must consider in their sequencing decisions.

The basic idea is quite simple. When sequencing interventions, it seems natural to take as a primary guide the most usual sequence in the input-output production process. In this process, land and business registries are mostly intermediate steps. They use information on the identity of individuals (rightholders and company shareholders and officers) produced by civil registries and the identification system and deliver outputs to be used primarily by courts, contractual parties, and administrative agencies. Therefore, before policymakers undertake the costly deployment or improvement of land and company registries, it will often be best for them to develop or upgrade the institutions used for identifying individuals, such as civil registries.[10] For a similar reason, with respect to real property, they might opt to invest in systems for identifying buildings and land parcels, such as unified nomenclatures of postal addresses and place names.[11] Similar considerations would lead them to develop or reform contractual registries before the court system or at least not to intervene in courts before registries.

Benefits from the Identification of Individuals

Dealing with the identification of individuals and civil registries before contractual registries also makes sense for other reasons. Information on individuals' identity facilitates impersonal trade based on notoriety, all types of public enforcement, and private enforcement of contract rights, the latter by allowing the market to develop palliatives based mainly on private records of reputational assets.

First, effective identification of individuals automatically "formalizes" individual entrepreneurs with respect to commercial transactions, since courts are able to enforce market-enabling contract rules on the basis of notoriety without proprietorships having to be formalized as firms. Exceptions arise only when entrepreneurs want to separate their personal and business assets, as this partition would affect their personal and business creditors and, therefore, requires registration. (For instance, granting limited liability to proprietorships is viable without the usual complexities of incorporation. However, it will still require some public registration to make it verifiable and therefore viable.) Thus, in the absence of such asset partitioning, the registration of individual entrepreneurs is not necessary for courts to be able to enforce contract rules in commercial transactions.

Moreover, the identification of individuals by means of civil registries and identity cards facilitates public enforcement. For instance, identifying contractual parties becomes easier, making it less necessary to rely on witnesses and other third parties as authenticators. Similarly, it greatly facilitates finding and punishing defaulting parties, which is otherwise particularly hard in societies with substantial mobility.

However, enforcing contract rights by these public means requires an independent and effective judiciary, an achievement that has been elusive for many countries. For this reason, perhaps the most important benefit of effective identification of individuals might be that it indirectly facilitates private enforcement of contractual obligations by means of private record-keeping systems, such as, for example, bank accounts and credit registries. These allow market participants to keep track of individuals' contractual performance, building what, in fact, amounts to private "registries of reputational assets," which they can then use to safeguard transactions with those who trust the record keepers. All sorts of economic agents can thus report more easily on their contractual partners' creditworthiness through both formal and informal arrangements. This demand for information was traditionally served by reference letters written by banks on the solvency of their small-firm clients, who could then use such letters in their dealings with third parties. Banks also used to request other banks to report on the solvency of their clients' potential debtors (Arruñada, 2011, 390). The same demand is now increasingly served by formal credit registries, which are often promoted by banks.

These private enforcement solutions allow transactions between parties who do not know each other to be treated as personal transactions, given that reputation developed in previous transactions is put at stake in the new transactions. Even if transactions remain personal, since the firm acting as an intermediary record keeper usually knows all parties, the parties themselves may be strangers to each other. These registries of reputational assets therefore make it possible for reputation to safeguard partly impersonal transactions. Moreover, a similar argument applies more generally to trademarks and business names. And they are equally applicable in developing economies. For example, the Msanzi account launched by the major South African banks in 2004 to provide entry-level banking services relied on an exemption allowing small accounts to be opened without a physical address but with an identification card. This reliance confirms that, as with all the other solutions, personal identification is still necessary.[12]

Building Up the Institutions Supporting Trade in Contract Rights

Spending scarce resources on developing or extending a titling system for property, *in rem*, rights should be weighed against the best alternative option. Considering the interactions just discussed, the main "opportunity cost" of such reform often lies in improving the environment for contract, *in personam*, rights by clearing the way for reputational intermediaries.

This strategy of reducing the transaction costs of contract rights may often be easier and more effective than that of reducing the transaction costs of property rights because it requires less public involvement. The hardest task, that of keeping an updated record, lies in the hands of private registries; thus, it is the market that provides incentives and self regulation. It is also easier because civil registries do not require the expensive evidencing and purging of rights that often plagues registration of property rights to land. Finally, it is also easier because government departments will benefit from the synergies that civil registries and identification cards provide for tax, police, and military uses.

Moreover, a strategy that facilitates contract rights may be more effective because it relies on private enforcement instead of state judicial enforcement. Titling systems are useless if courts are unable or unwilling to properly enforce property, *in rem*, rights. For example, the collateral value of land is close to nil if parties expect courts not to enforce foreclosure effectively after the mortgagor defaults, which is a common occurrence. To be effective, court enforcement has to compete with informal enforcement by the local community of which the debtor is often a member. Imagine, for example, a bank repossessing a home in an urban slum that has recently been occupied by organized squatters, or a family farm in a rural village. Compare this to the case of debtors defaulting on their personal obligations. Their default would enter the credit registry and would likely leave traces even in their bank records. Sanction is automatic as their reputational capital is immediately debited, with little chance that a court may delay the proceeding.

Because of easier enforceability, developing credit records for individuals might often be a more viable strategy than allowing them to use their assets as collateral, especially for the poor. Even when the poor have assets (e.g., land) usable as collateral, enforcing repossession after debtor default is often impossible for an outsider. In such situations, outsiders are reluctant to rely on collateral for lending, and access to credit requires systems of collective responsibility such as those used in microcredit schemes. Registries of reputational assets overcome these problems by extending the effective scope of market enforcement to partly impersonal transactions. There is indeed some evidence that the volume of credit grows when banks share more information on debtors and when the quality of credit registries improves.[13]

This advantage is also consistent with the observation that, after developing costly titling systems for land, owners continue to obtain most of their credit on a purely personal basis. "Banks are ultimately more interested in a loan applicant's salary and other income streams than in his/her ownership of a small piece of land in a marginal urban neighborhood or rural area" (Bruce et al 2007b, 38). And the effects of titling on credit seem small or nil (Bledsoe 2006, 155–58). When considered from the perspective of property versus contract rights, this underuse of available real guarantees suggests that the relative emphasis or the sequencing of reforms may have been misplaced, focusing too early on facilitating property rights rather than contract rights, which is a much cheaper proposition.

Reforming Registries before Courts

Considering the most usual flows in the input-output production process also would lead policymakers, in principle, to place priority on developing or reforming contractual registries before or at least at the same time as the courts.

As analyzed in chapter 1, contractual registries either produce a public reallocation of property rights or reliable evidence on which to base such a reallocation in the future. Even when registries of rights are legally structured as administrative bodies, many of their registration decisions involve quasi-judicial outcomes. These decisions can be litigated but this is also the case with decisions made by lower courts. Moreover, some registry decisions involve final consequences, mainly in relation to the enforcement of contract rules in favor of innocent third parties so that they are allocated *in rem* property rights.

Some registry services provide evidence for judicial decisions: for example, that used for establishing the priority between conflicting *in rem* claims, allowing courts to use streamlined procedures. A clear example is provided by mortgage foreclosures, which tend to be harder and slower in countries with weaker registries or when registry evidence is disputed, as in the 2010 foreclosure crisis in the United States. (In chapter 5, I present empirical data confirming this correlation between property registration and repossession of mortgaged land in case of default.)

These quasi-judicial roles of registries mean that organizing them is in a sense equivalent to reforming an integral part of the judicial system. Even for countries where courts are not working properly, better registries will substitute for courts and will produce judicial inputs that will allow courts to be more effective. And registries will also deter litigation: mandatory registration of certain transactions has even been justified as a way of discouraging subsidized litigation (Barzel 2002, 196).

Identifying the Key Attributes and Users of Registry Services

Although it might seem obvious, it is often forgotten that property and business registries provide a valuable service only when they are reliable enough for judges to confirm registry decisions or to base their decisions on registry information. Only then can economic agents also rely on registry information for contracting, thus reducing their information asymmetry and facilitating impersonal transactions. The documents filed in contractual registries must therefore be properly dated, contain the legally required information, and be preserved and accessible.

The Priority of Registry Independence

In particular, registries must be independent of all the parties to originative and subsequent transactions and free of corruption; not only the mild corruption that leads to selectively speeding up the processing of documents but also the much more serious practice of faking the date when the documents are filed, which makes registry certificates useless as proof. When such incidents are suspected to be frequent, judges will disregard registry decisions and certificates. Economic agents will soon follow judges, relying instead on personal safeguards, which will drastically limit their trade and specialization opportunities. They will also have little interest in registration because it will not save on transaction costs but will increase still further their tax and regulatory burdens.

Unfortunately, corruption is not a rare event. It is prevalent and has serious consequences,[14] though it is often disregarded. The United Nations Commission on Legal Empowerment of the Poor (CLEP) considered that "assuming that the state is strong and trustworthy and that therefore property titles and registries as well as the guarantee of transactions are reliable and corruption proof" has been one of the most serious mistakes of formalization reforms. Furthermore, land titling corruption involves large amounts of money. For example, bribes paid annually in India to land administration services have been estimated by Transparency International at USD 700 million, an amount equivalent to three-quarters of the public spending on science, technology, and the environment (CLEP 2008b, 82).

Independence from both registration applicants and users of registries' information and certificates is no less necessary for company registries, as argued in chapter 3. Even when a registry performs little review, it is essential that it exercises its independence with respect to, especially, dating and preserving the documents and issuing copies and certificates. In many countries, the registry staff is willing to take side payments to alter the priority of filings, often using urgency fees as an excuse, as illustrated by company registries in Venezuela (Arruñada 2010a, 186–87). Understandably, judges in such countries will be skeptical about the value they should place on registry certificates. Not by chance, there is considerable legal uncertainty in Venezuela about the legal effects granted by judges to registry entries. This uncertainty, in itself and whatever the prevalence of corruption, considerably reduces the value of the registered information for transacting parties.

Policy Consequences of Considering the Value of Formalization Services

When planning and evaluating reforms, these requirements of reliable and independent registries hold important consequences for identifying key users and setting priorities. Above all and to focus on the main contribution of registries—lowering future transaction costs by making originative contracts verifiable by judges, therefore reducing the information asymmetry suffered by parties to subsequent transactions—reformers should consider judges as the key users of registries' services. Of course, judges only occasionally interact with registries. But they are the fundamental last-resort users because the weight that judges give to the registry in their decisions determines the value of the registry for all market participants.

An advantage of emphasizing judges as key users is that it is a way of implicitly treating all affected rightholders as users even when they are not filing anything but are passive third parties to transactions initiated by others. This is easier to see in registries of rights that, before accepting a filing for registration, must make sure it does not violate the rights *in rem* of third parties. Registration failure at this crucial step would damage the interests of these holders of potentially affected rights. Understandably, judges dislike damaging innocent rightholders and thus would be wary of registration failure. If frequent, they might even disregard the registry. Therefore, focusing on judges' opinion is an indirect way of taking into account the holders of potentially affected rights, who might be hard to identify and may know little about such filings.

Unfortunately, many reform projects totally overlook judges. When diagnosing the situation before a reform is planned or when evaluating its achievements after completion, reformers often seek the opinions of registry filers, such as owners and entrepreneurs, but rarely those of judges. This behavior would be equivalent in a manufacturing process to surveying the opinion of suppliers while disregarding clients. This fixation on direct filers amounts to taking registry filings as an end in themselves, forgetting that filings, together with all other registry processes, must serve to facilitate future contracts, which will only be possible if registry outputs are truly taken by judges as judicial inputs.

By focusing on filing parties, reformers therefore risk setting wrong priorities, minimizing initial private costs, and neglecting not only value but also future and public costs. In contrast, paying heed to judges will draw reformers nearer to their efficiency goal by reminding them that, if forced to simplify the efficient balancing of costs and benefits, the priority should not be to reduce the private, initial cost of formalization—a cost paid only once—but, rather, to reduce transaction costs in the future. Although most of these future transaction costs are "opportunity costs" related to unprofitable exchanges that fail to materialize, and thus are hard to see, they are recurring and usually much larger than the costs of initial formalization. Therefore, as a first approximation, it often makes sense to grant them priority.

In other words, the priority when setting up new registries or reforming existing ones should be to have them providing useful legal services. Ensuring this minimum legal quality is generally much more important than reducing initial formalization costs. For example, it is nonsense to spend resources on refining systems that are all but useless by computerizing or speeding up the production of potentially partial information. Only reliable, independent registries are able to reduce transaction costs and act as catalysts for economic activity. Similarly, reaching economies of scope between contractual and administrative formalization serving public agencies, such as tax authorities, should generally be considered as a second-order objective. This is especially so because, in pursuing such an objective, policies tend to subordinate contractual registries, reducing their specialization and endangering the incentives of private parties to register.

Evidence on the Effects of Property Titling

Confused priorities and mistaken key users have not been the only errors in formalization reform, which, for instance, has often been promoted as a tool for accelerating economic development and alleviating poverty. However, inflated expectations about the ease and short-term achievements of reform are a sure recipe for failure and risk causing backlash. In fact, available evidence on the consequences of property and business formalization for development, which I review in this and the following sections, suggests that these promises exaggerated the potential benefits; inevitably, many subsequent reforms were based on flawed ideas.[15]

In the area of real property, a large number of empirical works have examined the effects of land titling on many social and economic variables, such as investment, credit, employment, violence, market beliefs, and even health.[16] A sample of the most important works shows an inconclusive picture of modestly positive but nuanced effects. Unsurprisingly, most works observed positive effects of titling on land value. However, their estimates vary widely from the modest percentages of around one-quarter found by Freidman, Jimenez, and Mayo (1988) in Manila or Lanjouw and Levy (2002) in Ecuador, to the doubling of value observed by Alston, Libecap, and Schneider (1996) in Brazil, with others obtaining numbers in between (e.g., Jimenez 1984, who finds a 58 percent effect in the Philippines). Correlations between land titling and other economic outcomes (e.g., credit, investment, and labor) also often, but not always, showed the predicted signs. Furthermore, their levels were modest. For example, Feder et al. (1988) found that Thai farmers who had been given titles were able to borrow and invest more, and their land increased in value. Positive effects on access to credit were also found by Carter and Olinto (2003) in Paraguay, as well as by Dower and Potamites (2007) in Indonesia, on both access and amount of credit. However, titling was relaxing credit constraints in Paraguay only for the wealthier landowners (Carter and Olinto 2003). Galiani and Schargrodsky (2010) also found only modest positive effects on access to mortgage credit in their Argentinean evidence, with no impact on access to other forms of credit. On investment, Besley (1995) observed some positive effects in Ghana; Do and Iyer (2008) found that additional land rights granted to Vietnamese farmers led to significant, but small, increases in the share of land devoted to long-term crops and in labor devoted to nonfarm activities; and Galiani and Schargrodsky (2010) observed substantially greater investment both in homes and children's education in a sample of randomly titled squatters in Buenos Aires. However, Migot-Adholla et al. (1991) found, at best, a weak relationship between land rights and land improvements, as well as productivity and credit access, in farm data from Ghana, Kenya, and Rwanda. Even worse, Brasselle, Gaspart, and Platteau (2002) observed that titling did not affect investment in Burkina Faso, as "the traditional village order, where it exists, provides the basic land rights required to stimulate small-scale investment" (373). And, when comparing titled and untitled plots of land cultivated by the same households in Madagascar, Jacoby and Minten (2007) found no significant effect on plot-specific investment and correspondingly little effect on land productivity and land values. Lastly, on labor, Field (2007) observed that titling in Peru appeared to increase supply, which allegedly shifted away from work at home to work in the outside market, and also caused substitution of adult for child labor (Field 2007). Galiani and Schargrodsky (2004) also observed in an Argentinean slum better weight-for-height scores among children and fewer teenage pregnancies in households that had been given titles. However, they found no significant effects on labor market performance.

Overall, this evidence fails to provide a universally positive judgment on titling efforts. Controversy, therefore, subsists for three reasons: (1) the modest, inconclusive and mixed results obtained, (2) the difficulties to identify causality in these complex social interventions, and (3) a relative disregard of opportunity costs and sustainability. First, as expected, titling seems to have positive effects at least sometimes. But in many other cases these positive effects are elusive, modest, or nonexistent, especially with respect to access to credit, which was often claimed to be the main benefit.

> There is evidence, albeit not uniform, of enhancement of tenure security through land registration with benefits manifesting themselves in higher levels of investment and productivity and a reduced need to defend land rights. Land registration has also been shown to increase activity in land

rental markets, leading to higher efficiency overall. Evidence of improved access to credit, due to formalization of land rights, is scant. (Deininger and Feder 2009, 233)

In addition to these conflicting results, this empirical literature encounters difficulties because titling decisions and formalization policies are often endogenous, and hidden causal variables may influence both the titling of land and its supposed consequences. For example, the implementation of titling projects often starts with the regions that have the best economic outlook. In other cases, reverse causation may also be present, as when investments enhance the quality of title, a phenomenon observed, for example, in Ghana with respect to the planting of trees (Besley 1995). Conversely, under voluntary titling, it may happen that those with insecure titling (and therefore less incentive to invest) are more inclined to title (in a manner similar to that discussed about Cook County in chapter 2), which could bias results toward underestimating a positive effect of titling.

To solve these problems, analysts apply econometric corrections, based on exclusion restrictions, the time variability of policy implementation or instrumental variables, but they often fail to provide a fully reliable solution. Only a few studies have been lucky enough to examine data with an almost random allocation of titles across the sample of households, which lends more confidence in identifying causal relationships instead of mere correlations. For example, Di Tella, Galiani, and Schargrodsky (2007) use data from a fortuitous distribution of titles to part of a population of squatters in the suburbs of Buenos Aires. As noted above, in their data titling seems to substantially affect home investment and children's education, as well as to have some modest effects on credit access, but no effect on labor income.

However, even these studies face a problem of "external validity"—that is, the samples on which these studies are based are idiosyncratic in terms of, for instance, geography, culture, and institutions. This uniqueness makes their results difficult to apply to cases subject to different geographical, cultural, and institutional circumstances. Success seems to be highly case specific. More work and a different emphasis might be needed to identify which environmental and design variables are driving success.

Moreover, most of the studies evaluating the effects of formalization policies pay little attention to the costs of such policies. Two exceptions are as follows: (1) Miceli, Sirmans, and Kieyah (2001), who confirm with aggregate data that demand for registration in Kenya is greater for more valuable land; and (2) Jacoby and Minten (2007), who perform a cost-benefit analysis to conclude that formal titling is not worthwhile in rural Madagascar.[17] Results obtained in studies that disregard the costs of titling policies are at most suggestive of the effectiveness of titling but reveal little about efficiency. Furthermore, the same argument has been made about the sustainability of formalization efforts (Deininger and Feder 2009). Greater emphasis on measuring costs and ensuring sustainability would therefore be welcome. However, it is unlikely to come from the reform industry because their omissions tend to exaggerate the net benefits of reform.

Evidence on the Effects of Business Formalization

In a fashion similar to land titling, extensive immediate effects also were argued early on by De Soto et al. (1986) for reforms in the business formalization area. Since then, these reforms have even been claimed to provide all sorts of macroeconomic benefits, such as increasing investment, entrepreneurship, employment, productivity, education, and gains from trade liberalization, as well as reducing informality and corruption (e.g., Djankov 2008 and 2009).

This view also exaggerates the benefits of formalization, since it generally focuses on initial formalization, whose cost in most cases is just a tiny component of both total entry costs and even of the total costs that a firm must incur to remain formal. The alternative view is that entrepreneurs remain informal mainly because formalizing their businesses increases their tax burden without—in many developing countries—significantly reducing their transaction costs. In this view, one should expect, at best, modest effects from reducing the costs of initial formalization.

To calibrate the low potential impact that initial formalization cost can exert, two sets of common mistakes must therefore be avoided, whereby the cost of registering a company is taken as the only factor of business firm formality and as a main barrier to entry. First, the cost of initial formalization is in fact a minor part of the total cost of formality. Most informal firms remain informal to avoid taxes and regulation rather than the initial formalization process. For a similar reason, many formal firms remain proprietorships instead of becoming corporations. For example, the difference between personal and corporate taxes is statistically highly significant in determining incorporations in Klapper, Laeven, and Rajan (2006), and the economic effect is likely to be several times greater than that of formalization costs. Moreover, it is not only the cost of formalization but also its value that determine entrepreneurs' decisions, and both may be positively correlated. When little value is added, businesses tend to remain informal, as shown by the high proportion of companies that remain unregistered

in developing countries. Furthermore, the link between initial formalization of companies and overall formality in the economy also breaks down
because legalization of a firm does not preclude informality in many of its
future transactions: for example, most tax evasion in developed economies
is carried out by formal firms. In addition, many informal firms are small
or comprise self-employed workers. But popular indexes such as the World
Bank's Doing Business indicators measure the costs of registering midsize
companies, which are rarely informal.[18] Lastly, the costs of formalizing a
proprietorship or a company differ substantially because, in most countries,
individual merchants—proprietorships—are not required to register with
a commercial registry[19] and often enjoy different tax treatment in terms of
both rates and enforcement. Overall, the cost of registering a midsize company can, at best, be a proxy of institutional quality but not a main cause of
key macroeconomic outcomes.

Second, the cost of initial formalization is also a minor component of
total entry costs. In the past, formalization may have been an important
roadblock for entry but this is no longer the case. For example, until the
mid-1800s a governmental charter that was discretionarily granted was often
required for incorporating a company.[20] However, since then most countries have allowed administrative incorporation, which means freedom to
incorporate subject to minor requirements and also provides the benefits of
company registration.

This is not to deny that entry barriers may be a major deterrent for economic development; and serious entry barriers do remain in many markets,
probably more so in developing economies. But the binding ones are not
located now in the legal formalization process, which is generally open to
all at a low cost, too low in fact to qualify as a significant barrier to entry.
Mixing serious entry barriers with trivial ones entails the risk of setting mistaken priorities and implementing distractive policies. In particular, misuse
of the "entry" label for initial formalization costs, which is common in the
business start-up literature, causes confusion and exaggerates their importance.[21]

Once entry barriers and initial formalization costs are properly distinguished, it becomes clear that business formalization reforms can hardly
be a panacea for economic development, especially when considering that
such reforms often narrowly focus on reducing the initial private costs of
company incorporation. Therefore, results of empirical studies estimating
that these costs of incorporation have substantial effects on macroeconomic
variables are doubtful. In fact, they suffer grave structural weaknesses.

Primarily, most of these studies use data that try to measure the private cost of mandatory procedures in initial formalization, without considering other costs and benefits or the structural characteristics of formalization systems (e.g., the extent, timing, and location of public review). Econometric models relying on such data strive to control for some of these other factors, but their results are inconclusive because other variables remain uncontrolled, among them the quality and enforcement of taxation and regulation, the cost and effectiveness of other public services, including the courts, and the efficacy of civil and criminal liability for punishing wrongdoers.

It is also difficult for such studies to identify causal effects, and the influence of hidden variables on both formalization cost and the regression outcomes cannot be ruled out. In particular, cross-country regressions cannot control for many unobservable country characteristics that might drive the results. For instance, economies with good institutions or more developed financial markets tend to perform well in all dimensions, making it hard to estimate the impact of a particular institutional variable. In these circumstances, the significance obtained in econometric models by the parameter associated with the cost of initial formalization is likely to represent something else and therefore provides no guide for policy. This risk is made greater by the doubts that arise regarding the quality of some of the measures used in these empirical studies. Some of these indicators are unreliable because of their subjective selection of sources, nonreplicability and unexplained retroactive changes.[22] To the extent that, after so many ad hoc adjustments, these indicators are mere confirmations of subjective valuations, they are not even measuring what they aim to measure but something else.

Cross-industry, cross-country studies, which follow Rajan and Zingales's methodology (1998), only resolve some of these problems. For instance, Klapper, Laeven, and Rajan (2006) used industry-level data from the United States as a reference for optimal rates of industry entry, but they relied on country incorporation data for measuring industry effects, even though much entry regulation is industry specific. They found that, in countries where incorporating a company is more expensive, fewer companies were incorporated, especially in industries for which a high incorporation rate is observed in the United States. However, industry-specific entry constraints vary significantly across countries (e.g., Nicoletti and Scarpetta 2003) and might be related to the general costs of business formalization and the potential of entry in each industry. Many variables, from politics to administration failure, could thus be causing both costlier formalization procedures and tougher entry constraints in all industries or high-entry ones. Their results cannot therefore reveal whether the observed effect is due to the cost of general formalization procedures (e.g., company incorporation) or to specific industry constraints (e.g., regulations for opening retail outlets). Consequently, they cannot indicate whether reform should restructure formalization procedures or relax industry constraints.

These models also suffer from the possible presence of hidden costs and benefits, as well as difficulties for identifying the direction of causation. For instance, the estimated effects remain subject to caveats like those cited by Klapper, Laeven, and Rajan (2006): "to the extent that . . . other benefits—such as the provision of greater information to the authorities—can be captured even with reduced costs (for example, by automating the process)" (622). This ability to capture other benefits with reduced costs seems overly optimistic. Similarly, reliance on instrumental variables such as legal origins for identifying causality and correcting a possible omitted-variables bias is open to doubt, even for those who pioneered their use. According to La Porta, Lopez-de-Silanes, and Shleifer (2008), "legal origins influence many spheres of lawmaking and regulation, which makes it dangerous to use them as instruments" and "we do not recommend such [instrumental variables] specifications since legal origins influence a broad range of rules and regulations and we cannot guarantee that the relevant ones are not omitted in the first stage" (291 and 293–94).

Limited and hard-to-quantify effects of business formalization should not, however, discourage serious reform efforts. More effective—not merely low initial private cost—business formalization should have beneficial effects by reducing transaction costs and facilitating taxation and regulation. The efficiency of these beneficial effects, however, depends on many factors, including the cost of achieving more effective formalization, the extent of the demand for the sort of impersonal trade that stands to benefit most from reducing transaction costs, and, in the public area, proper use by the state of its additional taxation and regulatory powers.

FIVE

The Choice of Title and Registration Systems

Substantial variety exists among systems of land and business formalization both over time and across countries. For instance, England relied on private titling and delayed land registration for centuries. In contrast, land recordation was imported into American colonies early on, and land registration was adapted to Australia. Similarly, in most of the world, governments used to allow voluntary land titling, in which owners decide whether they register their land. However, governments and international agencies often opted for universal titling, aiming to register all land in a certain region. Also, processes for administrative formalization such as, for instance, registering firms for taxes, have traditionally been separate from contractual formalization, but it later became fashionable to integrate both types of process.

Because of this variety, choosing the right formalization system in a particular context is not easy. The previous two chapters explain how the different types of land and business registries work, as well as their functional equivalencies and organizational requirements, and how their performance depends not only on their presumed advantages and disadvantages but also on contextual, regulatory, and organizational variables. I now discuss the main design choices, drawing the main branches of the decision tree and discussing the essential costs and benefits of the different options. In this chapter, I examine the following: the decision whether to create a public titling system or to rely exclusively on private titling; the choice between voluntary and universal titling; the theoretical and empirical consideration of recordation of deeds and registration of rights; and, lastly, since all other sections focus on real property titling, the mostly parallel choices for business registration.

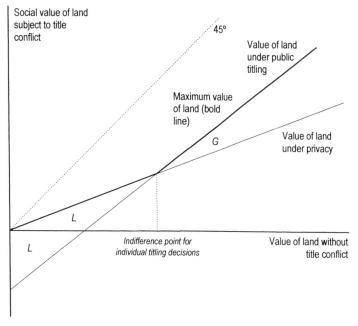

Social value of land subject to title conflict

45°

Value of land under public titling

Maximum value of land (bold line)

G

Value of land under privacy

L

L

Indifference point for individual titling decisions

Value of land without title conflict

NOTE: Figure represents how the social value of land (*vertical axis*) is a function of the theoretical value of land without title conflict (*horizontal axis*) and the type of titling institutions available, which incur different costs. Social choice of titling institutions will be driven by these costs and the distribution of land in the economy along the horizontal axis. Area G represents the potential gain from titling high-value land and area L the potential loss from overtitling low-value land. (*Source*: Adapted from Arruñada and Garoupa 2005, 717, figure 2.)

Figure 5.1. Titling options (I): Choosing between private and public titling to maximize the social value of land

Private versus Public Titling

To structure the analysis, figure 5.1 represents the social value of land under different institutions, assuming that prices of titling services are set optimally and owners are free to choose between keeping their land claims private and using the public titling system chosen by the government. Following Arruñada and Garoupa (2005), the social value of a parcel of land (represented on the vertical axis) depends on the probability that claimants with better legal rights may appear and is thus a fraction of its value in an ideal world with no conflicting claims (represented on the horizontal axis). This fraction will depend on the available institutions and will likely be lower if, whatever such institutions, the land remains under private titling—privacy, for short. To simplify matters, I am assuming that the figure represents all land in an area to be served by only one registry that costs an amount F to put in place. Titling a parcel of land means that, by incurring a given additional cost, the probability of a conflicting claim on that parcel being successful falls. I assume that, by titling, the value of the land increases by a certain percentage: with respect to the privacy line, the titling line has a negative intercept but is steeper.

If the government creates the registry, it must also choose between voluntary and universal titling. Under voluntary titling (often dismissively referred to as "sporadic" titling[1]), land rights are formalized at the request of individuals claiming to be owners. Since owners must pay a certain fee for publicly titling their land, they will choose not to title the less valuable parcels: those below the indifference point in the figure. Social gains arising from public titling are therefore represented by the area G. Under universal titling, often referred as "systematic" titling, all land in an area is publicly titled, and social gains fall to $G-L$.

Focusing now on voluntary titling and forgetting momentarily about area L, the decision to introduce public titling should be based on comparing titling gains G to the fixed costs of establishing the titling system, F. I now explore the main determinants of these gains and costs, while addressing universal titling later.

Determinants of the Gains from Titling

Title uncertainty reduces incentives to invest and increases the adverse selection suffered by potential acquirers of land rights, whether buyers or mortgage lenders. Public titling should improve the incentives to invest and reduce adverse selection (Arruñada and Garoupa 2005, 721–23). In terms of figure 5.1, the greater the value of potential investment and trade opportunities, the more the indifference point will be positioned to the left, and, for a given distribution of land in the economy, the larger the social gains from public titling, represented by area G.

These gains, however, depend on the true existence of such opportunities, which has therefore to be confirmed before embarking on the costly introduction of public titling. Unfortunately, the effects of public titling on investment and trade are hard to estimate even after titling has been introduced, as summarized in chapter 4. But estimating the demand for public titling is even harder before a titling system is introduced: the little information available is dispersed and specific, and participants do not necessarily reveal their true valuations. A main drawback is that those who know the level of demand best are likely to benefit the most from formalization projects, because they will either be subsidized users or privileged suppliers and thus tend to exaggerate demand.

Difficulties for Truthful Demand Revelation

In particular, suppliers of reforms and new formalization systems often commit two types of misrepresentation to exaggerate the demand for formalization. As analyzed in chapter 4, they tend to promote land titling and business formalization as silver bullets for growth, while disregarding that underdevelopment and poverty are mainly a cause, not a consequence, of informality.[2] In addition, they tend to present the demand for security of tenure as demand for public titling capable of facilitating transfer and credit transactions. In this, they are often helped by owners, who, in expectation of subsidized titling, are also prone to present their demand for greater security of tenure, which could be easily satisfied without creating expensive registries, as a demand for titles enabling land transfer and credit transactions, which do need such registries.

Security of tenure can indeed be provided more cheaply by simpler legislative and administrative measures, such as lessening the legal requirements for prescription and adverse possession or explicitly recognizing the legality of some contracts or the property rights of some squatters.[3] In part, this reflects a difference between which institutions are required for supporting investment and which for supporting trade: security of tenure often suffices to support investment, whereas trade in land tends to require public titling. However, when titling is subsidized, both land tenants and suppliers of titling services have an interest in exaggerating the demand for titling by presenting the demand for security of tenure as demand for titling. Consequently, the expectation of obtaining rents from titling may distort the opinions voiced in surveys and reports, making it more necessary for benevolent prospective reformers to rely on contractual and market signals as a source of information. Through these signals, individual transactors are more likely to reveal their true valuations because, unlike surveys and mere opinions, they result from real transactions and are backed by the real expenditures that transactors incur to carry them out.

Several types of signal meet these requirements for truthful demand revelation: use of inefficient contracts, confused and unreliable jurisprudence, and, especially, market prices. In the same vein, benevolent prospective reformers should also consider whether some components of titling projects must be interpreted as implicit recognitions that socially valuable demand is lacking. This is often the case when information campaigns are thought to be necessary to publicize the value of titling: in principle, owners should know better than reform suppliers, as discussed below. It is also the case with two other measures that are designed to palliate the bad consequences of titling, such as expropriation abuses and improvident sales. When such damage control is deemed necessary, reformers should start by asking themselves why titling is a good idea in the first place.

Role of Market Signals for Appraising Titling Demand

Paying attention to actual contractual and organizational behavior and to market prices will help identify fake claims in titling demands, as people reveal their preferences more faithfully in their conduct. In particular, the presence of costly private contracting that would be effectively facilitated by public titling could be taken as an indication that investment in public titling is needed. For example, substantial demand for using land as collateral for credit would be signaled by the widespread use of vicarious contractual solutions, such as including repurchase agreements in contracts for the sale of land, as would mortgages formalized by depositing the chain of written deeds with the creditor. If such arrangements or other functionally similar ones are frequent, demand for public titling or for better registries is more likely to be real. A similar market signal in business formalization would be the presence in business contracting of unincorporated companies, such as in eighteenth- and nineteenth-century England and currently in, for example, Bolivia.

A second source of hard evidence on the demand for change is provided by the inputs used and the consistency shown by judicial decisions. If judges rely on secret documents for deciding on conflicts involving third parties, this reliance often signals a lack of proper institutions. (Although judges are involved in these cases, their reliance on secret documents can still be considered to be a market signal because it is based on existing contracts.) In more developed countries, the subordinate role of the law of impersonal transactions can be inferred from the prevalence of law that is full of exceptions and contradictory jurisprudence. Some of the palliative organizational solutions analyzed in chapter 4, such as the creation of the private registry of mortgages in the United States (Mortgage Electronic Registration Systems [MERS]), can also be taken as evidence of institutional demand. Their existence is a strong signal, since they require substantial investment and overcoming a collective action problem among market participants.

Lastly, market prices are also especially revealing for detecting the need to reform existing, but dysfunctional, registries. This is the case, in particular, of the spread or difference in interest rates between secured and unsecured (i.e., personal) credit. When this difference is small, as in even some developed countries, it is a definite indicator that registries and likely land law need a radical upgrade, because they are unable to realize the collateral value of land. Some other prices are also informative but they are noisier signals and thus need closer scrutiny, such as the market price of shelf companies. The same happens with other indicators of the need for stronger contractual registries, such as mandatory intervention (both legally or de facto) by conveyancers; the relative price paid to conveyancers and registries; the use, cost, and legal complexity of lawyers' title reports; and the reliance on extensive legal opinions for ordinary company transactions.

Risk of Titling Abuses

When deciding to introduce public titling, the encouragement of private investment and contracting might be offset by enhanced possibilities of exploitation, rooted in land grabbing, fraud, and political failure. In terms of figure 5.1, these effects would move the indifference point to the right, thereby reducing the social gains from public titling.

First, individuals might take advantage of public titling to grab land and devise frauds. In particular, initial titling opens new opportunities for the powerful to grab land (Feder and Nishio 1998), a risk that is especially dangerous with respect to communal land. Community involvement is often proposed to reduce this danger (e.g., Bruce et al. 2007b, 3), but it is costly to operate and its results highly uncertain. Occasionally, artificial demand for titling is generated by the threat of the land being titled to someone else, often to elites or officials. Titling may also tend to degrade the rights of some specific classes of claimants, such as women, youths, and seasonal users (Meinzen-Dick and Mwangi 2009). Moreover, even if these frauds have been more common in connection with land, all registries are prone to suffer them, as exemplified by the European Trading Scheme, the world's biggest market in carbon emissions, which closed for several weeks in January 2011 after fraudsters stole about 62 million USD in carbon credits from several of its national registers.[4]

Similarly, information in the public records can also be used for planning various frauds and extortions, from the proverbial pursuit of wealthy heiresses by dowry-seeking bachelors that Victorian fathers feared (Anderson 1992, 46–47) to the present-day identity theft (Sibley 2006) or the sale of vacant houses after learning the identities of their owners in the public record (Sparkes 1999, 14). And this possibility of fraud is not exclusive of property registries, as shown by the company registry created in Bulgaria in 2008, which provided free access to the personal data of company owners, giving not only their names and various personal identifiers but also scanned copies of their identity cards (Kostadinov 2008). These risks of private abuse can be reduced by filtering the data to be disclosed (e.g., excluding personal identification numbers) or limiting access to the public record to those authorized by owners and those with a legitimate interest, which casts serious doubt on the current fashion of open registers (twenty-eight of the forty-two jurisdictions surveyed by the UN-ECE [2000] were wholly open to the public).

Lastly, in a political vein, there might be a risk that public titling could facilitate bad government. In principle, titling should facilitate law enforcement that includes, most prominently, the collection of taxes. But this may have positive or negative social effects depending on citizens' capacity to control their own government and impede excessive taxation. If citizens do not trust their government, they will tend to avoid public registries that might be used for collecting taxes. This holds two consequences. First, the weaker the political institutions, the less sensible it is to introduce public titling because it would be less likely to succeed. Second, it makes sense for the public titling system to be independent of the tax authority, even at the price of some duplication.

In all these cases, there are reasons to be doubly cautious in regard to the risks of abuse. To avoid such risks may require preventive measures but their presence should also alert policymakers that there might not be enough demand for titling.

Risk of Titling Facilitating Improvident Sales and Indebtedness

Studies of land titling have also often discussed the possibility that, by facilitating the sale and mortgage of land, titling efforts may lead the poor to improvidently lose their land. To avoid this risk, experts have advised that land marketability should be limited by different means, such as requiring the consent of spouses and administrative agencies (Bruce et al. 2007b, 37) or introducing sales moratoria during which the poor would receive education. According to the United Nations' Commission on Legal Empowerment of the Poor (CLEP), for instance, "ceilings on ownership and sales moratoria are considered a reasonably successful protective practice, provided that they are limited in time and that time is used for legal and financial education" (2008a, 67). However, my previous analysis suggests that such advice is misguided.

So far, I have implicitly assumed that owners are capable of maximizing their individual utility and hold consistent preferences across time. The improvident sales argument denies this assumption and therefore presumes some degree of irrationality, with owners being unable to look themselves. However, this view is incomplete, because such allegedly irrational behavior is induced by exogenous interventions that may be destroying the institutional basis of rationality. The lack of marketable titles—whatever its rationale—might perform a self-controlling function, committing owners to act in a manner consistent with their (or their families') long-term interests. This may be a valuable institutional arrangement to achieve rational self-control in an environment of extreme hardship. When family members are dying of hunger, being precluded from selling the land may guarantee the long-term survival of some whereas being free to sell it now might mean that all will perish. The deep reluctance that farmers feel in most societies about selling their land probably serves a similar long-term rationalizing purpose.

So, the question becomes why should such land be titled in the first place. One may think that a reasonable policy would have been to not introduce titling in that area or to introduce it on a voluntary, fee-for-service basis that would encourage only efficient titling, that is, titling by those deciding to be free of the commitment arrangement. (An argument along these lines could be made based on the "libertarian paternalism" promoted by Thaler and Sunstein 2008). However, the government often decides, first, to free the poor and then to introduce new constraints to prevent them from making mistakes and to teach them how to behave in the new environment. In a sense, it is replacing a simple legal constraint—the impediment to sell—with a hard-to-produce and harder-to-maintain education constraint. Titling efforts may well be premature in such life-threatening circumstances.

Poor people may be led to desperate sales, which titling may well facilitate. However, the best way of protecting them is not to constrain their behavior with moratoria and education just after granting them full titles. In a similar manner to the risk of titling abuse analyzed in the previous section, the expectation of improvident sales should instead alert us to the risk that the whole titling effort might be premature or its universal nature inappropriate.

Determinants of the Fixed Cost of the Titling System: Making Fixed Costs Variable

The fixed costs of introducing a titling system include legislative and administration costs. New legislation and judicial decisions will be necessary to reform land law, at least to solidly establish the legal effects of public titling (mainly, priority of filing in recordation and the contract rule in registration). It will be necessary not only to adapt the statute law, often in a new way, but also to train judges in the new law and to develop jurisprudence accordingly. Administration costs are involved in putting in place a titling service, which will require not only one or several registry offices but also a regulatory or managerial structure. Neither of these tasks is easy, and they are related: judges are often reluctant to enforce new principles of property law. Understandably, they are even more reluctant when the registries function imperfectly.[5]

Interactions between Legislative Decisions and Administration Costs

Furthermore, legislative and administration costs interact with each other. For example, defining by law a *numerus clausus* and eliminating the fragmentation of property rights in order to reduce administration costs will often be useful. However, this may conflict with the recognition of customary rights, thus providing another reason for voluntary titling. When such conflict is important, titling should be introduced only for those parcels or in those areas where keeping such customary rights as *in rem* rights has become inefficient, so they should be legally debased to mere contract rights.[6]

The solution adopted in England since the seventeenth century to transform the paralyzing property rights system inherited from feudal times can be understood in this way. At the start of the Industrial Revolution, owners had limited rights, as they could not mortgage, lease, or sell; many other people held property *in rem* rights on the same land; and land uses were often predetermined. These constraints made it impossible to use land in the most productive way, missing the valuable opportunities that were becoming increasingly available in a context of rapid economic change and growth. To be safe and avoid paying twice, acquirers had to gather the consent of all rightholders, but this was often impossible because only sellers knew about many of the rights.

Between 1660 and 1830, the English Parliament enacted numerous acts restructuring property rights by relaxing such constraints (Richardson and Bogart 2008; Bogart and Richardson 2009). With estate acts, sales, leases, and mortgages became legal, and all interests were recorded in a way that was accessible to the public. This eliminated information asymmetries, making it possible to transact impersonally. Statutory authority acts made construction of infrastructure possible by, among other measures, organizing procedures for expropriating land. And enclosure acts mainly served to transform common property into individual property.

The experience is interesting in terms of both efficiency and fairness. Consonant with my argument for voluntary titling, rightholders or communities had to apply for such restructurings, which led to these transformations occurring where they were most valuable. Moreover, damage to rightholders was minimized by procedures that granted them ample scope for opposition in several layers of review. Generally, rightholders who lost property rights received monetary compensation. The case therefore shows that it is possible to radically transform property rights in a manner that is fair, at least from the procedural point of view. But it also teaches a sad lesson, as England was the only European country able to achieve this transformation peacefully. Other countries had to endure their own versions of the French or Russian revolutions.

These English solutions required parliamentary acts but relied on specific administrative commissions. In general, purely legislative costs are mostly fixed with respect to the establishment of public titling. However, most administration costs can be made fixed or variable—and therefore, when variable, avoidable—depending on the titling policy being adopted. For example, considering only a given geographical area, voluntary titling allows for smaller registry offices and therefore incurs less fixed costs than universal titling. (Under voluntary titling, some titling costs are conditional on the decision by owners as to whether to title their land, a solution that, in combination with pricing decisions, helps to select which land should be titled first.) Conversely, under universal titling, all costs are fixed and unavoidable and are not conditional on owners' decisions. Similarly, fixed costs are smaller when titling is introduced only in the most promising areas. Imagine for a moment that the horizontal axis in figure 5.1 represents the land in a region that would be served by multiple registry offices, each incurring a fixed cost F. In this case, if land parcels of similar values are geographically concentrated in different areas within the region, it would make sense to introduce titling selectively, starting from the areas where the most valuable land is located, which should reduce the total fixed costs. In reality, this is the solution adopted when registry offices are opened only in urban areas or in the biggest cities. This was, for example, the solution chosen in England in 1897, which introduced compulsory registration following property transactions only in central London. It was as late as 1990 that the system was applied to all counties in England and Wales (Sparkes 1999, 1–3). Both selective demand and selective supply of titling services may therefore reduce fixed costs.

Variable Nature of Most Mapping, Surveying, and Similar Costs

The fixed or variable nature of costs also hinges on other policy options. First, establishing boundaries by surveying each land parcel is often considered to be a requirement for good titling (e.g., Kaufmann and Steudler 1998) and has been included in many titling programs. Investment to demarcate land by mapping the area and identifying parcel boundaries has therefore been treated as a fixed cost. But most of it can be transformed into a variable cost by allowing physical identifications of different quality, made on a voluntary basis, so that greater precision would be demanded either by owners for whom such precision in defining boundaries is really valuable or by the registry office in special circumstances in which it is deemed indispensable for titling. (The issue is important because 53.45 percent of the unit costs of land titling projects are being spent on physically identifying parcels.[7])

Centrally demarcating land in homogeneous, easy-to-measure units has been claimed to facilitate enforcement, reduce conflict and transaction costs, and produce positive externalities, increasing land value in a context of land allocation without preexisting property rights.[8] Some of these benefits may also accrue to surveying and mapping efforts in a steady-state context with preexisting rights. Furthermore, systematic mapping generally enjoys economies of scale and does not collide with vested interests. It is therefore understandable that titling projects tend to include or be preceded by mapping and surveying of land parcels. However, the value of this physical demarcation (as opposed to nonphysical, more purely legal demarcation) depends on the nature of the land. It is greater for rural, uniform land in areas lacking fixed boundaries,[9] as well as, given the fixed costs of surveying, for more valuable land. The latter explains why surveying and other due diligence studies are customary for commercial transactions in the United States but are rare for residential ones (Madison, Zinman, and Bender 1999, 14). Mapping is also costly and slow so that, above a certain frequency of transactions, even in developed economies it becomes almost impossible to keep the physical representation of the land universally updated at the speed needed today for economic activity, especially if the registry of rights is supposed to check boundaries before registration, to require neighbors' consent in case of collision and to indemnify claimants for boundary errors.

Scotland provides an interesting example of these difficulties. The 1979 Scotland Land Registration Act created a new registry of rights, the Land Register, to replace the old register of deeds, the General Register of Sasines, which had been created in 1617. The act burdened the new registry with a duty to maintain a physical description of each parcel of land, based on the Ordnance Survey map. More than thirty years later, only 19 percent of the landmass of Scotland and 55 percent of its titles had been transferred into the new registry (ROS 2010a, 5). Mapping had caused frequent refusals and delays in registration (see ROS 1999), often because of discrepancies between the plan in the deed and the Ordnance Survey map; it had also been the largest category of error in terms of indemnities (ROS 2010b, 26) and had been a major cause of the slow transition into the new registry, which suffered from long turnaround times and the accumulation of a considerable backlog, in which mapping issues figured prominently (ROS

2010b, 10 and 16). The Scotland Law Commission advised in 2010 to give discretion to the registry to replace the Ordnance Survey base map with some other system (ROS 2010a, 16).

Danger of Focusing on Average Costs for Making Sensible Technological Choices

Besides mapping, other policy options affecting the mix of fixed and variable costs are computerization and online registration, which are also often argued to reduce costs. For instance, CLEP (2008a) claims that the "costs of property certification can be considerably reduced and transparency improved by computerization and GPS systems, especially where comprehensive records do not yet exist" (66). This is partly true. Not only computers but also, in general, capital-intensive technologies achieve lower average costs. Formalization enjoys substantial economies of scale, as suggested by data such as those depicted in figure 5.2. However, these economies depend on the relative prices of capital to labor and, in any case, can only be reached at high levels of output. As it happens, most poor countries have plenty of labor, and their demand for formalization is limited to the most valuable urban land and corporate firms.[10] Therefore, extensive investments in computers and information technologies are often inappropriate.

Because average cost does not measure efficiency, it should be treated with extreme caution for comparisons and probably never set as an objective for reform efforts. Unfortunately, using average cost carelessly has been promoted by the popularity of international indicators that narrowly focus on them. In terms of the bottom panel of figure 5.2, they pay attention only to the vertical axis instead of considering the whole cost function. Consequently, when comparing such indicators across countries, institutions in countries with lower figures are seen as more efficient. However, countries at different levels of development have different demands for formalization and their optimum average costs should also differ. Therefore, a higher average cost in a country whose system functions at a lower scale does not necessarily mean that its institutions are less efficient. They may be functioning efficiently, at precisely the frontier of productive possibilities, but at a lower scale and perhaps with different, more labor-intensive technology. And vice versa, a richer country may show lower average costs only as a result of the scale, even though its system is inefficient.

Comparing average costs cannot resolve these doubts and may also lead reformers to pursue inefficient reductions in average costs (affecting, in fact, only part of them, as most indicators only measure expenses mandatorily paid by users, therefore producing only a partial estimate of *variable* average

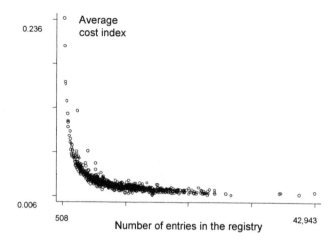

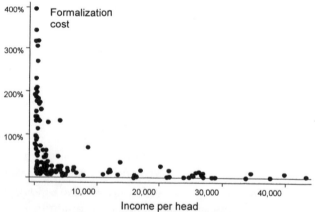

NOTE: *Top*, Average total cost index of property registries in Spain as a function of their volume of activity, measured by the number of annual entries in 1998 (based on data from DGRN 1998). *Bottom*, Income per head (in USD) and cost of business formalization (in percentage of income per head) in 2003 across countries worldwide (based on data from World Bank 2005).

Figure 5.2. Possible economies of scale in formalization processes

costs). This is yet another case of modern public management falling into an old trap of poorly applied managerial accounting, which for years had led industrial firms to choose capital-intensive technologies and to produce excessively large batches of products (Jensen and Meckling, 2009). It may help to explain why many formalization projects underestimate the fixed costs involved in building institutions (Wachter and English 1992; Holstein 1993).

Coming back to the main theme and considering that poor countries often have more labor than capital and limited demand for formalization, choosing labor-intensive technologies with higher average costs but little investment in fixed costs might be optimal. However, many have invested large amounts of capital while simultaneously trying to inflate demand and output by choosing a strategy of universal titling. I will now explore why this is generally a bad idea.

Voluntary versus Universal Titling

Under universal titling, where all land in an area is publicly titled, social benefits fall to the difference between the gains from titling high-value land (area G in figure 5.1) and the losses from overtitling low-value land (area L). Universal titling thus would be inferior to voluntary titling in the absence of positive externalities. I examine the causes of this inferiority before analyzing a possible justification of universal titling via externalities and discussing the real case of land titling in Peru. I close by questioning the direction of causality between informality and poverty.

Causes of "Overtitling" Low-Value Land

The negative effect, L, arises under universal titling because low-value land—that below the indifference point—is now titled, even if the cost of titling is higher than the resulting increase in land value. (Observe in the figure that for these parcels of land the value of land under the privacy line is above the value of land under the titling line). In practice, this situation normally results not from mandatory but from subsidized titling. Individual titling decisions are driven by the individual value of titling in terms of enhanced security of titles minus the price of titling services. Arruñada and Garoupa (2005) conclude that, in the absence of externalities, optimal titling fees should be *above cost* when social costs are lower than private costs.[11] The reason is that optimizing individuals tend to purchase too much title assurance, given that in their titling decisions they consider not social but individual losses, which are larger.

However, many development programs subsidize public titling by setting titling fees at nil or nominal levels and spending resources on informing owners about the benefits of public titling.[12] Most developing countries seem to follow the prescriptions of CLEP that "new and small landowners [should be] exempted from registration fees and taxes" (CLEP 2008a, 67). It coherently recommends institutionalizing "an efficient property rights governance system that *systematically and massively* brings the extralegal economy into the formal economy and that ensures that it remains easily accessible to all citizens" (60, emphasis added). Although it also aims for efficiency, CLEP's overarching goal seems to be a peculiar version of equality of results: "To ensure that a nation's property is recognized and legally enforceable by law, all owners must have access to the same rights and standards. This would allow bringing the extralegal economy into the formal economy systematically and massively" (66).[13]

Under registration, first titling of land previously held under privacy is in fact even more heavily subsidized because, given that unregistered titles are unclear, first registration is both more costly and more valuable.[14] Understandably, individuals are happy to go to the trouble of first registration, but they often do not file subsequent transactions and successions, even if the cost is less. They instead keep their titles private:

> Frequently, the record of land rights established in mass titling is not kept up-to-date, and the system falls into disuse. Keeping the system vital and current depends upon those who hold registered rights in land and those who acquire them registering their transactions and successions. Failure to do so is frequent and occurs for a number of reasons. The costs imposed, for instance, by fees or by taxing transactions, may be too high. The system may have become corrupt, driving away beneficiaries with heavy illegal charges. The landholders may not understand the system and its potential benefits to them or, if they do understand, they may not consider them worthwhile. They may simply be more comfortable with customary practices. (Bruce et al. 2007b, 42)

Titling therefore seems to be of so little value for these people that, even if they pay close to zero for it, it is not worth the time, trouble, and perhaps the possibility of being taxed, which are associated with registration. When this happens for the majority of subsequent transactions, despite subsidized prices, it is reasonable to ask if most of this land which returns to privacy after a subsequent transaction lies, in figure 5.1, to the left of the indifference point and therefore should not have been titled in the first place.

Positive Externalities of Titling

The above analysis assumes that the cost and value of titling each parcel of land is independent of whether other parcels are titled. In contrast, proponents of universal titling claim that there are substantial interdependencies, for instance, in clarifying boundaries and avoiding corruption, which should reduce the fixed cost of titling, F. For example, according to the United Nations Economic Commission for Europe (UN-ECE 2005), "the systematic [i.e., universal] approach. . . . is in the longer term less expensive because of economies of scale, safer because it gives maximum publicity to the determination of who owns what within an area, and more certain because detailed investigations take place on the ground with direct evidence from the owners of adjoining properties" (35).

Universal titling of an area might also produce positive externalities to the extent that the value gains produced by titling a parcel are not fully captured by its owner. Mainly, to the extent that titling encourages investments in building and renovation, some benefits of these investments will accrue to neighboring parcels.[15] Many other benefits are also possible. For instance, titling could modify in a promarket direction the beliefs of those receiving them, as observed by Di Tella, Galiani, and Schargrodsky (2007). Such a change might help stabilize political outcomes, even though this outcome has been questioned, considering that titling poor owners may be bad for the poorest tenants who lack ownership claims in slums: the poorest are often exploited not by the rich but by the poor.[16] Titles could also ease contracting for utilities, as emphasized by De Soto (2000, 58–61).

All these positive externalities would add to the benefits represented by the area G in figure 5.1. However, as often happens with externalities, their importance remains open to question. First, cost externalities are clear in mapping and surveying work but both activities may be unnecessary. They are also unsustainable, as "no project in the developing world has been able to implement and sustain high-accuracy surveys over extensive areas of their jurisdiction" (Burns 2007, 96). Second, positive externalities disappear when owners who have been given public titles decide to keep their titles private in subsequent transactions and successions. To this extent, universal titling is only universal for the initial first titling effort and all titling systems are de facto selective and voluntary. Lastly, there might be negative, as well as positive, externalities, for instance, by jeopardizing untitled customary rights to land.

Moreover, the empirical evidence on the effects of titling broadly supports applying voluntary instead of universal titling. Titling is more effective in areas where there are substantial investment opportunities, most commonly in cities, and when financial services have already developed (Bruce and Migot-Adholla 1994; Feder and Nishio 1998). Also, the benefits of titling, especially those related to the use of land as collateral for credit, accrue mostly to large landholders (Feder, Onchan, and Raparia 1988; Carter and Olinto 2003).

This evidence adds to the regularities observed in both the introduction of titling and the design of titling institutions, throwing some doubts on their real aims. With respect to the introduction of titling, it is common to find a symmetric failure to make sure, before the reforms, that a real demand exists, as has been admitted by CLEP (2008b, 84); and to check, after them, that such a demand has actually materialized. For example, most projects do not bother to monitor if subsequent transactions are being titled (Bruce et al. 2007b, 42). With respect to the structure of titling institutions, it is equally disturbing that most efforts rely on subsidized pricing, and policymakers are advised to continue relying on it (CLEP 2008a, 60, 67). No proper consideration is given to whether the need for subsidies is signaling lack of demand for titling.[17] Instead, policymakers are advised to educate beneficiaries on the benefits of titling and protect them from bad decisions (2008a, 67), even though it is unclear who knows best. Proposed policy changes share this disregard for demand. For instance, since credit does not evolve automatically from what are often supply-driven systems of property rights, CLEP advises the provision of "targeted credit" (2008b, 82), without considering whether demand (i.e., investment opportunities) for such credit really exists. Yet, after all these subsidies and advertising efforts, titling projects still fail to get subsequent transactions titled (CLEP 2008b, 84). In principle, all these features are consistent with the troubling hypothesis that, in spite of their empowering-the-poor rhetoric, these projects in fact serve the interests of the using-the-poor industry; mainly, the suppliers of titling and complementary services.

Land Titling in Peru: An Example

Peru has spent hugely on formalizing property—over 214 million dollars between 1991 and 2002 alone, in an effort financed with loans from the World Bank since 1998.[18] Positive effects on investment and on the supply of labor have been found by Field (2004, 2005, 2007), as titling supposedly allows squatters not to rely exclusively on physical possession to enforce their rights. However, a large proportion of the formalized properties leave the formal system when the land is sold again and hardly any commercial mortgages have been registered, despite many years of subsidized prices for registration.

Furthermore, several studies have concluded that titling has produced little, if any, security or value. Webb, Beuermann, and Revilla (2006) judge that formal titles add little additional security, and the difference has become smaller over time, from the perspective of owners. Kerekes and Williamson (2010) find that titling rural land has no effect on access to credit, even from public banks. Several reports conclude that "it is not clear that beneficiaries place greater value on a registered title than on other ownership documents, such as municipal certificates or sale and purchase contracts, which have not necessarily been purged and registered" (Morris 2004, 20, my translation). A report made for the promoters of the reform argues that "to some extent this can be explained by the widespread culture of informality among the population and also by the lack of knowledge of the benefits of having a registered title" (20). This argument is behind its observation that "a large percentage of the formalized population would not be placing any additional value on the fact that their ownership title has been properly purged and registered" (20). Also in line with this ignorance argument, the titling agency (Comisión para la Formalización de la Propiedad Informal [COFOPRI]) has been carrying out an extensive information campaign with the aim of "preventing the great effort at formalization from being wasted because a register that is not updated is of little use and everything seems to indicate that, once the COFOPRI title has been registered, *a large proportion of the beneficiaries have not registered second transactions*" (21, emphasis added).

It is, however, doubtful whether it is owners who underestimate the value of titles or, rather, title suppliers who overestimate it. It is hard to estimate true values in a dynamic context with possible collective-action effects, but data on credit suggest the latter:

> No important differences are noted for each type of title certificate, except for a slightly higher degree of approval of Cofopri applications (96%). . . . [nor] a higher use of the ownership title in access to credit, because this seems to be linked more to the applicant's payment capacity than to the holding of guarantees for the financial institution. The results show that the probability of approval of applications for loans is similar for those having a Cofopri title as for those having no ownership document as the two groups gained access to formal sources in the same proportion. (Morris 2004, 23–24)

What did increase slowly was the number of mortgages registered (between 4.18 and 5.59 percent, a tiny percentage considering that only 76,272 mortgages had been registered by the end of 2003 out of a total of 1,824,087 formalized parcels, for which 1,364,434 titles had been granted [Morris 2004, 98–99]). But it is unknown whether these mortgages effectively reduced the interest rate on the loans. More importantly, most of their lenders were public firms. According to Miranda (2002), "after six years work and more than one million registered land titles, . . . [most credit] is from the Banco de Materiales, a government credit system that provides credit to those with secure incomes and which is not based on those who have formal titles. There is not one private bank giving mortgage credit warranted by the titles registered" (263). These failures in subsequent transactions and mortgages have been blamed on the rising prices of notarial intervention (ILD 2007). However, even if notaries do make formalization more expensive, the problems with subsequent transactions and mortgages arose prior to the reintroduction of notarial privileges in 2002 and 2004. To make things worse, in later years, COFOPRI managers resigned amid allegations of prevalent corruption, including the hiring of thousands of political cronies and the sale of public land to friends at nominal prices (Miranda 2010).

Does Informality Cause Poverty or Is It Its Consequence?

Policies promoting titling and formalization efforts have become part of the conventional wisdom for fighting poverty. These efforts are grounded on the dual assumptions that the poor are poor because they are informal and that their informality is caused by high formalization costs. The argument goes that, as the poor cannot afford the fees required to register their land and their businesses, they lose economic opportunities. In particular, they are unable to use their land as collateral for credit and their businesses cannot rely on courts to enforce their contracts. The solution is simple: provide the poor with affordable—often meaning free or at least subsidized—formalization services, in the hope that this will increase the value of their land, allow them to use it as collateral, and expand their businesses.

However, these universal and affordable formalization policies may be misguided if causation between poverty and informality runs in the opposite direction—that is, the poor remain informal because they are poor. This might well be the case because their assets are of low value and their economic activities are of a personal nature; therefore, for most poor people the benefits of formalization are below its costs. According to this argument, informality is prevalent among the poor because formalization processes are costly, which makes access to all dimensions of legality—including the definition of property rights, written contracts, and litigation—less efficient for those who own fewer assets or subscribe smaller contracts. These costs of formality are real social costs, not arbitrary fees, and may well be higher than the benefits that the poor and society as a whole would obtain with formalization if the poor lack the impersonal trade opportunities for which formalization is really valuable. Individuals thus tend to formalize their activity more or less fully depending on their wealth: very poor people are not even registered as individuals; poor people are registered as individuals, but their assets are not valuable enough for their rights or titles to figure in a public record; and wealthier people have more valuable assets that are recorded in a more formal way. If registries in developing countries mainly serve the elite, far from being a problem, this is often an efficient outcome. Even though it does not justify their high costs and low quality, it is consistent with the priority of demand and value over costs. (Moreover, it might also be fairer than spending scarce tax or aid money on useless titling or formalization efforts.)

Consequently, focusing formalization efforts on the poor may well be inefficient, and governments and international aid organizations often invest too much in formalization projects and structure them badly, aiming for simple but, in the end, useless solutions. In fact, some formalization efforts may be no more than another way of exploiting the poorest—for example, those without land to entitle—for the benefit, not of those who have some land, but mainly of the suppliers of formalization solutions. It is also inevitable that many of these projects become unsustainable (Bruce et al. 2007b, 42): more often than not it is efficient not to sustain them and their inefficiency may even have been clear from the beginning.

Even if in many countries improving formalization institutions and lowering formalization costs is often a worthy objective, when properly based on costs and benefits, formalization policies should not focus on the poor. They should instead aim to improve registries for those already using them, focusing on improving the value of their services. And user fees should be levied so that charging beneficiaries at least part of the cost of formalization from the very beginning will provide a test on the social balance of costs and benefits and ensure sustainability, as argued in chapter 7. Such policies would benefit the poor by achieving more efficient formalization, via lower costs or greater benefits, which would increase economic growth and lead some of the poor to formalize.

This argument is applicable to both land and businesses. Firms tend to be informal when they are small and not the other way around. To the extent that some formalization costs are fixed with the size of the firm, it will be socially optimal that smaller firms remain informal and choose simpler contractual structures. This may be especially important when considering that formalization decisions influence the costs of public enforcement. For example, to the extent that incorporation facilitates tax evasion, easing the administrative burden of very small companies therefore increases the fixed costs of tax enforcement on the activities now channeled through these companies. From this perspective, policies that focus on reducing the regulatory burden (not mainly the initial but the recurrent costs) of smaller companies are misguided to the extent that, relative to their size, at least the smallest ones may impose greater costs on society.

Furthermore, protecting the poor by legal means often conflicts with developing the institutions needed for a market economy. In particular, a legal foundation for a market economy is equal treatment for all citizens, yet policies that "empower the poor" often include laws targeted to favor them (Bruce et al. 2007a, 5–6). For instance, governments are encouraged not only to provide land registration but also to recognize land occupants as owners, as well as provide advice and support to new small businesses, which distorts competition between firms of different sizes and promotes production at an inefficiently low scale. Governments are even advised to encourage workers' unionization efforts, as if unions did not have a dubious record in helping the really poor. And this is not to argue against redistribution to the poor in society. The criticism goes against implementing this redistribution by establishing unequal legal rights that at best benefit the poorest owners and not the poorest citizens.

Recordation of Deeds versus Registration of Rights

Theoretical Comparison of Recordation of Deeds and Registration of Rights

Choice between recordation and registration can be graphically represented by modifying figure 5.1 to introduce two titling systems—recordation and registration—instead of a generic one. Given the analysis in chapter 2, it is safe to assume that recordation is less effective than registration in avoiding title uncertainty. In the figure, the line representing registration will therefore be steeper, moving land values closer to the no-title-uncertainty 45° line. This greater effectiveness of registration is often considered to be rooted in greater unit costs. If true, the intercept of registration will be more negative than that of recordation.

Both assumptions are commonly found in the literature. However, even if these two assumptions hold, the choice of the best titling system may differ depending on the relative cost effectiveness of recordation and registration—that is, on the extent to which the additional cost of registration is justified by the reduction it achieves in uncertainty, relative to the same effect in recordation. The two possible cases are given by the possibility that recordation may be superior to privacy and registration for at least part of the distribution of land. They are shown graphically by the relative position of the indifference points between privacy and the two titling systems.

Figure 5.3 ("Titling Options [II]") represents the case where recordation is superior to both privacy and registration for part of the land distribution. Given that the indifference point between recordation and privacy is lower than the indifference point between registration and privacy, recordation is superior for land of intermediate value. If the government chooses to implement a recordation system, owners will record land above their indifference point for recordation. If the government chooses registration, owners will

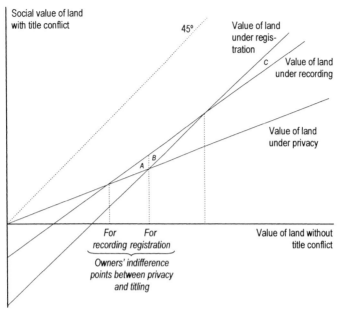

NOTE: Figure represents how the social value of land (*vertical axis*) is a function of the theoretical value of land without title conflict (*horizontal axis*) and the type of titling institutions available, which incur different costs. Social choice of titling institutions will be driven by these costs and the distribution of land in the economy along the horizontal axis. Area *A* represents the potential loss resulting when land that would be recorded under recordation is kept private under registration (*crowding out*); area *B*, the loss resulting when land that would be recorded under recordation is registered under registration (*overassurance*); and area *C*, the gain obtained when land that would be recorded under recordation is registered under registration (*underassurance*). (*Source*: Arruñada and Garoupa 2005, 717, figure 2.)

Figure 5.3. Titling options (II): Choosing between recordation and registration when registration incurs greater marginal costs

register land above their indifference point for registration. It is socially optimal to choose recordation or registration depending on the three effects represented in the figure by areas *A*, *B*, and *C*: crowding out, overassurance, and underassurance. (1) *Crowding out* happens under registration because its higher price leads owners to keep private some lower value land that otherwise would have been recorded (area *A*). (2) Similarly, some midvalue land that would have been recorded under recordation is registered under registration, causing *overassurance* (area *B*). Conversely, (3) recordation causes *underassurance* of land that is recorded under recordation but, given its greater value, would be registered under registration (area *C*). Recordation would therefore be socially preferable to registration if area *A* plus area *B* is greater than area *C*.

This conclusion assumes that the fixed costs of establishing the recordation and registration systems are the same. In fact, these fixed costs may differ in both directions, but the difference is unlikely to be decisive. Certainly,

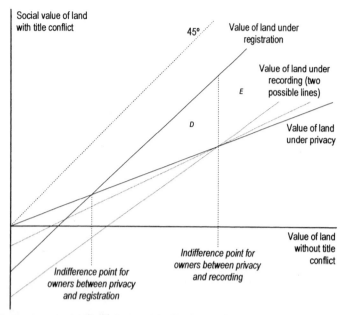

NOTE: The two alternative recordation lines are defined by the cost of recordation being lower or higher than the cost of registration. Area *D* represents the potential loss resulting when land that would be registered under registration is kept private under recordation (*crowding out*); and area *E*, the loss obtained when land that would be registered under registration is recorded under recordation (*underassurance*). (*Source*: Adapted from Arruñada and Garoupa 2005, 718, figure 3.)

Figure 5.4. Titling options (III): Choosing between recordation and registration when recordation incurs greater marginal costs

a registration system is probably more costly than a recordation system, but a large proportion of the cost difference is not fixed. It stems mainly from greater variable costs at the time of initially registering each land parcel rather than from the fixed costs of starting up the system. In other words, such costs are triggered by titling decisions and not by opening the registry office. On the other hand, when private title assurance is added to recordation, the recordation systems may incur larger fixed costs than registration, due to the duplication of title plants, which are private registries without legal effects, as explained in chapter 6.

Figure 5.4 ("Titling Options [III]") represents the case when recordation is inferior to at least privacy or registration for all parcels: the indifference point between recordation and privacy is higher than the indifference point between registration and privacy. Consequently, recordation is an inferior solution. Thus, if the government chooses to implement a recordation system or—more likely—is unable to move from recordation toward registration, owners will only record land above their (now higher) indifference point for recordation. There will be a social loss caused by the two effects represented by areas D and E in figure 5.4. Recordation causes both (1) crowding out of midvalue land that otherwise would have been registered (D); and (2) underassurance of the higher value land that is recorded under recordation but would have been efficiently registered under registration (area E). (In this case, there is no overassurance effect because registration is more effective than recordation.)

Palliatives in Titling Systems

The structure of pricing schedules and the legal solutions commonly adopted by titling systems are broadly consistent with the previous analysis, as they seem to be designed with a view to improving the efficiency of the title system in place. In particular, over-and underassurance, as well as crowding-out effects, are reduced through both corrective pricing and intermediate legal solutions.

First, transfer taxes, which are often linked to public titling, may serve to price private assurance and public titling services above social cost, limiting owners' inclination to overassure if losing the land has greater private than social costs. Similarly, charging minimum fees avoids the potential overassurance of low-value land. Lastly, using *ad valorem* titling fees, which increase with transaction value, motivates owners of midvalue land to register, thus limiting the crowding-out effect of registration.

Second, legal palliatives also minimize the specific disadvantages of both registration and recordation. Thus, recordation systems often provide a simplified judicial procedure to clear title (the French *purge* and the US "quiet title" suit), a solution to underassurance of the most valuable land. Conversely, registration systems usually allow some kind of inexpensive filing with lesser, or provisional, legal effects. This often takes the form of provisional registration of possessory title, which allows possessors to enter their claims in the register so that they are automatically upgraded into ownership if nobody has opposed them after a certain number of years. It can therefore be seen as a form of recordation within a registry of rights, and would substantially reduce the crowding-out and overassurance effects.

However, even if proper use of corrective pricing and legal palliatives may partly overcome the disadvantages of both titling systems, substantial differences are likely to persist in their relative performance. Not only are these palliatives costly and often applied sporadically but, being available to both systems, they enhance the performance of both. To choose between recordation and registration, it might be sensible to focus on their relative cost effectiveness in reducing title uncertainty. In terms of the analysis, the main question remains as to which of the two figures—either 5.3 or 5.4, "titling options" II and III, respectively—is more likely to represent the potential performance of both systems. The answer has to be empirical and should consider the specifics of each country.

Benchmarking of Recordation of Deeds Versus Registration of Rights

However, comparing the performance of titling systems is a daunting task. To illustrate the difficulties, I explore a tentative comparison based on data produced in a series of studies carried out by the European Mortgage Federation (EMF), and the European Commission and the University of Bremen's Centre of European Law and Politics (ZERP 2007), which put together the type of data suitable for clarifying these matters empirically.[19] At the price of a small sample size, these sets of data offer two main advantages over alternative sources. First, the EMF data measure not only titling costs—mainly, time and fees—but also titling benefits, as it estimates two indicators of legal certainty: mortgage repossession time after default and lenders' operating costs. Second, both the EMF and the ZERP consider all standard procedures rather than only those that are formally compulsory. For instance, they compute the cost of retaining professional conveyancers in countries where most transactors retain them, even if they are not obliged to do so and could instead prepare the contracts by themselves.

According to these two sets of data, European registration systems are not only more effective but also less costly than recordation systems, as summarized in tables 5.1 and 5.2. First, as expected, registries of rights exhibit far superior performance in regard to the value and quality of registration services. This can be seen in the indicators presented in panel A of table 5.1. Faster and safer registration and repossession are main drivers for (1) lower prices (i.e., interest rates) for mortgages, adjusted for differences in product mix, interest rate risk, credit risk, and prepayment risk, so that they represent a comparable price for borrowers, as well as (2) lower operating costs for mortgage lenders, measured as a percentage of outstanding loans.[20] They are informative indicators, as "the level of interest rates in capital markets is perhaps the most evident quantitative dimension of the efficiency of the institutional framework" (North 1990, 69). Moreover, the finding that mortgage repossession is faster in countries with registries of rights is fully consistent with the theory, since they are expected to provide better information on current valid rights and their priority. They therefore facilitate calculation of what is owed, establish priority among the various mortgages in a reliable way, and avoid litigation over the ownership and

Table 5.1. Performance indicators of eight developed titling systems

Performance indicators	Recordation of deeds[a]	Registration of rights[a]	Ratio of recordation: registration
A. Titling systems			
Mortgage adjusted price[b,c]	0.72%	0.63%	113.44%
Operating cost of mortgage provision for lenders, as percentage of outstanding lending[d]	0.59%	0.39%	150.64%
Mortgage registration time, in days[e]	37.19	13.40	277.50%
Mortgage repossession time, in months[f]	37.03	9.25	400.36%
B. Judicial systems (judicial enforcement of a contractual dispute related to sale of goods[g])			
No. of procedures	32.50	32.25	97.74%
No. of days from when the plaintiff files the lawsuit until actual payment	658.00	423.25	155.46%
Cost, in percentage of claim	21.48%	19.58%	109.71%

NOTE: Data are simple averages, drawn up by the author, for two samples of European Union countries with different titling systems.
[a] Classification of titling systems from UN-ECE (2000). Recordation countries are France, Italy, Portugal, and the Netherlands, whereas registration countries are Britain, Denmark, Germany, and Spain.
[b] Adjusted mortgage prices are based on a composite of prices for all lenders and are adjusted for differences in product mix, interest rate risk, credit risk, and prepayment risk, so that they represent a comparable price to the borrower.
[c] Data for 2006, from Mercer Oliver Wyman (2006, 4).
[d] Data for 2003, from Low, Sebag-Montefiore, and Dübel (2003, 34).
[e] Data for 2006, from EMF (2007, 11).
[f] Data for 2006, from EMF (2007, 174–91).
[g] Data for 2007, World Bank (2009).

capacity of the contracting parties, drastically reducing the number of legal defenses that can be used by the mortgagor after default. Remember, in contrast, that the 2010 US foreclosure crisis was partly caused by obscurity as to who really held the mortgages and the right to foreclose.

Certainly, these observations are open to alternative interpretations. On the one hand, part of the observed differences could be attributed to variables that have been omitted in the analysis, mainly differential court performance. In fact, data in panel B of table 5.1 comparing average judicial performance in both samples of countries lend some credit to this explanation. Nevertheless, the differences in judicial performance seem too small to account for the whole difference in repossession time. It is likely that registration improves the mortgage repossession process by providing it with better inputs. On the other hand, the choice between recordation and registration could be endogenous, having been influenced by the overall efficiency of the legal system, so that countries with less efficient legal systems should *optimally* rely on recordation rather than registration. European history provides a natural experiment that seems to refute this argument. The French region of Alsace-Moselle has a real property registration system (*Livre foncier*) because its three departments were part of the German empire between 1871 and 1918.[21] The system has two key features of registration: it is run by judges who examine the legality of each transaction, and the registered rights are presumed valid. Interestingly, French authors consider it safer than recordation (Piedelièvre 2000, 20) and generally advantageous (Simler and Delebecque 2000, 622). Something similar occurs in those areas of Northern Italy that enjoy a registry of rights introduced by Austrian authorities in the nineteenth century.[22] Italian authors consider it superior to the recordation system in place in the rest of the country (Gabrielli 1992), but several attempts to extend it have met with failure (Gazzoni 1998).

In addition, the data may also underestimate the beneficial effects of better titling because they do not consider some of its effects for the functioning of financial markets. For instance, within some of the European countries in the sample, the effectiveness of the institutions for mortgage collateral in Germany and Spain, as compared to France and Italy, may explain the differences observed in the average asset and financial structures of these countries' firms, as well as their differential reliance on formal bankruptcy procedures (Celentani, García-Posada, and Gómez-Pomar 2009).

Second, registries of rights also exhibit lower legal transaction costs than recordation of deeds, whatever the method used to compare them. Panel *A* of table 5.2 shows that, comparing costs for the average home transaction, a way of focusing on the transactions that are most relevant in each country, the typical home sale with a mortgage loan for 70 percent of the home value is 86.47 percent costlier in countries with recordation of deeds than in those with registries of rights. Moreover, only a small part of this difference could be attributable to lower average home values in countries with recordation, as shown in panel *B* of table 5.2, which compares across countries the transaction costs of buying homes of three different values. Lastly, a similar result is obtained when comparing the transaction costs of the same transaction in all countries (e.g., a €100,000 home) and then dividing such costs by a measure of each country's per capita income, as is done, for example, in the World Bank's *Doing Business* indicators (2004–11). Such an exercise is performed in panel *C*, expressing costs in purchasing power standard units of GDP per capita. Results are similar to those in panels *A* and *B*, because countries and average transactions in the sample are also similar.

As expected, the difference in total legal transaction costs between recordation and registration is caused by substantially lower conveyancing

Table 5.2. Legal transaction costs in twenty European Union countries

Legal transaction costs	Recordation of deeds[a]	Registration of rights[a]	Ratio of recordation: registration
A. For the average home in each country, as a percentage of home value			
Solicitors' or notary fees[b]	1.48	0.69	214.72
Property and mortgage registration[c]	0.30	0.26	112.67
Total legal costs	1.78	0.95	186.47
Average home value, €	150,737	164,724	91.51
B. For homes of different representative values, as a percentage of home value			
€100,000 home			
Solicitors' or notary fees[b]	1.74	0.94	185.50
Property and mortgage registration[c]	0.32	0.31	103.79
Total legal costs	2.07	1.25	165.23
€250,000 home			
Solicitors' or notary fees[b]	1.19	0.51	234.43
Property and mortgage registration[c]	0.26	0.24	109.71
Total legal costs	1.45	0.75	194.33
€500,000 home			
Solicitors' or notary fees[b]	0.93	0.35	268.72
Property and mortgage registration[c]	0.24	0.21	111.41
Total legal costs	1.17	0.56	208.65
C. For a €100,000 home, measured in terms of the GDP per capita of each country in purchasing power standards (EU-27=100)[d]			
Solicitors' or notary fees[b]	1,914.30	958.05	199.81
Property and mortgage registration[c]	340.31	266.78	127.57
Total legal costs	2,254.61	1,224.83	184.08

NOTE: Data for 2007, from ZERP (2007). Data are simple averages, drawn up by the author, for samples of twenty European Union countries with different titling systems and are given in percentages unless otherwise noted.
[a] Classification of titling systems from UN-ECE (2000). Recordation countries are Belgium, France, Greece, Hungary, Italy, Portugal, and the Netherlands, whereas registration countries are Austria, Czech Republic, Denmark, England, Finland, Germany, Ireland, Poland, Scotland, Slovakia, Slovenia, Spain, and Sweden.
[b] Solicitors' or notary fees, as well as legal fees charged by real estate agents in Denmark and Sweden.
[c] The transaction includes a mortgage loan for 70 percent of the value. Denmark's data were corrected to exclude transfer taxes.
[d] Data for 2007. Source of GDP data is Eurostat.

costs in registration, which are reduced by about half. This is consistent with the substitution argument between conveyancing and public titling. Results also show lower registration costs for registries of rights, but the differences here are much less significant. Taken together, these results suggest that registration offers lower variable costs than recordation, negating the common assumption to the contrary. This cost difference is also unlikely to be offset by the presumed advantage of recordation in terms of lower fixed start-up costs. As argued above, the fixed or variable nature of many of these start-up costs is a matter of design rather than principle.

If these comparisons of average performance and cost were confirmed, effective registration would be seen as the dominant titling system, justifying the general trend toward registration over recordation among development circles (e.g., Burns 2007, 120). Moreover, since in modern economies transactions are becoming increasingly frequent and property is increasing in value, pushing up the demand for security, this would also explain why many countries are creating or strengthening registries of rights. Two prominent examples are the transformation of the former Ontario recording system into a registry of rights and the English 2002 Land Registration Act. It would be premature, however, to interpret these empirical differences as causal effects, given the small samples involved. In addition, all countries in these samples are well developed, and the relative performance of titling systems might be different in less developed countries. For instance, they may find it harder to avoid a regression of registries of rights to de facto recorders of deeds.

The Legal System Does Not Determine the Titling System

The correspondence between legal and titling systems often creates substantial confusion, which may lead policymakers to exaggerate the difficulty of introducing a particular type of titling system in a given legal environment. For instance, according to Dale and McLaughlin (1999), "Roman law-based jurisdictions do not maintain 'positive' registers in the way that Torrens-based registration proves ownership" (1999, 42). This type of simplification disregards that Roman law corresponds to a system of private titling and, to some extent, to the recordation of deeds that exists not only in France but also in most of the United States. It also ignores the Germanic roots of registration of rights, which is present in countries with common and civil law traditions, such as England and Spain; and it forgets that Torrens registration is only one version of registration of rights, of scarce differential interest compared to the differences among privacy, recordation, and registration.

Understandably, when analyzed empirically, the number of property *in rem* rights is little affected by legal origin, since only socialist origin has a statistically significant influence, possibly due to underdevelopment of these systems. Similarly, legal origin at the civil versus common law level holds no explanatory power for the choice of titling system (Arruñada 2003a, 416–20). However, national origin within civil law is significant, as jurisdictions with German roots tend to have registration, whereas those with a French influence show a small, but significant, correlation with recordation. Registration was introduced, however, in some former French colonies. The United States also introduced Torrens registration in the Philippines (Iyer and Maurer 2009).

Choice of Business Formalization System

Similarity of Decisions in Property Titling and Business Formalization

This chapter has focused on the main choices in land titling. Part of the analysis is applicable to business formalization, as analyzed in chapter 3. Thus, contracting real property under privacy poses similar difficulties in terms of information asymmetry to the purely contractual formation of companies, as shown by the difficulties experienced by unincorporated companies.

Like landowners, for a given formalization system, entrepreneurs will also choose the degree of formalization that maximizes the value of their firms. Therefore, from the social point of view, the optimum formalization system for business firms will depend on the costs and value of the different systems and how the value of firms is distributed throughout the economy. And some elements of the decision between private and public land titling are also applicable to business formalization. When entrepreneurs are given a choice, their individual decisions will be to remain informal or to choose more simple contractual structures for lower firm values.[23] Similarly, social decisions as to whether to set up or improve a formalization system and, if so, which one, will depend not only on the formalization costs and the greater value resulting from the reductions in future transaction costs offered by each system but also on how the type and value of firms is distributed in each economy.

In general, policy decisions will therefore require substantial adaptation to local circumstances. For example, it would often make little sense to emphasize reforms of company registration procedures in a country with only a few companies. This logic seems less powerful for firms than for land since firms are human creations while parcels of land are fixed and it therefore seems more natural to take the distribution of land as given. However, appearances may be deceptive, because the key to the argument in both cases is the possible effect of cheaper formalization on the distribution of land and firms. Since many factors are involved, this effect might well be similar, if not smaller, for firms than for land.

There is also a correspondence between the types and effects of property and company registries, despite substantial differences in their functioning. In principle, recordation of deeds looks like a notice system in which companies simply file their documents in a passive public office, whereas registries of rights correspond to those company registries in which, in addition, the legality (or potential damage to third parties) of the documents filed is checked by a public official, resulting in more powerful legal effects. The different types of company registry also pose similar tradeoffs to those for property between recordation of deeds and registration of rights. However, some other features of land titling are not applicable to company registries. In particular, under both land recordation and land registration, owners exert their consent at the time of each specific subsequent transaction, while, in company registration, owners grant their consents in advance and, more generally, for a set of potential subsequent transactions.

Types of Company Registries

Company registries differ mainly in three dimensions: which information is required to be registered, the extent of review by the registry before the lodged documents are registered, and the discretion granted to filing parties to register limitations on the scope of contract rules.

All modern legal systems rely on a mix of informal notoriety (i.e., common knowledge) and formal registration to trigger contract rules in corporate law. The description in chapter 3 took as a reference the minimalist company registry defined by the US Model Business Corporation Act (MBCA). Most company registries require additional information and perform additional review of originative contracts. From the perspective of transaction costs, a main difference with respect to mandatorily registered information is the appointment of corporate directors and officers, which has to be registered in Europe to be used against third parties but not in the United States.[24] Consequently, there tends to be greater reliance in the United States on informal criteria, based on applying agency principles relating to the actual and apparent or "ostensible" authority of the firm's officers for exercising their functions. Such application often rests on the officer's position (e.g., Cary and Eisenberg 1988, 236–41). However, names and business addresses of directors and officers are also disclosed in the United States as part of the annual reports mandated by state rules adopting section 16.21(a) of the MBCA, under threat of administrative dissolution of the corporation (MBCA §14.20). Furthermore, this disclosure plays a role in ascertaining officers' authority,[25] a role that is likely to grow if the proposal to amend the MBCA is eventually adopted, as it includes a new duty to update the information in the annual report as soon as it becomes incorrect or incomplete.[26] Other differences among registries refer to disclosure requirements based more on an externalities rationale than a pure transaction-costs rationale. This is partly the case of the disclosure rules applied to listed companies in most countries, with the European rule mandating companies to file their financial statements annually (Arruñada 2011), and with, perhaps more clearly, the proposed disclosure of beneficial ownership in the United States.[27]

Similarly, registries differ in the extent of their review of originative contracts. The most passive registries only check that filings contain the required information with the prescribed formal attributes. This includes those US registries that follow the latest versions of the MBCA, whose section 1.25(d) has since 1984 treated the role of company registries as purely ministerial, assigning all checks of validity to the attorney general and the courts (ABA 2008a, 1–56). Conversely, more active registries, including most European registries and those in the United States whose state corporate laws follow earlier versions of the MBCA (ABA 2008a, 1–58), perform more substantive control, making sure that corporate documents conform with the law.[28]

Lastly, legal systems may allow parties to originative contracts a variable degree of discretion in tailoring the protection granted to third parties to subsequent contracts. The key difference in this respect lies in which effects are granted by law to limitative clauses in registered originative contracts. Originally, these limitations (introduced, for instance, in the objects clause or in the appointment of company representatives) were effective against third parties after being registered. However, the trend has been to make them effective only between parties to the originative contract, so that third parties remain protected whatever the limitations and without examining the content of the register.[29]

Tradeoffs between the Different Types of Company Registry

The main tradeoff, which is present in the three differential dimensions that I have just described, refers to the greater cost of registering more information on originative contracts and reviewing them more thoroughly versus the opportunity cost of missed trade opportunities and the need to put alternative safeguards in place to overcome information asymmetries in subsequent contracts.

On the one hand, more extensive registration or greater registration review should encompass greater costs and delays. This is consistent with the observation that registration fees, registration time, and registration refusals vary widely across countries. According to the detailed online data of the World Bank (2005), fees for company registration ranged from $3 to $3,200, with a mean of $275 and a standard deviation of $479. The time it took to register a company also varied substantially, from close to nil to 109 days, with an average of 15 days and a standard deviation of 17 days. Registration refusal rates also differed substantially across registries being, for instance, 3 percent in Canada and 8 percent in Britain (World Bank 2008, 13). Needless to say, dispersion in fees, times, and refusals of registration are grossly imperfect signals of the diversity of the scope of registration and its intensity of review. Lately, these variables have more often been interpreted as indicators of inefficiency, a view that is equally simplistic.

On the other hand, however, more comprehensive or better-verified registration should allow registries to produce greater legal effects in terms of, for example, creating a presumption of validity and correctness. Thus, in Spain, "the content of the Register is presumed to be accurate and valid. Entries in the Register are safeguarded by the Courts and shall have effect unless there is a court decision determining their inaccuracy or nullity" (article 20.1 of the Spanish Commercial Code). Conversely, more passive registries should produce lesser effects. For instance, section 1.25(d) MBCA states that

> the secretary of state's duty to file documents under this section is ministerial. His filing or refusing to file a document does not: (1) affect the validity or invalidity of the document in whole or part; (2) relate to the correctness or incorrectness of information contained in the document; or (3) create a presumption that the document is valid or invalid or that information contained in the document is correct or incorrect.

Consequently, less active registries should in principle save in the cost of registering originative contracts but lead parties to spend more when entering subsequent contracts, because of the need to produce additional safeguards. When the company registry only records company documents, provides copies, and certifies the date on which such documents are filed, legal counsels must examine more of the recorded documents of the companies with which they plan to contract. This effect is similar to the common practice under property recordation of deeds of performing title searches and producing title reports.

Corporate representation confirms this tradeoff. In Europe, where it is mandatory to register the name of company directors and primary officers, third parties can, in almost all cases, consult or get a certificate from the company registry to verify who the corporation's legal representative is. Providing protection for third parties against a possible lack of authority seems to require more paperwork in the United States, where the law relies more on apparent authority and less on registration. For instance, when buying in the United States a substantial part of the corporation's assets,

> most lawyers for the buyer would negotiate a rather specific contract for sale and would require the selling corporation's officials to produce at least all of the following: (1) a copy, certified by an appropriate state official, of the corporation's articles of organization, and a certificate of existence and good standing with respect to taxes, also from a state official; (2) an up-to-date copy of the bylaws, certified by the corporation's secretary; (3) a copy of the resolution of the board of directors authorizing the sale, accompanied by a certificate from the corporate secretary reciting that the action was taken by a proper majority of the directors at a meeting for which due notice was given and at which a quorum was present, and that there has been no substantive action affecting the resolution since then; and (4) miscellaneous certificates attesting to the validity of certain signatures, to the identity of certain officers, and to the up-to-date character of the other documents. (Clark 1986, 112)

Understandably, to avoid litigation about officers' authority, many US corporations "make it a practice to issue board resolutions authorizing officers to do specifically identified important tasks, even when the resolutions are not necessary" (Clark 1986, 117). More generally, the existence of a trade-off is further indicated by the different need for legal opinions in different legal systems:[30]

> The practice of asking counsel—one's own counsel or the counsel to the other party or both—for legal opinions originated in the United States. It is not a common practice for purely domestic transactions in other countries. This difference in practice can be explained by differences of custom and tradition and, in addition, by the fact that civil law countries have developed legal doctrines and methods that make it easier to verify matters such as due incorporation, the power to bind the corporation, etc., than it is in common law countries, such as the United States. (Gruson and Hutter 1993, xxvii)

This is not to suggest, however, that a system spending less on public registration and more on private due diligence is necessarily inefficient. It might well be that the cost of greater but selective due diligence is lower than the cost of more extensive and general registration. Similarly, the cost of more voluntary and more private compliance examination may be lower than the cost of mandatory and public review. Furthermore, the net balance may well vary for different countries and for different aspects. For instance, to the extent that differences in registration may cause more or less litigation, more extensive registration may be optimal in countries with less effective courts, especially given that less active registries can be expected to cause greater and costlier litigation, because they rely more on informal notoriety to trigger contract rules. Similarly, countries where company law has greater mandatory content may opt for registration review as a form of quality control to prevent formalistic breaches in corporate decisions from providing grounds for litigation, especially when judicial fees are far removed from optimal levels.

This might help explain why the most active company registries are responsible for protecting minority shareholders, acting as custodians of shareholders' rights (as in the Spanish registry). Their function becomes partly similar to that of property registries or rights, in which the registry verifies that rightholders have consented to each transaction. For example, if a wife sells the family home, the registry verifies that, if the husband is a co-owner, he has consented to the sale. Similarly, these registries verify that key company decisions have been made respecting legal and even company procedures. When doing so, it can be understood that they also are checking that shareholders have properly granted their consent to the intended transaction. However, even the most active company registries are less active and less specific in their review than property registries of rights.

The optimal tradeoff may also depend on which aspect is considered. I have just mentioned company representation where, considering both the historical trend and more recent moves in the United States,[31] the optimal solution is most likely to be one of registration. Conversely, it is less likely to be optimal to have registries enforcing rules on legal capital, as in most European registries, especially because preserving legal capital is costly but ineffective for ensuring companies' solvency.[32]

Lastly, another area where registration seems to be the preferred solution is that of companies whose shares are traded in the stock market. Securities regulation subjects open corporations to additional registration requirements, often subject to substantive review, as in the first decades of the US Securities and Exchange Commission (Easterbrook and Fischel 1991, 307). In fact, overall differences across countries are less pronounced when considering not only conventional company registries but also registries associated with securities regulation, which tend to exert a more active reviewing role. Interestingly, the intensity of this review and the extent of securities regulation seem to have been greater (at least originally) in countries with more passive company registries, such as the United States. This observation could be consistent with these two types of registries performing different functions—company registries, that of reducing transaction costs; and registries for issuers and traders in securities, that of avoiding negative externalities.

SIX

Conveyancing and Documentary Formalization

A major issue when designing and regulating contractual registries is the interaction with professionals whose services are used to define, write, and document private contracts. Some functions of these professionals may be made unnecessary or substantially simpler (and therefore less costly, less valuable for clients, and less profitable for the professionals), which is why, in various contexts, such professionals generally oppose the creation or improvement of public registries. Moreover, even though registries reduce the value of their services, palliative regulations mandating the use of these professionals in contracts are not always updated. It is not uncommon, even decades after registries are in place, for obsolete regulations to still explicitly mandate or implicitly force parties to retain lawyers or other professionals when contracting. For example, to sell a car in Italy until 2006, parties had to hire a notary long after a registry had been in place.

The present chapter analyzes the role played by these professionals in different institutional and market contexts, with and without different types of registries. This should help in regulating the professionals' functions and also in understanding the difficulties faced by policymakers when creating and reforming registries. The main argument has already been advanced in chapter 2. There is a potential conflict of interests between transacting parties on one side and third parties on the other. In the more general terms of chapter 1, there is a potentially serious conflict between participants in originative and subsequent transactions. This conflict explains why all such institutions organize their core public services, those which are of any consequence for third parties, as a monopoly, to preserve their independence. This applies to all types of registry as well as judges. Conversely, competition plays a greater role in documentary formalization of private contracts. Even where the provision of private legal services related to transfers of property (and, less often, incorporation) is regulated or reserved for the conveyancing professions (lawyers, notaries, title agents, and so on),[1] conveying parties are free to choose among individual professionals. This freedom encourages quality in the preparation of the private contract with respect to the dimensions valued by clients. However, protecting the interests of third parties whose property rights might be damaged by the intended transaction precludes free choice of registries and judges. Instead, cases are assigned to them based on an exogenous variable, such as geography, which amounts to granting them a territorial monopoly.

This difference is key for regulating titling and formalization systems. For a start, conveyancers and registries are serving the interests of different parties and must therefore be subject to different incentives. In addition, effective registries tend to make documentary formalization and, in particular, conveyancing services less necessary. For both reasons, it is understandable that they will often be in conflict, with lawyers and conveyancers impeding the development of registries, protesting their decisions, and, when possible, subjecting them to their own private interests—in a word, "capturing" them.

Here I analyze these issues, focusing on liberalization initiatives and the impact of institutional and market changes, but first, to clarify matters, let me start by nailing down the nature of documentary formalization.

The Palliative Nature of Documentary Formalization

Documentary formalization means subjecting private contracts to different procedures that improve their evidentiary quality. A written and signed contract is more formal, in this respect, than an oral agreement. In addition, the quality of the contract can be improved if it is prepared and authenticated by professionals and witnesses. Documentary formalization helps attest to the intention of the parties, which is helpful to judges who might be called to solve a conflict between the parties but also to parties themselves, as they tend to forget the terms of the agreement with the passing of time.

As judicial evidence, documentary formalization is more or less effective for different conflicts, with its effectiveness depending on which type of exchange, as identified in chapter 1, is at the origin of the relevant conflict. It works relatively well in conflicts related to "single exchanges" because all parties to the transaction receive and keep a copy of the contract; also, both parties can be present when preparing and formalizing it and thus can ensure that it is properly safeguarded. But documentary formalization is of little help for conflicts related to "sequential exchanges" because they typically arise in connection with subsequent transactions with third parties but they refer to some key element of a previous originative contract, and third parties are strangers to this originative contract. In such typical sequential-exchange conflict, documentary formalization is ineffective for the following reasons. First, because such third parties may lack access to the originative contract and cannot therefore present it to the judge. Second, because the total cost of getting access increases with the number of subsequent transactions. Third, because the subsequent third party, not being present at the time of the originative contract, cannot take precautions in order to avoid ulterior manipulations.

I have argued in chapters 2 and 3 that palliatives to these problems are not good either. Perhaps the most simple one is to give possession of the originative contract (often called "title" in this context) to the third party. This is how negotiable instruments work. Unfortunately, they face insurmountable difficulties when there are multiple rights. Another possibility, often used for land conveyancing, is for the originative contract to be kept by a specialist, usually the lawyer of the buyer. For instance, in traditional conveyancing before property registration had become prevalent, English solicitors used to keep the deeds of their clients. Something similar happens in civil law countries where notaries, despite acting usually in at least a nominally impartial capacity, are in principle chosen by the parties acting as acquirers, keep the deeds in their archives, and issue copies to grantees. To the extent that these professions sustain high standards of probity, their presence may provide some protection to third parties. For instance, when kept by lawyers and notaries, originative contracts should be harder to manipulate to deceive third parties. But possible hidden contracts may still prevail. Moreover, professional probity is always threatened by having parties choose lawyers and notaries, so that the strength of the whole system depends on the probity of the weakest link in the whole profession.

The obvious solution is to keep originative contracts under the custody of an independent agent and to make them public. But such an agent has to be independent not only of the parties to the originative transaction but mainly between them and the third parties entering subsequent contracts. This, in essence, is the key function that public registries must perform: making originative contracts public and verifiable.

The development of better registries therefore reduces and modifies the demand for complementary legal services and mostly dilutes the market failure arguments used to justify the restrictive regulation of conveyancing professions. Moreover, this tendency has been reinforced by the emergence of large operators and the growing standardization of transactions. Lately, new information technologies have been adding a third source of change by making it possible for contractual parties to dispense with the conveyance professionals in many of their remaining functions, in particular, in the authentication of documents to be lodged at the public registries.

I analyze these changes and their consequences for conveyancing in the next two sections before discussing policy options and future tendencies.[2] The analysis focuses on real estate, which is the most heavily regulated area. This makes its liberalizing conclusions even more applicable to the intervention of lawyers and other professionals in company registration. The reason is that the standardization of company charters provides an even stronger rationale for the liberalization of services involved in the documentary formalization of company transactions, an area already subject to less regulation in most countries. For example, even if lawyers are often retained to prepare incorporation documents, their intervention is not mandatory in most common law countries. Under civil law, notary intervention is also voluntary, for example, in France and Portugal.

Role of Conveyancers in Each Titling System

The three land titling systems analyzed in chapter 2—privacy, recordation, and registration—share functional similarities: all three are based on enforcing rightholders' individual consent as a requirement for their property rights to be affected. Consequently, contracting proceeds in two steps: first, conveying parties agree to the transaction; and second, they gather the consent of affected rightholders. By making this gathering of consents more or less difficult, the three titling systems induce different demands for conveyancing services, comprising the set of services provided by lawyers, notaries, title insurers, or other professionals in connection with contracts on real estate.

Conveyancing under Private Titling

Under privacy, property rights would eventually be enforced *in rem*—thus, against everybody, as rights *in rem* are defined directly on assets instead of persons—even if the transaction remained hidden. By themselves, private contracts could not damage third parties: the baseline principle *nemo dat quod non habet* ("no one can deliver what one does not have") fully applies. For instance, if second buyer B_2 is purchasing land from owner O, B_2 should be worried that O might have previously sold the land to first buyer B_1 or mortgaged the same land to lessor, L. However, first buyer B_1 is fully protected because, assuming neither of the two buyers took possession, the courts will establish title according to the date of the contract and give the land (i.e., thus the *in rem* right) to B_1 with B_2 being given only a contractual (i.e., an *in personam* or personal) claim on O. Buyer B_1 should be worried, however, about the possibility that O and B_2 may fraudulently antedate their contract.

This system maximizes the scope and complexity of conveyancing services. It first generates demand for lawyers to design and evaluate title guarantees offered by sellers and third parties that, even if they do not protect buyers *in rem*, at least provide some protection *in personam*. Second, reducing transaction costs when rights are embodied in titles also requires protecting the titles against fraud. From early times, legal systems required the presence of witnesses, surely the simplest solution, often qualified in terms of number, age, expertise, and authority. In addition, titles are protected by requiring that specialists (lawyers or notaries) are involved in producing them. A common solution making fraud difficult is for grantees and mortgagees to demand delivery of the full chain of title deeds from grantors and mortgagors, so that the risk of previous competing transactions is reduced and later transactions would require faking a full chain of deeds. In a sense, the chain of deeds is used as a private record but without any guarantee that it is exhaustive. In sum, the role of conveyancers is greatest under this privacy system, because they act as producers, depositories, and examiners of the main body of evidence used to establish title.

In this context, reducing competition between professionals may serve two purposes. First, the sharing among conveyancers of information on their contracts will save on the costs of structuring new deals and make them more secure. This process could still be observed at the end of the twentieth century in Andorra, a small country between France and Spain, which still applies a slightly modified version of Roman Law, including privacy for real estate transactions. The few Andorran notaries started to share information on mortgages after a new regulation was enacted in 1998.[3] This resembles the practice of Paris notaries who, during the ancien régime, also informally shared their information when referring their clients to other notaries. When lawyers or notaries enjoy a monopoly in writing deeds, the shared information is not mainly about creditworthiness but about the absence of previous and conflicting real estate transactions, which provides acquirers with a modicum of protection against adverse hidden sales and mortgages.

Second, reducing competition will lessen the incentives of conveyancers to cheat each other and may provide some support for the protection of third parties against fraud. But the system hinges on conveyancers dating deeds faithfully. For instance, notaries chronologically enter all documents into the notary's protocol, which provides an additional safeguard on the dating of documents. But the system may be prone to fraud as can be seen in some Latin American countries where, given the sorry state of property registries, judges tend to refer to the date of deeds, falling back de facto into a privacy system and thus increasing the motivation to fraudulently ante-date deed notarization, apparently a common occurrence.

Conveyancing under Recordation of Deeds

Under recordation, private contracts and other documents are lodged in a public office that only sets the lodgment date and reviews the formali-ties required to index it. The need to safeguard the contract is limited com-pared to privacy because recordation avoids one of the typical frauds under privacy—antedating a sale or a mortgage. The role of conveyancers as de-positories of documents also becomes less relevant and tends to disappear. Something similar happens to the demand for writing sophisticated title guarantees, to the extent that the filing system makes them superfluous.

Conversely, recordation does not avoid the risk of a double sale or mort-gage. In the above example, the recording office will not object to recording the second sale by O to B_2, even if the first sale to B_1 is already on record. Nor will it object to recording a sale to B_2 free of charges, even if a mortgage of the land to L has previously been recorded. Buyers will therefore be aware that the apparent owner might have sold or mortgaged beforehand, and this deed might have been recorded and gained priority.

Furthermore, finding the relevant information in the public record is not easy, because it contains a mix of relevant and irrelevant deeds result-ing from all the previous transactions, and the deeds are often indexed on a personal basis, using name or grantor-grantee indexes. To avoid nasty sur-prises and receive a report on the quality of title, transacting parties will retain some sort of title agent to search the record fully and detect any pre-vious sales or other title cloud. Consequently, the role of these title agents in searching and reporting on the quality of title remains important, creating a substantial demand for conveyancers.

However, the better the organization of the recording office, the less important the function of title agents. The two crucial improvements with respect to pure recordation are checking that the grantor's title is on record and using a tract index, though the importance of the latter diminishes with the computerization of land records.[4] First, the quality of the recorded infor-mation improves substantially when the recording office requires that only those already recorded as rightholders can be grantors in a new transaction, thus eliminating the risk of double sales. Similarly, a well-functioning recording office will require the lender's consent before canceling a mortgage. Second, the use of tract indexes, instead of relying on personal indexes of grantors and grantees, is essential for avoiding filing errors. When the records are poorly organized (as in many US counties), it seems natural for title agents to develop private title plants, that is, well-organized replicas of the public records. The investment required to build such plants moves the comparative advantage from individual title agents to the operators of the plants, who then start playing the leading role in the whole process.

Conveyancing under Registration of Rights

Under registration, the registry not only establishes the date but also performs a substantive review of the transaction, impeding any potential collision with property rights held by third parties. This drastically diminishes the demand and scope for high-value services in the preparation of the private contract. There is no role for title guarantees, and the registry itself performs the title search and produces a title certificate.

The data on real estate transactions in European countries with different titling systems (table 5.2) supports this substitution between registration of rights and conveyancing services, as it shows that, in countries with recordation of deeds, conveyancing services are substantially more costly. In countries with registration of rights, the cost of conveyancers was on average 0.69 percent of the value of the average property for contracting a purchase and its associated mortgage, whereas in countries with recordation of deeds, the cost was more than twice as large, reaching 1.48 percent. Thus, registration drastically reduces the value added by conveyancers.[5]

Moreover, registration provides indefeasible title, meaning that an innocent buyer who relied on the registry keeps the land to the detriment of the original owner. This switch from a property rule favoring owners to a contract rule favoring buyers drastically changes the incentives of lawyers and notaries, for a given degree of professional liability. These conveyancing professionals are no longer so strongly motivated by the interest of their clients to identify and avoid potential title defects, as they were under privacy and recordation. Rather, they often become the advocates of the transacting parties with respect to the registry, which is then the only element protecting the interest of third parties, whose property rights would turn into contract rights in case of registration error. In other words, since under registration courts adjudicate conflicting rights to innocent acquirers, transacting parties tend to encourage conveyancers and title examiners to disguise the facts before the registry instead of preventing such title conflicts, a change that further reduces the former gatekeeping function of these professionals.[6]

In particular, the function of notaries in civil law countries with registries of rights becomes more similar to that of notaries in common law countries, in that they often act merely as authenticators of contracts, ensuring the identity of the parties.[7] However, even this demand for authentication changes. On the one hand, authentication becomes more important because fraud would have more serious consequences than under privacy or recordation: fraud now leads to expropriation of legal owners when the contract rule is enforced to protect innocent third parties. On the other hand, effective new authenticators have also appeared. First, registries are now well placed to authenticate documents by themselves. In contrast to mere recording offices, registries of rights perform a highly technical task when reviewing the legality of private contracts. The knowledge and safeguards necessary to perform such a task can easily be applied to a less technical task such as authentication. This is exemplified by Scandinavian registries, which require neither notarized deeds nor intervention by lawyers but simply rely on witnesses for authentication and real estate agents for legal service. Second, banks are now the real experts at identifying individuals, which also diminishes the role of lawyers and notaries in contracts to which banks are parties. (This expertise also makes sense of judicial decisions that increasingly consider financial institutions liable for failing to detect the fake identity of fraudsters in mortgage fraud cases.[8]) Furthermore, digital signatures allow parties to dispense with notaries, other conveyancers, and witnesses for authenticating purposes.[9]

Nor is it necessary for lawyers to be involved in the start-up stages of a registration system. Given that start-up costs are high, if a reliable supply of party-independent (and, therefore, monopolistic) conveyancing services is available, a way of saving on start-up costs could be to make use of conveyancers to purge titles and improve the quality of deeds, as claimed by solicitors in the transition between titling systems in Ontario (Troister and Waters 1996). However, provisional registration of possessory rights provides an alternative, cheaper, and probably more effective solution (Arruñada 2003b). Furthermore, reliance on conveyancers for the start-up stage poses the risk that this mandatory intervention may extend beyond their useful life, as a functional, steady-state registry clears titles on registered land effectively and at low cost without such intervention.

This shrinking of conveyancing under registration helps to explain why conveyancers tend to oppose registration. As summarized by Simpson, "in the expense and delay the common run of lawyers had, of course, a vested interest: simple cheap conveyancing and certainty of titles do not increase the emoluments of attorneys" (1986, 273). Indeed, conveyancers have often managed to impede the development of registries, monopolizing entry into existing registries or debasing their legal effects—mainly, by supporting the effects of possession or title deeds against those of the registry. For example, several authors have argued that one of the reasons why Torrens registration failed in the United States was the opposition of lawyers, abstracters, and title insurers.[10] In the first decades of the twentieth century, when Torrens registration was being introduced, the title industry "organized to put up the best opposition possible against it" (Henley 1956). Similarly, English solicitors stopped registration in the seventeenth (Kolbert and Mackay 1977, 291) and nineteenth (Anderson 1992) centuries and finally delayed its expansion for a century by exploiting the veto power of local authorities (Bostick 1987, 59, n. 7; Sparkes 1999, 2–3; Mayer and Pemberton, 2000, 9–10). Also, "there clearly was bitter opposition to the introduction of the [Torrens] system in South Australia from almost all members of the legal profession, including the judiciary" (Whalan 1982, 5). After lawyers in South Australia did not cooperate with the Torrens system following its introduction in 1858, another act in 1861 set up a new profession of land brokers who were not legal practitioners but took over most of the conveyancing market there (Whalan 1966–67, 419–20; Mills 2002, 219). Recollection of this experience helped to ensure lawyers' cooperation with the introduction of Torrens registries in other Australian states (Whalan 1966–67, 420). Notaries' resistance to change has often also been linked to their monopoly.[11]

Partly as a consequence of this opposition, many real systems are hybrids in transition. In particular, registration systems are often plagued by the presence of "overriding interests": rights that are enforced *in rem* despite not being registered (e.g., due taxes and possessory rights) or rights filed in separate administrative registries (as happens often with municipalities' zoning and preemption rights). This implies that in many countries the role of conveyancers is also a hybrid one, in which they play a greater role with respect to unregistered rights. For example, French notaries play a preventive role, similar to that of US title insurers, with respect to the preemption rights held by tenants and municipalities (Willman and Pillebout 2002), but different with respect to ownership rights, because the French recording office checks that the grantor figures on record as rightholder of the right being conveyed, in application of the *règle de l'effet relatif*.

Market-Driven Changes in the Conveyancing Industry

In parallel with the development of titling systems, changes in the characteristics of parties and transactions have substantially reduced the comparative advantage of conveyancers for helping parties to property contracts. In fact, many professional structures of the conveyancing industries were set up in the nineteenth century, when most contracting took place between more equal, smaller parties, mostly individuals, who were freer to contract according to their wishes in the shadow of default law. These features of party equality and contractual freedom have changed dramatically since then, altering the kind of conveyancing services needed and making it possible to provide them more cheaply. First, the growing dominance of large parties has modified the information asymmetries between parties to the private contract and the locus of economies of scale in contract preparation. Second, the standardization and mandatory regulation of transactions has lessened the demand for tailoring private contracts to the parties' specific circumstances.

Changes in Parties' Characteristics

Today, in a large number of property contracts, at least one of the parties is a repeat player, mainly lenders, property developers, and real estate agents. The size and continuous presence of these players makes it possible for them to reach economies of scale in the preparation and safeguarding of contracts, reducing the demand for professional conveyancers.

Consequently, many property contracts have in fact become standard form contracts. This is especially so for mortgage loans, most of which are now written by lenders or, in the United States, involve standardized loan forms approved by secondary mortgagee lenders (DOJ 1999, 7) and filled in with the help of specialized software packages.[12] Consequently, the role of professional conveyancers in drafting the contract tends to disappear, as is often admitted by the professionals, who consider that it has debased their function. For instance, back in 1994 a prominent Spanish notary complained that:

> the massive granting of certain types of contract, especially deeds of sale and mortgage loans, as well as company incorporations and transformations, has had a dual effect: on the one hand, it has deprived the Notary of an essential part of his function, the writing of the document, which is invariably granted

on the basis of a draft produced by the legal services of the granting organization; on the other, it limits participation by the Notary, throughout the "transaction path," to the single moment of authorizing the deed. (López Burniol 1994, 129, my translation)

Similarly, because of their repeated presence in the market, large parties have additional incentives to invest in reputation and to act more fairly than nonrepeat transactors. They are therefore in a good position to act impartially with respect to their counterparties, as they expect to enter similar contracts with similar counterparties in the future.[13] In fact, the contractual functions of these repeatedly present agents sometimes go further than the preparation of documents. Consider, for instance, the procedures for nonjudicial foreclosure of mortgages in the United States, the traditional functioning of US banks as notaries,[14] or the unilateral setting of the final debt by lenders within the foreclosure procedure in Spain. Participation by reputed parties thus diminishes the role of lawyers in both the preparation and safeguarding of all but the highest-value contracts.

Nevertheless, even large and well-reputed parties often find it difficult to act impartially when drafting or safeguarding transactions. Standard form contracts cause new information asymmetry that calls for expert advice in some circumstances or for some contract attributes, such as nonsalient clauses. Katz (1990) has argued, for instance, that standard form contracts pose a typical "lemons problem." Competition should motivate drafting firms to improve the clauses in such contracts efficiently—that is, including actual information and the learning costs suffered by all parties (e.g., Hynes and Posner 2002; Schwartz 2008). But competition may work imperfectly, for example, when uninformed parties suffer bounded rationality, which is alleged to lead drafters to include inefficient clauses (Korobkin 2003).

Similarly, firms may find it hard to be impartial when they act through agents, even if acting impartially would forward firms' long-term interests. The subprime mortgage crisis that started in 2007 saw many firms fail to reach an effective position of impartiality because they were unable to solve agency problems within and between firms. For instance, some banks provided too powerful, short-term incentives to employees, motivating them to mislead borrowers even when this was detrimental to the bank. Also, the incentives of mortgage originators, lenders, and investors in securitized loans were often poorly aligned.[15]

In a competitive environment, the incentives are surely present for firms to trade off the different contractual problems with customers, employees, and agents, choosing the right mix of safeguards. Competition should therefore play a major safeguarding role. However, to the extent that competition is imperfect, failures might create a demand for independent professional services to fill the information gap suffered by small parties to the contract who are less informed, in both drafting and safeguarding. And firms might demand the presence of independent professionals to check on their agents and employees.

Unfortunately, professional conveyancers in many countries are poorly motivated to satisfy this potential demand and fill the gaps left open by imperfect competition among firms. This is first and foremost because of their dependence on large parties, mainly banks and real estate developers, who are repeat clients and often bring additional transactions. For instance, in Spain, when a bank imposes one of "its" notaries for a mortgage loan, the same notary will likely notarize the transfer deed, a situation often leading the notary to grant price discounts and kickbacks to the bank. Notaries complain that they cannot "change a single comma in the clauses" of mortgage deeds (Berná and Crehuet 2001, 121). Similar situations are common in other countries.[16] In some, it is even becoming increasingly common for several notaries to represent the interests of different parties to the same transaction.[17] There is thus no basis to the suggestion by Shiller (2008, 134) that the problems of information asymmetry allegedly prevalent in the US mortgage market can be solved by requiring professional intervention resembling that provided by civil law notaries. In particular, this suggestion does not stand up to observation of contractual practices during the housing bubble in civil law countries. For instance, in Spain, notaries' intervention did not avoid a wave of litigation by debtors alleging, for example, that at the time of signing the mortgage loan they had not been properly informed of the "recourse"—that is, unlimited liability—nature of the loan and of the existence of a "floor" on its variable interest rate.[18]

In addition, conveyancers suffer substantial information asymmetry of their own because they provide an ancillary service to the fundamental real estate or mortgage transaction. Consequently, the market for conveyancing services is prone to suffer from cognitive failure on the part of customers, given that they purchase conveyancing services jointly with a much costlier purchase. According to "prospect theory" (Kahneman and Tversky 1979), a cognitive bias may arise because the cost of conveyancing is only a small loss integrated into a much greater loss. Furthermore, the addition of a relatively small amount to the huge cost of most real estate transactions could make such small amounts difficult to perceive (Thaler 1980). These and other problems, mainly related to obscure pricing and undisclosed kickbacks among service providers, have led to recurrent regulatory efforts, with apparently little success in avoiding what authors criticizing the American title insurance industry have labeled as "wealth dipping," that is, the extraction of rents by providers of complementary services from transactions in which comparatively large amounts of money change hands.[19]

Changes in Transaction Characteristics

Demographic change has also impacted the conveyancing industry, as growing urbanization means that most real estate transactions now deal with urban property, which, once built, is more homogenous and generally presents fewer complications (e.g., it is easy to identify). Moreover, given that finding the seller becomes harder when people move more, title guarantees also become less valuable and, therefore, demand for them diminishes.

Standardization also comes about because of the more mandatory nature that the law has adopted since the first decades of the twentieth century. In the nineteenth century, the law mainly provided a set of default rules to the parties, allowing them to tailor their contracts freely to their particular needs. Mandatory law, in contrast, obliges parties to contract using fixed terms. The phenomenon is widespread: consider, for instance, the mandatory nature of legislation on mortgage foreclosures in most US states. A similar effect has been caused by the legal provision of standardized articles of incorporation, which can be registered faster.

Consequently, the demand for legal services to support the transaction changes in nature: instead of lawyers being required to tailor specific clauses to parties' desires, they are increasingly retained to formally comply with but in fact circumvent mandatory rules. In this context, the relevance of civil law notaries has suffered more than that of other lawyers, as they often have less incentive to satisfy the demand for circumvention, because they enjoy a profitable monopoly. This is protected not only by entry barriers—as with many other legal professions—but also by a closed number of notaries and has been made even more profitable by the lower costs brought about by standardization. In these favorable circumstances, they are happy providing routine services, even if such services add little value and could instead be produced by paralegals or replaced by standardized clauses.

As an example, both phenomena are consistent with the statistical evolution of the mix of services provided by Spanish notaries and their productivity. During the twentieth century, standard services such as mortgages grew more than those that require more individualized tailoring—the estimated proportion of standardized documents increased from 38 percent to 62.5 percent between 1930 and 1998 (Arruñada 2007b, 107–8). Consistently, the apparent productivity of notaries increased more than sixfold in terms of documents and almost tenfold in terms of sheets, a clear indication that theirs has become more an industrial and clerical activity than a truly professional one. Spanish notaries processed an average of 10.67 documents a day in 1998, whereas the standard number of deeds per notary in Berlin was only 325 documents *a year* (Kuijpers, Noailly, and Vollaard 2005, 61), about one per working day.[20]

Finally, consumer protection and foreclosure regulations also affects the demand by large parties for lawyers and notaries to leverage their position in future judicial proceedings. This demand is stronger for mortgage loans, because lenders often face difficulties in enforcing foreclosures, especially at times of economic crisis and generalized financial distress. Having lawyers or notaries nominally draft mortgage loans, explain them to debtors, and formally authenticate their signatures helps convince judges that debtors were aware of the commitments, making judges less reluctant to enforce loan terms that are harmful to debtors.

Regulation of Conveyancing Services in the Twenty-First Century

Situation of Conveyancing

In contrast with the territorial allocation of users and the resulting monopoly of registries, which aims to ensure independence, legal systems allow parties to the contract to freely choose the individual professional who is to provide them with conveyancing services. Even in countries in which a particular class of professional must be retained (namely, a lawyer or notary), parties can choose the individual professional within that class. The reason for this freedom is simple. Given that private contracts in both real estate and companies affect transacting parties alone, parties have good incentives to choose the professional who will help them prepare their contracts and the extent to which they will help. Therefore, free choice and competition between providers of contractual services encourage service quality without harming third parties who have no influence on the choice of professional.

This same logic makes mandatory intervention by professionals hard to justify, either in terms of information asymmetry or externalities. First, mandatory intervention by individual professionals is not the best way of solving the problem of information asymmetry between transacting parties, especially considering that their services could alternatively be produced by professional or business firms with longer lives and greater reputational assets. However, professionals' regulation often hinders innovation in this regard. Second, externalities are also elusive. Under privacy and recordation, where a property rule favoring the legal rightholder is applied, the consequences of bad conveyancing fall on the transacting parties and not on the third-party rightholders. This even applies to the cost spillovers that may appear between successive transactions. For instance, searching title for subsequent transactions can be simplified or even omitted if the previous conveyancers are trustworthy. (As US title insurers seemingly do when insuring land that the same company insured in the previous transaction.) Under registration, a contract rule is applied and transactions are examined by the registry to make sure that registration does not cause any damage to third-party rightholders, whatever the quality of conveyancing services. Bad conveyancing could increase registries' costs and endanger their effectiveness. However, both the diminishing comparative advantage of conveyancers, who now often do not personally know the transacting parties beforehand, as well as the availability of new and effective alternatives (the registries' staff, as well as that of banks and, for digital signatures, the certifying authorities), suggest that intervention by lawyers and notaries can be substituted with cheaper and at least equally effective alternatives.

Despite this lack of clear justification, in many countries parties are still required to retain lawyers when contracting real estate and forming companies. In others, lawyers or licensed conveyancers are the only professionals who can help parties write contracts for sale, transfer deeds, or both. Notaries enjoy an even wider reserved practice. Their monopoly as a profession is grounded on the legal requirement of prior notarization for filing many documents in public registries and on the privileges enjoyed by notarized deeds in some judicial procedures; and it is typically protected by a full set of restrictions, including a fixed number of notaries, fixed prices, and prohibitions on advertising and organization of notary offices. Similarly, the preparation of company incorporation documents is reserved for lawyers or notaries in 93 of 137 countries (World Bank 2005).

These constraints are particularly important for transition and developing economies, where such mandatory intervention is claimed to increase transaction costs exorbitantly, as forcefully argued by De Soto (1989, 2000). As a consequence, it could hinder formalization, the enforcement of property rights, the use of land as collateral for credit, and the incorporation of companies. However, developed economies also suffer poor regulation in this area, as analyzed below.[21]

Reform Proposals on Conveyancing

As argued in previous sections, both the private and social value of legal assistance in conveyancing services has been declining with the development of more-effective public titling, the emergence of large firms, and the growing standardization of transactions. Regulation should be adapted accordingly and should be consistent with the reduced functions required of professionals. For example, Spanish notaries are paid a fee that partially depends on the number of pages. This could have made sense when they drafted the documents (at the cost of corrupting the legal language, as pointed out by Adam Smith [1776, 721]). It does not make much sense now that most documents are standard or are drafted by firms and lenders. In fact, it seems to be used only to circumvent regulated price ceilings, as some notaries use unnecessarily large fonts. More generally, restrictive professional licensing is less justified to the extent that comparative advantage in eliminating asymmetries in the quality of title and provision of externalities now lies with public registries, and that of safeguarding against information asymmetries within contracts lies with large private firms. Regulation should also be consistent in preserving or, where needed, enhancing the effectiveness of public registries.

Understandably, conveyancing has been liberalized in many countries. The requirement of mandatory intervention has been relaxed or revoked, barriers to entry lifted, prices liberalized, and vertical and horizontal integration has increased. Everywhere, lawyers have opposed these changes on the grounds of preserving quality. Prominent examples are the controversy over "unauthorized practice of law" in the United States and the parallel debate in Europe about mandatory notarial intervention in standard transactions. Evidence on a drop in quality, however, is lacking. For instance, Palomar (1999) finds that the incidence of failures is not greater in US states where nonattorneys are allowed to prepare the deeds and close the deals. The cross-estate evidence provided in Arruñada (2007b) also supports the claim that involvement in conveyancing by US lawyers adds little value. In this case, greater freedom of entry in the provision of conveyancing services is associated with *lower* title insurance premiums, whereas lawyers' monopoly is associated with higher premiums. Given that title insurance premiums can be considered a proxy for the cost of detecting potential title problems, higher premiums might indicate that poor quality is provided by the conveyancing process in the long term.

Various international initiatives have also argued that mandatory intervention and current professional regulations are inefficient. The World Bank suggested that notaries are one of the main culprits for the greater cost and longer duration of company incorporations in civil law countries (World Bank 2004, 26–27). And, together with pharmacists, notaries were considered to be the most regulated profession by the European Commission's Directorate General for Competition (ECDGC) in its efforts to move toward the liberalization of professions.[22]

Both of these initiatives make a good case but also neglect key points. First, by focusing on civil law notaries, the World Bank disregards that the same should be argued about lawyers in jurisdictions—mostly under common law—where their intervention is still *de iure* or *de facto* mandatory for preparing property and company contracts and where they often collude to prevent their impartial intervention. For example, "do-it-yourself" conveyances, in which no lawyers or licensed conveyancers intervene, are legal in England and other countries. But their number is trivial because at least one mortgage is usually involved (either to finance the purchaser or to redeem the seller), and lenders insist on having professionals handling the transaction. The situation in the United States is also heavily regulated in many states: sixteen states still require lawyers' intervention in conveyance, and lawyers are generally precluded by the bar from providing their services impartially. However, no greater problems have emerged in states where the role of lawyers has almost disappeared and other economic agents intervene in an impartial capacity. Constraints on lawyers' intervention (both mandatory and impartial) should therefore be revised, as should both legal and de facto constraints on vertical integration.

Impartial assistance, in which experts represent the interests of several parties, is also becoming more usual in common law jurisdictions. Increasingly, brokers, lenders, and title and escrow companies represent more parties to the transactions in the United States. Something similar started to happen in Britain (Silverman 2001, 52–56). In some US states, real estate agents also act as dual agents of sellers and buyers (Pancak, Miceli, and Sirmans 1997). It is doubtful that users benefit from the prohibition that the lawyers' professional associations impose on their members, preventing them from providing impartial assistance to more than one party to the transaction.[23] Users seem well prepared to know when they need partial or impartial assistance and the prohibition seems to serve only the interests of the professionals.

Lastly, more careful attention needs to be paid to de facto mandatory intervention as a result of the development of e-conveyancing services, which in some countries has been strengthening the position of conveyancers in two ways. Some countries have granted them exclusive rights to use the new technologies when dealing with registries,[24] precluding direct contact by users and making do-it-yourself conveyance more costly or even impossible.

Second, by paying insufficient attention to the nature of the service in question, the ECDGC risks advancing incomplete reforms that might be inconsistent with the public functions that professionals are still entrusted to perform.[25] These reforms typically liberalize some rules on professional conduct, such as prices, organization, and advertising, but keep the practice reserved for the professionals. Such partial liberalization is inconsistent if licensing is now unnecessary for professionals to provide quality private services, while freeing conduct makes it well-nigh impossible for conveyancers to provide external effects.

This is confirmed by observing the consequences of liberalization in the Netherlands, where most notaries' prices were freed after 1999 and some freedom of entry allowed into each other's reserved markets. The result was that cross subsidies were reduced, resulting in higher fees for family services and lower fees for high-price transactions (Kuijpers, Noailly, and Vollaard 2005). Yet, there were hardly any entries, with most new notaries joining established offices (CMN 2003), an observation consistent with the empirical assessment by Noailly and Nahuis (2010) that the reforms did not affect entry decisions. Consistent with my argument, no change was detected in perceived quality by notary clients, but the quality attributes controlled by the property registry did decline (Nahuis and Noailly 2005), confirming that greater competition leads to weaker control of externalities. Moreover, several Dutch notaries have also been involved in mortgage and real estate fraud.[26] Subsequently, supervision of the profession has been tightened, adding newer regulations to the set introduced after the reform, to the point that, instead of deregulation, "the amount of regulation . . . increased dramatically" (Verstappen 2008, 21).

Most importantly, the Dutch experience suggests that the ECDGC may have been setting the priorities wrongly. Rather than merely liberalizing the price of conveyancing services, what is required for both reducing conveyancing costs and truly liberalizing conveyancers (i.e., not merely prices but also entry) is to make public titling more effective. This may require a movement toward registration of rights or, at least, adding to mere recordation of deeds the two key elements introduced in 1955 in France: tract indexes and a check by the registry that grantors are on record, two features that are still absent not only in most of the United States but also in, for example, Italy and Belgium (Nogueroles Peiró 2007).

This confusion of priorities is inevitable when the conveyancing market in a country is seen as independent of its public titling institutions. This was, for instance, a main error in a report produced for the ECDGC on the reform of legal services in real estate transactions (ZERP 2007), which classified conveyancing systems according to a formal and minor feature—intervention by different kinds of conveyancers: notaries, lawyers, or real estate agents. A much more substantive criterion is the type of public titling existing in each country, which defines by default the *functions actually performed by conveyancers*, whether these are lawyers in common law countries, notaries in civil law countries, or real estate agents in Scandinavian countries. Consequently, the report expressed surprise when finding that some highly regulated conveyancing systems, such as those of Germany and Spain, exhibited low legal costs. But this finding was surprising only within the report's misleading framework: conveyancing costs depend mainly on the nature of the property registry in place. For the same reason, the report was widely off the mark when considering that the Netherlands has a unique titling system. It is simply a well-organized recordation system in which registrars control the cadastre and make sure that grantors are on record (Nogueroles Peiró 2007, 124), with mandatory intervention by notaries, whose prices and organization—but not entry—have been liberalized, with the difficulties just examined.

In sum, it is important to keep in mind that the key social problem is not that of regulating a given market for conveyancing services but, rather, building and managing property registries so that a high level of security is obtained and most palliative services traditionally provided by conveyancers become superfluous.

A Possible Future for Conveyancing Services

For standard transactions, the horizon of the industry is a sort of industrialized production of property rights with low costs and no defects. This lean and "zero-defects" manufacturing of property rights requires fewer changes in countries with properly-functioning registries: simplifying overriding interests, standardizing forms, and enabling digital filing at the registry. In this way, standard rights in real estate would end up being contracted as legal commodities, in a way resembling financial derivatives in organized exchanges, with much lower transaction costs than those of today. This horizon seems even closer for company incorporation, relying on standard formation documents.

Automatic lodgment of documents that follow the standard forms is a prominent element of this future. In registration systems, this will tend to include automatic checks for previous rights, as well as for parties' identities and capacities, greatly facilitating and improving preregistration. It will also include authenticating the lodged electronic documents with rightholders' digital signatures, dispensing with or at least complementing conveyancers as authenticators, and removing a major source of error and fraud.

Governments play a key role in these transformations, not only in updating the registries but also in preparing default standard form contracts for real estate conveyance, mortgage loans, and company registration, as well as allowing for parties (e.g., lenders) to prepare alternative contracts suited to their needs. Both types of contract could be registered in a public registry of standard contracts (already available in some countries[27]). This would allow them to be subjected to a generic compliance review, thus enhancing the scope of automatic checks and speeding up registration of subsequent contracts.

The role of law professionals in preparing these standard transactions would be small and market driven. Changes in this direction have already been happening for a long time, focusing the use of lawyers only on the transactions for which they are really needed. In most of the United States, it is not lawyers but title companies' lay employees who search the title, prepare the documents, and close residential transactions (Braunstein and Genn 1991; Palomar 1999; ALTA 2000). Consequently, in many areas of the United States, "attorneys are not normally involved in the home sale.[28] For example, escrow agents or escrow companies in western states handle the paperwork to transfer title without any attorney involvement" (HUD 2000, 2). Similar tasks have been performed in England by "licensed conveyancers" since the Administration of Justice Act (1985) and with the arrival of the so-called factory conveyancing offered by several large national law firms for lender clients. The fact that property titling relies on recordation of deeds in the United States and on registration of rights in England suggests that these changes are viable under both systems.

Liberalization does not therefore mean that lawyers' and notaries' offices and firms have to give up providing conveyancing services, but it does require them, rather, to specialize and focus their services on market segments, with a few tailoring high-value transactions and others providing simple services with little legal content for the mass market. More legal work will also be needed for exceptional cases of lower value but, in these, professionals will tend to intervene within an organized hierarchy that filters cases, matching their complexity with the human capital of the professionals handling them (as happens widely in the United States, as explained in the previous paragraph).

Liberalization also encourages all sorts of providers to offer additional services, including a fuller guarantee—for example, strict liability and no-fault errors and omissions insurance—and the gathering of additional information (e.g., on the material quality of residential real estate and zoning restrictions), both of which may now be underprovided in many countries.

Trends in countries that have been pioneers in liberalization indicate that there will also be a good deal of vertical integration of conveyancing with real estate mediation, title assurance and insurance, and credit provision, with competition among organizations that combine different mixes of legal, insurance, financial, distribution, and mediation services. Freedom to choose among legal professionals is therefore being substituted by freedom to choose the fundamental service. That is, instead of choosing lawyers or notaries, users choose the bank, the real estate agent, or the title company, and these entities provide the legal services themselves or contract them out. Competition not only among different firms but also among different, more or less integrated, vertical structures even holds the promise of inventing alternative ways of tackling the residual asymmetries and conflicts of interest that appear in these industries, conflicts that conveyancers' monopoly and consumer protection regulation seem unable to tackle effectively.

Role of Title and Credit Insurance

The above discussion on the role of conveyancers would be incomplete without at least briefly considering the role to be played by the insurance industry in ensuring and enforcing property and contract rights. Not only is title insurance a main component of the US property market but its function is also present, under the same or different names, in other countries.

Preventive Nature of US Title Insurance

Title insurance indemnifies real estate rightholders for losses caused by pre-existing title defects that are unknown when the policy is issued. It emerged in the United States in the last third of the nineteenth century to complement the errors and omissions insurance provided by conveyancers when examining title quality and then expanded massively after World War II to satisfy the demand for title security in the secondary mortgage market. Poor organization of public records has led many US title insurers to integrate title examination and settlement services, given that their residual claimant status motivates these insurers to screen, cure, and avoid title defects.[29]

The salient attribute of US-style title insurance is that the risks it covers have already occurred when the policy is issued, as a standard clause explicitly excludes coverage of any defects arising after the date of the policy. This makes title insurance different from other branches of insurance, where most risks are related to future and uncertain events. On the contrary, title insurance covers against risks associated with facts that already exist but that are unknown when the policy is issued and may or not be discovered in the future.

Consequently, title insurance is based not on risk spreading and loss compensation but on risk and loss avoidance. To this end, insurers attempt by all means to identify preexisting title defects and to carefully perform closing services. The rationale behind title insurance is therefore not mere risk aversion on the part of the insured, but the provision of powerful incentives for the screening of preexisting risks and the correct performance of closing services, thus avoiding the emergence of new risks. Title insurance is thus better seen as an arrangement for reducing transaction costs, by motivating the production of information and the enforcement of liability in order to, respectively, reduce information asymmetry and moral hazard.

This preventive function of title insurers explains why the total losses paid out to their clients or spent in defending insured titles add up to a small proportion of their total revenue, around 6 percent (6.32 percent between 1968 and 2009; practically the same average as in each of the last two decades of the period), a much lower percentage than in other branches of the insurance industry (around 77 percent in property and casualty and 41 percent in boiler and machinery and surety).[30] The "insurance" label might even be slightly misleading, as title insurers provide much more "assurance" than "insurance" services, reversing the proportions of these components in more conventional types of insurance.

This emphasis on prevention and risk avoidance may also explain why title insurers have increasingly taken on the production of title information and the provision of closing services. No one has greater incentives to detect past risks and to avoid new ones than the insurer who, if the worst comes to the worst, will have to pay out losses resulting from either of these risks. Thus, it is the insurer who is in command of the process and he will organize the task of risk screening and avoidance using whatever means he thinks fit, from branch offices to independent agents.

Title insurers have every incentive to devise the means to discover in advance and to correct any defects in the titles before they provide coverage. In order to improve the efficiency of title searches, since the nineteenth century most title companies have kept private title plants that are better organized than the official records in two main respects. On the one hand, by using tract indexes, they provide fast and reliable access to all relevant information on each property. On the other, many of them are constantly updated with changes in the content of not only the deed recording office but also all other public files containing information of interest. However, although these title plants are well organized, they only serve companies' internal administrative functions, as they have no legal effect. This lack of legal effects is necessarily the case given the poor incentives of the title plant owner with respect to third parties.

Casualty Nature of Title Insurance Out of the United States

Outside the United States, title insurance has taken three main forms. US title insurers have been selling "international policies" mainly to US firms operating in unfamiliar foreign markets. These international policies provide less coverage than the standard policies sold in the United States. They also have limited use in the applicable jurisdictions, as they exclude risks that would require cover. This commonly happens for all sorts of legal interests that have legal force *in rem*, despite being unrecorded—"overriding interests"—, which are typically excepted. They also cover other risks in terms that are vague and are often written for a different jurisdiction. It seems that, lacking knowledge about which risks are insurable, which clauses are efficient and which prices are reasonable, insurers opt for excluding hard-to-ascertain risks. Therefore, it is doubtful whether they provide the insured with a reasonable expectation of cover or, instead, lull them into a false sense of security. Defensive lawyering on the part of the insured's attorneys may also partly explain the demand for these policies.

In countries where they have direct operations, title insurers have also developed country-specific policies more tailored to the specific risks faced by investors in each market. This has occurred in Canada since 1956. By 1999, most banks were prepared to accept title insurance instead of the lawyer's opinion for routine transactions. Canadian lawyers reacted by offering their own complementary insurance to standard no-fault errors and omissions insurance. Title insurance policies have also been sold in Puerto Rico to cover mainly the risk during the long period between lodgment and registration and to meet the demand derived from the US secondary mortgage market.

In Britain, "defective title insurance" has commonly been used when defects in titles are discovered, usually as a result of long-standing errors and lost deeds (Cribbet 1975, 309). This is similar to the practice of US insurers of charging an extra premium to bear the risk of a minor title defect on a casualty basis. Later, UK insurers have been covering against a set of unknown defects related to possible fraud and other failures in the conveyancing and registration process. There have been several attempts to sell similar policies in other European countries with seemingly little success thus far, as they have concentrated on the segment of cross-border purchases.

The common denominator of all these policies is that, relative to US policies, they are issued more on a casualty than a preventive basis. Mostly in business transactions, the preventive element is present, as the insurer requires that the due diligence for the transaction be performed by professionals chosen from a list of approved attorneys. However, policies for residential transactions are issued on a purely casualty basis, as the insurers rely fully on the conveyancing and titling process of the country. Furthermore, no title plants have been built out of the United States.

The role of these title insurance policies is more that of complementing and enforcing the liability of conveyancers and registries, which is often limited to negligent conduct and, in most countries, is difficult to enforce in practice. It may also play an important function in filling security gaps left open by the slowness of conveyancing and titling systems to adapt to changing market conditions, such as greater anonymity in transactions and the increasing presence of foreign nationals as parties to transactions.

Role of Credit Insurance: Differences and Similarities

The role that title insurance plays for real property resembles the role played by credit insurance for company credit. The main difference between them lies in the nature of the risk being covered. Title insurance covers against the risk that the legal title might be defective, while credit insurance covers the risk that the debtor may default on its obligations. This lesser legal nature of the credit risk may explain why credit insurance seems to be more widespread than title insurance, the latter being more dependent on unpredictable judicial decisions and perhaps more prone to adverse selection on the part of the insured.

Credit insurers have vertically integrated into producers of business information, using similar tools to title insurers. For small and midsize companies, their work is now based on building databases that collect information from different public registries and private sources, therefore resembling the title plants built by title insurers. Typically, these databases contain all sorts of information relevant to assessing credit risk, such as legal data from company registries; financial statements from lenders or, in Europe, company registries; filings in securities regulators; reports on secured transactions; abstracts on land ownership and mortgages; credit reports from credit bureaus; judicial records on pending litigation; and even press clips.[31]

This information is then used to evaluate credit risk and sell credit insurance policies or is sold to clients without insurance. It makes it possible to assess credit risk on a wider, anonymous scale, whereas risk assessment traditionally relied on mediators with some personal knowledge at both ends of the transaction, a role that was mainly played by banks when reporting on the solvency of their customers.

Lastly, both title plants and business information services are highly relevant for ascertaining how to simplify administrative procedures for business formalization. They are good examples of what might be called "private single windows": private firms providing a single interface with several public agencies. I examine this issue in chapter 7, arguing that these private single windows are potentially more efficient than single windows organized by government with a similar purpose. And they can be active in both sending information to public agencies—for example, on business formalization and tax filing—or, as in this case, in extracting information from them.[32]

SEVEN

Organizational Challenges

The performance of registries and, in general, of formalization systems depends not only on the type of registry but also on how it is organized and managed. For example, in the United States, poor organization in record offices led to the creation of duplicate private registries, such as title plants for issuing title insurance policies, and of the private registry of mortgages (Mortgage Electronic Registration Systems, known as MERS) for keeping a record of mortgage loan transfers. Poor incentives for registrars also cause registration delay, during which registries of rights, in fact, act as mere recordings of deeds. This has been the case in, for example, Puerto Rico. Worse still, whatever the type of registry, when registries are so unreliable that judges do not base their decisions on the registered information, then the whole registration system may become useless.

This final chapter focuses on the three key elements of organization: information, technology, and incentives. I first consider the information required for sensible decisions, that which illuminates the essential flows of the production process and the main tradeoffs between costs and benefits. Next, I examine two technological issues: the interaction of contractual and administrative registries and the impact of new technologies on performance. Finally, I discuss the design of incentive systems, at both the divisional and individual levels, and consider the tricky issue of self-interest.

Producing Useful Information for Decisions on Formalization Systems

In fall of 2010, mortgage foreclosures were all but frozen in the United States because of lawsuits about the status of the intermediary (MERS) that lenders had created to circumvent a decentralized, heterogeneous, and slow deed recordation system.[1] However, in the middle of the crisis, a World Bank publication, the 2011 *Doing Business* report, still placed the United States in the twelfth position worldwide in its *Registering Property* index, an index supposed to measure the performance of property institutions. The reason for this strange mismatch between real and reported performance is that these reports measure only a few costs and none of the benefits of such institutions, excluding effects on future litigation and transaction costs, such as the differential difficulties for foreclosure after debtors' default.

Structure of Information and Decision Making: Dispersed Information and Decision Strategies

The incompleteness of this type of index is only one manifestation of a more general problem: the difficulty of gathering the essential information on the values, inputs, and outputs of contractual registries. The value of their services and the demand for them are particularly hard to evaluate, both before registries are created and even once they are in operation. And, like productive processes in any other activity, different registry systems use different technologies to transform their inputs into outputs. They therefore incur different costs to provide more or less valuable services to users, more or less effectively reducing their future transaction costs. Different registry systems thus offer different mixes of costs and benefits, and their costs are incurred at different moments in the contractual process. They also require different complementary services and are financed with different sets of private and public funds.

Registries, of course, are not unique with respect to information difficulties. Making the best possible use of the knowledge available in society is hard for all sorts of goods and services (Hayek 1945). Information is in the hands of a multitude of individuals who have at most an incomplete view of the market, and their knowledge is often highly local and specific, which makes it hard to transfer. But this information problem is even harder for registries due to the nature of their productive process and the flows involved: their main output, legal certainty, and at least one key input, law quality, are hard to evaluate because both are intangible and highly qualitative in nature. Moreover, most effects of legal certainty are hidden and delayed. When registries are effective, their output is implicit and may seem unnecessary. When they are ineffective, this very ineffectiveness mainly causes a loss of trade opportunities, which, being invisible, is hard to recognize.

To utilize the information available in society, economic systems rely on two strategies, with specific solutions moving information or decision rights. This leads to different levels of centralization and the subsequent need to transfer more or less information: market solutions allocate decision making authority to those individuals with the relevant information, and political and regulatory solutions try to transfer such information to those with authority.

For deciding on registries, a variable mix of both strategies is commonly used. Price signals are sent to users, in the form of registration fees and transaction taxes; to registries, via service fees; and to registrars, through their compensation function. In turn, these prices elicit decentralized decisions by participants, by which they convey their information on, for example, their personal valuations and effort costs. But centralized decisions are also made about the creation and functioning of registries, given their nature as a public good, and even prices are centrally fixed. For registries, both strategies therefore rely on transferring information to central decision makers. Price signals have decentralized effects but are administered by government and not freely determined in the market; and most other decisions, such as those on registry creation and reform, are even more fully centralized. These decisions are made by political, regulatory, and administrative bodies, and are based on a variety of information systems, ranging from elections to quantitative indicators of performance, which aggregate disperse information and transfer it to decision makers.

Below I revisit the use of price signals. But first I discuss the design and use of these information systems by describing the dispersion and incompleteness of the information available to participants, examining the systematic failures of available information systems, and exploring how to improve them.

Dispersion and Incompleteness of Information on Registries

The *Doing Business* indicators mentioned at the beginning of this section are not alone in their incompleteness and partiality. Implicit and decentralized judgments on registries, such as users' knowledge of the value and costs of registries' services, also suffer serious biases, which differ from country to country depending on whether they have functional registries, ineffective registries, or none at all. When registries are in place, there is a tendency to take their services for granted and to consider their costs an unnecessary burden. In contrast, when registries are lacking, the benefits of creating registries are often exaggerated and their costs minimized.

Direct users—that is, those who must file documents at registries—often find it difficult to visualize the benefits of registry services. For instance, entrepreneurs are much more aware of the costs of procedures to register a company than of the private benefits afforded by the register in terms of lower transaction costs in their subsequent dealings with other firms. This asymmetry in the visibility of different costs and benefits inclines reform toward low-cost but low-value registries. It is compounded by a perception common in countries with functional registries that registries are simpler than they really are because they have been functioning for a long time, their complexity is underestimated, and their organizational requirements are neglected. When these biases are taken together, it becomes easier to understand why risky reforms are sometimes promoted to advance minor objectives. For example, in Spain in the early 2000s, the Ministry of Finance seriously pondered introducing free choice of land registrar by users. Freedom to choose was supposed to encourage registries (which, in Spain, are fully financed with users' fees) to compete among themselves for a greater share of total fees, by relaxing registrars' review and providing faster processing. The policy was rejected only when lenders realized the risks of debasing the register. They were happy with the idea of choosing registrar for their own mortgages but worried about competitors having the same ability to choose, as they could use it, for instance, to manipulate mortgage priorities. The ministry was using a sledgehammer to crack a nut and, in the process, putting the viability of the registry at risk.

In contrast, in developing countries, the case for a massive effort in property titling and business formalization reform was exaggerated in some influential accounts, such as those of De Soto (1986, 2000).[2] For instance, the size of the informal assets held by the poor and the potential value of formalizing them have been shown to be much lower than was claimed (Rossini and Thomas 1987, 1990; Woodruff 2001). Information was also poor because it was unrelated to the mixed record of real experiences. This did not, however, prevent such claims from achieving a substantial impact in the media and then on policy, so that for a while title and formalization became main items on the agenda of governments and international aid agencies. These expectations were often frustrated, moving the pendulum of fashion in the opposite direction. A realistic evaluation is therefore necessary, especially to consider two related aspects that have already been repeatedly emphasized in this book: the need to adopt a long-term view for design and evaluation purposes, as well as a focus on voluntary instead of universal formalization, so that resources are spent more efficiently. Both aspects are broadly consistent with the evidence: reforms show a poor record for universal titling; and registries in developed countries often took decades, even centuries, to prevail over private titling.

Moreover, users' perceptions of registries' costs are heavily influenced by the way registries are financed and, consequently, by the visibility of such costs to users. For example, governments in developing countries often subsidize land titling efforts, charging owners nominal fees and financing them instead with resources from general taxation and foreign aid. Similarly, when governments create single windows or one-stop shops for company incorporation, they rarely charge users for the additional investments that the new electronic systems require. More generally, some countries opt to tax land mainly through transaction or transfer taxes with correspondingly lower tenure or property taxes (e.g., France and Spain), whereas others opt for levying lower transfer taxes and greater property taxes (e.g., most of the United States and Britain). Likewise, some countries charge taxes on company incorporation (again, many European ones), while others prefer to tax incorporation with an annual franchise tax (again, most of the United States).

Because users are more conscious of costs when registries are financed from user fees than from general taxation, their position on registries will tend to be different and may lead to different decisions. From this perspective, and without considering possible externalities, fee-for-service systems are more transparent and thus likely to lead to better-informed decisions, whereas systems financed from general taxation will suffer the two failures characteristic of bureaucracies: excessive scale and chronic scarcity, as described below.

But it is not only users that pose information problems. Handling expert knowledge on registries is also difficult, because it is dispersed and there are vested interests. This technical knowledge is held by several legal professions (lawyers, notaries, registrars, and judges), different government departments (ministries of justice and finance, at least), and even different scientific disciplines (law, economics, and organization, most clearly), so that every type of expert knows about different aspects and there are substantial asymmetries between them. As a result, ideas about registries suffer from incomplete perspectives, rooted in the interdisciplinary nature of the problems registries solve and the private interests of participants. Decision makers must therefore be cautious when buying ideas and must structure decision bodies with a view to channeling different sets of knowledge effectively toward the decision-making process.

Systematic Failures of Available Information Systems

These defects are also suffered by explicit information systems on contractual registries, including performance indicators, case histories, best-practice guidelines, and surveys of user satisfaction.

First, cross-country quantitative indicators of registries' institutional performance, epitomized by the *Doing Business* indicators on starting business and registering property, were originally devised as a warning system on excessive red tape and thus consider only some costs. When used for broader policy analysis, they risk prejudicing the results in several ways.[3] Mainly, by considering only the initial formalization costs, they tend to blind policymakers to the tradeoff between initial and future transaction and administrative costs. Similarly, by considering only mandatory procedures, they tend to preclude comparing the costs of mandatory and voluntary, but often indispensable, procedures. Likewise, by computing only the private costs paid by entrepreneurs and property owners, they obscure the costs incurred by the government for providing better formalization services. Lastly, by disregarding private intermediaries between users and public formalization agencies, they lead reformers to overlook relevant tradeoffs when determining the optimal degree of public and private involvement—that is, how much of the formalization process should be vertically integrated in the state bureaucracy. In particular, this tends to bias their choice between public and private solutions, favoring public, vertically integrated single windows. Overall, the information they provide on initial costs might be useful if it were made reliable,[4] but should in any case be used with care, bearing in mind its partial nature.[5] Failure to do so explains why the use of these indicators has been falling into the old "management by numbers" trap into which many large firms fell in the 1950s and 1960s.[6]

These defects of quantitative indicators make case analyses more necessary. However, the growing literature on exemplary reforms must also be taken with caution, as it focuses on an equally limited set of variables and therefore suffers similar biases. Moreover, judgments of reforms as successes do not always survive scrutiny. For example, in the simplification of administrative formalities, some success stories have been shown to be real failures and best-practice standards to be both premature and based on partial viewpoints.[7] Evaluations of reforms in this area therefore appear to be erring often and systematically in favor of their intellectual or financial sponsors.

Best-practice guidelines must be taken critically too, as they are produced within the same limited assumptions. This is exemplified by the fad of administrative simplification, focused on initiatives to accelerate procedures for business start-ups.[8] Most of these initiatives also consider only the costs incurred by entrepreneurs for the incorporation of companies, disregarding all other costs and benefits, especially the value of formalization services for reducing future transaction costs. Consequently, they lead reformers to reduce the average time and cost of initial formalization when the priority, especially in developing countries, should be to achieve functional business registries—that is, registries sufficiently reliable for their services to inform judicial decisions and therefore reduce parties' transaction costs.

Lastly, surveys of users usually focus on land owners and entrepreneurs, who are often asked about their satisfaction in the context of titling projects and business single windows that have been heavily subsidized. Because they have no idea of either the costs that they will end up paying via taxes or, more importantly, the legal quality and, therefore, the value of registries' services, their responses are biased toward apparent quality and do not provide a reliable indicator of performance. More generally, something similar also happens with business lawyers, who are almost the only informants for some cross-country indicators:[9] it may be expedient to use them for estimating private direct costs, but not for other costs or benefits. Moreover, there is a conflict of interests with registries, in that lawyers are the main providers of documentary formalization.

These structural failures of information systems have had serious consequences for policies, which were aggravated by the perverse incentives created by development agencies when using quantitative indicators to channel aid funding;[10] and by the media that treated rankings of institutional performance as a sports league and reduced institutional reform to a mere simplification of administrative processes. Unsurprisingly, despite the doubtful results obtained in the field, such recipes gained credence among policymakers, and some countries even redesigned their policies merely to rise in the rankings, without addressing the real problems (e.g., Channel 2007).[11]

Developing Meaningful Information Systems for Decisions on Contractual Registries

Given the substantial centralization of decisions on registry organization and pricing, information systems should ideally cover the whole productive process of registries in order to clarify the essential attributes of the elements involved: especially, costs and values of inputs and outputs, as well as the main tradeoffs. The most basic of these tradeoffs is the intertemporal substitution between formalization costs and subsequent transaction costs incurred both to prevent and to cure conflicts. All registration systems spend resources on processing originative contracts to facilitate future subsequent transactions, but different registries make different intertemporal substitutions. For example, as analyzed in chapter 2, property registration is believed to be initially more costly than recordation but more effective in reducing future transaction costs. In general, better formalization of originative contracts should reduce future transaction costs in subsequent contracting, with less need for title reports, legal opinions, and due diligence work. Similarly, litigation should be less prevalent and eventually faster and cheaper, as suggested by the data presented in chapter 5 about mortgage repossessions, which is also consistent with the MERS experience mentioned above.

A second set of substitutions, highly relevant for choices between systems, comparisons across countries, and regulatory decisions, takes place between compulsory and voluntary services and, therefore, their costs, as different formalization systems require different complementary services to be provided by different agents before formalizing a transaction. Moreover, while in some countries these requirements are *de iure* compulsory (whatever the real need for them), in others they are only *de facto* indispensable to achieve a satisfactory level of legal certainty. For example, land title examination, which is mandatorily performed by notaries in France and can only be professionally provided by lawyers in several US states, is voluntary in other US states. However, most US parties retain professionals—not necessarily lawyers—to perform it. All these possibilities pose tradeoffs that should be contemplated when planning reforms and evaluating the performance of existing systems.

Full consideration of these tradeoffs is difficult because it requires information on many costs and benefits produced at different moments of the contractual process. However, current practice could at least be substantially improved, as many reform efforts only consider a narrow set of initial costs. A broader perspective would at least estimate, first, some major later costs and benefits by measuring, for example, the incidence of litigation and those contractual and judicial processes (such as the data on the value and cost of land titling services analyzed in chap. 5), whose effectiveness can be attributed to registries' performance. Second, instead of considering only mandatory procedures, all those followed by most users should be considered. Third, any costs paid by government agencies, including investment expenditures, should be added to the costs paid by entrepreneurs and property owners. In addition, paying attention to all components of the productive process also indicates which variables should be considered and which participants hold relevant information and must therefore be consulted. Consequently, the *user* concept would be changed to include judges.

Similarly, the prices charged by competitive private facilitators would be regarded as a market valuation of the total private costs incurred (more on this below).

Building more comprehensive measures is obviously costly, and some of the new elements will also be less precise. However, an imprecise but more comprehensive set of indicators is often preferable to a partial set. It would at least discourage naive management-by-numbers. Perhaps the main difficulty in this broader measurement scheme is that of gathering information on qualitative variables, such as legal security or, in cost terms, the opportunity costs of legal insecurity. Considering these qualitative variables requires a fuller set of complementary talents. Qualitative information is hard to codify and thus hard to transfer. To ensure that such information is available for decision making, it will be necessary to place knowledgeable people on reform teams. On the other hand, additional quantitative measures are not harder to produce or less precise than those being estimated. For example, the later costs of legal due diligence are not harder to measure than the initial costs of compliance with formalization requirements. In any case, relevant costs and benefits do not cease to exist when they are ignored and, if they are ignored, the discussion will tend to focus too narrowly on the few measured variables.

Integrating Contractual and Administrative Registries

My analyses of property and business formalization have focused on its core private and contractual function: that of reducing market transaction costs. This is accomplished mainly through land and company registries, which are generally considered to be public because they are open to everybody and are both based on publicity. However, their function is essentially private in the sense that they reduce parties' transaction costs.

Lately, reform policies in this area have also included a truly public side of formalization, which serves government agencies—what I call "administrative formalization"—and affects, among others, processes connected to tax formalities, social security, and the issuance of business licenses and land-use permits. These policies have often treated contractual and administrative formalization as if they were one single phenomenon. In so doing, they fail to distinguish their diverse private-public nature. Instead, they mainly see both as mere bureaucratic processes or even as barriers to economic activity and end up overestimating their similarities and disregarding their diverse organizational requirements. It is therefore necessary to deal with this administrative formalization here in order to clarify how it interacts with the contractual and private formalization that land and company registries perform.[12]

Concept and Rationale of Administrative Formalization

The theory in the first three chapters makes clear the differences between both types of formalization. Like contractual formalization, administrative formalization also imposes a set of mandatory requirements on private contracts. However, while contractual formalization reduces transaction costs in the market, administrative formalization aims to facilitate public interventions in order to avoid negative externalities or to favor the production of public goods. Such interventions can be justified by the insurmountable difficulties that individuals face for contracting in the market on such externalities and public goods.

Taxes are the most prominent manifestation of administrative formalization, as they can be seen in terms of the need to gather resources for providing public services. Understandably, tax formalities are ever-present in both property and business. Most countries charge a transfer tax or "stamp duty" on land transactions, some of them also tax company incorporations, and everywhere owners and firms are registered in cadastres and tax registries to facilitate collection of future tax on property and on firms' profits, sales, and value added.[13]

In addition, all kinds of externalities are also controlled by different forms of administrative formalization. Land transactions often have to comply with land-use rules to prevent owners of neighboring parcels from damaging each other. Business firms are also heavily constrained, especially when they are involved in potentially dangerous activities. In both cases, in order to ensure compliance, it is usual to subject private transactions and business operations to different sorts of authorization or registration.

Costs and Benefits of Integrating Contractual and Administrative Formalization

The coexistence of these two types of formalization poses questions about how they interact with each other, as both economies and diseconomies arise when they are integrated. There is, first, a general issue about which type of formalization should be given priority in that one may be a condition for the other; and, in particular, to what extent they should be organized independently, even at the price of wasting potential economies of scope that might be attainable by merging some of their processes.

Setting Priorities between Contractual and Administrative Formalization

Because contractual registration provides private benefits, governments have always been using the interest of individuals in registering their contracts to enforce administrative formalization, by requiring it before contractual registration. For example, in many countries buyers of land and founders of companies must pay land transfer and company incorporation taxes, respectively, before their property transactions and new companies can be duly registered. However, the social value of this greater enforcement might be small or even negative if it deters the registration of some property transactions or business activities that it would have been efficient to formalize contractually, even without formalizing them administratively (such as, e.g., registering a sale of land or incorporating a company without paying the corresponding transfer or incorporation taxes).

For this reason, it will often be advisable to place greater priority on contractual than administrative formalization, especially in the initial development of registration institutions. By facilitating market transactions, this priority should encourage growth, which will produce social benefits even without administrative formalization.

This solution is also consistent with historical evidence, to the extent that the main and oldest type of administrative formalization, related to taxes, has traditionally been run by separate government bodies. In modern times, at least, most property registries are assigned to the courts or—within the executive power—to ministries of justice and general administrative departments, but seldom to treasury or economic departments.[14] Company registries also tend to be independent of the executive, especially those that are administered by semiprivate bodies, such as chambers of commerce.

Contextual variables also play a role when establishing these priorities. If political institutions are weak, regulation and taxes are likely to be less efficient and enhanced enforcement is less likely to be beneficial in the long term. Moreover, when formalization institutions are nascent, they will also be less valuable and thus it will be less costly for users to remain informal. So greater priority should be placed on contractual registration in the first stages of the institutions. This is also consistent with historical evidence. In many developed countries, land and company registries have gradually been assigned an increasing array of administrative enforcement tasks but only at later stages, that is, since the last decades of the twentieth century and once they were well established and parties had become accustomed to doing such transactions formally, both contractually and administratively.

Mirage of Synergies

More recently, modern information technologies highlight the possibility of integrating different elements of the production processes in contractual and administrative formalization, from entering data to controlling registration or even merging the records. The benefits of greater integration, which may affect only the user interface, only the back office, or both, stem from the two processes relying on the same information and performing some similar activities. Separate registries will duplicate both entry and control procedures, as well as some of the information on record. For instance, owners and entrepreneurs may have to file documents in two or more offices, and some of the information in these documents may be the same. Duplication occurs in both single and repeated filings. For example, part of the data in company incorporation documents is the same as data given when registering a firm with the tax authority or the social security agency. Most European companies also are obliged to compile two different sets of financial accounts and to file them every year, one set with the company registry and another set with the tax authority, supposedly adapted to the different users of the information and with different legal effects.

However, integration also involves substantial risks because processes are not so similar as a process-engineering perspective may assume. The theory of contractual registries developed in the first chapters suggests that, given their different purposes, contractual and administrative formalization often rely on different resources and organizations. In particular, they use different types of specialized knowledge and implement different incentive structures. For a start, the data on file often serves different functions. For example, real property registries can work effectively with less precise geographical identification than cadastres, which are often used for planning purposes, such as building roads. Consequently, the type of knowledge necessary for exercising their functions is substantially different. This knowledge tends to rely on the law for contractual and company registries; on geography, taxation, and related fields for cadastres; and on the specific tax, labor, consumer, or safety regulations affecting each of the other administrative registries.

These different purposes entail different demands. For instance, delays are often more costly for entering documents in contractual registries than in administrative ones. The outputs of both contractual and administrative registries are inputs in subsequent processes but these processes differ, consisting respectively of bilateral contracting and unilateral enforcement. Hence, delays in formalization have the potential for precluding further contractual transactions, whereas they merely postpone administrative enforcement. Similarly, entry in contractual registries can be kept on a voluntary basis, whereas entry in administrative registries must be obligatory, as they are designed to avoid negative externalities. Moreover, specific issues arise for different registries. For instance, company registries deal with companies regardless of the industry in which they are operating, while many regulatory agencies and their registries deal with specific industries and often work at an establishment instead of at a firm level.

Consequently, organizational constraints and incentive structures are also different. Registration procedures need to be stricter in contractual registries to ensure independence, because they bestow rights, not only obligations, on the filing users or their future contractual parties. Cadastres, for instance, are declarative: if someone claims to be in possession of land, most cadastres will have no trouble believing that person because their entries only create obligations for declarers. In contrast, property registries have to implement more rigorous registration procedures to check the quality of title or the date of filing because they bestow rights on filers or, more commonly, concede economic benefits to filers by bestowing rights on subsequent third-party innocent acquirers. In addition, the incentives necessary to operate their processes are also different: contractual registries need to be impartial with regard to the transacting parties, on the one hand, and third parties, on the other; whereas administrative registries serve and are run by one of the parties, the government.[15]

Bureaucratic versus Market-Driven Administrative Simplification

Creating public single windows has been popular lately, especially for company registration, which was even considered "the most popular reform in 2005/06" (World Bank 2007, 11). Similar initiatives have been undertaken with many purposes and functions, as well as under different names, such as "one-stop shops," "service counters," "single access points," and "information kiosks," among others (OECD 2006, 62–65). Several options are available,[16] as coordination may be limited to having several public formalization offices located under the same roof but acting independently (which might be properly called a "one-stop shop"), or may integrate them functionally, so that they share one or several tasks (offering a "single window" to users, rather than a one-stop shop). Also, when opting for functional integration, it is possible to assign the shared functions to a new agency or to an old agency, in which case this is typically done by extending the tasks performed by the old contractual registry and providing them through a single window. Moreover, with functional integration, the central agency can perform different administrative functions. If these include some administrative control, it is usually necessary to enhance its competencies. If not, it will just receive information from users, transfer it to the administrative agencies, which will check compliance, and return their decisions before the central agency proceeds or refuses the requested registration. Alternatively, administrative control can be postponed until after contractual registration. In this case, the typical role of the central unit is to communicate the formalization request to the interested administrative agencies. Hybrid solutions are also possible. For example, administrative agencies may be granted a temporary right to block contractual registration, working under a silence-is-consent rule.

However, these initiatives share a puzzling feature: the new single windows are integrated in the public administration. They therefore purport to solve a problem in public bureaucracies by creating a new public agency— the single window—or expanding a preexisting one in order for it to act as such. This way of solving the problems of bureaucracy with still more bureaucracy should be met with skepticism, especially since they are often financed in a way that exaggerates their benefits and disguises their costs.

Public single windows indeed promise faster service and minimum costs to users. However, they are costly to create and run, and their costs often remain hidden to users in the form of higher taxes, distorting their judgment. For example, the cost of just the central data processing unit for the single window helping to formalize a new type of small company (the *Sociedad Limitada Nueva Empresa* [SLNE]) in Spain was 11.1 million Euros for the period 2003–6, during which its main accomplishment was to digitally transport from notaries to registries the incorporation documents of 2,001 new companies, at an average cost of 5,560 Euros per company. This amount was much greater than their average legal capital or the price quoted by private facilitators for shelf companies that had been registered in the old system (between 1,100 and 1,312 Euros). The gain in time was minimal, the performance appalling, and, in 2007, five years after the system was started, 99.07 percent of companies were still incorporated using the conventional paper system, despite the fact that companies using the new single window not only did not pay any additional formalization fee but also enjoyed a minor tax advantage and received some advisory services.

This is not a unique case: most public single windows reduce the number of contacts between final users and public agencies only by increasing the number of contacts between such agencies. Deep down, this type of public one-stop window vertically integrates into the public administration functions that have traditionally been performed by private intermediaries, or "facilitators." Those who implement these new bureaucratic machineries choose to ignore how the market has been helping to solve the bureaucratic problem and just replace it, adding yet more bureaucracy in the form of the public single window. (There is a modicum of irony in this, in that these policies have been promoted by economic libertarians but end up expanding governmental bureaucracy.)

The theory in the first three chapters of the book and the analysis of the choice of business formalization system in chapter 5 advise an alternative strategy: improving the interaction between public agencies and private facilitators, preserving the independence of the different agencies and exploiting the strengths and specialization advantages of public and private operators. This would enable private single windows to be competitively designed by market forces, such as the business information services that were described in the last section of chapter 6.

The organizational patterns observed in the facilitating industry argue in favor of this alternative strategy. This industry comprises a variety of professionals, including lawyers, accountants, tax agents, and administrative specialists, and in the most developed countries is organized with a complex mixture of franchising, subcontracting, and referral structures, instead of vertically integrated firms. Arguably, these structures tie in with the presence of different human capital and the importance of local information. They suggest that the optimum means for mediating between users and public bureaucracies is probably a variety of specialized intermediaries with different degrees of vertical and horizontal integration, rather than a fully integrated formula. They also suggest that public single windows and one-stop units, being part of a vertically integrated public organization, would find it doubly difficult to provide the right incentives. Not only would they be public agencies providing professional services but they would also have a poorly adapted organizational structure.

A sensible policy would therefore be to focus reform on developing flexible public-private interfaces with the bureaucracies in charge of the public core of formalization services while—and this is the key aspect—allowing the free market to organize a multifaceted intermediate sector, comprising all sorts of intermediaries offering final users a variety of more or less integrated services. Public agencies could then focus their efforts on building such virtual interfaces that private providers of support services can then integrate in a modular fashion. Tax authorities in many countries already have experience with this type of solution, as most tax returns are prepared and filed by tax experts, and most business firms deal only with their advisors, without interacting directly with the tax authority. One of the previous examples, that of European companies being obliged to file two different sets of financial accounts, one for the company registry and the other for corporate taxes, suggests the power of market solutions and the slowness of public agencies. The costs of this duplication have been drastically reduced by developing accounting software packages that easily produce the two sets of accounts based on one common data set, limiting the duplication to the output and filing process. However, public agencies have been slow in easing the filing processes. Instead, efforts have been directed toward reducing the disclosure obligations and designing a unified set of accounts, which risks being unsatisfactory for both business and tax purposes. Conversely, less attention has been paid to the more modest but less controversial possibility of reducing the costs of compliance (in this case, the cost of filing) in a manner that might encourage the development of market solutions: for example, by making it possible for account preparation software to dialogue directly with public agencies and cheaply provide different outputs adapted to their needs (Arruñada 2011).

Exploiting Technical Change

Electronic and communications technologies have made possible new ways of contracting and registering property and corporate transactions. In essence, they allow automation of many registry processes, including not only lodging and archiving but also some routine compliance checks, as well as many tasks performed by conveyancers when preparing and authenticating contracts and communicating with each other and with the registries.

Main Decisions

The least problematic changes are those using these new technologies for accessing and archiving information, by keeping the register in digital form and providing online access to those elements of the register that are open to conveyancers, transacting parties, or to the general public. A second and harder change is to make it possible for users to lodge documents electronically. In principle, these documents could be the digital version of those in the paper system. However, to fully exploit the potential of new technologies, electronic lodgment is often accompanied by substantial standardization of documents and transactions. To this effect, common transactions must be catalogued and forms preapproved by the registry.[17] For these standardized transactions, parties themselves or their legal representatives may start to complete the forms in an electronic workspace by entering the specific data on the transaction that they want to contract and register (e.g., the identity of the buyer or mortgagee, or the name and incorporators of a new company), often "prepopulating" them with data from registry databases that identify each property and its owner or identify each company in subsequent filings. If necessary, documents in the workspace can be electronically shared by parties and their representatives for review, amendment, and approval, which is especially useful in conveyancing. Automated systems can also generate reminders and reports on, for instance, who has missed a deadline to input data or perform a step. Eventually, after all parties have granted their consent, the document is submitted electronically to the registry. The most ambitious systems also provide for transferring funds between parties to property transactions.

Focusing now on property transactions, the main issues relate to the following: (1) who is allowed to lodge documents at the registry; (2) the nature of the review performed by the registry staff before registration; and, encompassing both of these aspects, (3) how the new system ensures that rightholders have granted their consent.[18]

First, to speed up reform, reduce opposition to it, and, allegedly but doubtfully, enhance security,[19] the new system may be reserved for lawyers or professional conveyancers by granting them exclusive lodgment access to the registry. For example, in New Zealand, Singapore, and British Columbia, only conveyancers may lodge documents electronically. Alternatively, the system may be open to other participants, at least to those who meet certain conditions and register for that purpose, as is the case with the Ontario Land Registration Reform Act R.S.O. 1990, which also allows the registry staff to electronically enter documents lodged by "onetime" users, a practical solution close to the "do-it-yourself conveyancing" contemplated by the English 2002 Land Registration Act. In practice, however, much depends on how strict the conditions for professional licensing and registration access are.

Second, lodged documents may be subject to a variable mix of automated and human preregistration checks for compliance with the law and respect for preexisting property rights. Most systems that have instituted electronic lodgment retain manual review by registrars before registration. Therefore, they allow conveyancers to lodge their instruments electronically but reject the possibility of allowing them to alter the register after automatic controls have been performed but without manual intervention by the registry staff (an automatic solution often called "agency registration"). Thus, the pioneering Electronic Land Registration System in Ontario maintains ultimate control by registrars, and the same solution has been adopted in British Columbia and Singapore (Low 2005) and proposed for Australia (ARNECC 2011, 3). The system under development in England also introduces validation by the registry prior to execution and completion. In this, the New Zealand *Landonline* system is exceptional because it is conveyancers who directly alter the register, subject only to automated checks for some impediments to registration, such as caveats and pending dealings, with no manual intervention by registry staff prior to registration.[20] Thus, New Zealand provides the paradigm case of agency registration.

Third, reforms introducing electronic conveyancing differ in how they ensure that rightholders have granted their consent to the transaction. Expediency has led some reformers to allow and even require conveyancers to sign documents electronically on behalf of their clients; so clients sign only the authorization documents to be kept by conveyancers. (Interestingly, in some countries conveyancers were happy to sign on behalf of their clients, whereas in others they were opposed to bearing the risks of such representation. A major factor here seems to be previous practice, as both solutions are in place in paper-based systems [Low 2005].) Alternatively, the system may require the digital signature of rightholders on any document lodged, which is not only safer but may also allow parties to dispense with witnesses, including conveyancers, for authenticating purposes. In addition, security may be enhanced by having the system notify rightholders and even request their consent before registering any relevant alteration in their rights.

Lessons and Possibilities

As analyzed in chapter 2, a registry of rights comprises a registry of deeds (the lodgment or presentation diary) and the register of rights *stricto sensu*, in which only purged, clean titles are entered. Automated lodgment, allowing conveyancers or subscribers to the electronic system to file their application without human intervention by registry staff, is easy to accomplish, whatever the type of registry.

Conversely, automating the registration decision in a registry of rights, that is, substituting the human registrar by computer software, is much harder. It is costly in terms of both the effort required to develop the system and the additional contractual constraints that will be imposed if a stricter *numerus clausus* is necessary to make greater automation viable. It is also risky in terms of fraud and the overall design of the registry. In particular, reforms introducing electronic registration could inadvertently interfere with the broader decision about the choice of titling system, since registration of rights or its main attribute, indefeasibility, would be endangered by granting registration powers to conveyancers.

This risk is compounded for a registry of rights with genuine deficiencies in terms of productivity, delay, and registration gaps, a set of failures that makes agency registration attractive, as it promises immediate results. However, this promise may be illusory because it is likely that agency registration will debase such a registry of rights into a recordation of deeds. That is, empowering conveyancers to directly alter the register should speed up *registration*, but would inevitably reduce the legal quality of *claims* registered in such a way—that is, rather than speeding up registration, it would most likely suppress it, "backsliding" into recordation.[21] This transformation of the title system might be a sensible move in itself, but, whatever its merits, it should be decided explicitly, considering many factors, instead of being an unintentional byproduct of introducing new technology. The alternative course of action to debasing the registry is to directly tackle its deficiencies. New technology helps here, but, to obtain durable results, registrars' incentives must be changed, linking their compensation to performance in terms of both speed and risk.

In addition to this speed versus legal-quality tradeoff, electronic registration poses other dilemmas. They relate to the standardization of property rights and the partly consequent transfer of costs between conveyancers and registries. Reducing the intervention of the registry staff in checking transactions for legal compliance and the presence of pertinent consents by affected rightholders is safer for standard transactions, which are thus easier to automate. It is therefore more viable for systems with abstract property transactions and fewer types of property rights. But there are costs involved in such standardization. Generally, the more abstract and summarized the content of the register, the more parties will have to rely on contract documents, which will be kept by conveyancers and parties. This in itself leads to difficulties. In some solutions, there is not even a real simplification but a mere transfer of paperwork, and access to the documents may even constrain some transactions. For example, mortgage refinancing may be hindered by the need to access documents in the hands of lenders.

Moreover, in automation reforms, registries often reduce their future variable costs only at the price of heavy fixed investment or by transferring such variable costs to conveyancers. Both these tradeoffs should be carefully examined. For instance, savings at the registry are not necessarily good if they are obtained by lowering quality or increasing the costs incurred by conveyancers. And both of these effects are likely when the chosen option is agency registration, moving the titling system from registration of rights to recordation of deeds. Conveyancers' costs would increase in two ways because (1) they would bear more responsibility for the transaction being filed and (2) they would need to search the title by examining the chain of title deeds for the parcel.

Understandably, there would be a parallel transfer of risk and liability between registries and conveyancers. This would tend to pose additional constraints on the structure of the conveyancing market. In general, conveyancers' ability to ensure compliance in the aspects not verified by a registry depends on their incentives, which are mainly defined not only by their position vis-à-vis their clients and third parties (e.g., their independence with respect to large parties) and their effective liability regime but also by the intensity of competition among conveyancers. This suggests a tradeoff between competition in conveyancing and conveyancers' ability to check transactions for compliance: the greater the competition, the lesser the ability of conveyancers to preserve the interests of third parties. The same argument applies to conveyancers' fraud. It is intrinsic to competition that some professionals are brought at least close to bankruptcy. This proximity greatly modifies their incentives to lower standards in aspects that are not rewarding to clients and even leads them, in some cases, to commit fraud. When these effects are observed, a logical reaction is to reinforce rules and to reduce competition (as in the Dutch case covered in chap. 6). Thus, the price of greater functions, especially those related to externalities, ends up being reduced competition.

Empowering Rightholders

The most promising contribution of new technologies is to enhance property enforcement in a radical and fundamental manner. By ensuring the exercise of rightholders' consent, they have the potential to avoid fraud and, in particular, overcome an essential weakness in all systems with registration of rights: the risk that owners may lose their property without having granted their consent. This feat can now be accomplished in several complementary ways: mainly, by dispensing with conveyancers and enhancing security through codes and notices.

Dispensing with Conveyancers

In many sectors of the economy, the role played in the productive process by different types of intermediaries, such as conventional distributors or banks, has been decreasing, as new technologies allow manufacturers and lenders to interact more directly with customers or borrowers. This "disintermediation" is also active in conveyancing, as new technologies allow parties to interact more directly among themselves and with the registry. Digital signatures provide a way of authenticating the will of the parties that can be used to complement or substitute the authenticating function of conveyancers and witnesses. The identification task passes to the certifying authority, which has to check individuals' identity when first issuing signatures to them. This makes it possible for rightholders to communicate directly with the registry to formalize their consent to the intended transaction. Digital signatures save time and money because they allow individuals to physically interact just once with the authenticator, the digital signature's certification authority, for all transactions during the life of the identity certificate, instead of once for each transaction. Furthermore, rightholders' consent can be safely gathered without any need for the rightholder to be present at the closing. In fact, there is no need for a physical closing act. Digital signatures may also be safer than traditional methods, especially now that conveyancers do not personally know most of the transacting parties, as they used to do in the past, and have to rely on indirect proof such as identity cards that are easy to manipulate. As concluded by a committee of the United Nations, "electronic signatures can be used to authenticate deeds. When they are used there must be certainty of authorship, guarantees that there has been no change in transit, the signatures cannot be repudiated, and the data remain confidential" (UN-ECE 2005, 15). Moreover, digital signatures are compatible with all sorts of conveyancers' intervention, which could be either superseded or complemented in a general way or on an optional basis, for all or some types or transactions or parties. For example, it is easy for banks to communicate cancellations of mortgages directly to the registry in this way. Digital signatures also have the potential for facilitating do-it-yourself (DIY) conveyancing, at least for the most routine transactions.

Enhancing Security with Codes

A modest way to improve security is to provide rightholders with digital identifier codes (right and person specific), known only to the holder and the registry, which they must assign to their conveyancing representatives in order to allow representation or must produce in some other form before registration (Thomas 2003b and 2003c). This would provide a safer version of the paper certificates of titles used in Torrens registries, which have been eliminated in reforms such as that in New Zealand. Its workings are similar to the "two-key" system used for electronic transactions in financial securities, in which both the owner and the broker must provide their unique identifier codes before a transaction takes place (Thomas and Grinlinton 2005). Moreover, two- or three-key systems tie in perfectly with the theory of property titling developed in chapter 2, since they ensure that no property right is affected without its rightholder giving consent to a specific conveyancer or, more directly, to the transaction itself.

Enhancing Security with Electronic Notices

Similarly, electronic technology reduces the cost of policies requiring the registry to notify affected rightholders of any change in the status of their rights before or even after registration becomes effective, something that could be implemented as a parallel safeguard in most systems. The value of such notification is shown by the emergence of private providers of this type of information in countries where registration fraud has become a serious concern, even if in this case it takes place after registration. For instance, in Costa Rica, since 2007 a private firm called PPR daily checks a mirror database of the public register to identify transactions that have been registered in the last twenty-four hours and, if any have not been authorized automatically, files a caveat.[22] At the least, registries should be allowed to notify registered rightholders about intended changes in their registered rights, as covered by Section 23 of the Ontario Land Registration Reform Act after its 2006 amendment. The English Land Registry has traditionally notified rightholders about intended changes to the register when the Registry perceives a possibility of fraud or undue influence.[23] Moreover, notification is becoming standard security in all types of computerized registries. For example, the fraud alert systems introduced by Section 112 of the 2003 US Fair and Accurate Credit Transactions Act (FACTA) allow consumers to instruct credit-reporting bureaus to notify users that the consumer is or might be a victim of identity fraud. Users of consumer reports are then restricted in the type of credit they can extend to that consumer. Some credit bureaus also provide consumers with a monitoring service that alerts them whenever someone asks about their credit (Zetter 2009). Working on a similar basis is the security trick used by some websites that send an email to all new registrants requiring them to validate their registration before they can start interacting with the website. These are just three examples of the possibilities that, at low cost, new technologies have opened up for protecting individuals and developing customized protection schemes.

The reasons of expediency and cost that are often given against empowering rightholders when introducing electronic systems do not hold much water. Empowering rightholders does add a complication and would take additional time and money to implement. Furthermore, many citizens do not yet use information technology. But registration systems are not developed for the short term and should be designed on the understanding that in the near future most, if not all, citizens will use digital signatures. Furthermore, the issuance of electronic signatures linked to the renewal of identity cards, which is well advanced in many countries, would avoid most of these difficulties, whatever their other merits. Digital signatures will increasingly be seen as a type of contractual infrastructure similar in nature and importance to the civil registry. Similarly, the costs of empowering rightholders differ substantially with the type of empowerment and, more importantly, there is scope for empowering rightholders in a self-sustained way, as they could be given the choice of, for instance, paying a fee to subscribe to a notice service from the registry. In systems of agency registration like New Zealand's, they could also be allowed to choose whether a registration application should include their digital signature before it can be registered or request that transactions affecting their rights be subject to manual examination by the registrar. These options could be offered on a fee-for-service basis, reducing the burden for the registry and maximizing their value for users.

Structuring Incentives for Effective Public Registries

The above section has argued that successfully introducing information technologies without endangering the legal function of contractual registries requires these registries of rights to be effective. This is only one more manifestation of a recurrent problem: when they lack proper incentives, registries of rights tend to become de facto recordings of documents, and recordings of documents tend to lose their ability to independently date and keep the filings. In general, to produce greater, faster or more reliable legal effects, registries require stronger and well-suited incentives.

Different sections of the book already have provided many insights into the requirements, possibilities, and difficulties faced when trying to organize public contractual registries. This section discusses some solutions relying on organizational theories to frame the argument, taking traditional solutions as a source of evidence. The aim is to extract some of the knowledge gained from these solutions over centuries of trial and error. I first examine the organization of the market for formalization services, focusing on the interaction between users and registries, and then discuss the internal organization of registries.

Managing the "Market" for Registration Services:
The Interaction between Users and Registries

Traditionally, public services have been organized as a bureaucracy with the features of a "discretionary expense center," a way of arranging economic activities within organizations in which both users and providers have few or no explicit incentives.[24] Users do not pay anything for the services they consume, and providers are allocated a budget to serve users following pre-scribed procedures but without their performance being subject to detailed evaluation. Understandably, users tend to demand too much, and providers try to expand the budget under their control.

Subjecting producers to this arrangement makes more sense when their services are easily standardized, so that they can be hierarchically controlled. Also, zero pricing is more viable when services have no value for users (as, e.g., with a tax audit), so they do not consume excessively. Otherwise, when services are complex and directly valuable, the poor incentives of both providers and users tend to cause a structural disequilibrium characterized by excessive production but permanently unsatisfied demand, a disequilibrium that is only partly adjusted through rationing and recurrent budget cuts. When this happens, local decisions by each expense center are suboptimal, as users demand too much and providers are happy to collude with them in requesting more resources from the budget unit. The latter suffers information asymmetry, as only users and providers know the value and cost of services, respectively; thus, budget allocation tends to be driven by political and strategic considerations. For example, when budget crises arise, allocations are often equally cut across the board, without considering the marginal value of each service.

These structural problems can only be tackled at the root by modifying the incentives of both users and providers, granting them some freedom to decide and, correspondingly, making them responsible for their actions. In particular, the users of many public services (those without serious externalities) can bear part or all the cost of the service and be allowed to choose provider. Their freedom to choose will in turn discipline providers, especially when the latter are given freedom to organize their activities and are paid for performance. Such changes modify the incentives for the bureaucracy, creating what is sometimes called an "internal" (i.e., organizational and somehow more artificial) market. It is hoped that, by having users paying for services, they will reveal their true utility; and, by motivating providers better, they will reveal their true costs. Both these revelations are expected to lead to more efficient allocation of resources. In many countries, this type of solution has been guiding efforts to rationalize the provision of the valuable services that are typical of the welfare state, such as education and healthcare.[25]

Interestingly, the traditional organization of many contractual registries partly relies—since their creation mostly in the nineteenth century—on some of these economic incentives, which sets them apart from the standard bureaucratic arrangements characteristic of general public administration. For registries, it has been common to rely on more independent agencies, which are not financed with taxes but with user fees, and to pay at least the key professional providers—the registrars—according to performance.

For example, in England, the Land Registry was organized as a nonministerial government department in 1862, as an executive agency in 1990, and as a trading fund in 1993. The 1990 reform improved productivity (Sparkes 1999, 18), even though it did not always avoid registration delays;[26] and, since 2003, it was set the objective of achieving a minimum 3.5 percent return on average capital employed. It is staffed by civil servants but has its own pay bargaining and pay and grading structures, suited to its requirements (Land Registry 2008). Since 2009, different British governments have even considered privatization as a possibility for future organization.[27] Similarly, Companies House is organized as an executive agency with trading fund status and, as such, is subject to business-like organizational patterns, including also a 3.5 percent return on capital and performance pay (Companies House 2009). As such trading funds, they have standing authority under the Government Trading Funds 1973 Act to use their receipts to meet their expenditures.

In France, the land registry is also financed with user fees and run by the *conservateurs d'hypothèques* who are civil servants but have enjoyed a special status with variable compensation, substantial deferred compensation in the form of pensions, and personal liability for registration errors (Cour des comptes 2008, 2009). Likewise, the *greffiers du Tribunal de Commerce* who maintain the French company registry are public officers endowed with public authority (CNG 2010) and also liberal professionals (Cointat 2002, 231; Girod 2002, 19) and, as such, are compensated with the net revenue of the registries.

A similar solution is applied in Spain where both land and company registries are run by registrars who are civil servants (*registradores*). A government department regulates entry, procedures, and prices. But each registrar manages a registry office, bears its costs, and earns its residual profit. In particular, each registrar recruits the office employees, who are not civil servants and some of whom are typically paid with a share of the office's profits.[28]

This arrangement therefore resembles but goes much further than the solutions being applied in modern reforms of public services in introducing stronger incentives. The latter often have grander plans but weaker incentives, as shown by the paradigmatically weak incentives of the "internal market" introduced after the 1989 reform of the British National Health Service.[29]

Stronger incentives have also been introduced in registries in many countries such as, for instance, the Netherlands in 1994 (de Jong 1998). Other jurisdictions, such as New Brunswick, have relied on state-owned companies (Dale and McLaughlin 1999, 132), and others on specific public-private partnerships. Changes in the Ontario registry have also been achieved by a firm, Teranet, founded in 1991 for this purpose as an alliance between the Ontario government and the private sector (Teranet 2008). Even the conversion of American private title plants into registries of rights, once defended by Janczyk (1977, 226–27), ties in with these experiences, as does the possible transformation of the private MERS mortgage registry into a federal registry (Cha and Dennis 2010).

Furthermore, registries' incentives are often strong in other dimensions. Thus, it is common for user fees to be so high that registries are not only self-financed but also become net sources of revenue for governments. Individual providers are also subject to strong incentives, especially in countries where registrars, despite being civil servants, are compensated with the net revenue of the office, after hiring and paying for all other resources. (In contrast, titling efforts in developing countries have often deviated from these patterns, charging users a small fee or none at all for service and paying fixed salaries to providers. Unsurprisingly, they tend to suffer the common problems of discretionary expense centers: excessive size, unsatisfied demand, low productivity, and budgetary crisis.)

In line with these strong incentives of some registries, both users and providers are subject to administrative constraints and economic incentives designed to provide automatic control. Thus, users are not free to choose providers, and providers must follow a detailed set of procedures, which substantially limits their discretion.[30] This arrangement is broadly similar to the one found in privately organized franchising networks, in which the discretion of franchisees is constrained in order to produce a homogenous service across the whole network but at the same time they are strongly motivated to make efficient use of local resources.[31] It makes sense in registries, given that their outputs are the inputs of further judicial and contractual processes, which makes standardization of quality a key attribute.

In addition, economic incentives are adapted in several ways to automatically control service quality. First, subsequent providers are often subject to contrary incentives, creating a system of checks and balances. Registries are monopolies and users cannot choose between registrars, who are thus placed in an independent position, suitable to protect the interest of third parties. Yet, conveyancers are in competition and clients are free to choose among conveyancers, who are encouraged to place the interests of their clients before those of third parties. Understandably, these contrary incentives cause a productive structural tension between registries and conveyancers. Similarly, when registrars are subject to strong performance incentives, their regulators and supervisors (including judges) tend to be paid fixed salaries, a difference that also generates opposing views and fruitful tensions between registrars and their controllers.

Second, some quality attributes, such as service time and even legal quality, are often internalized by specific incentives. For example, providing speedy service is motivated by making fees collectible only after the service is completed. Following this pattern, users of registries of rights pay lodgment fees after applying for registration but only pay registration fees after registration, thus reducing the perennial tendency of these registries to delay registration decisions.[32] Postponing payment in this way seems to provide weaker incentives than urgency surcharges, but it is also less prone to abuse (e.g., urgency surcharges encourage the registry to delay its standard processing). On the other hand, the legal quality of registration decisions is automatically controlled by subjecting registrars to strict, instead of negligent, liability. This method ensures law enforcement by the registry, which risks causing a backlash against the registry when the law itself is inefficiently mandatory, which is the case in those European countries that have more interventionist company law. Personal liability is also hardly viable unless registrars are paid as liberal professionals, as confirmed by repeated observations. In Italy, strict liability was transformed into a weaker, negligence-based regime ten years after suppressing residual compensation (Mariconda 1990, 156, n. 15). In Puerto Rico in 1914, the inability of registrars to indemnify parties damaged by registration failure put an end to residual compensation; since then, the registry has suffered considerable delays. In France, the reform planned for 2013 simultaneously transfers to the state the civil liability previously borne by individual registrars and modifies their compensation, from a variable amount linked to volume to a fixed salary.[33]

All these characteristics—administratively regulated procedures, strong legal outputs, fees for service, compensation with a residual profit, strict personal liability, and organizing providers as State franchisees—constitute a hybrid organizational form between public administration and private provision of registry services. This hybrid nature is probably more effective, sustainable, and flexible than the more extreme solutions in which registries are either purely private or part of standard public administration. Private registries may enjoy stronger incentives but lack public effects (remember the MERS case). And public registries have stronger effects but weaker incentives, especially when organized as standard public agencies, which often causes substandard performance or, in the case of registries of rights, mortally debilitates them. The solution seems to lie in hybrid organizational forms, which can produce public effects while keeping strong incentives for performance.

Added Difficulties of Organizing Registries of Rights

Long-established contractual registries also hold a lesson on how to organize their key resource: registry personnel. Registries acting as pure recorders of deeds, which mostly perform ministerial duties consisting of the simpler administrative tasks of dating and filing lodged documents, as well as issuing copies and certificates, are damaged less if organized as standard bureaucracies. However, even for them, it is necessary to ensure speedy processing and preclude corruption, so they perform better when bureaucrats are paid for performance and with deferred compensation.

Conversely, given that registries of rights must make sure that filings respect third parties' property rights and conform to law before they are accepted for registration, their performance crucially depends on the application of legal knowledge by competent registrars. Unsurprisingly, successful registries of rights tend to adopt some of the features of law firms. Registrars' competence must be at least comparable to that of the conveyancers who prepare the filings that registrars have to examine. Therefore, registries must pay registrars competitive salaries to recruit and retain competent lawyers. Registrars must also play the key role in organizing all other resources, as their contribution defines the performance of the whole registry. Given the importance of their registration decisions, the organization of registries of rights tends to be focused on supporting them by subordinating other resources that take care of administrative tasks and routine checks. Variable compensation provides a direct link between pay and performance, even though it requires additional mechanisms such as stricter personal liability. Moreover, rising compensation based on seniority helps parallel the accumulation of human capital and the consequent increase in outside opportunities.

Finally, having part of the compensation deferred in time (by paying below the compensation the registrar could make in the best alternative job during the first years and above it later or by requiring "specific" investments—that is, only valuable for that job—in the form of entry exams), helps motivate compliance by encouraging self-selection and increasing the expected cost of noncompliance. First, deferred compensation motivates professionals with a lower subjective discount rate to self-select themselves, as such deferral is less costly for them, and they are also likely to be relatively averse to fraud. Second, it additionally motivates registrars to comply once they are paid more than they could earn in the best alternative job (Becker and Stigler 1974).

These features are hard to sustain within the standard organization of public administration, especially without financing the registry through user fees. For instance, the public sector often finds it difficult to keep compensation levels competitive. When the economy is expanding, private salaries tend to increase faster, opening an earnings gap that leads the best professionals to leave their public posts. Moreover, budgetary crises often lead to across-the-board wage cuts that consider neither market conditions nor the alternative of reducing staff. Even worse, the range of salaries may be reduced in an equalizing effort that expropriates the deferred compensation of professional civil servants. The expectation that such expropriation may happen makes deferred compensation hard and expensive to introduce, as registrars will have to be paid competitive salaries from the beginning (Arruñada 2004b, 389–96). Systems thus often end up in a damaging "revolving door" equilibrium: public-sector salaries attract talented young professionals who leave for the private sector after some years of training. This increases the risk that registries may be "captured": subjugated to the private interests of those professionals interacting with them.

Making these features sustainable for managing registries' human resources therefore requires adopting patterns similar to those found in professional firms. In particular, linking pay to performance and having registries structured as independent agencies and financed by users' fees should make their earnings and compensation policy more independent of the budget cycle, protecting them against budget freezes and, as an added benefit, making their capacity easier to adjust to market demand.

Application to a Poorly Organized Registry of Rights: The US Patent and Trademark Office

The consequences of ignoring many of these organizational patterns can be observed in the poor performance of the US Patent and Trademark Office

(PTO), which, as a registry of intellectual property is, from an organizational viewpoint, more similar to a registry of land rights than to a recorder of deeds. After inventors apply for a patent, claiming that their idea provides a new, useful, and non-obvious solution for a given problem, examiners check these claims, granting the patent only if it meets those requirements and therefore does not collide with the state of the art or, as it is often known in patent law, the "prior art": that set of information that is publicly known when the patent is claimed and is thus pertinent to judge its originality. Furthermore, most jurisdictions have arranged for a "patent opposition" process in which interested parties can bring information pertinent to the granting decision. If a patent is denied, applicants can often redraft their applications more narrowly.

Patent registries thus share several features with real property registries. First, the patent application resembles a request for first registration of land, so that examiners act as registrars do in land registration, checking possible affected rights. For patents, the equivalent of potentially affected rights on land is the prior art in private hands, if previously patented, and in the public domain, if not patented.[34] Affected rightholders are those with a previous patent that would be infringed by the new one or those using knowledge in the public domain that would be privately appropriated by unduly obtaining a patent on it. Procedures are also similar: public announcement of patent applications before the granting decision plays a similar role to the publication of edicts announcing a judicial purge or an application for first registration; subsequent submissions by interested parties denouncing interference with prior art serve the same function as allegations by affected rightholders in a quiet title suit and similar purging proceedings in land; and redrafting a patent application is akin to, for example, redrawing the boundaries of the parcel being registered after an overlap has been detected by the registrar. Lastly, they even share vested interests, as the legal profession is also the main interest group, to the extent that patent lawyers gain from bad granting decisions that increase demand for litigation, similarly to land conveyancers, who also enjoy greater demand for their services when land registries work poorly.

Despite these analogies, patents and real property differ in many respects. For instance, a patent does not grant an absolute right to its holder but its validity can be denied by a judicial decision. This makes sense. In land, first registrations give absolute title only after an exhaustive review that includes audience to potentially affected parties, such as neighbors and past owners. Otherwise, without such exhaustive procedures, what is registered is a possessory right, not ownership; this possessory right only becomes absolute ownership after a certain period without objections having been raised by affected parties. Similarly, given the possibly incomplete nature of the examination, the right defined by a patent is less than absolute. Nevertheless, if a patent has been subject to examination before being granted, it usually enjoys a presumption of validity, meaning that the burden of proof lies with those trying to invalidate it.

The PTO is theoretically organized along these lines, but its examination procedures have become increasingly weak because its political masters seem to hold a mistaken assumption as to its main users, wrongly believing that the PTO must serve only patent applicants and not the public.[35] At some point, the PTO's mission was even changed from "issue valid patents" to "help customers get patents" (Jaffe and Lerner 2004, 137). Consequently, examiners have been encouraged to process applications faster, which often endangers examination quality. For example, the prior art considered is mostly the set of patents already granted, with little attention being paid to nonpatented knowledge and practices. This risk is compounded by the limitations for effective patent opposition by interested parties. The system has therefore been transformed into a de facto recordation system (which, in the intellectual property context, is confusingly called a "registration" system). Nevertheless, to make things worse and despite this weak examination procedure, a US patent still enjoys a presumption of validity, which is hard for alleged infringers to destroy in court because, among other reasons, they should provide "clear and reasonable evidence" proving that it is invalid.

Understandably, these inconsistencies have triggered an explosion of litigation, as the PTO grants numerous patents that interfere with prior art. Bessen and Meurer (2008, 130–45) estimate that firms spend 19 percent of their research and development budgets in defending patent lawsuits. And the system is unpredictable for all parties involved. Even district courts seem unable to predict the interpretation of the Federal Circuit court that sets most patent standards. For instance, the latter reverses the claim constructions of district courts in more than a third of cases (Moore 2005). And lawyers are equally unable to ascertain the scope and validity of patents. Their legal opinions, which cost between 20,000 and 100,000 USD, provide little assurance as to whether firms' technological choices protect them against infringement and are at best effective only to deny the willfulness of infringement. Overall, in many industries, it is impossible for innovators to find out whether they are infringing and to obtain clearance (Bessen and Meurer 2008).

The PTO therefore provides a paradigm of registry mismanagement by showing how registration systems can be transformed into recordation when registrars are encouraged to sacrifice quality and emphasize quantity. The PTO's priority has been that of maximizing its net revenue, an objective easy to achieve by granting patents fast, increasing gross revenue, and, with little review, minimizing PTO's costs; but causing substantial costs to other economic agents in terms of insecure intellectual property. It thus illustrates the tradeoff between, on the one hand, cheaper and worse registration and, on the other, greater litigation later.

The solution is simple but conflicts with powerful private interests: modifying the objective of the agency and the incentives of examiners, reducing their emphasis on quantity, and making it possible for affected rightholders to defend their rights effectively and inform examiners' decisions. Apparently, the difficulty faced by these changes comes only from the opposition of the patent bar, whose demand would be reduced by the improved system (Jaffe and Lerner 2004, 159–69). The long period of time taken for examinations in patent offices (years) when the examination itself only takes a few hours suggests that incentives should be strengthened to avoid the chronic backlog and to speed up decisions. The procedure would benefit from introducing stronger incentives for examiners, giving more weight to variable compensation and introducing some degree of agency and examiners' liability for mistaken decisions. More intense pay for performance should reduce the now exceedingly long examination period, and stronger personal liability should lead to better decisions by patent examiners and align them with those of the courts, thereby reducing litigation.

Reconsidering Self-Interest

In essence, in the above section I was trying to design incentives capable of aligning registrars' incentives with the public good. The same logic can be applied more generally to aligning the private interests of other participants or counterbalancing them for the benefit of the common good.

The analysis developed in previous chapters provides the basis for identifying gaps between private and public interests or, in other words, for exposing the private-interest rationale that lies behind many public-good arguments used to disguise private interests in titling and business formalization discussions. What follows aims to chart some regular manifestations of private interests and encourage comprehensive and impartial treatment in line with the arguments developed in this and previous chapters.

First, building effective formalization institutions tends to be opposed by professionals providing palliative services, in the vein of the opposition to reform showed by US patent lawyers discussed in the previous section.

The most prominent and recurrent case is the opposition of conveyancing lawyers and notaries to the development of land registration systems, which has been documented in many countries. This opposition is understandable, considering that, as argued in the two previous chapters, both recordation and, especially, registration reduce the demand for conveyancing services.

Given this conflict of interests, registries are at permanent risk of being "captured" by the private interests of legal and conveying professionals, whether they are lawyers, notaries, or licensed conveyancers, and, as a consequence, of ceasing to perform their essential functions. This capture is facilitated by the organization of registries as state agencies, with registrars being paid a fixed salary as standard civil servants, which makes them interested in minimizing their workload and, therefore, the scope and functions of the registry, by ceding functions and responsibilities to professionals, even when this is socially inefficient. In this way, registries of rights easily "backslide" into registries of deeds, as analyzed in the previous "Lessons and Possibilities" section with respect to electronic registration. Also fitting this picture are the efforts made by the American Bar Association to define as purely ministerial the role of secretaries of state with respect to company registries, a recommendation that has been partly followed by the states.

To avoid this risk of registries being captured by professionals and to make them sustainable, the powerful incentives of professionals should be counterbalanced with powerful incentives for the registrars, paying them for performance, an arrangement seldom available when using the standard civil-service structure. Applying the line of argument in North, Wallis, and Weingast (2009), paying some rents or quasi-rents to registrars will help to ensure that they work in a viable equilibrium with professionals, especially when the latter also enjoy rents.[36]

Second, reform efforts are also affected by private interests that may cause them to depart substantially from the common good. Some puzzling regularities observed in modern formalization projects are prime suspects in this regard, including specific policy choices such as the following: (1) opting for universal titling in areas where little demand for transactions exists; subsidizing titling efforts, especially in these same areas; (2) advertising the benefits of titling in countries where owners are reluctant to formalize subsequent transactions; (3) subsidizing mapping and surveying land even where these maps and surveys offer questionable utility and are in any case unsustainable; (4) choosing capital-intensive technologies in countries with plenty of labor; and (5) focusing the improvement of the business environment on the registration of companies in countries with very few companies. Moreover, newly created bureaucracies soon evolve into vested interests themselves. A prominent example has been provided by the degeneration of the *Comisión para la Formalización de la Propiedad Informal* (COFOPRI), the Peruvian land formalization agency, as mentioned in chapter 5.

These and other policies, to the extent that they stem from the argument that informality leads to poverty (which I have argued above might well be incorrect), could be interpreted as a privately interested instrumentation of poverty to benefit those providing the different components of such a faulty solution, from the United Nations representatives to aid agencies' bureaucrats, and consultants. The reason for this interpretation is that defining informality as the cause of poverty directly promotes demand for grandiose formalization policies. Conversely, the opposite argument, according to which it is poverty that causes informality, leads to more modest formalization policies and, consequently, to little demand for such providers.

Furthermore, the interaction of old vested interests and new emerging interests poses at least two challenges for policymakers related to how to hold a balanced view on participants and how to avoid an antisocial coalition of old and new interests. The presence of private interests should be treated as natural in all participants. Transaction costs related to private interests are only part of the price we pay for having specialized resources and institutions:[37] one more cost to consider in the quest for efficiency. Manichean visions, especially if reformers focus on only some of these interests, are damaging. They often come about from the proclivity of reformers to see private interests in established operators, while negating them in promoters of reform efforts or suppliers to them. This biased view prevents the information of the excluded experts from being considered in the decision process and provides a ready excuse for failure. Moreover, it often ends up in an awkward coalition of interests when reformers, being unable to achieve any result, reach a falsely modernizing consensus with vested interests: professionals then keep their privileges and rents as the price for letting reformers show off some apparent results, such as speedier procedures or the introduction of new computer systems. Meanwhile, more fundamental deficiencies remain untouched: for instance, the unreliability of registries that increases demand for lawyers and notaries, as well as their mandatory intervention in transactions. A common consequence of such consensuses is to entrench old monopolies into new technologies. This happened, for instance, when reforms introducing electronic conveyancing granted lawyers a privilege in using digital signatures, a technology that could substitute for part of their authenticating activities.

Avoiding these risks of biases and socially damaging coalitions requires policymakers truly interested in the public good and not only in showing apparent results. It requires policymakers who, considering the private interests of all participants, confront these interests to obtain information and rely on consensuses only if they enable rather than preclude meaningful institutional changes.

Third, given the need for a monopoly as the core of the formalization process—the registry—it is natural that not only conveyancers but all kinds of agents who contribute complementary services to private contracting make every effort to extend this monopoly to their own services, by having the law defining such services as a requirement for registration. This likely explains the diversity of requirements observable in mandatory procedures, as different countries may, or may not, require the intervention of, for instance, lawyers for conveyancing services, surveyors for land surveys and maps, or accountants for certifying company accounts. Regarding these requirements, the conclusions obtained in chapter 6 on the regulation of conveyancing lawyers are applicable to the other agents; because these professional services at best only produce legal effects among the parties to the originative contract, parties are in a good position to choose whether to buy the service and from whom.

For example, surveyors help define more precisely the land being transacted by reducing information asymmetry, but this definition is only effective between the parties. It is efficient to make it more or less precise depending on different circumstances—mainly the land's value—but there is generally no need to mandate a single (high) level of definition. This would increase the cost and delay originative transactions without facilitating subsequent transactions, given its lack of effects with respect to third parties. To achieve such effects, an independent agent, whether a court or a registry of rights, would have to verify that all affected parties (mainly, neighboring landowners) consent, making registration much more costly and slow. This independent procedure should be available for parties in need of such a "physical" purge, but the "legal" purge implicit in registration (which should also, in principle, be voluntary) should not be conditioned by such a physical purge. Regulation should therefore make surveyors' intervention voluntary and its provision competitive.

Lastly, politicians find it hard to support sensible, long-term policies because their time horizon is often shorter, something that also plagues international donors. Understandably, they demand and favor policies that promise short-term results. It comes as no surprise that some authors present these institutional reforms as low-effort panaceas for development, ranging from proposals emphasizing the need for "unlocking" capital owned by the poor (De Soto 2000) to those "simplifying" administrative formalities (World Bank 2004–11). These labels suggest that all that is needed is an easy negative action: freeing capital or reducing procedural complexity. Instead, building these institutions demands much harder, positive, and sustained actions, as many of them, especially property registries, often require several decades, if not centuries, to become established. The mismatch between these simplistic approaches and the long-term nature of institutional development helps to explain why a backlash against institutional change often results when these reforms fail to deliver on their inflated promises. It also provides a simple rule of thumb for benevolent policymakers: they should be skeptical about any recommendation promising short-term substantial benefits for the economy.

In the fall of 2010, the main US mortgage lenders all but stopped fore-closure proceedings against their defaulting debtors because of lawsuits al-leging that they had improperly registered mortgage transactions and there-fore lacked a legal right to foreclosure. When the ensuing crisis threatened another collapse of the financial system, which was still recovering from the 2008 meltdown, attentive observers started realizing that contractual regis-tries play a key role in a modern economy. Their lack of previous awareness is far from unique. For more than a century, developed nations have been enjoying these typical institutions of the liberal state, which provide the legal infrastructure for impersonal markets, such as mortgage lending and securitization.

Analysts and policymakers have taken them for granted, focusing their attention instead on newer welfare-state interventions, such as pensions or healthcare. Their disregard for the institutional foundations of markets goes a long way toward explaining why most of the US registries that I have ana-lyzed in this book are stunted, shaky institutions whose functions are partly provided by private palliatives. In land, the public county record offices have been unable to keep up with market demands for speed and uniform legal assurance. Palliative solutions such as title insurance duplicate costs only to provide incomplete *in personam* guarantees or even multiply costs, as Mortgage Electronic Registry Systems (MERS) did by being unable to safely and comprehensively record mortgage loan assignments. In company regis-tries, their lack of ownership information means that they are of little help in fighting fraud, and their sparse legal review implies that US transactions require more extensive legal opinions. In patents, a speed-oriented US Pat-ent and Trademark Office combines with a strongly motivated patent bar to cause an upsurge of litigation of arguably dangerous consequences for innovation.

The 2008 financial crisis unveiled yet another case, as it was exacerbated by weaknesses in the markets for financial derivatives, related to a possible deficit in central clearinghouses and organized exchanges, which also commoditize transactions by eliminating personal characteristics, therefore performing similar functions to contractual registries. Traders in organized exchanges are indifferent about their counterparties' solvency because they do not deal with each other but with the exchange, in contrast with traders in informal over-the-counter (OTC) transactions (Telser 1981; Pirrong forthcoming). Similarly, acquirers of real estate need to worry mainly about the content of the register. In a sense, they do not deal with sellers but with the registry. Unsurprisingly, similar private interests are involved, as both the dealers selling OTC derivatives and conveyancers examining land-title quality and customizing title guarantees are displaced by the more industrial production of, respectively, exchange trading of financial derivatives and truly *in rem*, real, property rights. To overcome the collective action problem in the creation of both organized exchanges and contractual registries, more effective public interventions are necessary.[1]

Behind these weaknesses in public registries lies a misunderstanding about the role of registries in the economy and the proper role of the state in providing services for the registration of private contracts. For markets to function, it is often thought that a minimal state is good. This confuses the liberal-state institutions *supporting* markets with the welfare-state institutions *replacing* markets. Registries are conceived as unnecessary barriers instead of as facilitators of transactions. Such disregard for registries' value and their organizational complexity leads to policies that, by minimizing public registries, give way to the overgrowth of industries providing ineffective palliative services, such as those of lawyers, notaries, title insurers, or financial dealers.

Recapitulation

The alternative view presented in this book is that, far from being unnecessary burdens on market participants or, at most, trivial and easy-to-build depositories of data, functional property and business registries are valuable market facilitators. They are costly and fragile institutions that must be well designed and wisely managed to be effective in reducing transaction costs and thus make truly impersonal (that is, asset-based) exchange possible.

In fully impersonal exchange, parties do not need information on personal characteristics, such as solvency or reputation. Instead, they rely on the exchanged assets themselves. For this reliance to be effective, innocent acquirers must be granted strong property rights on the acquired assets, what the law considers *in rem* rights, valid against everybody, including other potential claimants, even true legal owners.

This concept of strong property rights comes from the legal distinction between property (real, *in rem*) and contract (personal, *in personam*) rights, which has been overlooked in economic analyses of "property rights" but lies at the core of the basic conflict between property enforcement and transaction costs that registries are designed to solve. Rights *in rem*, on things, enjoy an enforcement advantage and are therefore more valuable than rights *in personam*. For land, the difference ranges from full value for the party being adjudicated the land to zero for the one being given a claim against an insolvent person. And for business and corporate assets, similar differences arise in terms of legal priorities.

Given this enforcement advantage, individuals and legal systems rely heavily on rights *in rem*. However, enforcing rights as rights *in rem* endangers either trade or property. If owners are protected *in rem*, aspiring acquirers of rights suffer an informational disadvantage and are subject to the risk of acquiring less than they pay for: they may pay the seller for an asset but eventually obtain only a claim against the seller, while the asset is kept by the owner. On the contrary, if acquirers are protected *in rem*—if, for example, they are given the asset even when the seller was not the owner and lacked authority to sell—it is owners who suffer the risk of being dispossessed.

In principle, this conflict between protecting owners and acquirers, between the *in rem* strength of property and the costs of transacting, is inescapable. Given a certain set of information, if the law were to decide in favor of owners, it would endanger trade, as buyers would be reluctant to buy. Conversely, if the law decided in favor of acquirers, it would endanger property security, and owners would be reluctant to invest and specialize (e.g., to hire agents). At a cost, contractual registries avoid such conflict by producing verifiable information, so that the law can attain both strong enforcement and low transaction costs, benefiting both owners and acquirers. The law thus overcomes the tradeoff of property enforcement and transaction costs by protecting acquirers while preserving the crucial element of owners' (in general, rightholders') consent. This consent is exercised by rightholders either at the time of contracting, by choosing if they want the law to protect property or trade, or by following a course of action that implies one of these two types of protection. Preserving this element of consent is essential to protect property rights and to allow them to be diluted only when owners judge that protecting trade is more valuable than protecting property. But the granting of consent needs to be verifiable by judges, to prevent rightholders from opportunistically denying their previous choices. When these choices are not publicly known as an automatic byproduct of economic activity, independent contract registration is essential to make them verifiable by judges, ensuring that rightholders remain irrefutably committed to their choices.

The theory highlights that independence is an essential attribute of registries. By incurring a registration cost, they make private originative contracts verifiable, allowing courts to apply market-friendly rules to subsequent contracts, thus eliminating parties' information asymmetry and enabling truly impersonal—that is, asset-based—exchange. Registries are not ordinary processes, however, because such asset-based, *in rem*, property rights are valid against everybody and therefore affect not only the transacting parties but also third parties. These third-party effects are quasi-judicial: registries produce undisputable judicial evidence on legal priorities or a final reallocation of rights; their nature is therefore intrinsically public. Private provision of palliative services (not only traditional conveyancing but also title insurance or mortgage registries such as MERS) lacks the independence necessary to be granted public effects. Thus, it falls short of enabling impersonal asset-based exchange.

The theory also provides an analytical toolkit for setting priorities when establishing new registries, both in developing and developed countries. In developing countries, the main risk stems from registry projects that are often premature and poorly designed. The aid industry sells such projects as drivers instead of as contributing factors for economic development, favoring a universal-titling, minimum-average-cost approach that spends gaily on creating huge but unsustainable registries producing low-quality services. To avoid creating such large but weak registries, it would be preferable to follow the economic rationale that can be drawn from past experience. Historically, registries have been developed on a selective, demand-driven, fee-for-service basis, ensuring that the most valuable transactions and assets are registered first and that proper legal quality is achieved.

Similarly, in many developed countries, registries are dysfunctional. If they are to be reliable, there must be both independence from parties and effective processes. Independence can be achieved by making registries territorial monopolies, similar to courts, but, as often happens in the public sector, monopoly endangers effectiveness and calls for strong corrective incentives. Most registries were created more than one hundred years ago and their design and organizational basis have often been debased as a consequence of mismanagement and capture by the private interests of both the registries' own bureaucracies and the palliative industries set up by lawyers and conveyancers. Registry reform therefore requires a drastic change in the incentives of both users and providers, often reinventing old structures such as user fees, public franchising, pay for performance, and the professional career and stricter personal liability of registrars.

The Challenge of Public Registries

Organizing registries therefore is harder than it might seem at first sight. But the rewards are greater than ever due to their enhanced potential, related to technological changes that both increase demand and reduce costs.

This challenge is not new. Throughout history, solutions enabling impersonal exchange have developed unequally across countries and economic activities. Although market-enabling contract rules covering commerce and finance were applied in business trade since the medieval law merchant, it has taken almost ten more centuries to apply similar rules enabling impersonal markets in property and company law.

The difference has mainly been linked to different trade opportunities and, therefore, differential *demand* for institutional change across economic activities and legal areas. But something else must also have been going on, since market-enabling and, in particular, contract rules were applied earlier in areas in which judges could safely base their decisions on the publicity produced as an unintentional byproduct of contractual and economic processes. This gap suggests an additional *supply* explanation: enabling rules are applied later where applying them requires the support of registries.

Indeed, both property and company registries were first proposed by cities and merchants during the Middle Ages, but they were generally created later and often unsuccessfully. As described in the historical references in previous chapters, governments have struggled for almost ten centuries to organize reliable registries that could make enabling rules safely applicable to real property. Similarly, company registries were adopted by most governments only in the nineteenth century, after the Industrial Revolution. Moreover, though most countries have now been running property and company registries for more than a century, only a few have succeeded in making them fully functional, as shown by the fact that in most countries adding a mortgage guarantee to a loan does not significantly reduce its interest rate. Furthermore, registry development has imperfectly matched demand across countries, as illustrated by the late creation of the company register in Britain.

The introduction of registries has been protracted because it involves multiple difficulties, not the least substantial being that their value depends on solving a collective action problem among beneficiaries, because part of the benefits of registering accrue to others. And even functional registries are fragile creatures, as the value of their services disappears altogether when corruption or incompetence lead to fraud, error, or, most often, delays and gaps in registration. They also have to fight against private producers of palliative services (i.e., documentary formalization) who usually prefer weak or dysfunctional registries, as they increase the demand for their services. Moreover, they suffer the added drawback that mainstream law first developed for facilitating personal exchange. Consequently, most legal resources, including not only the human capital of judges, scholars, and law practitioners but also other intangible assets, such as conceptual frameworks and academic curricula, were originally—and to a large extent, still are—adapted to personal exchange. Institutional delay is thus partly caused by path dependency.

Today, these two sets of factors—demand for institutions supporting impersonal market transactions and the difficulties involved in supplying them—are being affected by technological changes that both increase such demand and reduce the costs of contractual registries. On the one hand, communications technologies have made new possibilities for impersonal trade potentially profitable, thus increasing the demand for the institutions, such as registries, that support impersonal trade. On the other hand, computerized databases lower registries' operating costs, telecommunications dramatically facilitate access, and digital signatures not only reduce costs but also enhance security by ensuring parties' agreement without any need for having every contract authenticated by a third party. Economic development therefore hinges, more than ever, on governments' ability to overcome the difficulties and private interests that are holding back the effective registries needed to enable impersonal exchange and exhaust trade opportunities.

NOTES

INTRODUCTION

1. Property enforcement could also be considered a different type of transaction cost, that which is incurred to possess, rather than to trade, resources. For clarity, however, I will label as "transaction costs" only those costs related to trade and not to enforcement.
2. Demsetz (2000) makes this point effectively in connection with his previous works on property rights.
3. See, e.g., Rubin (1995) and Williamson (1996, 2005). In the subject area of the book, it is not so much that the functioning of contracts beyond the "shadow of the law" is disregarded, as argued by Rubin and Williamson, but the possibility that this shadow is made darker.
4. For example, Cooter and Ulen (2008, 159–61); Shavell (2004, 52–55); and Posner (2007, 80–81).

CHAPTER ONE

1. On the importance of impersonal exchange, see mainly North and Thomas (1973), Granovetter (1985), North (1990), Seabright (2004), and, for a more foundational treatment, Hayek (1982).
2. The old hypothesis linking secure property rights and growth (e.g., Smith 1776) was reformulated by North (1981, 1990) and tested by, among many others, Knack and Keefer (1995); Chong and Calderón (2000); Acemoglu, Johnson, and Robinson (2001); and Rodrik, Subramanian, and Trebbi (2002).
3. Moral systems are important in this regard. For instance, current survey data suggest that Protestant values are more supportive of impersonal exchange than Catholic values (Arruñada 2010c). Most parties, however, can do little to modify them, and conversion, in addition to having dubious effects, is out of the question in many situations.
4. See Greif (2002, 2004, 2006a, 2006b).
5. See, for instance, North (1990, 34–35; 1991). See also Wallis (2011), who emphasizes equal treatment of citizens by courts.
6. This sort of legal commoditization effort can also be seen as part of a greater modularization process (see, in general, Simon 1962; and, in law, Smith 2006, 2007, 2008, 2009, and 2011).

7. I focus on the survival-to-adverse-transactions attribute of *in rem* rights because it is central to the function performed by contractual registries. See Merrill and Smith (2001b, 780–89) for an analysis of other attributes, such as the right to exclude others.

8. This is often a consequence not of narrowly defined property law but of specific regulations on, for instance, residential leases that aim to protect current tenants. The mixed property and contract nature of US landlord-tenant law is analyzed by Merrill and Smith (2001b, 820–33).

9. Indicative of this potential equality in asset uses is the practice of naming rights *in personam* as rights *ad rem* (rights *to* things), as opposed to rights *in rem* (rights *in* things).

10. The tradeoff between the strength of one's rights and their transferability at low cost is more or less explicit in, among many others, Calabresi and Melamed (1972), Baird and Jackson (1984), Epstein (1987), Levmore (1987), and Rose (1988), as well as in later works which have mostly focused on the role of the *numerus clausus* of property rights, such as Heller (1999), Merrill and Smith (2000, 2001b), Hansmann and Kraakman (2002), and Dnes and Lueck (2009).

11. This public-versus-private characterization overly simplifies matters. Registries are needed because of "market failure"—i.e., a failure of the hypothetical market of price theory, short of adequate institutions. But governments also fail by often being unable to provide functional registries, a pillar of such institutional support.

12. See mainly North and Thomas (1973), North (1981, 1990), and North, Wallis, and Weingast (2009).

13. This perspective has illuminated a variety of issues, including, among many others, the following: the forces behind the emergence and precision of private property rights, such as increases in the value of resources (Demsetz 1967; Libecap 1978; Smith 2002), the costs of exclusion (Anderson and Hill 1975), and the costs of measuring different resource attributes (Barzel 1997); the political forces behind alternative outcomes from common pool problems (Libecap 1989); informal regimes of common property (Ostrom 1990); specific situations, such as homesteading (Anderson and Hill 1990; Allen 1991) and frontiers (Alston, Libecap and Mueller 1999); particular contractual arrangements, such as sharecropping (Cheung 1969; Allen and Lueck 2003); and a variety of institutional solutions, from first possession (Lueck 1995) to restrictions on alienability (Epstein 1985; Rose-Ackerman 1985; Barzel 1997). Lueck and Miceli (2007) provide a comprehensive survey. Being interested in different issues, such as the boundaries of firms, the mostly unrelated literature pioneered by Grossman and Hart (1986), which is often also given a "property rights" label, focuses on how the allocation of residual claims on assets affects parties' incentives, whereas possible asset transactions with third parties only define parties' bargaining power, a particular problem with no connection to those I am analyzing here.

14. Some aspects of property law are clearly public (e.g., eminent domain) but it mostly deals with private transactions. A sample of property law handbooks reveals that the public element only dominates in at most a quarter of chapters (mainly those dealing with zoning, social policy, forbearance, and takings) and often much less than that.

15. These failures may go a long way to explaining why "economic analysis of property law has not been as welcome among property law scholars as it has been among legal scholars of antitrust, contracts and torts" (Lueck and Miceli 2007, 249). Merrill and Smith (2007, 2010) provide a path-breaking introduction to property law, solidly grounded on economic analysis.

16. This is only a particular case of the proclivity of economic analysis to focus on exceptions, already mentioned in the introduction when explaining that this book will focus on general rules.

17. The identification of ownership with possession (as in, e.g., North 1990, 33; Demsetz 1998, 144) therefore simplifies key elements of the economic system.

18. My analysis of multiple rights includes as a particular case the "anticommons" situation identified by Heller (1998), in which several individuals hold exclusion rights with respect to the same good or the same rights. These are situations of joint entitlement, such as, e.g., multiple ownership. I also consider the effect of the much more numerous cases in which different individuals hold separate and, in principle (i.e., before adverse transactions), nonconflicting rights on the same asset.

19. The relative roles of specialization and enforcement may cause confusion. For example, the work by Dnes and Lueck (2009) on servitudes emphasizes a tradeoff between specialization advantages and information asymmetry. However, in principle, the same specialization advantages could be obtained without causing any additional information asymmetry for future buyers if the land uses defined in the servitudes were enforced *in personam*, as contract rights; the differential advantage of servitudes lies not in specialization but in the fact that they are enforced *in rem*.

20. Note that in economic contract theory "verifiability" generally refers to the observation of contractual performance by third parties and, in particular, by judges. I am referring here to the verifiability of contracts themselves, in particular, to the ability of judges to verify the consent given by principals in originative contracts with respect to the rules (property or contract) that will be applied by judges when adjudicating subsequent contracts.

21. The importance of sequential exchange does not mean, however, that analyses of single transactions are irrelevant. Indeed, all sequential exchange is composed of a series of single transactions. Moreover, when parties are unable to improve the institutions needed to solve title problems, or when these institutions work well, it may be appropriate to focus on the interparty conflicts that characterize such single transactions.

22. For instance, Jensen and Meckling (1976).

23. As analyzed, for instance, by Kaplow and Shavell (1996, 757–63) in a situation of single exchange in which a disputed resource must be allocated between its owner and a second-party taker (instead of an innocent third party) and the liability (instead of contract) rule has this second party compensating the owner.

CHAPTER TWO

1. Criticisms on the positive net social value of secured credit, centered on its negative effects on unsecured and tort-related credit (e.g., Jackson and Kronman 1979; Bebchuk and Fried 1996), miss the point by assuming that unsecured credit is viable and that the allocation of asset ownership remains unaffected by the possibility of using assets as collateral.

2. Ellickson (1993) provides a detailed analysis of the variety of rights voluntarily defined on land. In addition, multiple claims also arise as an unintended consequence of most transactions. Stake (2000) reviews the literature on the decomposition of land rights in common law.

3. The analysis draws on the material presented in Arruñada (2003a).

4. A couple of terminological notes. First, the term "title" may refer to a legal right, as here, or to the evidence of it, often a deed. Any ambiguity is easily clarified by con-

text. Second, for the remaining discussion on real property, I will mostly use intuitive concepts such as "seller," "buyer," "conveying parties" and "affected rightholders" rather than the more generic ones coined in chap. 1, which were necessary to establish equivalencies between property and business transactions. Given the long life of real property, current subsequent transactions are the originative transactions of future subsequent transactions on the same asset. Consequently, the terms "originative" and "subsequent" transactions, which are appropriate in the general context of chap. 1, might be counterintuitive when describing property.

5. Incidentally, this is a reason why the legal construct that equates the transfer of possession—one of the requirements for transferring property in many traditional legal systems—with the granting of a title deed exaggerates the latter's function. Deep down, full ownership against all claimants is not transferred until some other *public* requirements (transferring possession, recording the deed or registering the right) are fulfilled. In the few (necessarily marginal) instances when this is not the case, the rights of third parties may lose enforceability *in rem* and remain prone to fraudulent maneuvers. This still happens, for example, in Spain, with the legal exception allowing a grantee in a nonregistered but previous deed to override a registered judgment lien.

6. For descriptions of the procedures used in these transactions, see, e.g., Sparkes (1999, 76–77 and 479–82).

7. This link between privacy and concentration is consistent with the fact that in the nineteenth century the landed gentry joined the solicitors in successfully opposing the land registry (Anderson 1992), which was finally introduced only on a gradual and geographic basis, starting with the city of London in 1897.

8. See, e.g., Picod (1999, 535), on their opposition before the revolution; Weill (1979, 548), on the opposition of nobles and practitioners to make transfers public in 1804; and Patault (1989, 212), who mentions the strong opposition still existing to the 1855 law.

9. Two further steps are often distinguished in what I call the private contract: (1) the preliminary contract and (2) the agreement or mode of conveyance, which create, respectively, contractual and property claims *between the transacting parties.* (Agreement or mode could also be distinguished as two steps [as in Garro 2004, 56].)

10. See, e.g., §9 of the Hammurabi Code in Levmore (1987, 51).

11. See, e.g., Hoebel (1979, 107, 231) for primitive societies; Finley (1965) for classic Greece and Rome; and Silver (1995) for the Middle East. Debt-slavery practices are still common in West Africa ("Slave-ships in the 21st Century?," *The Economist,* April 19, 2001).

12. See Aghion and Hermalin (1990), as well as Hynes, Malani, and Posner (2004), who provide a historical and empirical analysis of property exemption laws in the United States.

13. See, e.g., Anderson and Hill (2004, 139–41 and 149–51) on how the branding of cattle evolved in the US West.

14. Marriage contracting poses problems and relies on solutions similar to those found in real property. Incentives to invest are affected by information asymmetries caused by possible hidden claims and alternative adjudication rules, related to multiple conflicting rights held by spouses, children, and families on spouses themselves and their wealth. Contracting also takes place in two steps, with the private engagement producing legal consequences only for the parties. It is the public wedding that commits everybody, thanks to its use of an array of devices, including the following:

registries of marital status; publicity by banns and processions; presence of priests who act as notaries, registrars, and gatekeepers; and even a purge of previous claims ("speak now or forever hold your peace"). This publicity allows the law to grant priority to rights arising from formal, nonclandestine marriage, thus providing strong incentives to invest. There has been some evolution toward "contract" marriage, but without any change, for instance, in the treatment of second marriages, which are the equivalent of double sales of land.

15. Posting of notices and advertisements also were used to claim land in the US West (Anderson and Hill 2002, S500).

16. See, for France, Patault (1989, 205–8) and, for some Hanseatic German cities and old Spanish kingdoms, Oliver y Esteller (1892).

17. This happened, e.g., with the Scottish Register of Sasines between 1503 and 1693 (Kolbert and Mackay 1977, 280–84), the French *Conservation des Hypothèques* between 1798 and 1855 (Weill 1979, 547–52), and the Spanish *Contadurías de Hipotecas* between 1768 and 1861 (Oliver y Esteller 1892).

18. Some important caveats are in order. First, this ideal completeness of the public record has often remained unfulfilled because of organizational and legal problems, as exemplified by the traditional problems of land records in the United States (Cross 1957; Straw 1967). Moreover, in most jurisdictions, the priority-of-recording rule applies only to innocent or good-faith acquirers for value, and judges infer that such good faith is lacking when the acquirer knew (had "notice") of the previous transactions, an aspect that is also illustrated by the different systems being applied in different states in the United States (Dukeminier and Krier 1998, 675–77; and Merrill and Smith 2007, 919–23). Finally, acquirers must usually inspect the land to find out about physical possession, as this inspection provides actual notice as to the existence of a claim or right. (Baird and Jackson [1984] summarize the role played by possession in the transfer of property rights in different kinds of assets.) I will sideline these caveats, however, to focus on registries and, generally, on the solutions that facilitate the predominant transactions rather than exceptional ones.

19. See, similarly, Article 291 of the New York Real Property Law and Articles 2146–56 of the French Civil Code.

20. The rationale here is similar to the theory of the *numerus clausus* of property rights in Merrill and Smith (2000), who argue that the possibility that parties might invent idiosyncratic rights *in rem* would raise the information cost and thus the cost of contracting for all other participants (mainly, 26–34).

21. See, on these French reforms, Piedelièvre (2000, 12–14, 34–37, 40–45) and Simler and Delebecque (2000, 659–62 and 670–74).

22. This ambiguity derives from the polysemy of the word "title," which means both deed and right, as explained in n. 4.

23. In jurisdictions with Torrens registries, this is often referred to as "title by registration" (e.g., Stein and Stone 1991, 31). On the difference between publicity of claims in recordation and titling by registration, see, e.g., Méndez González (2008b, mainly 15–28); and Nogueroles Peiró (2008, 861–63).

24. Referring to recordation but in a similar vein, Epstein (1987) asserts, "[t]he basic system of recordation is best understood as an *institutional* response to the structural weaknesses in *any* common-law resolution of the ostensible ownership problem. Common-law solutions attempt to reduce the total loss by assigning it to one party or another. Institutional responses seek to eliminate the loss by a more comprehensive system of social control" (18, emphases in the original).

25. Acquirers often remain unprotected *in rem* by registration against their own sellers, but only third parties are protected, after a further registered transaction, following the principle of "deferred indefeasibility." For instance, if seller *S*, who is not the legal owner, sells land owned by *O* to buyer *B*, who partly finances the purchase with a mortgage loan provided by *L*, and the transaction is registered, the land would be kept by *O*, even if often burdened with the mortgage. The buyer would end up only with a contractual obligation against the seller. In principle, many Torrens registries have curative effects on the transaction itself and thus protect innocent second parties in the position of *B* in the above example. For instance, this doctrine of "immediate indefeasibility" is now established in Australian jurisdictions, even for registration of an instrument that is void for any legal reason (O'Connor 2003), after initial vacillation by the judiciary (Whalan 1982, 293–317). In other jurisdictions, exceptions have often reduced this curative effect. For example, cases of fraud were excluded in Cook County (Shick and Plotkin 1978, 127).

26. Compare, e.g., Shick and Plotkin (1978, 20), who focus on the Torrens version, or Piedelièvre (2000, 20), who considers that registration attacks consensual contractual traditions.

27. The main precedent of modern land registration is the old German institution of *Auflassung*, in which documents on the conveyance were presented and examined by the town council then the court before being noted in a territorial registry (Oliver y Esteller 1892, 86–94). Hints of land registration activities by palaces and temples date from the third millennium BCE in Babylonia (Silver 1995, 126–27), and the state kept a registry of land in Egypt as early as 2350 BCE (Powelson 1988, 17). But the role played by these registries in land allocation, private land conveyance, and taxation is open to discussion.

28. There is controversy as to the origin of the Torrens registration system. Robinson (1979, 11–25) attributes the greatest credit to Ulrich Hübbe, a German lawyer living in South Australia at the time when the system was launched in the 1850s, who would have transplanted methods from the Hanseatic registration system that had been in place in Hamburg for centuries. Whalan spreads the credit more widely and disputes the leading role of Herr Hübbe (Whalan 1982, 5–6, mainly n. 15). Esposito (2003) concludes, based on new sources, that Hübbe was the main drafter of the 1858 Act creating the system, but Taylor (2008) attributes to Torrens the credit for conceiving the principles of the system, drafting the bill, and convincing the public and politicians to support it.

29. On the rationale for the *numerus clausus* principle and its importance, even in common law jurisdictions, see Heller (1999), who points out the role it plays in solving the "anticommons" problem; Merrill and Smith (2000), who argue that it serves to reduce the information costs in transfers of property; and Hansmann and Kraakman (2002), who emphasize the verifiability costs faced by acquirers.

30. See Arruñada (2010d). In general, the argument about the *numerus clausus* is consistent with econometric results, suggesting that registration systems with stricter *numerus clausus* also produce stronger effects (Arruñada 2003a, 416–20, 423).

31. See, e.g., the opinions along these lines of Cribbet (1975, 318); Janczyk (1977); Baird and Jackson (1984, 305); Bostick (1987); and Miceli et al. (2002). Other authors, considering the US experience with Torrens registration, conclude that registration is costlier and less effective (Shick and Plotki 1978). The issues have been controversial almost everywhere. See, for Australia, Whalan (1982, 3–12); England, Anderson

(1992); France, Picod (1999, 535); Spain, Oliver y Esteller (1892); and, for the US controversy of the 1930s, Powell (1938) and McDougal and Brabner-Smith (1939).

32. This can be seen as an example of the "anticommons" analyzed by Michelman (1982); Heller (1998); Heller and Eisenberg (1998); Buchanan and Yoon (2000); Schulz, Parisi, and Depoorter (2002); and Parisi, Schulz, and Depoorter (2005).

33. As Dukeminier and Krier (1998) assert, "title registration puts title assurance in the hands of the government whereas the recording system puts title assurance in private hands using the public records" (721). This might allow recording to produce better information on title quality, supposedly overcoming its information difficulties, as "the private company with a profit motive will do a better job of identifying flaws up front as compared to the government" (Miceli and Sirmans 1995, 86).

34. I will analyze this issue more generally in the second section of chap. 5, "Causes of 'Overtitling' Low-Value Land."

35. For private title plants, relying on their own old title reports is risky because the law may have changed since the previous examination (Johnson 1966, 401). In fact, even if a new insurer is retained in a later transaction, it will frequently examine the full chain of title again. These problems are shown by the diversity of practices and proposals regarding reliance on prior examinations (McCormack 1992, 126) and reissue discounts (Boackle 1997).

36. See ZERP (2007), for the regulation of European notaries; Suleiman (1987) for French notaries; and GAO (2007) and the last section of chap. 6 for US title insurance. Eaton and Eaton (2007) are highly critical of the antitrust immunity enjoyed by US title insurers since 1945, their allegedly rent-extracting practices, and their ability to capture regulators.

37. The costs of building and maintaining title plants are fixed (Lipshutz 1994, 28) and account for up to half the total costs of title insurance companies (Plotkin, cited by Villani and Simonson 1982, 274, n. 6).

38. See FTC (1999) for references to two acquisitions that led to consolidation of title plants in several markets. Divestures were required by antitrust authorities later. The US title insurance industry is heavily concentrated, with the largest four groups holding 87.4 percent of the market share in the first quarter of 2011 (ALTA 2011).

39. Rose (1988) summarizes this tendency graphically when she points out the repeated failed attempts at clarifying property law: "[L]egislatures pass new versions of crystalline record systems—only to be overruled later, when courts once again reinstate mud in a different form" (580). For history and references, see mainly Rose (1988, 585–90). The resistance of judges to apply contract rules appears in many forms and contexts. For instance, New Zealand (and, to a lesser extent, Australian) courts have constructed a fraud exception with apparently little justification in the statute when judging that a rightholder has registered an interest with the intention of defeating an unregistered interest (Blanchard 2003). A further example is provided by the position held by the Paris courts regarding seventeenth-century company registers, discussed in chap. 3.

40. See, e.g., the position of the Forum Group on Mortgage Credit, which recommended that the European Commission "ensure that all charges affecting real estate must be registered in a Public Register in order to be binding on and take effect against third parties, regardless of their nature" (FGMC 2004, 29).

41. This tension between courts and registries is perhaps why some of the most complete registries have traditionally fallen under the responsibility of judges. This happens,

for instance, with the German *Grundbuch* and the land court of Massachusetts, which is responsible for administering its Torrens registry. Interestingly, "unlike other jurisdictions, the Massachusetts courts have not carved out any additional exceptions to the legal conclusiveness of the certificate of title" (Shick and Plotkin 1978, 106). Furthermore, the register is relatively complete with, e.g., mandatory registration of boundaries (Shick and Plotkin 1978, 118).

42. See Kraakman (1986) for a theory of legal gatekeeping.

43. For unregistered land, the Spanish system offered these three options between 1861 and 1944 (Arruñada 2003b).

44. See, respectively, Miceli et al. (2002, 2011) and Arruñada and Garoupa (2005).

45. MERS used to charge $6.95 for every loan registered, compared to about $40 to file a mortgage assignment with a local county (Cassens 2010).

46. See, on the creation of MERS, Slesinger and McLaughlin (1995) and Forte (2007).

47. See Peterson (2010, 1368–72) for descriptions of the different arrangements for contracting and recording mortgages before and after the creation of MERS and with MERS acting either as the first assignee or as the original mortgagee.

CHAPTER THREE

1. The analyses in this chapter are largely based on §§2–6 of Arruñada (2010b).

2. This Roman law rule is fully valid in common law but has been toned down, or even derogated, in many civil law jurisdictions. For a historical approach to good-faith purchasers in different jurisdictions, see, in general, Levmore (1987). Sauveplanne (1965) offers a thorough comparative analysis, and Merryman (2008), as well as Schwartz and Scott (2011), summarize the legal treatment in common and civil law.

3. Protection of the good-faith purchaser in commercial law was already a universal rule in the *lex mercatoria*, since its principles were consolidated from the eleventh to the thirteenth centuries, at a time of great expansion and internationalization of trade (Berman 1983, 348–50). See Murray (1960, mainly 29–34) for ancient law and Benson (1998) for a summary of medieval and modern law merchant. There is, however, substantial discussion about the nature, enforcement mechanisms, and timing of the institutions characteristic of medieval law merchant; e.g., Epstein (2004) and Kadens (2004).

4. Compare, e.g., for Germany, the German Civil Code or *Bürgerliches Gesetzbuch* (BGB), §§932 and 935, with the German Commercial Code or *Handelsgesetzbuch* (HGB), §366.

5. Other typical exceptions violate basic assumptions of the general problem under analysis. This happens in particular for the good faith and knowledge exceptions, which relate to the breakdown of the information asymmetry assumption; and the theft case, which violates the assumption of voluntary agency. Understandably, many jurisdictions, including most of the United States, apply the property rule to commercial purchases of stolen goods, but the contract rule to goods that have been separated through fraud, deceit, or coercion, where a voluntary, though imperfect, element is present.

6. See, e.g., Caruso (2000), as well as Landes and Posner (1996), for a defense of application of the property rule, and Merryman (2008), who argues in favor of granting legal entity status to the register of lost works of art.

7. For example, Article 464 of the Spanish Civil Code, partially amended by Article 61.1 of Law 7/1996 on the organization of retail trade.

8. Therefore, the argument considers the effects of the allocation rules on both property enforcement and transaction costs. These two effects have been extensively analyzed

in the literature on good-faith purchasers (see, e.g., Medina [2003, 344] for an introduction), often under extreme and opposite assumptions minimizing one of the two effects. For instance, many works assume that third parties' willingness to pay remains unaffected by the choice of legal rule since they will also become principals and thus will be affected by both rules. This assumption seems particularly inadequate for situations of voluntary agency (instead of a fraud or theft), as it is principals' decisions that trigger rule switching and it is therefore principals' performance in, for instance, selecting agents that defines the costs they will bear. The relative optimality of rules thus hinges on the comparative ability of merchants to select agents when acting as principals as compared to their ability to select counterparties when acting as acquirers.

9. As argued, e.g., by Weinberg (1980, 588–91), for cases in which there is fraud and the owner's agent behaves incorrectly.

10. The difficulties increase with the complexity of originative contracting, driven by the diversity—owners and managers—and the number of participants involved, as well as the degree of specialization in their functions—mainly, the separation of ownership and control. The reference for the analysis is today's dominant type of business company with many owners, most of whom are not empowered to commit the company. This means that priorities between the firm's and the owners' creditors need to be clearly defined. In the extreme case of what used to be a general partnership under common law, these problems hardly existed. When all the partners may commit the firm and there is little asset partitioning among them or with regard to the firm, they may function on the basis of the de facto publicity provided to third parties by the partners signing on behalf of the partnership. However, this solution is limited to firms with a small number of owners, all of them empowered to commit the firm and, originally, with no asset partitioning. In particular, it provides little organizational flexibility, especially when partners wish to distribute decision-making rights among them in a nonuniform or restricted way (see the comparison between France and the United States below). Safe asset partitioning is also hard to achieve. For instance, in the United States during the first decades of the nineteenth century, there was often litigation involving personal debtors trying to prove the existence of a partnership, even when what really existed was just a pact to share profits (Lamoreaux 1995).

11. For the purpose of clarification, I will examine these three elements sequentially even though they overlap, because of the following: (1) both corporate will and asset partitioning presuppose incorporation; (2) effective asset partitioning is a consequence of the initial endowment of resources at incorporation and the subsequent exercise of the corporate will; and, perhaps most important, (3) incorporation and corporate will most often boil down to asset partitioning in terms of the efficacy of remedies for lack of contractual performance.

12. For example, Articles 7–9 of the 1968 First European Directive 68/151/EEC on Company Law (now Articles 8–10 in Directive 2009/101/EC) are relevant in this respect. Protection is also strong in the United States, since all that is needed for the third party to be protected against possible irregularities is for the corporate secretary to attest that a decision was duly adopted by the board (Cary and Eisenberg 1988, 221–22; Grossfeld 1973, 45; and Lutter 1997, 131–35).

13. The protection afforded to third parties contracting with a corporation when the board of directors goes beyond its powers—*ultra vires*—now varies little from country to country. Traditionally, German legislation afforded the strongest protection since the board's power is unlimited and cannot be restricted (Grossfeld 1973, 39–

45). Article 9.1 of the First European Directive (Article 10.1 in Directive 2009/101/ EC), now implemented across the European Union, establishes that *ultra vires* decisions by corporate organs are binding unless they are illegal, with some countries also requiring that third parties be in good faith and without knowledge. In the United States, it is no longer an issue because of the evolution of both case and statute law (e.g., MBCA §3.04), as well as statutory acceptance of object clauses that allow corporations to engage in any lawful business (MBCA §3.01).

14. Entity shielding is a slightly more complex case because it involves at least three transactions and four parties: personal creditors are the principals in an originative transaction, with at least two subsequent transactions between the borrower and the company, and between the company and its creditors. However, this last transaction is hardly relevant for the analysis, as it can even take place before the originative transaction.

15. See, mainly, the pioneer work by Simon (1962), and, closer to our topic, Smith (2006, 2007, 2008, and 2009).

16. In the past, however, individual merchants often were required to register. Even if one of the aims might have been to facilitate the enforcement of guild rules and restrictions, this registration actually altered merchants' legal status. It was, for instance, used to distinguish between "burghers" and mere inhabitants, who had fewer rights and were required to provide additional safeguards (Kadens 2004, 46–47, n. 34). Registration of merchants therefore played a role in supporting the personal jurisdiction of merchant courts, including their community responsibility as analyzed by Greif (2002, 2004, and 2006a), and it lasted for centuries, until the nineteenth century in most of Europe. For example, it was still required by the Spanish Commercial Code of 1829 to distinguish merchants from nonmerchants, even though this formal criterion had been dropped in practice somewhat earlier (Garrigues 1943, 69 and 182). Even now, it is still required at least in some Latin American countries, including Bolivia, Colombia, and El Salvador (Arruñada 2010a, 304–5).

17. See §§2.01, 2.02, and 3.01 on actual authority and §§2.03 and 3.03 on apparent authority in *Restatement (Third) of Agency* (ALI 2006).

18. See, e.g., World Bank (2004, 17) and Wallis (2011).

19. The term "externality" refers to the positive or negative spillovers that impact third parties when a decision maker, respectively, produces or consumes goods without in principle collecting or paying appropriate compensation, thus lacking proper incentives for producing or consuming what would be the optimal level from a public interest perspective.

20. See Arruñada (2010, 550, n. 35), citing Girón Tena (1955, 130–31; 164–65). The difficulties faced by the French registry are analyzed later in the chapter.

21. Negotiable instruments are also products of the medieval law merchant revolution and were adopted as from the eleventh to the twelfth centuries (Berman 1983, 350–52), even if full negotiability probably only developed in the fifteenth century (Kadens 2004, 41, citing Munro 1994, 58–59 and 71–75). Ellinger (2000) analyzes historical and contemporary practices.

22. See Kötz (1992, 96–97) for an international comparison.

23. See, for instance, Hayek (1982, 44). Also Barzel (2002), who considers mandatory registration of assets and transactions a way to facilitate disputed agreements, with the scope of private registries being limited by the need for neutrality (169, 185–86).

24. See Zingales (2004) for an introduction and Arruñada (2011) for the disclosure of company accounts.

25. Harris's work contradicts a long-standing historiographical tradition. See, e.g., Getzler and Macnair (2005).
26. See Harris (2000) with additional details at 85–109 and, on financing, at 124–27.
27. See, e.g., the "Response of the Paris Court to the *députés de commerce*," May 20, 1748, reproduced in Girón Tena (1955, 195–201).
28. See, e.g., Girón Tena (1955, 127–32); Freedeman (1979, 4); and Kessler (2007, 165).
29. See, in general, Supple (1977) and, especially for France, Kessler (2007).
30. This is in stark contrast with the communitarian spirit present in England at about the same time, allegedly rooted in Calvinist theology and thought to be important for the success of joint-stock companies (Berman 2003, 341–43).
31. My translation from Girón Tena (1955, 200, emphasis added).
32. The *Ordenanzas de Bilbao* were adopted with some exceptions as Spain's commercial law until enactment of the 1829 Commercial Code (González Huebra 1867, 15–16). They regulated much more than just companies, covering most aspects of commerce, and were drawn up and enforced by the merchants' corporation, although their enactment by the Consulate of Bilbao led to litigation that ended in a Royal Provision in 1740 (Petit 1979, 101, 104).
33. Mainly Coase (1937); Alchian and Demsetz (1972); Jensen and Meckling (1976); Williamson (1975, 1985); Klein, Crawford, and Alchian (1978); Grossman and Hart (1986); and Holmstrom and Milgrom (1994).
34. See, e.g., Symposium (1989), as well as Black (1990).
35. Registration is thus understood as a fundamental pillar of corporate law rather than a mere device to inform third parties, as seen, e.g., in Armour and Whincop (2007), who describe it as a complementary strategy for disseminating information to be used in the selective, case-by-case, enforcement of alternative rules, and emphasize the role of the law in supporting property rights against third parties (for the latter, see esp. 451–52).

CHAPTER FOUR

1. See, for instance, the solutions described in the first two sections of chap. 2.
2. De Soto (2006) identifies eighteen archetypes or "patterns of interaction" in Tanzania. Nine (i.e., documentation, collateral, testament, association, redundancy, attestation, representation, standardization, and contract) refer to purely private contracting. Four are means to reduce not transaction costs but contractual outcomes, either final (division of labor and management) or intermediate (transparency and liability), so they play no role in the analysis. The last five arrangements do consist of public solutions. These are as follows: adjudication by third parties who resolve disputes and therefore create property rights (e.g., Council of Elders); village repositories of property and business documents (e.g., Village Council Chairmen, known as *Mwenyekiti*); paper certificates of occupancy title issued by a local marketplace; personal identification documents issued by local authorities; and cattle marking.
3. An important factor was that the legal design of MERS provided a ready excuse for borrowers to delay and often block foreclosure procedures by questioning MERS's standing: because MERS was not the mortgage holder, borrowers claimed that it had no right to foreclose. Advocates for borrowers also complained that, by acting as a representative for lenders, MERS made it difficult for borrowers to get in touch with lenders when seeking to renegotiate their loans individually, as well as to structure wide-scale modification programs. Moreover, the mortgage industry did not help itself when it exhibited systematic failures in its processes, was often unable to rec-

oncile the paper-based public record with its electronic data, and showed disdain for legal niceties, such as its practice of recreating paper loan assignments long after the fact or having employees certify documents they had never seen. For details on the crisis, see COP (2010).

4. In the same crisis, another version of this conflict between legal orders took place between property and commercial law when parties tried to apply principles of commercial law to what are, at least formally, property transactions: e.g., when mortgage notes have been treated as negotiable instruments in securitized transactions.

5. The crisis has even led to proposals for a gradual federalization of land records (Marsh 2011).

6. Current—as opposed to prospective—debtors may find against their interest a system that publicizes land charges and, indirectly, informs on their real indebtedness. This was a serious concern, for instance, for English gentlemen of the nineteenth century at a time when commercial lists of debtors were beginning to be produced (Anderson 1992, 46–47).

7. The good-faith third parties who are unaffected by private contracts are, e.g., company creditors of unregistered companies, personal creditors of their founders, or purchasers of land from the owners on record who have previously sold to persons who did not record their deeds.

8. This is most visible when good-faith third parties are themselves considered to be exceptional. For example, Armour and Whincop (2007) assert that "transactions with third parties that are entered into by directors in breach of their fiduciary duties. . . . may leave the outsider liable either to have an executory contract set aside or to a proprietary claim by the organization for restitution of its property, *unless the counterparty is in good faith and gives value*" (456, emphasis added).

9. For instance, in Spain, deferred indefeasibility of registered property titles was enacted by law with the creation of the land registry in 1861 but was not really enforced until a reform in 1944–46, which also added a requirement of good faith. Arguably, the Supreme Court did not support it fully until 2007 (Méndez González 2008a, 2008b).

10. Focusing on British history, Szreter (2007) argues that developing civil registries had a substantial impact on development and that they are a requisite for other institutions, such as social security or property registries. The UN Commission on Legal Empowerment of the Poor (CLEP) has also advised countries to improve identity registration systems (CLEP 2008a, 60–61) but has focused on more sophisticated institutions. For example, CLEP's working group reports (2007b) covered civil registries in 8 pages but devoted 268 to dispute resolution and property, labor, and businesses' rights. Zeyringer (1995) describes the history, difficulties, and solutions used for registering civil status.

11. Note that this has little to do with generalized mapping of land and drawing of parcel boundaries, which is a much more costly and less justified proposition, as argued in chap. 5.

12. The Msanzi account reached more than six million customers in four years, two-thirds of whom had previously never had a bank account, and thus greatly raised the proportion of people with accounts and was often considered to be a success, even if its stand-alone profitability was in doubt (BFA 2009).

13. See Pagano and Jappelli (1993); Jappelli and Pagano (2000, 2002); Brown, Jappelli, and Pagano (2009); as well as Djankov, McLiesh and Shleifer (2007), who also argue that in less-developed countries credit volume depends more on the availability of information on debtors' quality than on the strength of creditors' rights.

14. See, e.g., Okoth-Ogendo (1999); Wily and Mbaya (2001); and Hunt (2004).
15. Formalization projects were not alone in this failure: broader attempts to promote the "rule of law" have also been disappointing. See the analyses of these attempts in, e.g., Dezalay and Garth (2002); Tamanaha (2004); Carothers (2006); and Trebilcock and Daniels (2008).
16. Only a sample of representative works is mentioned here. For extensive surveys, see Besley (1998), who focuses on the effects on investment; Bruce at al. (2007b) for an evaluation (83–85) and a summary of main works (99–118) with an emphasis on the effects on the poor; and Deininger and Feder (2009) for policy implications.
17. Emphasis on the substantial opportunity costs of land titling is also prominent in Atwood (1990).
18. The Doing Business indicators are a set of annual reports produced by the World Bank that are based on a survey of mostly lawyers whose aim is to quantify the bureaucratic obstacles to business activity. See http://www.doingbusiness.org/ (accessed November 24, 2010), as well as, for a critique, Arruñada (2007a).
19. See on this the discussion on the registration of individual merchants in chap. 3, as well as that in this chapter on the role of civil registries.
20. The historical interpretation by North, Wallis, and Weingast (2009) is apparently close to the formalization argument, a proximity that should not lead to confusion in this regard. They distinguish between "natural state" and "open access" societies. In natural states, elites respect each other's property rights, distribute rents among themselves, and impede access of non-elites to the legal order, including the free formation of organizations. Violence is partly contained by an unstable balance of interests. In contrast, open access is capable of preventing manipulation of economic interests and controlling the state better, which is then in a better position to act as an enforcer and prevent violence. Whatever its merits, their argument also hinges on free entry and not on formalization.
21. For example, the costs of initial business formalization or start-up play practically no role in Alesina et al. (2005), who "look at the effects of regulation on investment in the transport (airlines, road freight, and railways), communication (telecommunications and postal) and utilities (electricity and gas) sectors" (792). To do so, they "measure regulation with different time-varying indicators that capture entry barriers and the extent of public ownership, among other things" (792) and these "[e]ntry barriers cover legal limitations on the number of companies in potentially competitive markets and rules on vertical integration of network industries" (801). This work thus refers to all types of entry barriers. However, it has been interpreted by Djankov (2009) that "Alesina and others (2005) find that *business start-up reforms* have had a significant positive impact on investment in the transport (airlines, road freight, and railways), communication (telecommunications and postal), and utilities (electricity and gas)" (196, emphasis added).
22. As shown, for instance, by the internal evaluation of the World Bank's *Doing Business* indicators (IEG 2008). Consequently, the indicators have been making recurrent mistakes, such as the grossly inflated position of the United States in the "Starting a Business" index (Arruñada 2007a, 743–44).

CHAPTER FIVE

1. See, e.g., Dale and McLaughlin (1999); UN-ECE (2005); and Bruce et al. (2007a and 2007b). The term "sporadic" suggests randomness, though, in fact, it results from rational value-maximizing decisions by owners.

2. See the last two sections of chap. 4, "Evidence on the Effects of Property Titling" and "Evidence on the Effects of Business Formalization."

3. Atwood (1990, mainly 666–68) analyzes different alternatives, pondering their suitability and costs. See also Payne (2002, 18).

4. This fraud was seemingly caused by lenient registration of market participants, so that, after opening accounts, fraudsters then took advantage of lax security to transfer credits from companies' accounts into their own accounts, from which they were immediately sold to third parties ("Carbon Trading: Green Fleeces, Red Faces—A Theft of Carbon Credits Embarrasses an Entire Market," *The Economist*, February 3, 2011).

5. See references in notes 27 and 39 of chap. 3.

6. After decades of ignoring customary rights, their recognition has become common in development programs. For example, CLEP advises the "recognition of a variety of land tenure, including customary rights, indigenous peoples' rights, group rights, certificates, etc., including their standardisation and integration of these practices into the legal system" (2008a, 60). Recognizing such customary rights may or may not be efficient, but it seems contradictory with other recommendations made by the same commission, especially those for universal titling and for establishing "simplified procedures to register and transfer land and property" (2008a, 60). Customary rights are complex, and recognizing them as property rights makes titling less simple and more costly. In the vein of the preceding section, the need for such recognition could also be understood as a sign that the titling effort is premature.

7. The unit costs incurred for physical identification in the seven projects on which sufficient detail is given in Burns (2007, 94–95) amount to 38.74 percent of total costs, whereas costs are 37.17 percent for other activities and 24.09 percent for administration and management. Allocating the proportional share of administration and management, the costs for physical identification increase to 53.45 percent. Physical identification includes the following tasks: building a geodetic network, developing cartography, investigating boundaries, surveying and marking, and preparing cadastral maps and plans. The remaining 46.55 percent is spent on compiling existing records, publicity, acquiring government equipment, collecting claimant information, mediating in conflicts, controlling quality, legal validation, publicly displaying field results, resolving conflicts, preparing land records, designing cadastral and registry databases, entering data, registering property rights, and issuing titles to beneficiaries.

8. See Libecap and Lueck (2011a). Their seminal empirical work on land demarcation systems (2011b) compares the value of adjacent land in thirty-nine counties of Ohio that, due to an historical accident, were demarcated by metes-and-bounds (MB) or the rectangular survey (RS) around 1784–85. They find that, for otherwise identical land, the RS system is associated with higher land values, more roads, more land transactions, and fewer legal disputes. However, it is unclear to what extent these significant and persistent differences can be attributed to physical land demarcation. In fact, the two sets of parcels differ not only in the demarcation technique but also in the way the land was allocated to settlers.

    The processes for demarcating *and claiming* land in Ohio were different for RS and MB lands. For farmers to obtain RS land, the federal government first surveyed parcels into square 640-acre sections, as the law required, and then made them available to individuals at the local land office, often the county seat. Individuals located a square parcel or collection of squares and obtained title through purchase and registration of the transaction . . . Under MB there was no presurvey by the government and *no external constraint on individual plot demarcation*. Claimants first located a plot of land of any shape, marked its perimeter on trees or other natural or human monuments, filed the claim or "entry" at the local land office (again at the county seat), hired a surveyor to formally measure the boundaries, and then *recorded* the surveyed plot at the land office and received title. (Libecap & Lueck 2011, 433, emphases added)

Therefore, it seems that, where land was demarcated by the RS, settlers were granted specific parcels, guaranteeing no overlaps or conflicting claims. But, where land was demarcated by MB, settlers were given a right to appropriate a certain area, which then was freely chosen by each settler, privately surveyed and recorded, without, in principle, undergoing any purging procedure to avoid overlaps and clear the title. Consequently, whether the observed differences capture the effects of the different demarcation systems or those of alternative allocation and titling procedures is unclear. To isolate both effects, it would have been necessary for the land under MB to have been divided using MB before being granted to settlers, like the land divided under the RS. Therefore, the results obtained by Libecap and Lueck (2011b) probably overestimate the relative importance of physical demarcation by including those of the different allocation procedures used in that case for RS and MB lands. In particular, they might reflect the fact that the boundaries of plots under MB have not been purged and are therefore likely to overlap with those of neighboring plots. In this case, both contracted and reported acreage under MB would systematically overestimate the legal acreage really sold, as parties would try to keep their boundary claims alive. Consequently, the acre prices that they observe under MB would underestimate real prices. This hypothesis is consistent with the fact that they observe such value differences in farmland but not in urban land, whose boundaries are usually more precise. Finally, the case poses the usual doubts in terms of external validity and disregard for fixed costs: e.g., whatever the benefits of an RS system, the cost of introducing it is greater in an area with preexisting property rights.

9. Libecap, Lueck, and O'Grady (2012) use a similar contextual argument to explain the variation in the land demarcation systems adopted in various British colonies.

10. Individual proprietorships do not need contractual registration, as shown in chap. 3.

11. The enforcement of land claims generates not only private but also social costs when transferred from current owners to rightful claimants (in privacy and recordation) or from current owners to wrongful owners (in registration). Nonconsensual transfers are socially costly because they trigger rent seeking and, generally, transaction costs, especially to make future consensual transactions possible and to protect against fraud. For instance, real resources are spent on fabricating frauds and litigating disputes on current ownership. In addition, future land sales become more difficult when titles are unclear. The situation poses the typical problem of excessive care when private benefits are higher than social benefits (e.g., Kaplow and Shavell 1992; Shavell 1997), characterized in a wider context as "excess measurement" by Barzel (1982). Feder et al. (1988) suggest several reasons why the private value of formalization is greater than the social value. Sterk (2008) explains along these lines several exceptions in the application of property rules to both real and intellectual property, exemplified by the tendency of courts to deny injunctive relief in cases of good faith boundary encroachments and to limit such relief in patent and copyright cases.

12. According to the responses to the *Doing Business in 2005* survey, user fees accounted for an average of 32.12 percent of the cost of public titling in 113 countries, with governments financing 63.90 percent and other sources (mostly aid agencies) the re-

maining 3.98 percent. Moreover, user fees financed the whole costs of titling systems in only 23 countries.

13. The United Nations Economic Commission for Europe has proposed an intermediate approach whereby the initial establishment of the registry would be mainly financed from general taxation while user fees would provide for the cost of maintaining the registry in the future (e.g., UN-ECE 1996, 8). But even this intermediate solution is not necessary under voluntary titling when most of the fixed costs of setting up the registry are made variable, as discussed above in this chapter.

14. The inclination to register shown by holders of less secure titles when both registration and recordation are available in the same jurisdiction suggests that the value of titling is generally greater the less clear the title.

15. For the same reason, diluting property rights may cause negative externalities. For example, a number of foreclosures above a certain threshold reduces the value of all houses in a neighborhood (Schuetz, Been, and Ellen 2008), potentially triggering a snowball effect when reduced home values lead to additional foreclosures. Harding, Rosenblatt, and Yao (2009) estimate that each foreclosure reduces the value of neighboring family homes between 0.6 and 1.3 percent, an effect that decreases with distance and is caused by the visual impact of deferred maintenance and neglect; and Campbell, Giglio, and Pathak (2011) estimate that in Massachusetts a foreclosure at a distance of 0.05 miles lowers the price of a house by about 1 percent. Accumulated average reductions may reach up to $159,000 (Immergluck and Smith 2006).

16. See, e.g., Ward's analysis of the Mexican case (1990, 193), and, more generally, Davis (2006, 79–82).

17. The recommendation to subsidize first registration and mapping but to recover recurrent operating costs (as in UN-ECE 2005, 25) is hardly viable unless titling triggers a substantial increase in land values.

18. ILD (2007, 65). In 2006, the World Bank granted an additional loan of twenty-five million dollars, subsequent to a previous one of thirty-eight million that ended in 2004 (*COFOPRI al día*, November 28, 2006; http://tinyurl.com/37jm7zy; accessed November 14, 2010, 1).

19. Mainly EMF (2007); and Low, Sebag-Montefiore, and Dübel (2003).

20. See Low, Sebag-Montefiore, and Dübel (2003, 43–44).

21. See, e.g., Piedelièvre (2000, 17) and Simler and Delebecque (2000, 620–22).

22. They include Trentino-Alto Adige, Trieste, and Gorizia, as well as some areas of Udine, Belluno, Vivenza, and Brescia (Cuccaro 2010, 1).

23. In this context, the response of small entrepreneurs in Lima was revealing in that they claimed they would prefer to be formal. However, when given the opportunity of formalizing for free with the added benefit of being given guidance for the procedures, almost three in four did not formalize their activities (Jaramillo 2009). Less than a third of those who remained informal did so because they did not comply with zoning or safety regulations. In contrast with their claims, the behavior of the rest suggests that they prefer to remain informal.

24. Articles 2.1(d) and 3.5 of the First European Directive 68/151/EEC on company law [Articles 2(d) and 3.6 in Directive 2009/101/EC].

25. See a list of cases in Arruñada (2010b, n. 26).

26. See 16.21(e) in ABA (2008b).

27. See the reports by MLTAG (2005, mainly 47–50); FCEN (2006); and GAO (2006); as well as the US Incorporation Transparency and Law Enforcement Assistance Act (S. 569), available at http://tinyurl.com/35gzhvj (accessed November 14, 2010).

28. In the United States, surveys in fact obtain different results as to the scope of registries' compliance review. According to the Government Accountability Office, the registries of all US states control the availability of company names, forty-five states check articles of incorporation, and thirty-six states check annual reports for conformity with the law, of a total of forty-eight states responding (GAO 2006, 21–23). However, in a survey by the National Association of Secretaries of State, thirty-one states, of a total of thirty-nine states responding, define their filing role as ministerial, two as regulatory, two (including Delaware) as a mix, and five as other (NASS 2007, 23–24).

29. See n. 13 of chap. 3.

30. See Arruñada and Manzanares (2011) for an empirical test.

31. See n. 26.

32. See, e.g., Manning and Hanks (1990) and Armour (2006) and, on the situation in the United States, Booth (2005). A report to the European Commission concluded that "legal capital is criticised for failing to protect creditors: it is a poor indication of the company's ability to pay its debts. The current regime is arguably inflexible and costly" (Winter 2002, 13).

CHAPTER SIX

1. Because most of the chapter focuses on the role of lawyers, including notaries public, in land transactions, I will refer to these professionals as "conveyancers," even if most of the analysis is also applicable to lawyers writing company contracts and to other professionals assisting parties in both land and company contracts, such as, respectively, surveyors and accountants.

2. The analysis in these sections partly draws on the material presented in Arruñada (2007b).

3. Section 12 of the Andorran 1996 Notary Act (*Llei del notariat 28–11–1996*, BOPA, December 27, 1996) and Temporary Rule 2 of the Andorran 1998 Notary Regulation (*Reglament general del notariat 20–2–1998*, BOPA, February 25, 1998).

4. Both improvements have been applied in France since 1955 (*règle de l'effet relatif* and *fichier immobilier*) but not in most of the United States. See, on France, Piedelièvre (2000, mainly 12–13 and 50–55) and Simler and Delebecque (2000, 659–62 and 670–74); and, on the United States, Dukeminier and Krier (1998, 653–57).

5. Complementarily, in countries with recordation of deeds, conveyancers may have been successful in both impeding the introduction of the seemingly most efficient technology (registration) and in rent seeking, therefore enjoying higher fees.

6. This crucial difference is often disregarded for those who focus on the alleged duplication in the transaction review tasks performed by conveyancers and registrars (e.g., Law Commission and HMLR 1998, 253).

7. This seems to follow a historical tendency, because notaries' functions in common law were also broader in the past: see, e.g., Closen and Dixon (1992, 875, n. 10), on how United States notaries prepared and kept copies of documents around 1900; Pulling (1862, 10, n. *u*), on preparation of documents by nineteenth century English notaries; and Brockman (1997), for the case of British Columbia.

8. See Aaron (2008) and BLG (2009) for some benchmark cases in Ontario and British Columbia; and, for a deeper analysis focused on Australia, see Griggs and Low (2011).

9. Digital signatures are cryptographic procedures used to sign electronic documents. I use the terms "digital signature" and "electronic signature" interchangeably. "Elec-

tronic signature" has often been used as a more generic term or to refer to the less secure versions, whereas "digital signature" has been reserved for the most secure cryptographic procedures. For a description of these technologies, see, e.g., Lim (2002).

10. See, e.g., Johnstone (1957, 513) and Dukeminier and Krier (1998, 721).

11. See, e.g., the cases of France in Suleiman (1987, 92–106); Belgium in Raucent (1998, 129); and Spain in Arruñada (2001a).

12. For many years, firms such as International Document Services (http://www.idsdoc .com; accessed July 15, 2011) have been providing online software that serves to prepare mortgage forms that are updated regularly to comply with the requirements of secondary lenders (see, e.g., "Partnership links doc prep and RE," *Origination News*, February 13, 1999).

13. For empirical analyses of this "asymmetric contracting" in other industries, see Arruñada (2000) and Arruñada, Garicano, and Vázquez (2001). Note that the expectation of repeat transactions is unlikely to protect third parties—i.e., strangers to the transaction at hand.

14. Understandably, banks have been prominent in developing authenticating technologies. For instance, DST, an affiliate of a US bank, Zions Bancorporation, became the first licensed Certification Authority in the United States, therefore being a pioneer in providing digital signatures. It was thought at the time that "banks' capital strength, fiduciary tradition, and long involvement with electronic services and data base management create a natural affinity for providing electronic authentication services" (Corwin 1998). DST was later integrated into IdenTrust, a company founded by major financial institutions and allegedly "the global leader in trusted identity solutions . . . [and] the only bank-developed identity authentication system" (http:// tinyurl.com/3ylp6wl; accessed November 18, 2010).

15. Mortgage securitization was a driver of subprime lending (Mian and Sufi 2010) and also resulted in multiple lenders holding rights with different priorities and conflicting interests. Some have argued that, after the bursting of the real estate bubble in 2007, this fragmentation made it more difficult to renegotiate mortgages (e.g., White 2009; Dana 2010), which was necessary to contain foreclosures. Agarwal et al. (2011) estimate that, after default, renegotiation is one-third less likely for securitized loans. It is unclear, however, to what extent the problem is one of fragmentation of property, *in rem*, rights or ill-designed contract rights: even when mortgage servicers have the legal authority to renegotiate, they seem to lack proper incentives to do so.

16. See, e.g., Lankhorst and Nelen (2004, 170–71) for a description of the situation in the Netherlands.

17. See, for France, Paterson, Fink, and Ogus (2003, 208) and Murray (2007, 31–32), and, for British Columbia, Strandlund (2000). On the role of impartiality in the traditional position of notaries public, see Arruñada (1996, 9–10), Malavet (1996), and Knieper (2010). Furthermore, it is important to understand that civil law notaries are not generally used *in addition to* but *in place of* lawyers (compare, e.g., Dale and McLaughlin 1999, 158).

18. Some pioneer judicial rulings were those of the Navarra Appeal Court (Section No. 2), December 17, 2010 (AC 2011\1027), and the Seville Commercial Court No. 2, September 30, 2010 (AC 2010\1550); later overruled by the Seville Appeal Court (Section No. 5), October 7, 2011 (JUR 2011\365269). See also Daley (2010).

19. On wealth dipping, see Eaton and Eaton (2007, 5–6). Miles (2004, especially 27–44) analyzes the difficulties suffered by borrowers when contracting mortgages in Britain. An example of regulation trying to protect consumers are the rules adopted

in November 2008 by the United States Department of Housing and Urban Development (HUD 2008), modifying the changes to the regulatory requirements of the Real Estate Settlement Procedures Act (RESPA), first passed by the US Congress in 1974. The new regulator created by the financial reform of 2010 to protect consumers of financial products is expected to issue simplified disclosure forms for mortgage loans before the middle of 2012. The European Commission has also proposed a Directive [COM (2011) 142 final] defining a "European standardised information sheet (ESIS Model)" with the minimum precontractual information to be given by lenders to home loan borrowers.

20. There are numerous accounts by notaries themselves of this trivialization of their work: see, e.g., López Burniol (1994, 113–149) and Berná and Crehuet (2001, especially 119–122). In the same vein, from outside the profession, Paz-Ares (1995, 48–49), who also explains how little variation was found in the 1990s within a sample of five hundred clauses included in articles of incorporation to constrain the alienability of company shares (48, n. 84).

21. Moreover, intervention by notaries has often been mandatory for other contracts, in addition to real estate conveyancing and company incorporation. For example, authenticating documents for corporate loans entitled Hungarian notaries to 0.1 percent of the sum involved ("Your Papers Please," *The Economist*, November 20, 1997). In another notorious example, Italian notaries not only intervened until 2006 in all sales of used cars, but their prices for real estate transactions were so high that transacting parties often avoided them by the old and cumbersome technique of filing a simulated lawsuit, a primitive technique similar to the English "fine," explained in chap. 2.

22. See Paterson, Fink, and Ogus (2003, 51–57); Monti (2003, 2); and CEE (2005) for the original general effort; as well as ZERP (2007) for a subsequent study focusing on conveyancing.

23. On the possibilities and restrictions faced by US lawyers to act as impartial agents, representing not one but several parties, see Hazard (1978, 56–68), Dzienkowski (1992), as well as an early analysis of the impartial role of some escrow agents in Burke and Fox (1976, 333–45). English solicitors face similar restraints for representing several parties in a conveyance as a consequence of Rule 6 of the Solicitors' Practice Rules 1990 (Law Society 2007, 6–21), but with some exceptions, which require parties' consent, lack of conflict of interest and that the seller is not selling as a builder or developer. There is no conflict of interest in acting for cosellers, for copurchasers, for the seller and seller's mortgagee, or for the purchaser and the purchaser's mortgagee, if the mortgagee is not a private person (Sarton 2000, 23–24). The rule was strengthened in October 1999 and additional rules were introduced at the same time by *The Lenders' Handbook*, a voluntary code of conduct adopted by the association of mortgage lenders to reduce conflicts of interest and instructing conveyancers acting on lenders' behalf in residential conveyances (available at http://www.cml.org.uk/handbook; accessed November 19, 2010).

24. This has happened, e.g., in Spain with respect to notaries since Act 24/2005 on productivity enhancement reforms (*Ley de reformas para el impulso a la productividad*), *Boletín Oficial del Estado*, November 19, 2005); in British Columbia, where only lawyers can lodge instruments using a particular digital signature (Christensen 2004); and in New Zealand with respect to, in practice, only lawyers (Thomas 2003a). Other countries have left access open to all parties who comply with a given set of conditions (see, e.g., the regulation of Ontario, Canada, at OMGCS 2011).

25. Arruñada (2006) applies this argument to professions in general.

26. The most common forms of culpable involvement of Dutch notaries are insufficient questioning when setting up legal entities, lack of due care when executing property deeds, maintaining a misleading appearance, and using third-party accounts as safe havens (Lankhorst and Nelen 2004, 176–79). More cases and regulations are described by Preesman (2008) and Macintyre (2008). It remains unproved whether fraud has increased with liberalization: fraudulent behavior has also been common in countries in which notaries have not been liberalized. For instance, some notaries were prosecuted for participating in money-laundering schemes discovered in the south of Spain (Bejarano 2005; Viúdez 2008).

27. For example, in Spain, chap. 3 of Act 7/1998, on standard form contracts (*Ley sobre condiciones generales de la contratación*), *Boletín Oficial del Estado*, April 14, 1998.

28. On the activities of U.S. competition authorities counseling against restraints on lay provision of closing services, see Schechter and Wilson (2006, 575–76).

29. Topics in this section have been discussed extensively at Arruñada (2001b, 2002, and 2004a). See also GAO (2007).

30. These numbers compute the losses and loss-adjustment expense ratios and are taken from A. M. Best's annual reports on the title industry (e.g., 2010, 4).

31. See, e.g., the product overview at the US website of D&B Worldwide, a major network of business information providers (http://tinyurl.com/34ax94f; accessed November 14, 2010).

32. Another example of this type of private single window is the service provided by firms, such as World-Check, that rely on public sources to build databases on individuals and businesses likely to be engaged in dubious or criminal activities and then sell enhanced due diligence services to clients eager to screen their customers, associates, transactions, and employees for potential risk (World-Check 2010).

CHAPTER SEVEN

1. As described in different sections of chaps. 2 and 4.

2. For a long list of laudatory reviews and an equally long list of critical analyses of De Soto's works, see the references in Ahiakpor (2008). See also Bruce (forthcoming) for an enlightened account of the tendency of policy circles to embrace simplistic solutions.

3. See Arruñada (2007a) and the ensuing replies (Djankov 2008; Arruñada 2009) and, for additional analyses, the references in Arruñada (2009, n. 2).

4. The evaluation of *Doing Business* by the World Bank's own Independent Evaluation Group (IEG 2008) points out so many deficiencies in the application of the methodology that it makes it hard to trust even the numbers obtained. This suspicion has been repeatedly confirmed for such a prominent number as the one given by *Doing Business* for the time needed to start up a business in the United States, for which *Doing Business* departs from its own methodology, artificially reducing it from twenty-six to six days (Arruñada 2009, 559).

5. Partiality also plagues the development of indexes of institutional performance in other areas. For example, because they hide the complex interactions between the measured variables and corporate performance (Bhagat, Bolton, and Romano 2008) and miss key aspects such as the presence of a controlling shareholder (Bebchuck and Hamdani 2009), indexes of corporate governance have been claimed by these authors to be counterproductive.

6. Pioneered by managers such as ITT's Harold Geneen or Ford's Robert McNamara (later at the US Department of Defense), management-by-numbers already showed

its limits at that time: probably its most influential critique, Hayes and Abernathy's article in the *Harvard Business Review*, dates from 1980.

7. For example, *Doing Business* publicized as successful reforms that are in fact failures in at least Afghanistan, Bulgaria, Colombia, El Salvador, and Spain, and drew from them unfounded policy conclusions (Arruñada 2007a, 2009). And the World Bank is not alone in praising failure. For example, the single window created in Spain for small companies was evaluated as an "impressive achievement" by the European Commission (CEE 2004, 6), but the system failed, as will be explained below.

8. These initiatives have proliferated in parallel in several international organizations, such as the OECD (2003, 2006); the European Commission, with its "Charter for Small Enterprises," drawn up in 2000 (CEE 2008); and the World Bank, with its *Doing Business* indicators (2004–11).

9. For example, 70 percent of informants to the World Bank's *Doing Business* survey were private sector lawyers (IEG 2008, 15).

10. The Millennium Challenge Account, a mechanism devised by the United States to channel aid to developing countries, used a battery of indicators to identify the countries that most deserved aid, which was then given with few strings attached (MCC 2005). Linking aid to performance indicators of business climate has also been advised by the Center for Global Development, an independent think tank (2010).

11. Again, something similar happens in the area of corporate governance, where indexes have been claimed to lead corporations to introduce cosmetic changes in their governance in order to improve their rankings (Bebchuck, Cohen, and Ferrell 2008, 787), as well as to mislead investors and regulators (Rose 2007; Bhagat, Bolton, and Romano 2008).

12. However, my purpose is just to analyze how administrative and contractual formalizations interact. This book is not about administrative formalization, and the objective of this section is not to analyze administrative registries in depth but only with respect to how they interact with contractual registries. This explains why administrative formalization is not given a chapter to itself but is discussed here as one more decision to make when designing or reforming contractual registries.

13. "Cadastre" refers here to a public register identifying for the purpose of taxation each parcel of land, indicating its value and naming the corresponding taxpayer. In land administration, the term is sometimes used as a synonym of registry, and distinguishing among "juridical cadastre," "fiscal cadastre," and "multipurpose cadastre" (e.g., Dale and McLaughlin 1999), the latter being the sort of integrated agency that encompasses both contractual and administrative registries and is the subject of this section. Both contractual and administrative registries are legal constructs and are therefore equally "juridical," another label often used to describe mainly property registries.

14. This is especially so for registries of rights as seen in the survey of forty-three national land administration systems prepared by UN-ECE (2000). Allocating the registry to a land ministry or similar department also generates conflicts of interest, as such departments often act as both landholders and land managers.

15. This helps to explain why even authors who argue that land administration systems should provide complete information on all rights on land and manage land use, tenure, and development, claim that different land interests should be registered in different ways, with less valuable rights, such as those held by government to access and manage land, run in separate administrative registries with the information being made available by using communication technology (e.g., Bennet, Wallace, and Williamson 2008a, 2008b).

16. The analysis in this section summarizes the main points in Arruñada (2010a, 307–20), where several real cases are analyzed in some depth.

17. See, e.g., a list of the 221 electronic forms available at the New Zealand land registry at http://tinyurl.com/2usmdjr (accessed November 14, 2010).

18. What follows is largely based on my analysis of the reforms adopted in Ontario and New Zealand, as well as those planned in England and Australia (Arruñada 2010d, 116–18), where I examine the possibilities for substitution between the tasks performed by humans and computers in different titling systems and the main tradeoffs that these possibilities involve.

19. To avoid the greater possibilities for fraud created by electronic conveyancing, some analysts have called for restricting access to registered professionals and having them certify the identity and authority of parties (e.g., Christensen 2004). This might be safer than giving such rights to a broader class of specialists but not safer than allowing direct interaction between the rightholders and the registry. In particular, professionals' access facilitates two forms of fraud: identity fraud by third parties, especially when rightholders are not required to sign, and direct fraud by conveyancers who may abuse their certification powers (Low 2006).

20. See Christensen (2004) and Low (2005) for summaries of these and other systems.

21. A joint recommendation issued by the New Zealand registry agency, LINZ, and its Law Commission confirms this danger, as it would allow courts to reverse immediate indefeasibility and would make mortgagees responsible for verifying the identity of mortgagors. In their joint proposal for a new land transfer act, their advice was to "confirm the current system of immediate indefeasibility upon registration, but modify it by introducing judicial discretion as a means of avoiding manifest injustice in limited cases." They also recommended that "the title of a mortgagee should be defeasible if the mortgagee fails to take reasonable steps to check the identity of mortgagor and the mortgage was executed by a person without lawful authority" (NZLC 2010, 4). See Thomas (2011) for a critical analysis.

22. See "¿Qué haría si un día se da cuenta de que su casa, lote o finca *ya no le pertenece?* [What would you do if one day you realize your house, plot or estate no longer belongs to you?]," http://www.propiedadsegura.com (accessed November 14, 2010).

23. However, at least one UK law firm has started providing additional protection by placing restrictions at the Land Registry, so that the firm's consent is required for any dealings with the land ("Gatekeeper: Title Theft Protection," http://www.gatekeeper protection.co.uk/; accessed July 27, 2011). It has been accused of scaremongering and charging hefty fees: owners could file their own restrictions for a fraction of the cost (Lyndon 2011).

24. For complementary analyses of the economics of bureaucracy, see Niskanen (1968), Kaplan and Atkinson (1989, 531–33), and Jensen and Meckling (2009).

25. A pioneering example of this type of reform was the introduction in 1990 of an internal market in the British National Health Service, which assigned fund-holding and purchasing functions to general practitioners with a view to introducing competition among within-system providers (e.g., Enthoven 1991; Bartlett and Le Grand 1993; SSH 2010).

26. See, e.g., the responses to a public consultation by the Land Registry (2003, 95).

27. See O'Connor (2009), as well as the "Feasibility Study Regarding Land Registry" (http://tinyurl.com/2bdf4k6; accessed December 19, 2010). In this vein, ministerial responsibility for the Land Registry was moved on July 18, 2011, from the Ministry of Justice to the Department for Business, Innovation and Skills.

28. For a description of the organization of Spanish registrars, see Nogueroles Peiró (2006); a similar hybrid organization—that of notaries public—was analyzed in Arruñada (1996).

29. See, e.g., the difficulties and eventual failure suffered by reformers who in 2011 tried to introduce stronger incentives and greater competition in British public services ("The Profit Motive: Where Lucre is Still Filthy" and "The NHS: Sweetened Pill, No Cure," *The Economist*, May 19 and June 16, 2011).

30. Jensen and Meckling (2009) explore the key role played by the difficulties for controlling quality when setting up different types of divisions within organizations.

31. See, e.g., Rubin (1978) and Blair and Lafontaine (2005).

32. See, for an example, Cour des comptes (2008, 452). When the registry is not allowed to charge for registration refusals, some applicants tend to abuse the system through repeated applications in legally doubtful cases. A decreasing price scale would probably make more sense, to the extent that the cost of repeatedly examining modified versions of the same transaction also decreases.

33. Article 30 of the *Loi 2009-1674 du 30 décembre 2009 de finances rectificative pour 2009* and *Ordonnance* 2010-638.

34. See Bessen and Meurer (2008, 46–72) for an analysis of the role of boundaries in patents that includes a comparison with real property. Their reform proposal emphasizes the need to improve notice by defining patent boundaries better.

35. My description of how the PTO works is based on Jaffe and Lerner (2004), reinterpreting their analysis in the conceptual language of the book. The PTO was originally created as a recording system, without any review prior to granting the patent, but it was soon transformed into an "examination" system. Since 1836, applications have been reviewed and granted only if they meet substantive requirements of novelty, usefulness, and the like. In addition, the US system also has some features of a privacy regime: e.g., it gives priority to the first to invent, while elsewhere priority is given to the first to file.

36. This solution is also in line with Barzel's argument about how paying fixed salaries to state bureaucrats places state enforcement at a disadvantage (2002, 69 and 159).

37. As emphasized, e.g., by Barzel (1997, 14).

CONCLUDING REMARKS

1. The financial reform bill passed by the US Congress in July 2010 moved in this direction by regulating the OTC derivatives market, requiring routine transactions to be traded on exchanges and routed through clearinghouses, as well as customized swaps to be reported to central repositories (mainly, Title VII of the Dodd-Frank Wall Street Reform and Consumer Protection Act).

REFERENCES

A. M. Best Research. 2010. "Results Partially Recover in 2009 and 2010; Job Market to Influence 2011." *A. M. Best Special Report*, December 13. http://bit.ly/v6s9ja (accessed November 30, 2011.

Aaron, Bob. 2008. "House Fraud Decision Rocks Industry: Bank 'Did Not Take Steps to Scrutinize the Power of Attorney,' Judge Rules." *Toronto Star*, January 5.

ABA (American Bar Association), Committee on Corporate Laws. 2008a. *Model Business Corporation Act Annotated*. 4th ed. Chicago: American Bar Association.

———. 2008b. "Changes to the Model Business Corporation Act Providing Increased Transparency." Draft of June 1, 2008. http://bit.ly/tcLjOm (accessed October 16, 2009).

Acemoglu, Daron, Simon Johnson, and James Robinson. 2001. "The Colonial Origins of Comparative Development: An Empirical Investigation." *American Economic Review* 91:1369–401.

Agarwal, Sumit, Gene Amromin, Itzhak Ben-David, Souphala Chomsisengphet, and Douglas D. Evanoff. 2011. "The Role of Securitization in Mortgage Renegotiation." Federal Reserve Board of Chicago Working Paper 2011–02.

Aghion, Philippe, and Benjamin E. Hermalin. 1990. "Legal Restrictions on Private Contracts Can Enhance Efficiency." *Journal of Law, Economics, and Organization* 6:381–409.

Ahiakpor, James C. W. 2008. "Mystifying the Concept of Capital: Hernando de Soto's Misdiagnosis of the Hindrance to Economic Development in the Third World." *The Independent Review: A Journal of Political Economy* 13. http://tinyurl.com/3xjnd60 (accessed December 14, 2008).

Akerlof, George A. 1970. "The Market for 'Lemons': Quality Uncertainty and the Market Mechanism." *Quarterly Journal of Economics* 84:488–500.

Alchian, Armen A., and Harold Demsetz. 1972. "Production, Information Costs, and Economic Organization." *American Economic Review* 62:777–95.

———. 1973. "The Property Rights Paradigm." *Journal of Economic History* 33:16–27.

Alesina, Alberto, Silvia Ardagna, Giuseppe Nicoletti, and Fabio Schiantarelli. 2005. "Regulation and Investment." *Journal of the European Economic Association* 7:791–825.

ALI (American Law Institute). 2006. *Restatement (Third) of Agency*. St. Paul: ALI.

Allen, Douglass W. 1991. "Homesteading and Property rights; or, 'How the West Was Really Won.'" *Journal of Law and Economics* 34:1–23.

Allen, Douglas W., and Dean Lueck. 2003. *The Nature of the Farm: Contracts, Risk and Organization in Agriculture*. Cambridge: MIT Press.

Alston, Lee J., Gary D. Libecap, and Bernardo Mueller. 1999. *Titles, Conflict and Land Use: The Development of Property Rights and Land Reform on the Brazilian Frontier.* Ann Arbor: University of Michigan Press.

Alston, Lee J., Gary D. Libecap, and Robert Schneider. 1996. "The Determinants and Impact of Property Rights: Land Title on the Brazilian Frontier." *Journal of Law, Economics and Organization* 12:25–61.

ALTA (American Land Title Association). 2000. "Real Estate Closings by Non-Attorneys or Title Agents/Title Insurers." Mimeo. Washington, DC: ALTA.

———. 2011. "Comparative Family/Company Summary (1st Quarter 2011 vs. 1st Quarter 2010)." http://www.alta.org/industry/financial_TeMp.cfm (accessed July 15, 2011).

Anderson, J. Stuart. 1992. *Lawyers and the Making of English Land Law, 1832–1940.* Oxford: Clarendon Press.

Anderson, Terry L., and Peter J. Hill. 1975. "The Evolution of Property Rights: A Study of the American West." *Journal of Law and Economics* 18:163–80.

———. 1990. "The Race for Property Rights." *Journal of Law and Economics* 33:177–97.

———. 2002. "Cowboys and Contracts." *Journal of Legal Studies* (issue 2, part 2) 31:S489–S514.

———. 2004. *The Not So Wild, Wild West: Property Rights on the Frontier.* Stanford: Stanford University Press.

Anderson, Terry L., and Dean Lueck. 1992. "Land Tenure and Agricultural Productivity on Indian Reservations." *Journal of Law and Economics* 35:427–54.

Armour, John. 2006. "Legal Capital: An Outdated Concept?" *European Business Organization Law Review* 7:5–27.

Armour, John, and Michael J. Whincop. 2007. "The Proprietary Foundations of Corporate Law." *Oxford Journal of Legal Studies* 27:429–65.

ARNECC (Australian Registrars National Electronic Conveyancing Council). 2011. "Proposed Electronic Conveyancing National Law." Discussion Paper, May 24. http://bit.ly/tX1ujP (accessed November 30, 2011).

Arruñada, Benito. 1996. "The Economics of Notaries." *European Journal of Law and Economics* 3:5–37.

———. 2000. "The Quasi-Judicial Role of Large Retailers: An Efficiency Hypothesis of their Relation with Suppliers." *Revue d'economie industrielle* 92:277–96.

———. 2001a. "Pasado, presente y futuro del notariado." *Folio Real: Revista Peruana de Derecho Registral y Notarial* 2:135–53.

———. 2001b. "A Global Perspective on Title Insurance." *Housing Finance International* 16:3–11.

———. 2002. "A Transaction-Cost View of Title Insurance and its Role in Different Legal Systems." *The Geneva Papers of Risk and Insurance* 27:582–601.

———. 2003a. "Property Enforcement as Organized Consent." *Journal of Law, Economics, and Organization* 19:401–444.

———. 2003b. "Vías de acceso al Registro de la Propiedad: La experiencia española." *Revista Crítica de Derecho Inmobiliario* 79:3271–89.

———. 2004a. "El seguro de títulos de propiedad." *Revista Crítica de Derecho Inmobiliario* 80:53–141.

———. 2004b. *Sistemas de titulación de la propiedad: Un análisis de su realidad organizativa.* Lima: Palestra.

———. 2006. "Managing Competition in Professional Services and the Burden of Inertia." In C.-D. Ehlermann and I. Atanasiu, eds., *European Competition Law Annual 2004:*

The Relationship between Competition Law and the (Liberal) Professions, 51–71. Oxford and Portland: Hart Publishing.

———. 2007a. "Pitfalls to Avoid when Measuring the Institutional Environment: Is 'Doing Business' Damaging Business?" *Journal of Comparative Economics* 35:729–47.

———. 2007b. "Market and Institutional Determinants in the Regulation of Conveyancers." *European Journal of Law and Economics* 23:93–116.

———. 2009. "How Doing Business Jeopardizes Institutional Reform." *European Business Organization Law Review* 10:555–74.

———. 2010a. *Formalización de empresas: Costes frente a eficiencia institucional*. Cizur Menor, Spain: Thomson Reuters.

———. 2010b. "Institutional Support of the Firm: A Theory of Business Registries." *The Journal of Legal Analysis* 2:525–76.

———. 2010c. "Protestants and Catholics: Similar Work Ethic, Different Social Ethic." *The Economic Journal* 120:890–918.

———. 2010d. "Leaky Title Syndrome?" *New Zealand Law Journal* (April): 115–20.

———. 2011. "Mandatory Accounting Disclosure by Small Private Companies." *European Journal of Law and Economics* 32:377–413.

Arruñada, Benito, Luis Garicano, and Luis Vázquez. 2001. "Contractual Allocation of Decision Rights and Incentives: The Case of Automobile Distribution." *Journal of Law, Economics, and Organization* 17:256–83.

Arruñada, Benito, and Nuno Garoupa. 2005. "The Choice of Titling System in Land." *Journal of Law and Economics* 48:709–727.

Arruñada, Benito, and Carlos A. Manzanares. 2011. "The Tradeoff Between Registration and Transaction Costs: Evidence from Legal Opinions." 15th Conference of the International Society for New Institutional Economics, Stanford University, June 17.

Arruñada, Benito, and Xosé H. Vázquez. 2006. "When Your Contract Manufacturer Becomes Your Competitor." *Harvard Business Review* 84:135–45.

Atwood, David A. 1990. "Land Registration in Africa: The Impact on Agricultural Production." *World Development* 18:659–71.

Ayotte, Kenneth, and Patrick Bolton. 2011. "Optimal Property Rights in Financial Contracting." *Review of Financial Studies* 24:3401–33.

Baird, Douglas G., and Thomas H. Jackson. 1984. "Information, Uncertainty, and the Transfer of Property." *Journal of Legal Studies* 13:299–320.

Bartlett, Will, and Julian Le Grand. 1993. *Quasi-markets and Social Policy*. London: Palgrave Macmillan.

Barzel, Yoram. 1982. "Measurement Cost and the Organization of Markets." *Journal of Law and Economics* 25:27–48.

———. [1989] 1997. *Economic Analysis of Property Rights*. 2d ed. Cambridge: Cambridge University Press.

———. 2002. *A Theory of the State: Economic Rights, Legal Rights, and the Scope of the State*. Cambridge: Cambridge University Press.

Bayer-Pacht, Emily. 2010. "The Computerization of Land Records: How Advances in Recording Systems Affect the Rationale Behind Some Existing Chain of Title Doctrine." *Cardozo Law Review* 32:337–72.

Bebchuk, Lucian A., Alma Cohen, and Allen Ferrell. 2009. "What Matters in Corporate Governance?" *The Review of Financial Studies* 22:783–827.

Bebchuk, Lucian A., and Jesse M. Fried. 1996. "The Uneasy Case for the Priority of Secured Claims in Bankruptcy." *Yale Law Journal* 105:857–934.

Bebchuk, Lucian A., and Assaf Hamdani. 2009. "The Elusive Quest for Global Governance Standards." *University of Pennsylvania Law Review* 157:1263–318.

Becker, Gary S., and George J. Stigler. 1974. "Law Enforcement, Malfeasance, and Compensation of Enforcers." *Journal of Legal Studies* 3:1–18.

Bejarano, José. 2005. "Cajas de seguridad sin secretos." *La Vanguardia*, March 15, 31–32.

Bennett, Rohan, Jude Wallace, and Ian P. Williamson. 2008a. "Organising Land Information for Sustainable Land Administration." *Journal of Land Use Policy* 25:126–38.

———. 2008b. "A Toolbox for Mapping and Managing New Interests Over Land." *Survey Review* 40:43–53.

Benson, Bruce L. 1998. "Law Merchant." In Peter Newman, ed., *The New Palgrave Dictionary of Economics and the Law*, 2:500–508. London: Macmillan.

Berman, Harold J. 1983. *Law and Revolution: The Formation of the Western Legal Tradition*. Cambridge: Harvard University Press.

———. 2003. *Law and Revolution (II): The Impact of the Protestant Reformations on the Western Legal Tradition*. Cambridge: Harvard University Press.

Berná, Joan, and Eladi Crehuet. 2001. *A l'infern de dos en dos: Cartes entre Joan Berná i Eladi Crehuet, notaris*. Pagès: Lérida.

Besley, Timothy. 1995. "Property Rights and Investment Incentives: Theory and Evidence from Ghana." *Journal of Political Economy* 103:903–37.

———. 1998. "Investment Incentives and Property Rights." In Peter Newman, ed., *The New Palgrave Dictionary of Economics and the Law*, 2:359–65. London: Macmillan.

Besley, Timothy, and Stephen Coate. 1995. "Group Lending, Repayment Incentives and Social Collateral." *Journal of Development Economics* 46:1–18.

Bessen, James, and Michael J. Meurer. 2008. *Patent Failure: How Judges, Bureaucrats, and Lawyers Put Innovators at Risk*. Princeton: Princeton University Press.

BFA (Bankable Frontier Associates LLC). 2009. "The Mzansi Bank Account Initiative in South Africa: Final Report." Report commissioned by FinMark Trust, March 20. http://www.finmarktrust.org.za/documents/R_Mzansi_BFA.pdf (accessed December 17, 2009).

Bhagat, Sanjai, Brian Bolton, and Roberta Romano. 2008. "The Promise and Peril of Corporate Governance Indices." *Columbia Law Review* 108:1803–82.

Bhole, Bharat, and Sean Ogden. 2010. "Group Lending and Individual Lending with Strategic Default." *Journal of Development Economics* 91:348–63.

BIS-IOSCO (Bank for International Settlements-International Organization of Securities Commissions). 2001. *Recommendations for Securities Settlement Systems, Consultative Report*. Basel: BIS. http://www.bis.org/publ/cpss42.pdf (accessed November 9, 2001).

Black, Bernard. 1990. "Is Corporate Law Trivial? A Political and Economic Analysis." *Northwestern University Law Review* 84:542–97.

Blair, Roger D., and Francine Lafontaine. 2005. *The Economics of Franchising*. Cambridge: Cambridge University Press.

Blanchard, Peter. 2003. "Indefeasibility under the Torrens System in New Zealand." In David Grinlinton, ed., *Torrens in the Twenty-First Century*, 29–49. Wellington: LexisNexis.

Bledsoe, David. 2006. "Can Land Titling and Registration Reduce Poverty?" In John W. Bruce et al., *Land Law Reform: Achieving Development Objectives*, 143–74. Washington, DC: The World Bank.

BLG (Bolden, Ladner, Gervais). 2009. "*Gill v. Bucholtz*: The British Columbia Court of Appeal and Mortgage Fraud." *Commercial Real Estate Law Alert*, May.

Boackle, Kenneth F. 1997. *Real Estate Closing Deskbook: A Lawyer's Reference Guide & State-By-State Summary*. Chicago: General Practice, Solo and Small Firm Section, American Bar Association.

Bogart, Dan, and Gary Richardson. 2009. "Making Property Productive: Reorganizing Rights to Real and Equitable Estates in Britain, 1660 to 1830." *European Review of Economic History* 13:3–30.

Booth, Richard A. 2005. "Capital Requirements in United States Corporation Law." University of Maryland Legal Studies Research Paper 2005–64. http://ssrn.com/abstract=864685 (accessed February 27, 2008).

Bostick, C. Dent. 1987. "Land Title Registration: An English Solution to an American Problem." *Indiana Law Journal* 63:55–111.

Brasselle, Anne-Sophie, Frederic Gaspart and Jean-Philippe Platteau. 2002. "Land Tenure Security and Investment Incentives: Puzzling Evidence from Burkina Faso." *Journal of Development Economics* 67:373–418.

Braunstein, Michael, and Hazel Genn. 1991. "Odd Man Out: Preliminary Findings Concerning the Diminishing Role of Lawyers in the Home-Buying Process." *Ohio State Law Journal* 52:469–80.

Brockman, Joan. 1997. "'Better to Enlist Their Support than to Suffer Their Antagonism': The Game of Monopoly between Lawyers and Notaries in British Columbia, 1930–81." *International Journal of the Legal Profession* 4:197–234.

Brown, Martin, Tullio Jappelli, and Marco Pagano. 2009. "Information Sharing and Credit Market Performance: Firm-Level Evidence from Transition Countries." *Journal of Financial Intermediation* 18:151–72.

Bruce, John W. Forthcoming. "Simple Solutions to Complex Problems: Land Formalization as a 'Silver Bullet.'" In Jan M. Otto and Andre Hoekema, eds., *Fair Land Governance: How to Legalize Land Rights for Rural Development*. Leiden: Leiden University Press.

Bruce, John W. (Team Leader), Omar Garcia-Bolivar, Tim Hanstad, Michael Roth, Robin Nielsen, Anna Knox, and Jon Schmidt. 2007a. *Legal Empowerment of the Poor: From Concepts to Assessment*. Washington, DC: United States Agency for International Development.

Bruce, John W., Omar Garcia-Bolivar, Michael Roth, Anna Knox, and Jon Schmidt. 2007b. "Land and Business Formalization for Legal Empowerment of the Poor." *Strategic Overview Paper*. Washington, DC: United States Agency for International Development.

Bruce, John W., and Shem E. Migot-Adholla, eds. 1994. *Searching for Security of Land Tenure in Africa*. Dubuque: Kendall/Hunt.

Buchanan, James M., and Yong J. Yoon. 2000. "Symmetric Tragedies: Commons and Anticommons." *Journal of Law and Economics* 43:1–13.

Burke, D. Barlow, and Jefferson K. Fox. 1976. "The *Notaire* in North America: A Short Study of the Adaptation of a Civil Law Institution." *Tulane Law Review* 50:318–45.

Burns, Tony. 2007. "Land Administration Reform: Indicators of Success and Future Challenges." Agriculture and Rural Development Discussion Paper 37. Washington, DC: The World Bank.

Buxbaum, Richard M. 1974. *The Formation of Marketable Share Companies*, In Alfred Conard, chief ed., *Business and Private Organizations*, chap. 3. Vol. 13 in *International Encyclopedia of Comparative Law*. Tubingen: Mohr Siebeck.

Cabrillac, Michel, and Christian Mouly. 1997. *Droit des sûretés*, 4th ed. Paris: LITEC (Libraire de la Cour de cassation).

Calabresi, Guido, and A. Douglas Melamed. 1972. "Property Rules, Liability Rules, and Inalienability: One View of the Cathedral." *Harvard Law Review* 85:1089–128.

Campbell, John Y., Stefano Giglio, and Parag Pathak. 2011. "Forced Sales and House Prices." *American Economic Review* 101:2108–31.

Carothers, Thomas, ed. 2006. *Promoting the Rule of Law Abroad: In Search of Knowledge*. Washington, DC: Carnegie Endowment for International Peace.

Carter, Michael, and Pedro Olinto. 2003. "Getting Institutions 'Right' for Whom? Credit Constraints and the Impact of Property Rights on the Quantity and Composition of Investment." *American Journal of Agricultural Economics* 85:173–86.

Caruso, Peter J., II. 2000. "To Buy or Not to Buy: Protecting Yourself from Stolen Art." *Arts Editor*, August. http://www.artseditor.com/html/august00/aug00_law.shtml (accessed February 2, 2009).

Cary, William L., and Melvin A. Eisenberg. 1988. *Cases and Materials on Corporations*. 6th ed. Westbury: Foundation Press.

Cassens Weiss, Debra. 2010. "Was Mortgage Registration System Built on 'Foundation of Sand'?" *ABA Journal*, October 19.

CEE (Commission of the European Communities). 2004. *Report from the Commission to the Council and the European Parliament on the Implementation of the European Charter for Small Enterprises*, February 2, COM(2004) 64 final. Brussels: CEE.

———. 2005. *Professional Services—Scope for More Reform*, September 5, COM(2005) 405 final. Brussels: CEE.

Celentani, Marco, Miguel García-Posada, and Fernando Gómez-Pomar. 2009. "The Spanish Corporate Bankruptcy Puzzle and The Crisis." FEDEA Working Paper, October.

Center for Global Development. 2010. "A Doing Business Facility: A Proposal for Enhancing Business Climate Reform Assistance." The Supporting Business Climate Reforms Working Group: Advancing Africa's Private Sector Series (Todd Moss, Chair), Washington, DC, March. http://www.cgdev.org/content/publications/detail/1423783 (accessed August 23, 2010).

Cha, Ariana Eunjung, and Brady Dennis. 2010. "Aggressive Lobbying Defends Mortgage-Trading System." *Washington Post*, November 18.

Channell, Wade. 2007. "Uses and Abuses of Doing Business Indicators." Washington, DC: United States Agency for International Development, Economic Growth Officers Workshop. http://www.businessenvironment.org/dyn/be/docs/149/Channell.pdf (accessed March 13, 2009).

Cheung, Steven N. S. 1969. *The Theory of Share Tenancy*. Chicago: University of Chicago Press.

Chong, Alberto E., and César A. Calderón. 2000. "Causality and Feedback between Institutional Measures and Economic Growth." *Economics and Politics* 12:69–81.

Christensen, Sharon. 2004. "Electronic Land Dealings in Canada, New Zealand and the United Kingdom: Lessons for Australia." *Murdoch University Electronic Journal of Law* 11. http://bit.ly/sFS4EM (accessed November 25, 2008).

Clark, Robert C. 1986. *Corporate Law*. Boston: Little, Brown and Company.

Clay, Karen. 1997. "Trade without Law: Private-Order Institutions in Mexican California." *Journal of Law, Economics, and Organization* 13:202–31.

CLEP (Commission on Legal Empowerment of the Poor). 2008a. *Making the Law Work for Everyone*. Vol. 1. New York: United Nations.

———. 2008b. *Making the Law Work for Everyone*. Vol. 2, Working Group Reports. New York: United Nations.

Closen, Michael L., and G. Grant Dixon, III. 1992. "Notaries Public from the Time of the Roman Empire to the United States Today, and Tomorrow." *North Dakota Law Review* 68:873–96.

CMN (Commissie Monitoring Notariaat). 2003. *Eindrapport Periode 1999–2003*. The Hague: Ministerie van Justitie.

CNG (Conseil National des Greffiers des Tribunaux de Commerce). 2010. "The National Council of Business Registrars and Commercial Courts." http://www.cngtc.fr/english.php (accessed June 5, 2010).

Coase, Ronald H. 1937. "The Nature of the Firm." *Economica* 4:386–405.
———. 1960. "The Problem of Social Cost." *Journal of Law and Economics* 3:1–44.
Coing, Helmut. 1996. *Derecho privado europeo, tomo II: El siglo XIX*. Translated by Antonio Pérez-Martín. Madrid: Fundación Cultural del Notariado.
Cointat, Christian. 2002. "Rapport d'information sur l'évolution des métiers de la justice." No. 345, Sénat, session extraordinaire de 2001–2002, July 3.
Companies House. 2009. *Annual Report and Accounts 2008/09*. London: The Stationery Office. http://www.companieshouse.gov.uk/about/pdf/annrep2008_9.pdf (accessed June 5, 2010).
Coornaert, Emile. L. J. 1967. "European Economic Institutions and the New World: The Chartered Companies." In E. E. Rich and C. H. Wilson, eds., *The Cambridge Economic History of Europe*, 4:220–74. Cambridge: Cambridge University Press.
Cooter, Robert D., and Thomas Ulen. 2008. *Law & Economics*. 5th ed. Boston: Pearson.
COP (Congressional Oversight Panel). 2010. *Examining the Consequences of Mortgage Irregularities for Financial Stability and Foreclosure Mitigation*, November 16. http://cop.senate.gov/documents/cop-111610-report.pdf (accessed November 19, 2010).
Copp, Stephen. 2002. "Company Law and Alternative Dispute Resolution: An Economic Analysis." *The Company Lawyer* 23:361–75.
Corwin, Phillip S. 1998. "Notaries in Cyberspace: A New Role for Banks." *American Banker* 163:4.
Cour des comptes. 2008. "Les conservations des hypothèques." In *Rapport public annuel*, February 6, 435–56. Paris: Cour des comptes.
———. 2009. "Les conservations des hypothèques." In *Rapport public annuel*, February 4, 109–12. Paris: Cour des comptes.
Cribbet, John E. 1975. *Principles of the Law of Property*. 2d ed. Mineola: Foundation Press.
Cross, Harry M. 1957. "The Record 'Chain of Title' Hypocrisy." *Columbia Law Review* 57:787–800.
Cuccaro, Michele. 2010 *Lineamenti di diritto tavolare*. Milan: Giuffrè Editore.
Dale, Peter F., and John D. McLaughlin. 1999. *Land Administration*. Oxford: Oxford University Press.
Daley, Suzanne. 2010. "In Spain, Homes Are Taken but Debt Stays." *New York Times*, October 27.
Dana, David A. 2010. "The Foreclosure Crisis and the Anti-Fragmentation Principle in State Property Law." *University of Chicago Law Review* 77:97–120.
Davis, Mike. 2006. *Planet of Slums*. London: Verso.
De Soto, Hernando. 2000. *The Mystery of Capital: Why Capitalism Triumphs in the West and Fails Everywhere Else*. New York: Basic Books.
———. 2006. "The Challenge of Connecting Informal and Formal Property Systems." In Hernando de Soto and F. Cheneval, eds., *Realizing Property Rights*, 18–67. Berne: Rüffer & Rub.
De Soto, Hernando, Enrique Ghersi, Mario Ghibellini, and Instituto Libertad y Democracia. 1986. *El otro sendero: la revolución informal*. Lima: El Barranco. (English ed.: De Soto, Hernando. 1989. *The Other Path: The Invisible Revolution in the Third World*. New York: Harper & Row).
Deininger, Klaus, and Gershon Feder. 2009. "Land Registration, Governance, and Development: Evidence and Implications for Policy." *The World Bank Research Observer* 24:233–66.
DeLong, James V. 1997. *Property Matters: How Property Rights Are under Assault—And Why You Should Care*. New York: Free Press.

Demsetz, Harold. 1967. "Toward a Theory of Property Rights." *American Economic Review* 57:347–59.

———. 1998. "Property Rights." In Peter Newman, ed., *The New Palgrave Dictionary of Economics and the Law*, 3:144–55. London: Macmillan.

———. 2000. "Dogs and Tails in the Economic Development Story." In Claude Ménard, ed., *Institutions, Contracts and Organizations: Perspectives from New Institutional Economics*, 69–87. Cheltenham: Edward Elgar.

Dezalay, Yves, and Bryant Garth, eds. 2002. *Global Prescriptions: The Production, Exportation and Importation of a New Legal Orthodoxy*. Ann Arbor: University of Michigan Press.

DGRN (Dirección General de los Registros y del Notariado). 1998. *Anuario de la Dirección General de los Registros y del Notariado*. Madrid: Ministerio de Justicia.

Di Tella, Rafael, Sebastián Galiani, and Ernesto Schargrodsky. 2007. "The Formation of Beliefs: Evidence from the Allocation of Land Titles to Squatters." *Quarterly Journal of Economics* 122:209–41.

Diamond, Arthur S. 1975. *The Evolution of Law and Order*. Westport: Greenwood Press (1st ed.; London: Watts, 1951).

Djankov, Simeon. 2008. "A Response to 'Is Doing Business Damaging Business.'" http://www.doingbusiness.org/features/response_to_arrunada.aspx (accessed September 26, 2008).

———. 2009. "The Regulation of Entry: A Survey." *The World Bank Research Observer* 24:183–203.

Djankov, Simeon, Rafael La Porta, Florencio Lopez-de-Silanes, and Andrei Shleifer. 2002. "The Regulation of Entry." *Quarterly Journal of Economics* 117:1–37.

Djankov, Simeon, Caralee McLiesh, and Andrei Shleifer. 2007. "Private Credit in 129 Countries." *Journal of Financial Economics* 84:299–329.

Dnes, Antony W., and Dean Lueck. 2009. "Asymmetric Information and the Law of Servitudes Governing Land." *Journal of Legal Studies* 38:89–120.

Do, Quy Toan, and Lakshmi Iyer. 2008. "Land Rights and Economic Development: Evidence from Vietnam." *Economic Development and Cultural Change* 56:531–79.

DOJ (Department of Justice). 1999. "Letter to Board of Governors, Kentucky Bar Association." Washington, DC: US Department of Justice, June 10. http://www.usdoj.gov/atr/public/comments/3943.pdf (accessed June 30, 2004).

Dower, Paul, and Elizabeth Potamites. 2007. "Signaling Credit-Worthiness: Land Titles, Banking Practices and Access to Formal Credit in Indonesia." Mimeo. New York: New York University Department of Economics, July 3.

Dukeminier, Jesse, and James E. Krier. 1998. *Property*. 4th ed. New York: Aspen Law and Business.

Dzienkowski, John S. 1992. "Lawyers as Intermediaries: The Representation of Multiple Clients in the Modern Legal Profession." *University of Illinois Law Review* 741–817.

Easterbrook, Frank H., and Daniel R. Fischel. 1991. *The Economic Structure of Corporate Law*. Cambridge: Harvard University Press.

Eaton, Joseph W., and David J. Eaton. 2007. *The American Title Insurance Industry: How a Cartel Fleeces the American Consumer*. New York: New York University Press.

Ellickson, Robert C. 1993. "Property in Land." *Yale Law Journal* 102:1315–400.

Ellickson, Robert C, and Charles D. Thorland. 1995. "Ancient Land Law: Mesopotamia, Egypt, Israel." *Chicago-Kent Law Review* 71:321–411.

Ellinger, Peter. 2000. "Negotiable Instruments." In Jacob S. Ziegel, chief ed., *Commercial Transactions and Institutions*, chap. 4. Vol. 9 in *International Encyclopedia of Comparative Law*. Tubingen: Mohr Siebeck.

EMF (European Mortgage Federation). 2007. *Study on the Efficiency of the Mortgage Collateral in the European Union.* Brussels: EMF.

English Registration Act. 1844. "An Act for the Registration, Incorporation, and Regulation of Joint Stock Companies. (5th September 1844)." In *A Collection of the Public General Statutes Passed in the Seventh and Eighth Year of the Reign of her Majesty Queen Victoria, 1844.* London: Owen Richards.

Enthoven, Alain C. 1991. "Internal Market Reform of the British National Health Service." *Health Affairs* 10:60–70.

Epstein, Richard. 1985. "Why Restrain Alienation?" *Columbia Law Review* 85:970–90.

———. 1987. "Inducement of Breach of Contract as a Problem of Ostensible Ownership." *Journal of Legal Studies* 16:1–41.

———. 1995. *Simple Rules for A Complex World.* Cambridge: Harvard University Press.

———. 2004. "Reflections on the Historical Origins and Economic Structure of the Law Merchant." *Chicago Journal of International Law* 5:1–20.

Esposito, Antonio K. 2003. "Ulrich Hübbe's Role in the Creation of the 'Torrens' System of Land Registration in South Australia." *Adelaide Law Review* 24:263–303.

EUTFLT (European Union Task Force on Land Tenure). 2004. "EU Land Policy Guidelines: Guidelines for Support to Land Policy Design and Land Policy Reform Processes in Developing Countries." European Commission, Directorate General for Development, November. http://tinyurl.com/30tzp2w (accessed July 27, 2011).

FCEN (Financial Crimes Enforcement Network). 2006. *The Role of Domestic Shell Companies in Financial Crime and Money Laundering: Limited Liability Companies.* Washington, DC: Department of the Treasury. http://fincen.gov/LLCAssessment_FINAL.pdf (accessed May 14, 2009).

Feder, Gershon, Tongroj Onchan, Yongyuth Chalamwong, and Chira Hongladarom. 1988. *Land Policies and Farm Productivity in Thailand.* Baltimore: Johns Hopkins University Press.

Feder, Gershon, Tongroj Onchan, and Tejaswi Raparla. 1988. "Collateral, Guarantees and Rural Credit in Developing Countries: Evidence from Asia." *Agricultural Economics* 2:231–45.

Feder, Gershon, and Akihito Nishio. 1998. "The Benefits of Land Registration and Titling: Economic and Social Perspectives." *Land Use Policy* 15:25–43.

Fernández del Pozo, Luis. 2008. "La publicidad registral de las sociedades civiles profesionales en el Registro Mercantil." *Revista de Derecho Mercantil* 267:7–59.

FGMC (Forum Group on Mortgage Credit). 2004. *The Integration of the EU Mortgage Credit Markets.* Brussels: European Commission, Directorate General for the Internal Market.

Field, Erica. 2004. "Property Rights, Community Public Goods and Household Time Allocation in Urban Squatter Communities." *William and Mary Law Review* 45:837–87.

———. 2005. "Property Rights and Investment in Urban Slums." *Journal of the European Economic Association Papers and Proceedings* 3:279–90.

———. 2007. "Entitled to Work: Urban Property Rights and Labor Supply in Peru." *Quarterly Journal of Economics* 122:1561–602.

Finley, Moses I. 1952. *Studies in Land and Credit in Ancient Athens, 500–200 B.C.: The Horos-Inscriptions.* New Brunswick: Rutgers University Press.

———. [1965] 1981. "Debt-Bondage and the Problem of Slavery." In M. I. Finley, *Economy and Society in Ancient Greece,* 150–66. London: Chatto & Windus. Originally published in *Revue historique de droit français e étranger* (1965) 43:159–84.

Fleisig, Heywood W., Juan Carlos Aguilar, and Nuria de la Peña. 1997. "Legal Restrictions on Security Interest Limit Access to Credit in Bolivia." *International Lawyer* 31:65–110.

Forte, Joseph P. 2007. "A MERS Primer." In American Law Institute-American Bar Association, The ACREL Papers, Fall. http://tinyurl.com/391pxv4 (accessed November, 21, 2010).

Freedeman, Charles E. 1979. *Joint-Stock Enterprise in France, 1807–1867: From Privileged Company to Modern Corporation*. Chapel Hill: University of North Carolina Press.

Freidman, Joseph, Emmanuel Jimenez, and Stephen Mayo. 1988. "The Demand for Tenure Security in Developing Countries." *Journal of Development Economics* 29:185–98.

FTC (Federal Trade Commission). 1999. *Annual Report to Congress. Fiscal Year 1998*. Washington, DC: Department of Justice Antitrust Division. http://www.ftc.gov/bc/hsr/98annrpt/hsr98annual.htm (accessed June 2, 2001).

Gabrielli, Giovanni. 1992. "La pubblicità legale nel sistema del codice civile." *Rivista di Diritto Civile* (Part 1) 38:455–80.

Galiani, Sebastián, and Ernesto Schargrodsky. 2004. "The Health Effects of Land Titling." *Economics and Human Biology* 2:353–72.

———. 2010. "Property Rights for the Poor: Effects of Land Titling." *Journal of Public Economics* 94:700–29.

GAO (United States Government Accountability Office). 2006. *Company Formations: Minimal Ownership Information Is Collected and Available*. Report to the Permanent Subcommittee on Investigations, Committee on Homeland Security and Governmental Affairs, US Senate, April, GAO.06-376.

———. 2007. *Title Insurance: Actions Needed to Improve Oversight of the Title Industry and Better Protect Consumers*. Report to the Ranking Member, Committee on Financial Services, US House of Representatives, April, GAO-07-401.

Garrigues, Joaquín. 1943. *Instituciones de derecho mercantil*. Madrid: S. Aguirre.

Garro, Alejandro M. 2004. "Recordation of Interests in Land." In A. Yiannopoulos, chief ed., *Property and Trust*, chap. 8. Vol. 6 in *International Encyclopedia of Comparative Law*. Tubingen: Mohr Siebeck.

Gazzoni, Francesco. 1998. *La trascrizione immobiliare*. 2d ed. Milan: Giuffrè.

Getzler, Joshua, and Mike Macnair. 2005. "The Firm as an Entity before the Companies Acts: Asset Partitioning by Private Law." In Paul Brandt, Kevin Costello, and W. N. Osborough, eds., *Adventures of the Law: Proceedings of the 16th British Legal History Conference—Dublin, 2003*, 267–88. Dublin: Four Courts Press. http://www.law.cam.ac.uk/docs/view.php?doc=2365 (accessed February 2, 2009).

Girod, Paul. 2002. "Rapport sur le projet de loi portant réforme des tribunaux de commerce." No. 178, Sénat, Session extraordinaire de 2001–2002, January 23.

Girón Tena, José. 1955. "Las sociedades irregulares." *Anuario de Derecho Civil*, Tome 4 (1951). Reproduced in *Estudios de derecho mercantil*, 125–201. Madrid: Editorial Revista de Derecho Privado.

González Huebra, Pablo. 1867. *Curso de derecho mercantil*. 3d ed. Madrid: Librería Sánchez.

Granovetter, Mark. 1985. "Economic Action and Social Structure: The Problem of Embeddedness." *American Journal of Sociology* 91:481–510.

Greif, Avner. 2002. "Institutional Foundations of Impersonal Exchange: From Communal to Individual Responsibility." *Journal of Institutional and Theoretical Economics* 158:168–204.

———. 2004. "Impersonal Exchange without Impartial Law: The Community Responsibility System." *Chicago Journal of International Law* 5:109–38.

———. 2006a. "The Birth of Impersonal Exchange: The Community Responsibility System and Impartial Justice." *Journal of Economic Perspectives* 20:221–36.

———. 2006b. *Institutions and the Path to the Modern Economy*. New York: Cambridge University Press.

Griggs, Lynden, and Rouhshi Low. 2011. "Identity Fraud and Land Registration Systems: An Australian Perspective." *Conveyancer and Property Lawyer* 75:285–308.

Grossfeld, Bernhard. 1973. *Management Control of Marketable Share Companies*, In Alfred Conard, chief ed., *Business and Private Organizations*, chap. 3. Vol. 4 in *International Encyclopedia of Comparative Law*. Tubingen: Mohr Siebeck.

Grossman, Sanford J., and Oliver Hart. 1986. "The Costs and Benefits of Ownership: A Theory of Lateral and Vertical Integration." *Journal of Political Economy* 94:691–719.

Gruson, Michael, and Stephan Hutter, eds. 1993. *Acquisition of Shares in a Foreign Country: Substantive Law and Legal Opinions*. London: Graham & Trotman and International Bar Association.

Hansmann, Henry, and Reinier Kraakman. 2000. "The Essential Role of Organizational Law." *Yale Law Journal* 110:387–440.

———. 2002. "Property, Contract, and Verification: The *Numerus Clausus* Problem and the Divisibility of Rights." *Journal of Legal Studies* 31:S373-S420.

Hansmann, Henry, Reinier Kraakman, and Richard Squire. 2006. "Law and the Rise of the Firm." *Harvard Law Review* 119:1333–403.

Harding, John P., Eric Rosenblatt, and Vincent W. Yao. 2009. "The Contagion Effect of Foreclosed Properties." *Journal of Urban Economics* 66:164–78.

Harris, Ron. 2000. *Industrializing English Law: Entrepreneurship and Business Organization, 1720–1844*. Cambridge: Cambridge University Press.

Hayek, Friedrich A. von. 1945. "The Use of Knowledge in Society." *American Economic Review* 35:519–30.

———. [1973–1979] 1982. *Law, Legislation, and Liberty: A New Statement of the Liberal Principles of Justice and Political Economy*. Chicago: University of Chicago Press (reprint; London: Routledge & Kegan Paul). Page references are to reprint edition.

Hayes, Robert H., and William J. Abernathy. 1980. "Managing Our Way to Economic Decline." *Harvard Business Review* 85:138–149.

Hazard, Geoffrey C. 1978. *Ethics in the Practice of Law*. New Haven: Yale University Press.

Heller, Michael A. 1998. "The Tragedy of the Anticommons: Property in the Transition from Marx to Markets." *Harvard Law Review* 111:621–88.

———. 1999. "The Boundaries of Private Property." *Yale Law Journal* 108:1163–223.

Heller, Michael A., and Rebecca S. Eisenberg. 1998. "Can Patents Deter Innovation? The Anticommons in Biomedical Research." *Science* 280:698–701.

Henley, Benjamin J. 1956. "Historical Highlights of ALTA®: The First 50 Years." *Title News*, November. Reproduced in *Title News* 86, January/February 2006. http://www.alta.org/publications/titlenews/07/01_01.cfm (accessed July 27, 2011).

Hermalin, Benjamin E., Avery W. Katz, and Richard Craswell. 2007. "Contract Law." In A. Mitchell Polinsky and Steven Shavell, eds., *Handbook of Law and Economics*, 1:3–138. Amsterdam: Elsevier.

Hoebel, E. Adamson. [1954] 1979. *The Law of Primitive Man: A Study in Comparative Legal Dynamics*. New York: Atheneum (1st ed.; Cambridge: Harvard University Press).

Hoffman, Philip T., Gilles Postel-Vinay, and Jean-Laurent Rosenthal. 2000. *Priceless Markets: The Political Economy of Credit in Paris, 1660–1870*. Chicago: University of Chicago Press.

Holmstrom, Bengt, and Paul Milgrom. 1994. "The Firm as an Incentive System." *American Economic Review* 84:972–91.

Holstein, Lynn C. 1993. "Review of Bank Experience with Land Titling and Registration." Mimeo. Washington, DC: World Bank.

HUD (United States Department of Housing and Urban Development). 2000. "Buying Your Home: Settlement Cost and Useful Information." Washington, DC: HUD. http://www.hud.gov/fha/sfh/res/sfhrestc.html (accessed June 3, 2001).

———. 2008. "Real Estate Settlement Procedures Act (RESPA): Rule To Simplify and Improve the Process of Obtaining Mortgages and Reduce Consumer Settlement Costs; Final Rule, 24 CFR Parts 203 and 3500." *Federal Register* 73, November 17.

———. 2000. "Buying Your Home: Settlement Cost and Useful Information." Revised version: July 2000 (first version: June 1997). Washington, DC: HUD.

Hunt, Diana. 2004. "Unintended Consequences of Land Rights Reform: The Case of the 1998 Uganda Land Act." *Development Policy Review* 22:173–91.

Hynes, Richard M., Anup Malani, and Eric A. Posner. 2004. "The Political Economy of Property Exemption Laws." *Journal of Law and Economics* 47:19–43.

Hynes, Richard, and Eric A. Posner. 2002. "The Law and Economics of Consumer Finance." *American Law and Economics Review* 4:168–207.

ICANN (Internet Corporation for Assigned Names and Numbers). 1999. "Uniform Domain-Name Dispute-Resolution Policy," August 26. http://www.icann.org/udrp/udrp.htm (accessed July 4, 2011).

IEG (Independent Evaluation Group; The World Bank). 2008. *Doing Business: Independent Evaluation (Taking the Measure of the World Bank/IFC Doing Business Indicators)*. Washington, DC: World Bank, June 15. http://bit.ly/uJSQma (accessed September 20, 2008).

ILD (Instituto Libertad y Democracia). 2007. *La guerra de los notarios*. Lima: ILD. http://www.ild.org.pe/download.php (accessed March 7, 2007).

Immergluck, Dan, and Geoff Smith. 2006. "The External Costs of Foreclosure: The Impact of Single-Family Mortgage Foreclosures on Property Values." *Housing Policy Debate* 17:57–79.

Iyer, Lakshmi, and Noel Maurer. 2009. "The Cost of Property Rights: Establishing Institutions on the Philippine Frontier Under American Rule, 1898–1918." Harvard Business School Working Paper 09–023.

Jackson, Thomas H., and Anthony T. Kronman. 1979. "Secured Financing and Priorities Among Creditors." *Yale Law Journal* 88:1143–82.

Jackson, Thomas C. 1908. *Justinian's Digest (Book 20) with an English Translation and an Essay on the Law of Mortgage in the Roman Law*. London: Sweet and Maxwell.

Jacoby, Hanan G., and Bart Minten. 2007. "Is Land Titling in Sub-Saharan Africa Cost-Effective? Evidence from Madagascar." *World Bank Economic Review* 21:461–85.

Jaffe, Adam B., and Josh Lerner. 2004. *Innovation and Its Discontents: How Our Broken Patent System Is Endangering Innovation and Progress, and What To Do About It*. Princeton: Princeton University Press.

Janczyk, Joseph T. 1977. "An Economic Analysis of the Land Systems for Transferring Real Property." *Journal of Legal Studies* 6:213–33.

Jappelli, Tullio, and Marco Pagano. 2000. "Information Sharing in Credit Markets: The European Experience." University of Salerno, Centre for Studies in Economics and Finance Working Paper 35.

———. 2002. "Information Sharing, Lending and Defaults: Cross-Country Evidence." *Journal of Banking and Finance* 26:2017–45.

Jaramillo, Miguel. 2009. "Is There Demand for Formality among Informal Firms? Evidence from Microfirms in Downtown Lima." German Development Institute Discussion Paper 12.

Jensen, Michael C., and William H. Meckling. 1976. "Theory of Firm: Managerial Behavior, Agency Costs and Ownership Structure." *Journal of Financial Economics* 3:305–60.

———. 2009. "Specific Knowledge and Divisional Performance Measurement." *Journal of Applied Corporate Finance* 21:49–57.

Jimenez, Emmanuel. 1984. "Tenure Security and Urban Squatting." *Review of Economics and Statistics* 66:556–67.

Johnson, Harry M. 1966. "The Nature of Title Insurance." *Journal of Risk and Insurance* 33:393–410.

Johnstone, Quintin. 1957. "Title Insurance." *Yale Law Journal* 66:492–524.

Jong, Jitske de. 1998. "Access to Geo-information in the Netherlands: A Policy Review." In J. Zevenbergen, *Free Accessibility of Geo-Information in the Netherlands, the United States and the European Community*. Delft: Delft University Press.

Kadens, Emily. 2004. "Order within Law, Variety within Custom: The Character of the Medieval Merchant Law." *Chicago Journal of International Law* 5:39–66.

Kahneman, Daniel, and Amos Tversky. 1979. "Prospect Theory: An Analysis of Decision Under Risk." *Econometrica* 47:263–91.

Kaplan, Robert S., and Anthony A. Atkinson. 1989. *Advanced Management Accounting*. 2d ed. Englewood Cliffs: Prentice-Hall.

Kaplow, Louis, and Steven Shavell. 1992. "Private versus Socially Optimal Provision of Ex Ante Legal Advice." *Journal of Law, Economics, and Organization* 8:306–20.

———. 1996. "Property Rules Versus Liability Rules: An Economic Analysis." *Harvard Law Review* 109:713–90.

Katz, Avery. 1990. "Your Terms of Mine? The Duty to Read the Fine Print in Contracts." *RAND Journal of Economics* 21:518–33.

Kaufmann, Jürg, and Daniel Steudler. 1998. *Cadastre 2014: A Vision for a Future Cadastral System*. Rheinfall: International Federation of Surveyors. http://www.fig.net/cadastre2014/translation/c2014-english.pdf (accessed January 2, 2009).

Ker, Henry Bellenden. 1837. *Report on the Law of Partnership*. London: House of Commons.

Kerekes, Carrie B., and Claudia R. Williamson. 2010. "Propertyless in Peru, Even with a Government Land Title." *American Journal of Economics and Sociology* 69:1011–33.

Kessler, Amalia D. 2007. *A Revolution in Commerce: The Parisian Merchant Court and the Rise of Commercial Society in Eighteenth-Century France*. New Haven: Yale University Press.

Klapper, Leora, Luc Laeven, and Raghuram Rajan. 2006. "Entry Regulation as a Barrier to Entrepreneurship." *Journal of Financial Economics* 82:591–629.

Klein, Benjamin, Robert G. Crawford, and Armen A. Alchian. 1978. "Vertical Integration, Appropriable Rents, and the Competitive Contracting Process." *Journal of Law and Economics* 21:297–326.

Knack, Stephen, and Philip Keefer. 1995. "Institutions and Economic Performance: Cross-Country Tests Using Alternative Institutional Measures." *Economics and Politics* 1:207–28.

Knieper, Rolf. 2010. *An Economic Analysis of the Notarial Law and Practice*. Munich: C. H. Beck.

Kohler, Jürgen. 1996. "The Law of Rights *in Rem*." In Werner F. Ebke and Matthew W. Finkin, eds., *Introduction to German Law*, 227–50. The Hague: Kluwer.

Kolbert, Colin F., and Norman A. M. Mackay. 1977. *History of Scots and English Land Law* (based on *The Principles of Scots and English Land Law* by Charles d'Olivier Farran). Berkhamsted: Geographical Publications.

Konig, David T. 1974. "Community Custom and the Common Law: Social Change and the Development of Land Law in Seventeenth-Century Massachusetts." *American Journal of Legal History* 18:137–77.

Korngold, Gerald. 2009. "Legal and Policy Choices in the Aftermath of the Subprime and Mortgage Financing Crisis." *South Carolina Law Review* 60:727–48.

Korobkin, Russell. 2003. "Bounded Rationality, Standard Form Contracts, and Unconscionability." *University of Chicago Law Review* 70:1203–95.

Kostadinov, Petar. 2008. "Corporate ID Worries: Managers Still Fear Losing their Property through Fraud." *Sofia Echo*, November 28. http://sofiaecho.com/2008/11/28/665096_corporate-id-worries (accessed November 30, 2009).

Kötz, Hein. 1992. *Rights of Third Parties: Third Party Beneficiaries and Assignment.* In Arthur von Mehren, chief ed., *Contracts in General*, chap. 13. Vol. 7 in *International Encyclopedia of Comparative Law.* Tubingen: Mohr Siebeck.

Kraakman, Reinier H. 1986. "Gatekeepers: The Anatomy of a Third-Party Enforcement Strategy." *Journal of Law, Economics, and Organization* 2:53–105.

Kuijpers, Nicole, Joëlle Noailly, and Ben Vollaard. 2005. "Liberalisation of the Dutch Notary Profession: Reviewing its Scope and Impact." Centraal Planbureau (CPB, Netherlands Bureau for Economic Policy Analysis), Discussion Paper 93, September. http://www.cpb.nl/nl/pub/cpbreeksen/document/93/doc93.pdf (accessed March 7, 2006).

La Porta, Rafael, Florencio Lopez-de-Silanes, and Andrei Shleifer. 2008. "The Economic Consequences of Legal Origins." *Journal of Economic Literature* 46:285–332.

Lamoreaux, Naomi R. 1995. "Constructing Firms: Partnerships and Alternative Contractual Arrangements in Early-Nineteenth-Century American Business." *Business and Economic History* 24:43–71.

Lamoreaux, Naomi R., and Jean-Laurent Rosenthal. 2005. "Legal Regime and Contractual Flexibility: A Comparison of Business's Organizational Choices in France and the United States during the Era of Industrialization." *American Law and Economics Review* 7:28–61.

———. 2006. "Entity Shielding and the Development of Business Forms: A Comparative Perspective." *Harvard Law Review Forum* 119:238–45.

Land Registry. 2003. "E-Conveyancing: A Land Registry Consultation Report." London, March 17. http://www1.1andregistry.gov.uk/assets/library/documents/eccir.pdf (accessed August 25, 2009).

———. 2008. "Framework Document." London, December. http://bit.ly/sfyF3D (accessed June 5, 2010).

Landes, William M., and Richard A. Posner. 1996. "The Economics of Legal Disputes Over the Ownership of Works of Art and Other Collectibles." In Victor A. Ginsburgh and Pierre-Michel Menger, eds., *Economics of the Arts: Selected Essays*, 177–220. Amsterdam: North Holland.

Lanjouw, Jean, and Philip Levy. 2002. "Untitled: A Study of Formal and Informal Property Rights in Urban Ecuador." *Economic Journal* 112:986–1019.

Lankhorst, Francien, and Hans Nelen. 2004. "Professional Services and Organised Crime in the Netherlands." *Crime, Law and Social Change* 42:163–88.

Law Commission and Her Majesty's Land Registry. 1998. *Land Registration for the Twenty-First Century: A Consultative Document.* London: The Stationery Office.]http://www1.1andregistry.gov.uk/upload/documents/lc254.pdf (accessed November 12, 2011).

Law Society. 2007. "Solicitors' Practice Rules 1990. Professional Ethics." Last amended 12 January 2007. London: Law Society. http://tinyurl.com/pyr8h (accessed November 26, 2011).

Levmore, Saul. 1987. "Variety and Uniformity in the Treatment of the Good-Faith Purchaser." *Journal of Legal Studies* 16:43–65.

Libecap, Gary D. 1978. "Economic Variables and the Development of the Law: The Case of Western Mineral Rights." *Journal of Economic History* 38:338–62.

———. 1989. *Contracting for Property Rights.* New York: Cambridge University Press.

Libecap, Gary D., and Dean Lueck. 2011a. "Land Demarcation Systems." In Kenneth Ayotte and Henry E. Smith, eds., *Research Handbook on the Economics of Property Law,* 257–95. Cheltenham: Edward Elgar.

———. 2011b. "The Demarcation of Land and the Role of Coordinating Property Institutions." *Journal of Political Economy* 119:426–67.

Libecap, Gary D., Dean Lueck, and Trevor O'Grady. Forthcoming. "Large-Scale Institutional Changes: Land Demarcation within the British Empire." *Journal of Law and Economics.*

Lim, Yee Fen. 2002. "Digital Signature, Certification Authorities and the Law." *Murdoch University Electronic Journal of Law* 9. http://www.murdoch.edu.au/elaw/issues/v9n3/lim93_text.html (accessed August 25, 2009).

Lipshutz, Nelson R. 1994. *The Regulatory Economics of Title Insurance.* Westport: Praeger.

López Burniol, Juan J. 1994. "Entre el servicio y el control: Contribución de la fe pública a la ordenación del mercado." *Iuris: Cuaderns de Política Jurídica* 1:113–149.

Low, Rouhshi. 2005. "Maintaining the Integrity of the Torrens System in a Digital Environment: A Comparative Overview of the Safeguards Used within the Electronic Land Systems in Canada, New Zealand, United Kingdom and Singapore." *Australian Property Law Journal* 11:155–78.

———. 2006. "Opportunities for Fraud in the Proposed Australian National Electronic Conveyancing System: Fact or Fiction?" *Murdoch University Electronic Journal of Law* 13:225–53.

Low, Simon, Matthew Sebag-Montefiore, and Achim Dübel. 2003. *Study on the Financial Integration of European Mortgage Markets.* Brussels: European Mortgage Federation and Mercer Oliver Wyman.

Lueck, Dean. 1995. "The Rule of First Possession and the Design of the Law." *Journal of Law and Economics* 38:393–436.

Lueck, Dean, and Thomas J. Miceli. 2007. "Property Law." In A. Mitchell Polinsky and Steven Shavell, eds., *Handbook of Law and Economics,* 1:183–257. Amsterdam: Elsevier.

Lutter, Marcus. 1997. "Limited Liability Companies and Private Companies." In Detlev Vagts, chief ed., *Business and Private Organizations,* chap. 2. Vol. 13 in *International Encyclopedia of Comparative Law.* Tubingen: Mohr Siebeck.

Lyndon, Rachel. 2011. "Property Title Theft Insurance: Is It Just Scaremongering?" *Today's Conveyancer,* March 11.

Macintyre, Iain. 2008. "Dutch Notaries Accused of Money Laundering." *Radio Nederland Wereldomroep,* July 15.

Madison, Michael T., Robert M. Zinman, and Steven W. Bender. 1999. *Modern Real Estate Finance and Land Transfer: A Transactional Approach.* 2d ed. New York: Aspen.

Malavet, Pedro A. 1996. "Counsel for the Situation: The Latin Notary, A Historical and Comparative Model." *Hastings International and Comparative Law Review* 19:389–488.

Manning, Bayless, and James Hanks, Jr. 1990. *Legal Capital.* 3d ed. Westbury: Foundation Press.

Manning, Joe G. 1995. "Demotic Egyptian Instruments of Transfer as Evidence for Private Ownership of Real Property." *Chicago-Kent Law Review* 71:237–68.

Mariconda, Gennaro. 1990. "La transcrizione." In Pietro Rescigno, dir., *Trattato di diritto privato,* Vol. 19, tome 1. Torino: UTET.

Marsh, Tanya D. 2011. "Foreclosures and the Failure of the American Land Title Recording System." *Columbia Law Review Sidebar* 111:19–26.

Masten, Scott E. 1988. "A Legal Basis for the Firm." *Journal of Law, Economics, and Organization* 4:181–98.

Mayer, Peter, and Alan Pemberton. 2000. *A Short History of Land Registration in England and Wales*. London: Her Majesty's Land Registry.

MCA (Massachusetts Conveyancers Association). 2001. "Deregistration Bill Passes." *The Conveyancer, Newsletter of the Massachusetts Conveyancers Association* 20.

MCC (Millennium Challenge Corporation). 2005. "Report on the Criteria and Methodology for Determining the Eligibility of Candidate Countries for Millennium Challenge Account Assistance in FY 2006." Washington, DC: MCC.

McCormack, John L. 1992. "Torrens and Recording: Land Title Assurance in the Computer Age." *William Mitchell Law Review* 18:61–129.

McDougal, Myres S., and John W. Brabner-Smith. 1939. "Land Title Transfer: A Regression." *Yale Law Journal* 48:1125–51.

Medina, Barak. 2003. "Augmenting the Value of Ownership By Protecting It Only Partially: The 'Market-Overt' Rule Revisited." *Journal of Law, Economics, and Organization* 19:343–72.

Meinzen-Dick, Ruth, and Esther Mwangi. 2009. "Cutting the Web of Interests: Pitfalls of Formalizing Property Rights." *Land Use Policy* 26:36–43.

Méndez González, Fernando P. 2007. "La inscripción como título valor o el valor de la inscripción como título." *Revista Crítica de Derecho Inmobiliario* 83:2059–164.

———. 2008a. "Ciento cuarenta y seis años después (1861–2007)." Asociación de Registradores Bienvenido Oliver (ARBO), February 2. http://tinyurl.com/yfejukn (accessed January 6, 2010).

———. 2008b. *De la publicidad contractual a la titulación registral: El largo proceso hacia el Registro de la Propiedad*. Cizur Menor, Spain: Thomson-Civitas.

Menéndez Menéndez, Aurelio. 1959. "Auxiliares del empresario." *Revista de Derecho Mercantil* 27:269–305.

———. 1990. "El Registro Mercantil español: Formación y desarrollo." In Ilustre Colegio de Registradores de la Propiedad y Mercantiles de España, Centro de Estudios Hipotecarios, *Leyes hipotecarias y registrales de España: Fuentes y evolución (tome 5, Vol. 1): Registro Mercantil*, 9–140. Madrid: Castalia.

Mercer Oliver Wyman. 2006. "European Mortgage Markets: 2006 Adjusted Price Analysis." Brussels: European Mortgage Federation and Mercer Oliver Wyman.

Merrill, Thomas W., and Henry E. Smith. 2000. "Optimal Standardization in the Law of Property: The *Numerus Clausus* Principle." *Yale Law Journal* 110:1–70.

———. 2001a. "What Happened to Property in Law and Economics?" *Yale Law Journal* 111:357–98.

———. 2001b. "The Property/Contract Interface." *Columbia Law Review* 101:773–852.

———. 2007. *Property: Principles and Policies*. New York: Foundation Press.

———. 2010. *Property*. Oxford: Oxford University Press.

———. Forthcoming. "Making Coasean Property More Coasean." *Journal of Law and Economics*.

Merryman, John Henry. 2008. "The Good Faith Acquisition of Stolen Art." In John Jackson, Maximo Langer, and Peter Tillers, eds., *Crime, Procedure and Evidence in a Comparative Context: Essays in Honour of Professor Mirjan Damaska*, 275–94. Oxford: Hart Publishing.

Mian, Atif R., and Amir Sufi. 2010. "House Prices, Home Equity-Based Borrowing, and the U.S. Household Leverage Crisis." National Bureau of Economic Research Working Paper Series 15283.

Miceli, Thomas J., Henry J. Munneke, C. F. Sirmans, and Geoffrey K. Turnbull. 2002. "Title Systems and Land Values." *Journal of Law and Economics* 45:565–82.

———. "A Question of Title: Property Rights and Asset Values." *Regional Science and Urban Economics* 41:499–507.

Miceli, Thomas J., and C. F. Sirmans. 1995. "The Economics of Land Transfer and Title Insurance." *Journal of Real Estate Finance and Economics* 10:81–88.

Miceli, Thomas J., C. F. Sirmans, and Joseph Kieyah. 2001. "The Demand for Land Title Registration: Theory with Evidence from Kenya." *American Law and Economics Review* 3:275–87.

Michelman, Frank I. 1982. "Ethics, Economics, and the Law of Property." In J. Roland Pennock and John W. Chapman, eds., *Nomos: Ethics, Economics, and the Law*, 24:3–40. New York: New York University Press.

Migot-Adholla, Shem, Peter Hazell, Benoît Blarel, and Frank Place. 1991. "Indigenous Land Rights Systems in Sub-Saharan Africa: A Constraint on Productivity?" *World Bank Economic Review* 5:155–75.

Miles, David. 2004. *The UK Mortgage Market: Taking a Longer-Term View, Final Report and Recommendations*, March. London: Her Majesty's Treasury. http://www.hm-treasury .gov.uk/d/miles04_470[1].pdf (accessed December 13, 2008).

Mills, Gordon. 2002. *Retail Pricing Strategies and Market Power*. Melbourne: Melbourne University Press.

Miranda, Liliana. 2002. "A New Mystery from De Soto?" *Environment and Urbanization* 14:263–64.

Miranda, Óscar. 2010. "Cofopri fue infectado por la corrupción." *Perú 24*, August 31. http://peru21.pe/noticia/631621/decadencia-cofopri (accessed October 18, 2010).

MLTAG (Money Laundering Threat Assessment Working Group). 2005. *U.S. Laundering Threat Assessment*. Washington, DC: Department of the Treasury. http://www.ustreas .gov/offices/enforcement/pdf/mlta.pdf (accessed May 14, 2009).

Monti, Mario. 2003. "Competition in Professional Services: New Light and New Challenges." Berlin: Bundesanwaltskammer, March 21.

Moore, Kimberly A. 2005. "Markman Eight Years Later: Is Claim Construction More Predictable?" *Lewis and Clark Law Review*, 9:231–47.

Morris Guerinoni, Felipe, with the collaboration of Víctor Endo D. and Rafael Ugaz. 2004. *La formalización de la propiedad en el Perú: Desvelando el misterio*. Lima: Comisión para la Formalización de la Propiedad Informal (COFOPRI) and Banco Mundial. http://www .cofopri.gob.pe/bdigital.asp?i=3 (accessed March 4, 2007).

Mueller, Milton L. 2001. "Rough Justice: A Statistical Assessment of ICANN's Uniform Dispute Resolution Policy." *The Information Society* 17:153–63.

Munro, John H. 1994. "The International Law Merchant and the Evolution of Negotiable Credit in Late-Medieval England and the Low Countries," chap. 10 in *Textiles, Towns and Trade: Essays in the Economic History of Late-Medieval England and the Low Countries*. Aldershot, UK: Variorum.

Murray, Daniel E. 1960. "Sale in Market Overt." *The International and Comparative Law Quarterly* 9:24–52.

Murray, Peter L. 2007. "Real Estate Conveyancing in 5 European Union Member States: A Comparative Study." Brussels: Conseil des Notariats de l'Union Européenne (CNUE), August 31. http://bit.ly/sK6NlJ (accessed October 29, 2009).

Nahuis, Richard, and Joëlle Noailly. 2005. "Competition and Quality in the Notary Profession." CPB Netherlands Bureau for Economic Policy Analysis, Discussion Paper 94, September. http://www.cpb.nl/nl/pub/cpbreeksen/document/94/doc94.pdf (accessed March 7, 2006).

NASS (National Association of Secretaries of State). 2007. "NASS Survey on Company Formation Processes in the States." Results as of July 25. http://www.nass.org/ (accessed March 2, 2008).

Nicoletti, Giuseppe, and Stefano Scarpetta. 2003. "Regulation, Productivity and Growth: OECD Evidence." *Economic Policy* 18:9–72.

Niskanen, William A. 1968. "Nonmarket Decision Making: The Peculiar Economics of Bureaucracy." *American Economic Review* 58:293–305.

Noailly, Joëlle, and Richard Nahuis. 2010. "Entry and Competition in the Dutch Notary Profession." *International Review of Law and Economics* 30:178–85.

Nogueroles Peiró, Nicolás. 2006. "El registrador." In Luis María Díez-Picazo, ed., *El oficio de jurista*, 183–218. Madrid: Siglo XXI.

———. 2007. "La evolución de los sistemas registrales en Europa." *Noticias de la Unión Europea* 265:121–34.

———. 2008. "La implantación del registro inglés: Enseñanzas de una lenta conquista." In Salustiano de Dios et al., eds., *Historia de la propiedad: Crédito y garantía*, 789–866. Madrid: Servicio de Estudios del Colegio de Registradores.

North, Douglass C., and Robert P. Thomas. 1973. *The Rise of the Western World: A New Economic History*. Cambridge: Cambridge University Press.

North, Douglass C. 1981. *Structure and Change in Economic History*. New York: W. W. Norton.

———. 1990. *Institutions, Institutional Change and Economic Performance*. Cambridge: Cambridge University Press.

———. 1991. "Institutions." *Journal of Economic Perspectives* 5:97–112.

North, Douglass C., John Joseph Wallis, and Barry R. Weingast. 2009. *Violence and Social Orders: A Conceptual Framework for Interpreting Recorded Human History*. Cambridge: Cambridge University Press.

NZLC (New Zealand Law Commission). 2010. *A New Land Transfer Act*. Report 116, June. Wellington: New Zealand Law Commission. http://tinyurl.com/3zk30ux (accessed April 7, 2011).

O'Connor, Pamela. 2003. "Registration of Title in England and Australia: A Theoretical and Comparative Analysis." In Elizabeth Cooke, ed., *Modern Studies in Property Law*, 2:81–99. Oxford: Hart Publishing.

O'Connor, Rebecca. 2009. "Land Registry to Shed 1,500 Jobs ahead of Possible Sale." *Times Online*, October 22. http://tinyurl.com/yj9msbu (accessed October 28, 2009).

OECD (Organization for Economic Co-Operation and Development). 2003. *From Red Tape to Smart Tape: Administrative Simplification in OECD Countries*. Paris: OECD.

———. 2006. *Cutting Red Tape: National Strategies for Administrative Simplification*. Paris: OECD

Okoth-Ogendo, H. W. O. 1999. "Land Policy Development in East Africa: A Survey of Recent Trends." UK Department for International Development Workshop, "Land Rights and Sustainable Development in Sub-Saharan Africa." Berkshire, February 16–19. http://tinyurl.com/39e5nfj (accessed November 24, 2008).

Oliver y Esteller, Bienvenido. 1892. *Derecho inmobiliario español: Exposición fundamental y sistemática de la Ley Hipotecaria*, Vol. 1. Madrid: Sucesores de Rivadeneyra.

OMGCS (Ontario Ministry of Government and Consumer Services). 2011. "Application Guide for the Application for Authorization to Submit Documents for Registration in the Electronic Land Registration System." Toronto, ver. 1.07 http://tinyurl.com/64ge25q (accessed July 16, 2011).

Onsrud, Helge. 2002. "FIG Agenda 21—Committing Surveyors to Sustainable Development." FIG XXII International Congress, Washington, DC, April 19–26. http://www.fig.net/pub/fig_2002/PL3/PL3_onsrud.pdf (accessed July 25, 2011).

Ostrom, Elinor. 1990. *Governing the Commons: The Evolution of Institutions for Collective Action*, Cambridge: Cambridge University Press.

Pagano, Marco, and Tullio Jappelli. 1993. "Information Sharing in Credit Markets." *Journal of Finance* 43:1693–718.

Palomar, Joyce D. 1999. "The War Between Attorneys and Lay Conveyancers—Empirical Evidence Says 'Cease Fire!'" *Connecticut Law Review* 31:423–546.

———. 2003. *Patton and Palomar on Land Titles*. 3d ed. St. Paul: Thomson West.

Pancack, Katherine A., Thomas J. Miceli, and C. F. Sirmans. 1997. "Real Estate Agency Reform: Meeting the Needs of Buyers, Sellers, and Brokers." *Real Estate Law Journal* 25:345–77.

Pardo Núñez, Celestino. 1993. "Entre la purga y la fe pública: Génesis del sistema hipotecario español." *Revista Crítica de Derecho Inmobiliario* 614:111–64.

Parisi, Francesco, Norbert Schulz, and Ben Depoorter. 2005. "Duality in Property: Commons and Anticommons." *International Review of Law and Economics* 25:578–91.

Patault, Anne-Marie. 1989. *Introduction historique au droit des biens*. Paris: Presses Universitaires de France.

Paterson, Iain, Marcel Fink, and Anthony Ogus. 2003. "Economic Impact of Regulation in the Field of Liberal Professions in Different Member States." *Final Report—Part 1*. Vienna: Institute for Advanced Studies. http://europa.eu.int/comm/competition (accessed May 10, 2004).

Payne, Geoffrey, ed. 2002. *Land, Rights and Innovation: Improving Tenure Security for the Urban Poor*. London: ITDG Publishing.

Paz-Ares, Cándido. 1995. *El sistema notarial: Una aproximación económica*. Madrid: Consejo General del Notariado.

Penner, James E. 1997. *The Idea of Property in Law*. Oxford: Oxford University Press.

Peterson, Christopher L. 2010. "Foreclosure, Subprime Mortgage Lending, and the Mortgage Electronic Registration System." *University of Cincinnati Law Review* 78:1359–1407.

Petit, Carlos. 1979. *La compañía mercantil bajo el régimen de las ordenanzas del Consulado de Bilbao 1737–1829*. Sevilla: Universidad de Sevilla.

Picod, Yves. 1999. *Sûretés: Publicité foncière*. 7th ed. In H. Mazeaud, L. Mazeaud, J. Mazeaud and F. Chabas, eds., *Leçons de droit civil*. Tome 3, Vol. 1. Paris: Montchrestien.

Piedelièvre, Stéphane. 2000. *La publicité foncière*. Paris: Librairie Général de Droit et Jurisprudence.

Pirrong, Craig. Forthcoming. "Exchanges: The Quintessential Manufactured Markets." In Eric Brousseau and Jean-Michel Glachant, eds., *Manufacturing Markets*. Cambridge: Cambridge University Press.

Posner, Richard A. 1976. "The Rights of Creditors of Affiliated Corporations." *University of Chicago Law Review* 43:499–526.

———. 2007. *Economic Analysis of Law*. 7th ed. New York: Aspen.

Pottage, Alain. 1998. "Evidencing Ownership." In S. Bright and J. Dewar, eds., *Land Law: Themes and Perspectives*, 129–50. Oxford and New York: Oxford University Press.

Powell, Richard R. B. 1938. *Registration of the Title to Land in the State of New York*. Rochester: Lawyers Co-Operative Publishing Company.

Powelson, John P. 1988. *The Story of Land: A World History of Land Tenure and Agrarian Reform*. Cambridge: Lincoln Institute of Land Policy.

Preesman, Leen. 2008. "Netherlands Tightens Measures Against Property Fraud." *IPE Real Estate*, November 3.

Pulling, Alexander. 1862. *A Summary of the Law and Practice Relating to Attorneys*. London: Stevens and Haynes.

Rajan, Raghuram G., and Luigi Zingales. 1998. "Financial dependence and growth." *American Economic Review* 88:559–86.

Ramseyer, J. Mark. 1998. "Corporate Law." In Peter Newman, ed., *The New Palgrave Dictionary of Economics and the Law*, 1:503–10. London: Macmillan.

Raucent, León. 1998. *Fonction et statuts des notaries*. 10th ed. Louvain: Académia-Bruylant.

Richardson, Gary, and Dan Bogart. 2008. "Institutional Adaptability and Economic Development: The Property Rights Revolution in Britain, 1700 to 1830." National Bureau of Economic Research Working Paper Series 13757.

Robinson, Stanley. 1979. *Transfer of Land in Victoria*. Sydney: Law Book Company.

Rodrik, Dani, Arvind Subramanian, and Francesco Trebbi. 2002. "Institutions Rule: The Primacy of Institutions over Geography and Integration in Economic Development." *Journal of Economic Growth* 9:131–65.

ROS (Registers of Scotland). 1999. "Registration of Title: A Basic Guide," April 3. http://www.ros.gov.uk/pdfs/basicguide.pdf (accessed November 9, 2010).

———. 2010a. "Land Registration (Scotland) Bill Consultation Paper." http://www.ros.gov.uk/lrbillconsultation/index.html (accessed November 9, 2010).

———. 2010b. *Annual Report and Accounts 2009–2010*. Edinburgh: ROS. http://www.ros.gov.uk/pdfs/rosannualreport_09–10.pdf (accessed November 9, 2010).

Rose, Carol M. 1988. "Crystals and Mud in Property Law." *Stanford Law Review* 40:577–610.

Rose, Paul. 2007. "The Corporate Governance Industry." *Journal of Corporation Law* 32:887–926.

Rose-Ackerman, Susan. 1985. "Inalienability and the Theory of Property Rights." *Columbia Law Review* 85:931–69.

Rossini, Renzo, and Jim Thomas. 1987. *Los fundamentos estadísticos de "El otro sendero": Debate sobre el sector informal en el Perú*. Lima: Friedrich Eber Foundation.

———. 1990. "The Size of the Informal Sector in Peru: A Critical Comment on Hernando de Soto's *El Otro Sendero*." *World Development* 18:125–35.

Rubin, Edward L. 1995. "The Non-Judicial Life of Contract: Beyond the Shadow of the Law." *Northwestern University Law Review* 90:107–31.

Rubin, Paul H. 1978. "The Theory of the Firm and the Structure of the Franchise Contract." *Journal of Law and Economics* 21:223–33.

Sackville, Ronald, and Marcia Ann Neave. 1971. *Property Law: Cases and Materials*. Sydney: Butterworths.

Sarton, Priscilla. 2000. *Conveyancing*. 3d ed. London: Macmillan.

Sauveplanne, Jean-Georges. 1965. "The Protection of the Bona Fide Purchaser of Corporeal Movables in Comparative Law." *Rabels Zeitschrift* 29:651–93.

Schechter, Mark C., and Christine C. Wilson. 2006. "The Learned Professions in the United States: Where Do We Stand Thirty Years After *Goldfarb*." In C.-D. Ehlermann and I. Atanasiu, eds., *European Competition Law Annual 2004: The Relationship between Competition Law and the (Liberal) Professions*, 555–81. Oxford and Portland: Hart Publishing.

Schuetz, Jenny, Vicki Been, and Ingrid Gould Ellen. 2008. "Neighborhood Effects of Concentrated Mortgage Foreclosures." *Journal of Housing Economics* 17:306–19.

Schulz, Norbert, Francesco Parisi, and Ben Depoorter. 2002. "Fragmentation in Property: Towards a General Model." *Journal of Institutional and Theoretical Economics* 158:594–613.

Schwartz, Alan. 2008. "How Much Irrationality Does the Market Permit?" *Journal of Legal Studies* 37:131–59.

Schwartz, Alan, and Robert E. Scott. 2011. "Rethinking the Laws of Good Faith Purchase." *Columbia Law Review* 111:1332–84.

Seabright, Paul. 2004. *The Company of Strangers: A Natural History of Economic Life.* Princeton and Oxford: Princeton University Press.

Serna Vallejo, Margarita. 1996. "La formación histórica del régimen hipotecario francés o mixto." *Revista Crítica de Derecho Inmobiliario* 72:943–1022.

Shavell, Steven. 1997. "The Fundamental Divergence between the Private and the Social Motive to Use the Legal System." *Journal of Legal Studies* 26:575–612.

———. 2004. *Foundations of Economic Analysis of Law.* Cambridge: Belknap Press of Harvard University Press.

Shick, Blair C., and Irving H. Plotkin. 1978. *Torrens in the United States: A Legal and Economic Analysis of American Land Registration Systems.* Lexington and Toronto: D.D. Heath and Company.

Shiller, Robert J. 2008. *The Subprime Solution.* Princeton: Princeton University Press.

Sibley, James P. 2006. "Is the Door to Public Records Slowly Closing?" *Title News* 85. http://www.alta.org/publications/titlenews/06/03_01.cfm (accessed July 18, 2011).

Silver, Morris. 1995. *Economic Structures of Antiquity,* Contributions in Economics and Economic History 159. Westport: Greenwood Press.

Silverman, Frances. 2001. *Conveyancing Handbook 2001.* 8th ed. London: Law Society Publishing.

Simler, Philippe, and Philippe Delebecque. 2000. *Droit civil: Les sûretés, la publicité foncière.* 3d ed. Paris: Dalloz.

Simon, Herbert A. 1962. "The Architecture of Complexity." *Proceedings of the American Philosophical Society* 106:467–82.

Simpson, Alfred William Brian. 1986. *A History of the Land Law.* 2d rev. ed. Oxford: Clarendon Press.

Slesinger, Phyllis K., and Daniel McLaughlin. 1995. "Mortgage Electronic Registration System." *Idaho Law Review* 31:805–18.

Smith, Adam. [1776] 1981. *An Inquiry into the Nature and Causes of the Wealth of Nations.* Indianapolis: Oxford University Press/Liberty Press.

Smith, Henry E. 2002. "Exclusion versus Governance: Two Strategies for Delineating Property Rights." *Journal of Legal Studies* 31:S453-87.

———. 2006. "Modularity in Contracts: Boilerplate and Information Flow." *University of Michigan Law Review* 104:1175–222.

———. 2007. "Intellectual Property as Property: Delineating Entitlements in Information." *Yale Law Journal* 116:1742–823.

———. 2008. "Governing Water: The Semicommons of Fluid Property Rights." *Arizona Law Review* 50:445–78.

———. 2009. "Modularity in Property, Intellectual Property, and Organizations." Harvard Law School Working Paper, September 17.

———. 2011. "Standardization in Property Law." In Kenneth Ayotte and Henry E. Smith, eds., *Research Handbook on the Economics of Property Law,* 148–73. Cheltenham: Edward Elgar.

Sparkes, Peter. 1999. *A New Land Law*. Oxford and Portland: Hart Publishing.

SSH (Secretary of State for Health). 2010. *Equity and Excellence: Liberating the NHS*. Report presented to Parliament. The Stationery Office Limited.

Stake, Jeffrey Evans. 2000. "Decomposition of Property Rights." In B. Bouckaert and G. de Geest, eds., *Encyclopedia of Law & Economics*, 2:32–61. Cheltenham and Northampton: Edward Elgar.

Stein, Robert T. J., and Margaret A. Stone. 1991. *Torrens Title*. Sidney: Butterworths.

Sterk, Stewart W. 2008. "Property Rules, Liability Rules, and Uncertainty about Property Rights." *University of Michigan Law Review* 106:1285–1335.

Strandlund, Wayne. 2000. "Canada Respected as a Global Model for Real Estate Practices." *Scrivener* 9. http://www.notaries.bc.ca/article.php3?206 (accessed July 6, 2001).

Straw, Jr., Ralph L. 1967. "Off-Record Risks for Bona Fide Purchasers of Interests in Real Property." *Dickinson Law Review* 72:35–90.

Suleiman, Ezra N. 1987. *Private Power and Centralization in France: The Notaries and the State*. Princeton: Princeton University Press.

Supple, Barry. 1977. "The Nature of Enterprise." In E. E. Rich and C. H. Wilson, eds., *The Cambridge Economic History of Europe*, 5:393–461. Cambridge: Cambridge University Press.

Suyono, H. Haryono, and Dodo Juliman. 1999. "Community-Based Low-Cost Housing Movement in Indonesia." Submission to the United Nations Best Practices Initiative of the Habitat II Conference, Jakarta, March 15. http://www.serd.ait.ac.th/umc/bestprac/cblwcst.htm (accessed October 28, 2008).

Symposium. 1989. *Contractual Freedom in Corporate Law*. *Columbia Law Review* 89:1395–773.

Szreter, Simon. 2007. "The Right of Registration: Development, Identity Registration, and Social Security—A Historical Perspective." *World Development* 35:67–86.

Tabarrok, Alexander, and Eric Helland. 1999. "Court Politics: The Political Economy of Tort Awards." *Journal of Law and Economics* 42:157–88.

Tallon, Denis. 1983. "Civil Law and Commercial Law." In Konrad Zweigert, chief ed., *Specific Contracts*, chap. 2. Vol. 8 in *International Encyclopedia of Comparative Law*. Tubingen: Mohr Siebeck.

Tamanaha, Brian Z. 2004. *On the Rule of Law: History, Politics, Theory*. Cambridge: Cambridge University Press.

Taylor, Gregg. 2008. "Is the Torrens System German?" *Journal of Legal History* 29:253–85.

Telser, Lester G. 1981. "Why There Are Organized Futures Markets." *Journal of Law and Economics* 24:1–22.

Teranet. 2008. "History." Teranet, Toronto. http://www.teranet.ca/corporate/history.html (accessed November 7, 2008).

Thaler, Richard H. 1980. "Toward a Positive Theory of Consumer Choice." *Journal of Economic Behavior and Organization* 1:39–60.

Thaler, Richard H., and Cass R. Sunstein. 2008. *Nudge: Improving Decisions about Health, Wealth, and Happiness*. New Haven: Yale University Press.

Thomas, Rod. 2003a. "Fraud, Risk and the Automated Register." In David Grinlinton, ed., *Torrens in the Twenty-First Century*, 349–67. Wellington: LexisNexis.

———. 2003b. "Lawyers Must Understand Land Registry System." *Law News* 16, May 9.

———. 2003c. "Issues Raised by Registrar-General's Article." *Law News* 22, June 20.

———. 2011. "Reduced Torrens Protection: The New Zealand Law Commission Proposal for a New Land Transfer Act." *New Zealand Law Review* (December): 715–47.

Thomas, Rod, and David Grinlinton. 2005. "Myths' E-Dealings and the Way Ahead." *Law News* 16, May 6.

Trebilcock, Michael J., and Ronald J. Daniels. 2008. *Rule of Law Reform and Development: Charting the Fragile Path of Progress.* Cheltenham: Edward Elgar.

Troister, Sidney H., and Kathleen A. Waters. 1996. "Real Estate Conveyancing in Ontario: A Nineties Perspective." Mimeo. Toronto: Lawyers' Professional Indemnity Company.

UN-ECE (United Nations Economic Commission for Europe). 1996. *Land Administration Guidelines with Special Reference to Countries in Transition.* New York and Geneva: United Nations.

———. 2000. *Study on Key Aspects of Land Registration and Cadastral Legislation.* London: Her Majesty's Land Register.

———. 2005. *Land Administration in the UNECE Region: Development Trends and Main Principles.* New York and Geneva: United Nations. http://bit.ly/tSvZGZ (accessed December 20, 2008).

Verstappen, Leon C. A. 2008. "Word of Welcome: The Dutch Situation on Regulation of Notaries." In Nicolle Zeegers and Herman Bröring, eds., *Professions under Pressure: Lawyers and Doctors between Profit and Public Interest,* 11–24. The Hague: Boom Juridische Uitgevers.

Villani, Kevin, and John Simonson. 1982. "Real Estate Settlement Pricing: A Theoretical Framework." *American Real Estate and Urban Economics Association Journal* 10:249–75.

Viúdez, Juana. 2008. "La juez del 'caso Hidalgo' reactiva la investigación contra los notarios." *El País,* August 12.

Wachter, Daniel, and John English. 1992. "The World Bank Experience with Rural Land Titling." World Bank Policy and Research Division, Environment Department Working Paper 1992-35.

Wallis, John Joseph. 2011. "Institutions, Organizations, Impersonality, and Interests: The Dynamics of Institutions." *Journal of Economic Behavior and Organization* 79:48–64.

Ward, Peter N. 1990. *Mexico City: The Production and Reproduction of an Urban Environment.* London: Belhaven Press.

Watson, Alan. [1968] 1984. *The Law of Property in the Later Roman Republic.* Aalen, Germany: Scientia (1st ed.; Oxford: Oxford University Press, 1968).

Webb, Richard, Diether Beuermann, and Carla Revilla. 2006. *La construcción del Derecho de Propiedad: El caso de los asentamientos humanos en el Perú.* Lima: Colegio de Notarios de Lima.

Weill, Alex. 1979. *Droit civil: Les sûretés, la publicité foncière.* Paris: Dalloz.

Weinberg, Harold R. 1980. "Sales Law, Economics, and the Negotiability of Goods." *Journal of Legal Studies* 9:569–92.

Whalan, Douglas J. 1966–67. "Immediate Success of Registration of Title to Land in Australasia and Early Failures in England." *New Zealand Universities Law Review* 2:416–39.

———. 1982. *The Torrens System in Australia.* Sidney: Law Book Company.

White, Michelle J. 2009. "Bankruptcy: Past Puzzles, Recent Reforms, and the Mortgage Crisis." *American Law and Economics Review* 11:1–23.

Williamson, Oliver E. 1975. *Markets and Hierarchies: Analysis and Antitrust Implications.* New York: Free Press.

———. 1985. *The Economic Institutions of Capitalism: Firms, Markets, Relational Contracting.* New York: The Free Press.

———. 1991. "Comparative Economic Organization: The Analysis of Discrete Structural Alternatives." *Administrative Sciences Quarterly* 36:269–96.

———. 1996. "Revisiting Legal Realism: The Law, Economics, and Organization Perspective." *Industrial and Corporate Change* 5:383–420.

———. 2005. "Why Law, Economics, and Organization?" *Annual Review of Law and Social Science* 1:369–96.

Willman, Raymond, and Jean-François Pillebout. 2002. *Buying or Selling a Home: The Notary's Mission*. 3d. ed. Paris: Mémos de Conseils par des Notaires.

Wily, Liz Alden, and Sue Mbaya. 2001. *Land, People and Forests in Eastern and Southern Africa at the Beginning of the 21st Century: The Impact of Land Relations on the Role of Communities in Forest Future*. Nairobi: Eastern Africa Regional Office of the International Union for Conservation of Nature (EARO-IUCN).

Winter, Jaap (Chairman). 2002. *Report of the High Level Group of Company Law Experts on a Modern Regulatory Framework for Company Law in Europe*. Brussels: European Commission.

Woodruff, Christopher. 2001. "Review of De Soto's *The Mystery of Capital*." *Journal of Economic Literature* 39:1215–23.

World Bank. 2004–11. *Doing Business*. Washington, DC: World Bank. (Year references in the text are for each annual report and not the year of publication.)

World-Check. 2010. "About World-Check." http://www.world-check.com/overview/ (accessed June 7, 2010).

ZERP (Centre of European Law and Politics, University of Bremen). 2007. *Conveyancing Services Market (Study COMP/2006/D3/003, Final Report)*. Brussels: ZERP.

Zetter, Kim. 2009. "Judge Rules LifeLock's Fraud Alert Service Illegal." *Wired*. http://www.wired.com/threatlevel/2009/05/lifelock/ (accessed December 17, 2009).

Zeyringer, Walter. 1995. "The Registration of Civil Status." In Mary Ann Glendon, chief ed., *Persons and Family*, subchap. 2.7, 148–66. Vol. 4 in *International Encyclopedia of Comparative Law*. Tubingen: Mohr Siebeck.

Zingales, Luigi. 2004. "The Costs and Benefits of Financial Market Regulation." European Corporate Governance Institute (ECGI)—Law Working Paper 21.

INDEX

Page numbers in italics refer to illustrations.

indirect liability, systems for, 16

individuals, identification of, 175, 252n14

Indonesia: *Kredit Triguna* or "triple function" loan, 112

industrialization: of contracting solutions needed for impersonal transactions, 117; of conveyancing, 181, 186–88; of trading in financial derivatives and property rights, 230

Industrial Revolution: situation of property rights in England, 140; triggering of the adoption of company registries, 233

industrial solutions in contracting, 117

informality, and poverty, 150–52, 226

information asymmetry: and contract rules, 5; and conveyancing professionals, 179; and corporate transactions, 81; high costs of, 77–78; and limited liability, 83–84; and multiple rights, 25; and property *(in rem)* rights, 3, 4, 11; and property rules, 37; and sequential exchange, 27–28, 34–38; and single exchange, 27; and specialization, 237n19; and third parties, 4, 5, 30, 116

information disclosure, by debtors, of their assets, 51; of accounts by European companies, 208, 244n24; in Bilbao company registry, 104; and collective action, 95, 101; and commitment, 96; of incorporation documents, 98; in mortgage loans, 253n19; of security interests, 53; in US company registries, 162–63

information systems: developing meaningful, 199–201; failures of available, 198–99

innocent (good faith) parties. *See* third parties, innocent (good faith)

internal market, 216

Internet Corporation for Assigned Names and Numbers (ICANN), 70

Internet domains, registration, 69–70

Italy: notaries, 253n21; registration of merchants in the Middle Ages, 87; and residual compensation, 219; superiority of land registration in former Austrian provinces, 158

Iyer, Lakshmi, 126

Jackson, Thomas H., 51, 58, 79, 86

Jacoby, Hanan G., 126, 127

Jaffe, Adam B., 223

Janczyk, Joseph T., 218

Jensen, Michael C., 144

Jimenez, Emmanuel, 125

judges: and allocation of *in rem* rights, 24, 37, 40–41; application of contract rule, 29, 36–37, 61–62, 241n49; assumed, 9–10; assumption on existence, 9–10; conditions for enforcement of loan terms that are harmful to debtors, 181; denial of conclusiveness of registration, 6; and documentary formalization, 169; and 1844 English Company Act, 100, 101; establishment of ownership based on a public register, 26; and French 1673 Registry, 102, 103; as key users of registry services, 124; nonelected versus elected judges in redistribution of wealth from out- of-state businesses to in-state plaintiffs, 111; and publicity requirements, 38–39; reliance on formal and informal solutions for different types of transactions, 85, 88, 91, 92; reluctance to enforce new principles of property law, 139–40; and two main types of contractual conflict, 26; and verifiability of contracts, 232, 237n20. *See also* judicial decisions

judgment proof, 16, 21, 23, 28

judicial decisions, 16, 23, 68; based on evidence provided by registry services, 29, 122, 199; considering financial institutions liable for failing to detect the fake identity of fraudsters in mortgage fraud cases, 175; as cost of introducing a titling system, 139; disputes over property rights, 5–6; equation of enforcement with, 23; focus on the prevalent cases and general rules, 9; in impersonal trade, 16–17; and incompleteness of registration, 66; inputs used and consistency shown by, 136; and MERS ruling in 2010 foreclosure crisis, 114; on patent rights, 222–23; performance in contractual disputes related to sale of goods, 157; and purging of title, 49, 51–52, 53, 56, 155; and "quiet title" suits, 56, 155; and reform of land law, 139; and registry reform, 121–22, 124; reliance on secret documents as indicator of